The Papacy

The
PAPACY

Bernhard Schimmelpfennig

translated by James Sievert

COLUMBIA UNIVERSITY PRESS
New York

Columbia University Press
New York   Chichester, West Sussex
Copyright © 1992 Columbia University Press
All rights reserved

Bernhard Schimmelpfennig
Das Papsttum. Von der Antike bis zur Renaissance.
Copyright © 1984, 3d ed. 1988
by Wissenschaftliche Buchgesellschaft,
Darmstadt, Germany

Library of Congress Cataloging-in-Publication Data

Schimmelpfennig, Bernhard.
    [Papsttum English]
    The papacy / Bernhard Schimmelpfennig.
    p.   cm.
    Translation of : Das Papsttum.
    ISBN 0-231-07514-6 (hard).—ISBN 0-231-07515-4 (pbk.)
    1. Papacy—History.   I. Title.
BX965.S3513   1992
262'.13'09—dc20   92-3696
⊛   CIP

Casebound editions of Columbia University Press books are
printed on permanent and durable acid-free paper.

Printed in the United States of America

c 10 9 8 7 6 5 4 3 2 1
p 10 9 8 7 6

Contents

Preface

The papacy is the only institution that connects the ancient and medieval past of Europe to the present. The papacy has often had a decisive influence on the course of European history. For these reasons, the papacy is fascinating for many who, without any religious intentions, are looking to gain access to bygone epochs. It is hardly surprising, then, that even many non-Catholic historians have devoted and are still devoting a major portion of their research to papal history.

Historico-critical investigations into papal history were stepped up considerably with the opening of the secret Vatican archives by Pope Leo XIII in 1881. This was followed by the founding of numerous foreign research institutes in Rome that chose the Vatican archives as the basis of their projects. As a result, multivolumed papal histories in German first appeared at the end of the nineteenth century, the one exception being the work of Leopold von Ranke.

As was common at that time—and as it still is somewhat today—the research was shaped by national aspects: German historians frequently concerned themselves with the papacy from the expansion of Charlemagne's empire to the end of the Hohenstaufens; French historians stressed the fourteenth century, when the popes resided in Avignon, since nowadays this city is part of French territory. Since the time of Petrarch, the Italians have viewed the Avignon period as the Babylonian Exile. Besides national interests, the research was frequently marked by disputes over the dogma of the infallibility of the pope in matters of faith and morality. This dogma was defined at the First Vatican Council in 1870 and caused intense controversy—even among historians. Among Italians with more of a "lay" character, other reservations are to be found, which have to do with the papacy's blocking of Italian unity until 1870 and its later partnership with Mussolini.

Even today, every pope is the "Bishop of Rome," "Patriarch of the West," "Supreme Shepherd of the Universal Church." As such, he asserts claims, rights, and obligations achieved in late antiquity and the Middle Ages that have been preserved ever since. In historical terms, the first title mentioned above is the oldest and was, for the first millennium, the most important. But even at the time when the popes had already become the recognized leaders of the Western church, their political policies were often determined by interests in Rome and Central Italy. Accordingly, in this book the bishopric and city of Rome as well as Central Italy will be duly taken into account.

As the bishop of Rome, the pope had to rule for centuries in Rome chiefly as the head liturgist. For this reason, the history of the liturgy will be given equal footing with political, legal, constitutional, and dogmatic history. Moreover, economic and social aspects are also taken into consideration as well as the mentality and the consciousness—as much as they can be discerned—of the popes and their assistants, for only then can papal ties to a certain social framework be made evident. And since the formulation of claims did not mean *eo ipso* their acceptance—a fact often overlooked in papal histories—it must be asked when and to what extent these claims were either partially or generally recognized. In this way, the book differs methodologically at the outset from an ecclesiologically or spiritually oriented presentation.

In contrast to many other papal histories, the individual chapters are arranged systematically, and the political disputes the popes had with other rulers, which often are presented in the foreground, will receive minimal attention, since they were not as important for the papacy as some other books might suggest.

A major portion of the text grew out of lectures and seminars. These made it clear that even Catholic students are unfamiliar not only with the developments of papal history, but also with the fundamental concepts of the church's structure. Therefore, an attempt was made to clarify the concepts when needed in order to facilitate an understanding. Unfortunately, it was not possible to deal more extensively with the general political history or other areas of church history (councils, heretics, etc.). This lies outside the stated range of this volume.

The book ends with only a segment that includes the beginning of the Reformation, chiefly because of quantitative reasons. In connection with this, however, it should be kept in mind that, by the fifteenth century, most of the foundations for the papacy's recognition in the modern era had been laid. In light of this, the book is certainly also useful as an orientation for those who are interested in the later era.

Also for reasons related to overall size, no annotations are included, the bibliographical references for the individual chapters offering a partial substitute. Maps and plans have not been added, and the index is relatively short.

In conclusion, I would like to thank, in addition to my former colleagues and students in Berlin, from whom I received numerous suggestions, Ludwig Falkenstein of Aachen, who read the manuscript with a critical eye. I would also like to thank the staff at the Chair for Medieval History in Augsburg for its help in the production of the manuscript, in the proof reading, as well as in the preparation of the bibliography and the index.

The Papacy

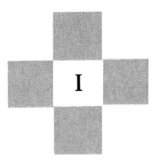

I

The Roman Congregation Before Constantine the Great

Early Christianity is characterized by several factors that are qualitatively different from all later periods. As far as is known, the Christian mission was mainly limited to the Roman empire, and therefore had to conform to the prevailing structures, habits, and ways of thinking. At the same time, this meant that in its initial development, Christianity was very much shaped by phenomena that were not genuinely Christian, since there was no fixed doctrine, and the form that the Christian communities would take only gradually emerged. Until the beginning of the fourth century, Christians were occasionally considered opponents of the Roman cult of emperors and, as such, seen as a danger to the state's stability. Because of this, they often were living beyond the law and had to be ready to prove their beliefs with their lives. The first persecutions were limited in both duration and location. Only from the middle of the third century, after Christian congregations had been established in almost the entire empire, did prosections begin on a larger scale, carried out by state organs. These pogroms were bound to fail, however, since at that time Christians already made up ten percent of the population, and they could hardly all be killed or deported. It was, therefore, a sagacious political move on the part of Constantine the Great and his ruling partners or adversaries, in the years 311 to 313, to legalize Christianity with the so-called Edicts of Tolerance.

This early period can be divided into two phases. In the first phase lived those witnesses of the faith who had received the teachings from Christ himself or from his disciples. The Christians believed that the second coming (parousia) of the messiah was imminent. This meant that the bearers of this message enjoyed the highest prestige in the communities, and that permanently fixed rules for community leadership were not yet needed. At the beginning of the second century, however, as Christians realized that the second coming might not materialize or could be a long time in coming, they had to organize themselves over the long run to the affairs "of this world" and find their own identity, without the help of the first believers, who by now were dead. This caused the dispute over the proper teachings to flare up stronger than ever. The second phase, therefore, is marked by the attempt to establish a canon of holy scriptures, as well as to construct a chain of apostolic succession to the first believers, giving to the communities a hierarchical order. This development also shaped the Roman congregation, of course, and the idea that people living there and in other congregations had of the works and importance of Simon Peter.

The Apostolic and Post-Apostolic Era
(until c. A.D. 110–130)

The traditional doctrine of the church has based the special position of the bishop of Rome on his being the successor to the apostle Peter, to whom Christ had entrusted the leadership of his "church" (Matthew 16:18). This interpretation of Peter's close connection with the Roman congregation is seen from the middle of the third century at the latest. Yet, in contrast to most of this kind of evidence, the reliability of which is still uncertain, there is a remarkable lack of interest in the works of the apostles in their lifetime. Thus the historian must ask what we really know about Peter so that historical reality can be separated from dogmatic fiction.

Recent research generally recognizes that in the forefront of the New Testament stood the preaching (kerygma) of the dawning of the Kingdom of God that had come with Jesus Christ. It has become evident to us that the authors of these scriptures did not want to write what they knew of the life and works of the historical Christ, but what they believed to be his teachings after the resurrection and the dispensation of the Holy Spirit that followed. It was even less important for them to portray realistically the lives of the first witnesses, including Peter's. It is hardly surprising, then, that we learn little about Peter in these writings. Moreover, most of what relatively little information there is (above all in the works ascribed to Matthew and Luke) was not written until decades after the apostle's death and is shaped by the situation in which the author lived at the time of the writing and by the audience for whom he was writing. We have no informtion from non-Christian writers.

It is more than likely that Peter was one of the oldest disciples and one of the first witnesses of Christ's resurrection. After Pentecost he led, together with James the Elder, the council of the "twelve," the leadership board of Jerusalem's Christian community, the "new convenant," which was modeled on the twelve tribes of the "old covenant" of Israel. The "twelve" presided over the entire community; their main work, however, was the mission among the ethnic Jews in Judaea and Galilee, that is, among the members of the twelve tribes. In addition, seven deputies (later called "deacons") were elected by the congregation to be responsible for missionizing (Stephen, for example) among the "Hellenistic," the non-Israelite Jews of the diaspora. Every member of the early congregation was, theoretically at least, an "apostle," a bearer of the new message. Making the "twelve" equivalent with the apostles came only later. Important questions were always decided by the whole congregation, even though the "twelve," Peter among them, were given special consideration because of their earlier relationship with Jesus. Thus Paul, the persecutor turned proselytizer, came to Peter, James, and the other "twelve" to coordinate his mission with theirs. For this same reason, the board sent representatives (Peter, Barnabas, and others) to other communities such as Caesarea and Antioch.

It was probably in A.D. 42 when the congregation at Jerusalem was persecuted for the first time (if we except Stephen's execution). James the Elder was killed, and Peter was barely able to escape with his life—a story later made legend. With this, the congregation was robbed of the core of its leadership. The Christian community, still viewing itself as a special group within the Jews, henceforth set up its directorate along the lines of the kinship-based custom the Palestinian Jews used in the recruiting of their ecclesiastics (Levites and high priests). Now Mary, James (the brother of Jesus), and their relatives stood at the head of the community. The stories later reported by Luke, and in apocryphal texts of Christ's childhood and of Mary's life and death, probably came out of this milieu. Yet for decades the community in Jerusalem remained the center for Christians, the place to which members of other congregations donated money and with which they had to agree in matters of teachings and congregational life. Only after the destruction of Jerusalem by Titus in A.D. 70, which brought about the dissolution of the Jerusalem congregation, did Christianity lose its center. It was logical, therefore, that other, specially qualified congregations would take the place of Jerusalem over time.

Little is certain about the life of Peter after he fled Jerusalem. It can be assumed that he missionized outside Jerusalem. That he was able to make it to Rome, however, is merely the view of later generations. It is clear from Paul's letters to the Romans that the congregation there was formed before the middle of the century, probably within the relatively large Jewish community. Paul knew Peter personally, though he never mentioned Peter's work in his letters to the Romans nor in his letters to the Philippians, which he wrote later, perhaps in Rome. If one assumes there was no rivalry between Peter and Paul, the reason for Paul's not mentioning Peter in his letters must have been that he knew nothing of Peter's stay in Rome; in other words, until approximately A.D. 55. Peter had not come to Rome. It is also unknown whether Peter was actually active in Rome in the following decades.

Only in circa A.D. 96, in a letter from the Roman congregation to the one in Corinth, is there reference made to the activity of Paul and Peter in Rome. This letter, which one hundred years later was almost made part of the canon of Holy Scriptures, is interesting in several respects. The sender, for example, is not an individual, but an entire congregation. Consequently, there was at that time in Rome no clearly accepted head of the congregation who was also recognized abroad. (Only after the middle of the second century was the letter ascribed to the presbyter and later pope Clement.) Many passages from the Old Testament and teachings of Stoic philosophy are quoted in the letter. This presupposes that the author or authors were very familiar not only with Jewish tradition but also with Roman philosophy, that they must have come from a relatively high social class in view of education at that time, and that the congregation was probably made up of former Jews and "pagans." The only information that can be taken for granted about Peter and Paul is that they worked and died in Rome. How they worked, how they died—and where they were buried—is not described. It would be misleading to say, however, that Peter and Paul, or one of the two, were leaders of the Roman community, since by the end of the first century the congregation still had no clear structure. "Bishop" Ignatius of Antioch, who wrote to Rome in circa A.D. 110, likewise knew nothing about a "monarchial" leadership of the community, referring to it instead as a "collective." Therefore, we can only assume that in the Roman congregation of the first century, as elsewhere, "spiritual representatives" acted as messengers of the gospel ("teacher," "apostle," "prophet"). Perhaps Peter and Paul also belonged to this group, while other members of the congregation ("episcopes," "deacons," and perhaps "presbyters") took care of matters relating to worship and administration, with the "spiritual representatives" holding preeminence.

As is well known, excavations have been made in an attempt to find the graves of both apostles, especially Peter's, despite the fact that the interest in and the possibility of burying the bodies of fellow believers and marking their graves was fairly slight. This can be assumed from the powerful sway the expectation of the second coming held over the congregation, from the so-called Epistle of Clement, and from the situation of those who had escaped Nero's persecution. It is hardly surprising, then, that the excavations under St. Peter's in Rome produced no clear evidence for Peter's presence in Rome. (Incidentally, the findings under St. Paul's from the first century offered no evidence of Paul's presence in Rome either, although in contrast to Peter, there are written accounts of his having been there.) Several of the graves found under St. Peter's were from the first century, though no Christians were buried in them. Under the Confessio, where tradition had it Peter was buried, graves were found which indicate that, from the middle of the second century, one grave was particularly venerated since it was the orientation point for the alignment of the other graves found there. This central grave itself, however, could not be discovered. Thus the question remains unanswered to which period this grave belongs and whether it was Peter's, let alone the question of whether those really are Peter's remains that Paul VI had venerated in a new reliquary. Even an inscription found at the excavation site left no sure indication, since it cannot be conclusively dated, and its condition is too fragmentary.

Thus the excavations revealed nothing that had not been known before, namely, that at the end of the first century the Roman community believed that Peter and Paul had been active in their circle. From the middle of the second century—by which time the congregations had stabilized and in places beyond Rome the graves of apostles were venerated as in the ancient hero cults—there were memorials (*tropaia*) to both apostles (to Peter in the Vatican, and to Paul along the Ostian Way). This veneration, which continues into modern times, is tied to theses two places. Soon this veneration was so widely recognized beyond Rome that no other place—not even Corinth or Antioch, where Peter was supposed to have been active—claimed to have Peter's grave. In later periods, apocryphal third-century texts, chiefly from the Middle East, depict Peter's life and death in legendary terms ("Quo vadis" encounter, crucifixion in the Vatican, etc.). At the same time—again initially outside Rome—Peter was beginning to be presented as the most esteemed of all the apostles in order to legitimize the preeminence of the bishop of Rome.

The Early Catholic Period (until c. 312–313)

As mentioned earlier, as Christians gave up waiting for the second coming, it was necessary for them to stabilize their congregational life. The Roman state made this easier with its policy, beginning with Trajan's reign (98–117), of persecuting Christians only when they had been formally charged and been found "guilty" by trial. Another important factor for future developments was the previously mentioned list of persons who, for the purpose of legitimizing the present teachings of a congregation, traced themselves back to the first believers. In addition, the canon of Holy Scriptures to be read during worship services was fixed. Besides the fact that these two actions helped the congregation adjust to the environment, as we shall see later, they also had the effect of making it easier to identify heretics and to exclude them from the community. A further effect was that Christian festivals took on the character of worship, which over time became the standard, and that the more spontaneous and inspired "spiritual representatives" were pushed into the background in favor of appointed officials, over time disappearing completely.

In the second half of the second century there arose, in the East earlier than in the West, a group of officials (*kleros*, which comes from *los*, in a personalized sense meaning "a group appointed by God through *los*") who distinguished themselves from the rest of the community members and stood in a hierarchical relationship among themselves. At their head stood the "episcope" (*episkopein* = to oversee or supervise, hence bishop). The "episcope" presided over the worship service, was the only person allowed to accept new members into the congregation through baptism, and secured for himself even at that time supreme control over discipline and doctrine in the congregation. He met with other episcopes of the same region to clarify questions of discipline and doctrine, from which developed the synod (*synodos*, meaning "assembly"), so important an institution for the church as a whole.

The episcope headed the board of "presbyters" (i.e., the elders, hence the word "priest") in his community. What their function was in every congregation is not clear. In a large congregation such as Rome's, the presbyters participated in the worship service together with the episcope on important days. They also presided over the eucharist ceremony in their communities, and prepared catechumens for baptisim. Through these actions, the presbyters attest to the fact that there was a federative merger of several local groups into a congregation, which was needed in larger cities in particular. Meanwhile, it was the "deacon" (messenger, servant) who made up the long arm of the episcope in questions concerning the running of the congregation and the needs of charity.

In third-century Rome, there were still other officials: subdeacons supported the deacons in their work; acolytes (*akolouthos* = servant belonging to the retinue) probably served as a link between episcopes and presbyters; exorcists were in charge of driving out demons (usually done before a baptisim); lectors (readers) read and sang liturgical texts; ostiaries (doorkeepers) controlled the access to the rooms in which worship services took place.

In addition to the episcope, the Roman clergy in the middle of the third century consisted of 46 presbyters, 7 deacons, 7 subdeacons, 42 acolytes, 52 exorcists, lectors, and ostiaries. These 155 clerics, along with 1,500 widows and other needy persons, were supplied with life's necessities by the congregation. This meant that, in effect, they probably gave up their jobs upon entering office. Other information can be deduced from these numbers. For example, in view of the large number of clerics and widows, the amount of donations taken in must have been considerable. It is also quite probable that the support was covered not only by donations, but also by tax revenues on real estate. Because of this, the community was easily injured financially in times of persecution. With more than 150 clerics, the number of believers in Rome must have been several tens of thousands. It would have been impossible for all these believers to attend the worship services conducted by the episcope; thus most of the pastoral work was entrusted to the presbyters. In this way, particular customs in the congregation, which are seen above all in the liturgy of later eras, got a head start in their development. The seven deacons and seven subdeacons corresponded to the proper number mentioned for deacons in the Acts of the Apostles. It was most likely for this reason that Rome was divided into seven ecclesiastical regions in late antiquity.

Other information in the sources offers further details about the Roman Christian community. From the end of the second century at the latest, the community included members from all classes, from slaves who even became bishop (Callistus I) to the mostly female members of the senatorial upper class. Even in the emperor's court there were Christians, several of whom held high positions. Of course, there was always the danger that if a dynasty fell, the Christian supporters of the dethroned emperor could also be affected in the ensuing purge, and with them the whole Christian community. The leading stratum of the congregation, especially in the third century, was recruited more and more from Latin-speaking Christians, whereas until that time Greek-speaking community members had set the tone, as was common outside Rome. The numerous Latin names of bishops, the letters of the board of presbyters and deacons from the middle of the century, and the texts of the presbyter Novatian (to be discussed later)—all are testaments to this change.

The size and structure of the congregation in the third century required an extensive administration. Not only were regions set up for the activities of deacons and subdeacons, but catacombs were

also obtained for burials, which took place in part under the supervision of the deacons. Worship services for burials probably took
place in buildings already on the site. Moreover, there was a turning away from the strict way of living of earlier times. Since most
of the upper-class persons who joined the community were women,
and Roman law allowed lawful marriage only between legal equals,
in 220 Callistus I recognized as lawful marriage the union of
women of the upper class with a Christian slave or simple freed-
man, which may have resulted in social problems regarding birth
control and the danger of abortion, or the exclusion of children
from inheritance. In addition, Callistus I also reduced the number
of so-called mortal sins, transgressions that had as a consequence
the exclusion from the congregation, while retaining for himself
the general absolution of such sins. To establish his measures, he
appealed to the authority of the *cathedra* (chair) of the Roman
church that he occupied and to the saying of Christ that God will
separate the wheat from the chaff (Matthew 13:29). Such measures
and motives show that the bishop already attributed a "monarchial" position to himself, but that it still was not justified in terms
of the apostolic succession.

Callistus' edicts showed an understanding for the contemporary
situation, though at the same time they also showed a factual
disregard for older Christian traditions, both of these positions
being quite common in late Roman times. To be sure, the Christian community did not fully support Callistus, as texts written
against him by the presbyter Hippolytus show. Although a personal rivalry with Callistus might have been the reason behind
Hippolytus' writings, this controversy is, more than anything, a
symptom of the changes in the community and of the tension in
the leading circles (Callistus was a deacon, Hippolytus a presbyter).
And if Callistus was the realistic pragmatist, then Hippolytus was
the theologian who was trusted with the traditional teachings, and
who was, at least in theory, the "better," but doctrinaire Christian
by standards of the apostolic period. In the end, the pragmatist
won. All memory of Hippolytus in Rome was wiped out, so that
his activities and his works are known only through texts from the
orient. Whether the conflict between Callistus and Hippolytus led
to a schism, to a division in the community, cannot be proven
beyond all doubt.

A further dissension, which caused the first confirmed schism
in Rome, arose after the first planned empire-wide persecution of

the Christian communities under Decius (249–251). Decius wanted to strengthen the cult of the emperor to guarantee the ideological unity of the empire. Every inhabitant of the empire was required to offer a sacrifice before an image of the emperor. Because many Christians were not, in contrast to earlier times, firm enough in their beliefs, there were many "fallen ones" (*lapsi*) among them. In Rome as well as in other congregations, the top echelon was divided over the issue of whether and how these *lapsi* should be taken in by the community again. In Rome, the conflict intensified with the defeat of Novatian, the leading presbyter during the time of the persecutions, at the hands of the pragmatic Cornelius in the episcopal election of 251. Novatian was then elected as antibishop and took up an even stricter position. The congregation he lead, the "pure" (*katharoi*, from which perhaps the concept "heretic" was derived), found followers in North Africa and the orient and continued in scattered regions until the seventh century. What is important here for later developments is that, because the Novatianists also spread to areas beyond Rome, communities in these regions had to take sides in the conflict so that—similar to Callistus' time—the following phenomenon became clear, as it would later in Rome: the preference for pragmatic persons over a theologically better founded but rather rigoristic elite. The belittling of the defeated opposition by the victorious was a scene that repeated itself often, and it was accompanied by a wiping out of names from the liturgical memory (*memoria*) in the congregation.

It became evident that Cornelius, with his forbearance for the *lapsi,* was more successful than his opposition when in 257 and 258 Emperor Valerian took up again and intensified Decius' persecution policy by threatening members of the clergy and Christian *honestiores* (senators, eques, and high officials) with the death penalty. What is more, the emperor wanted to make Christian congregational life impossible by confiscating ecclesiastical buildings and by prohibiting the right to assemble. Despite these harsh measures, there were fewer *lapsi* than there were under Decius; in fact, the number of martyrs was now greater. In Rome, for example, the ruling bishop at that time, Sixtus II, and his entire staff, the deacons, were killed. Lawrence, who was later much venerated, belonged to this group. But neither did this persecution bring with it the success the emperor had hoped for. Thus, in approximately 260, under the emperor's son and successor, Gallienus, the congregation's ecclesiastical riches were returned. And since the

Christian congregation, at least in Rome, was not disturbed by persecutions for another forty years, it was able to win over converts and build up both its organization and its wealth. Therefore, the great persecution begun in 302 by Diocletian and Galerius could not but fail in the end, even though the Roman bishop Marcellinus is supposed to have lapsed in faith temporarily. The hard line regarding penitential acts taken by Marcellinus' successors, Marcellus and Eusebius, led to tumult in the Roman congregation and to the expulsion of both of these bishops. These conflicts indicate, however, that what happened in Rome was but an aftershock of the actual persecutions, which had already ended by 308. Thus the Roman congregation was active again and its organization stabilized when, between the years 311 to 313, at the time of the new bishop Miltiades, the various *augusti* and *caesares* officially allowed, by edicts of tolerance, the practice of the Christian faith and cult within their sphere of power.

There was, however, not only an increase and a stabilization of the Roman community in the last century before the end of the persecutions; this period for the first time also left behind lasting signs in architecture and in the liturgy still visible today. The only older signs were the two commemorative markers for Peter and Paul on the site of the two later basilicas that bear their names. While he was probably still a deacon, Callistus I obtained for the Roman congregation the catacombs that were later named after him. In the middle of the third century, a special tomb for bishops was constructed that is still there today. It was not long before the two bishops who reigned in the most difficult period, Cornelius and Sixtus, were remembered in the canon, that part of the mass which underwent no changes. Also remembered was the beloved deacon Lawrence, while legendary female saints such as Agnes or Cecilia, along with the supposed first successors to Peter—Linus, Cletus, and Clement—were also included in the liturgical commemoration, but only later, probably in the sixth or seventh century. The most important festival for the papacy, the feast of Peter and Paul on June 29, also dates back to the middle of the third century. Starting with this time period, official registers were dated with the taking of office and the death of the bishops. Thus the first sure date handed down from the history of the Roman congregation comes from the third century: the year 235. All earlier dates are fictitious. Whether churches built after the fourth century are standing on the sites of earlier cult temples cannot be proved, except for St. Peter's, St. Paul's, and St. Sebastian's. For this reason, there is no information that indicates where the bishop of Rome resided. And yet, the importance of the third and fourth centuries in establishing a Roman tradition is evinced by the fact that churches of the fourth and fifth centuries were connected, if at times in error, with the names of earlier bishops such as Sixtus or Marcellus. In contrast, the bishops of the second century remained mere phantom figures in this regard. By the fifth century, Clement was the only one of these early bishops to become a patron of the church as a supposed follower of and successor to Peter.

Finally, a brief discussion is called for on how much importance the Roman community had outside Rome before the so-called Constantine turning-point. The solution to this problem is especially important for the historical and dogmatic solidification of later papal claims. Evidence is so slight, however, and the information it contains so ambiguous, that it is impossible to comment on this with certainty. At Paul's time, Jerusalem was still the center of Christianity. When Paul, in his letter to the Romans, referred to them as exemplary and strong of faith, this must be interpreted as praise for the Christian congregation of the capital. Admiration for Rome in the second century on the part of Ignatius of Antioch and others, as well as numerous visits to Rome by bishops, other Christians, and heretics, must also be viewed in this light: the Roman congregation was important, especially after the destruction of Jerusalem, because it was situated in the capital of the empire. Likewise, the Christian communities of other large cities and political metropolises—Antioch, Alexandria, Carthage—were also centers of Christianity for their surrounding regions. Later, this principle would also hold true with the increasing importance of cities such as Milan, Ravenna, and Constantinople. Rome's position as center of the empire was most likely one of the reasons that the Epistle of Clement from the Roman to the Corinthian congregation, though a letter of remonstrance that had not been requested, was long accepted as authoritative by the Corinthians. Of course, another reason was that the sending of such a letter was a custom taken from the Jewish tradition in which Jewish communities used to admonish each other in writing. However, when the Roman bishop Victor tried, in the latter third of the second century, to settle authoritatively a disagreement over the correct date for Easter, he was strongly criticized even by friends of Rome such as Irenaeus of Lyon.

Another reason for the gradually emerging preeminence of Rome was the claim to apostolic succession. In its original form, this did not mean in any way that the Roman bishops were Peter's successors in office; rather, such a claim was to give expression to the idea that, since the days of the apostles, there had always been leading members of the congregation who could trace the correct teachings back to apostolic times—similar to other communities such as Antioch and Smyrna. The important apostles for Rome were, as the Epistle of Clement shows, Peter and Paul together, not just Peter. This harking back to the two apostles would remain of importance to the papacy, at least in the liturgy, until well into the late Middle Ages. As a consequence of this well-formulated doctrine of apostolic succession, two concepts became part of papal dogma that are still in use today, even though they may not be of great significance: *cathedra* and *sedes apostolica*. In Rome as well as in other communities, these two concepts were supposed to indicate, with reference to Old Testament and Romano-pagan ideas, that the person who occupied the see was following in a particular tradition, in this case the tradition of the apostle. The concept of *cathedra* was used first in areas other than Rome and without naming a particular apostle in relation to the Roman church— such as in the writings of the North African Tertullian or those of Iranaeus, bishop of Lyon, at the end of the second century. But, from the middle of the third century, the concept of *cathedra* in particular was closely connected with Peter. This is attested to by Bishop Cyprian of Carthage and by those Romans with whom he exchanged letters or by his adversaries. The passages by Irenaeus, Tertullian, and Cyprian are referred to later by supporters of the papacy's primacy as the first positive evidence of this doctrine; in their context, however, the passages merely state that it is important for every congregation to have the same doctrines as the congregations with an apostolic tradition, among which Rome, being in the Western part of the empire, was often mentioned. And even if Rome's position from the time of Cyprian was based on the later so important passage from the Gospel of Matthew 16:18 ("thou art Peter, and upon this rock I will build my church"), the Roman congregation and its bishops were to have been given merely a special rank, not special privileges. It is just as tenuous to derive a primacy of jurisdiction, which later popes claimed, from the requests of non-Roman congregations to the Roman bishops to intervene in Gallic or Spanish conflicts, since requests of this kind were also made to bishops of other communities. Whenever Roman bishops such as Victor, Callistus, Cornelius, and Stephen tried to intervene in everyday Christian affairs, they were able to prevail only when their claims were recognized as justifiably essential. Demands for special privileges, on the other hand, were criticized or rejected. The only certainty that can be assumed in all this is that a close connection was made, beginning with the late second century, between the Roman congregation, its bishop, and the activities of Peter and Paul, and that a certain, though not clearly defined preeminence was recognized, especially in the Western half of the empire. This was enough, however, on which to base the development of the papacy's elevated position in the periods to come. The actual realization of this position, however, would have to wait until much later.

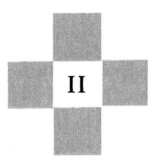

The Papacy and Rome Until the Death of Theodoric (526)

The title of this chapter and of the subsequent one emphasize the papacy's affiliation with political spheres of influence. In this way, it is indicated right from the start that the papacy's existence and function until the middle of the eleventh century was by and large shaped by political factors over which the papacy itself had little influence. That this chapter ends with the death of Theodoric, king of the Ostrogoths, in contrast to the usual division of papal history, can be justified in that the king saw himself as rightful successor to the Roman emperor in the West and ruled accordingly. The Byzantine epoch and, at the same time, the first medieval epoch of the papacy, began with the wars against the Goths following Theodoric's death.

From Rome's point of view, the fourth and fifth centuries were marked, in particular, by a complete Christianization of the city and by the bishop's elevation to the most important power in the city. At the same time, the most significant elements of the papal doctrine of primacy were developed.

To understand these three main tendencies, the following factors should be kept in mind. Until the end of this epoch, Rome was the theoretical capital of the empire, but the city's rulers usually lived elsewhere. This loss of political influence was especially noticeable after 324, when the new emperor Constantine and his successors in the East made Constantinople into the "new Rome," while the West was ruled mostly from either Milan or Ravenna. As a result of this shift of power, the Senate, which remained in Rome, sank to complete political insignificance, trying for a long time to regain its former prestige by opposing the policies of the ruler. For this reason, the Senate held on to the ancient Roman cults more tenaciously than other strata of society. Consequently, as the fifth century began, new "heathen" temples were built or old ones restored in Rome—in contrast to the East. The non-Christian temples shaped the city's image more than the recently victorious religion did. The Roman bishops, on the other hand, exploited the fact that the emperor lived far away to expand their own power and to make themselves, as much as possible, independent of the emperor.

The shifting of the center of power also had consequences for the Roman people. Some Greek-speaking inhabitants, whose ancestors had come to Rome because it was capital of the empire, were now leaving the city, with Latin again becoming the language of the majority. Revolts in North Africa and the successes of the Vandals from 429, coupled with bad harvests, made it impossible to guarantee the supply of grain from abroad beginning with the late fourth century, which also contributed to a contraction in the number of inhabitants. The conquest of the city by the Visigoths in 410 and by the Vandals in 455 had much graver consequences, however. While "new Rome" grew stronger both politically and economically and probably had, by the year 500, half a million inhabitants, the population of "old Rome" fell from approximately 500,000 to 100,000. Suffering the same negative effects, the population of the Roman ports of Ostia and Porto also fell, along with the Roman Campagna, where most of the land began turning marshy, a process which continued throughout the Middle Ages and was only turned around in the nineteenth century.

Special attention should ultimately be given to the changes in the West that came about through migration, since it was this dispersal of peoples that gave authority and legitimation to the bishop of Rome outside Italy. Roman rule in the fourth century stretched all the way to Britain and the lower Rhine, though most of these areas were only partly Christianized, chiefly the cities. Only in North Africa and Italy were there strong church organizations presided over by metropolitans, while similar administrative organizations for churches in Gaul and Spain were only in the process of being set up. This process nearly came to a halt in the fifth century, for outside of Greece and the Ostrogoth's sphere of power, which stretched from Sicily to the Danube and the lower Rhone, the Catholic congregations after circa 430 were for the time being either practically nonexistent (Gaul, Spain), were persecuted (North Africa and Sardinia), or nearly disappeared altogether (Britain, the lower Rhine, the upper and middle Danube). But when Constantine defeated his rivals and began promoting Christianity, the unfolding of events as we have just sketched them could have hardly been predicted.

The chief task of the Roman bishops in the first one hunderd years of the newly won freedom was to unite their city in one faith and form of worship. It was not just a matter of missionizing the greatest part of the population that belonged to another cult; rather, it was much more a matter of bringing to the various Christian congregations a single form of worship and creed under the supervision of the Roman bishop. As a result, the Christianization of Rome was shaped by an effort to make Latin the language of all congregations as well as an attempt to bring into the fold the smaller communities (Montanists, Novatianists, Donatists), which were in conformity with the true faith, but were somewhat rigoristic and had their own bishops. Furthermore, steps were taken to eliminate heretical communities, often labeled as "Manichaeans," though this plan was rather difficult to carry out. Nearly every pope of the late fourth and fifth centuries "discovered" heretics. This point alone makes it clear that the popes needed a long time to impose their doctrinal supervision in Rome. Little wonder that one of these was the first pope—the venerated Doctor of the Church, Leo I—who called on secular authorities to act with violence against these groups. Even earlier, at the end of the fourth century, the Jews were persecuted for the first time. Thus the Christianization of Rome was not completely peaceful; and more than ever it was impossible for the bishops to realize their projects without the backing of secular rulers. Their assistance was especially evident in the first decades of Constantine's rule and that of his sons.

One of the consequences of the legalization of Christianity in the years 311 to 313 was the restoration of property to the Christian congregations. For Rome, this meant the return of the catacombs located on the arterial roads and the restitution of the assembly rooms located in houses and in which the eucharist had been celebrated. The location of the catacombs is still known today since these places continued to be used and embellished in later times, and in modern times were excavated. About the community centers, on the other hand, we have no precise information. It had been assumed for a long time that the titular churches (about which more later), which were being built from the fourth century, were constructed on sites of early Christian assembly halls. Not one single example has ever been found, however, to verify this theory, not even in the cases in which after the fourth century titular churches were set up in homes. These new churches were established where the donor owned property. This also means that in the local dispersion of churches in the fourth century there are no indications that lead one to assume that Christians preferred certain perhaps socially differentiated residential areas. For this reason, a social history of Christians in Rome for this early period cannot be written. Since written sources for the first half of the fourth century are almost totally lacking, the buildings donated by Constantine and his family offer the most significant information about the first phase of Rome's Christianization after the persecutions.

Nearly all representative Christian places of worship were erected according to the standard multipurpose halls common in Rome at the time, the basilicas, and were therefore suited for various functions. Helena, the emperor's mother, had a private memorial built in the *sessorium* of her palace in which she kept a part of Christ's cross, which she had supposedly found. Hence, this place later received the nickname "Hierusalem" and is still called S. Croce in Gerusalemme today. Though it probably remained in private hands after the empress' death, only later was it possible to use the church for episcopal worship services. Six other buildings were used, principally for the burial of members of the imperial family and Roman Christians: SS Marcellino e Pietro on Via Labicana with the mausoleum of Helena; San Lorenzo on Via Tiburtina near the grave of Lawrence; S. Agnese on Via Nomentana near the grave of this saint and the mausoleum of the emperor's daughter Constantina; San Pietro in the Vatican; S. Sebastiano in via Appia; and possibly also a small structure over Paul's grave. These were covered catacombs in which only burials and *refrigeria* (wakes with feasts and drinking) took place, though initially no eucharistic celebrations took place, so that these structures did not have their own clergymen. Three of them were also used to honor the princely apostles who were regarded as the founders of the Roman congregation: S. Sebastiano for the worship of both saints, while St. Peter's and St. Paul's were used for the apostle who, according to the congregation's belief, was buried there. With this trend toward an increasing veneration and significance of the two apostles for the ideological foundation of the papacy, these structures, especially St. Peter's, were included more and more in the liturgy of the Roman bishops beginning with the middle of the fourth century. The pre-Constantine Roman community had neither a permanent cathedral nor a permanent episcopate.

The Lateran complex, including the Basilica of the Holy Savior and the bapistry, was initially the only place where the bishops could perform their rites. Corresponding to the still rudimentary state of development of the liturgical year at that time, the bishop celebrated in this basilica the most important fesitval, the resurrection, bapitizing new Christians the evening before Easter. The bishop also celebrated Sundays with these new Christians-to-be during their three-week (later six-week) prepatory period before baptism. In addition, the basilica was used for Roman synods and ecclesiastical court sessions. The bishop probably lived near the basilica, though vestiges of the episcopate can be identified only from the sixth century. The buildings were erected near the city walls, thus putting them at the time of Constantine, and even more so in the Middle Ages, outside of the city's residential area. For this reason, it was difficult for the bishop to have contact with the people, though this peripheral site proved to be advantageous when conflicts with parts of the population began in the middle of the fourth century. The church has remained to this day, hypothetically at least, the center of Christian Rome, which is seen most clearly in the Lateran basilica's title established in the following epoch: *caput et mater omnium ecclesiarum* (head and mother of all churches).

The Basilica of the Holy Savior surpassed in size all the state basilicas on the forum—there was room for 10,000 persons, or most of the adult Christians at that time—and in keeping with its importance for the community it was richly decorated by the emperor. Besides the main altar where the bishop officiated, there were seven other altars where the deacons, with the assistance of subdeacons, collected the offerings of the faithful (bread and wine) for the eucharist. For this, great patens (for the bread) and chalices or other containers were needed. Depending on the social rank of those who donated and those who received, the vessels were either of gold or silver, a total weight of 82 kilograms of gold and approximately 775 kilograms of silver. Additionally, there were images and lamps for the chancel as well as the fittings for the bapistry. The two episcopal houses of worship contained altogether about 330 kilograms in gold and 3.7 tons of silver, which could be melted down in case of emergency. Furthermore, there were landed estates, mostly in southeast Rome, set up for the production of wax (needed for worship at night) and other tribute. The other basilicas were similarly equipped, though perhaps to a lesser extent, while St. Peter's had agricultural estates as far away as Syria and Egypt. In general, the new structures were equipped very well. Income was bound by purpose, however, so that the bishop of Rome could not dispose of the wealth indiscriminately. Therefore, he was still dependent on the donations of the faithful, which the deacons made sure kept coming in.

The bishops of Rome and the presbyters, and later also wealthy lay persons, began from the late Constantine age—and perhaps even under Bishop Sylvester, probably since Mark—to build churches in houses which belonged to them. These are the so-called titular churches, of which there were about six in the middle of the fourth century, and about twenty-five at the beginning of the fifth century. Originally named after the owner and the donor (e.g., *titulus Equitii,* that is: "Ownership and donation of Equitius"), from the sixth century the churches began to be named more frequently after saints, or out of the donor's name a saint's name was made, suggesting a legendary background. Gradually, and in increasing numbers, the titular churches began replacing the old assembly halls, which were no longer needed. By the middle of the millennium, the new structures were so common throughout the city that the greatest distance between a residence and a titular church was five hundred meters. The faithful were most likely associated with certain titular churches that were in their neighborhoods, even though there were not any fixed parish districts in Rome until the end of the Middle Ages. An average of four or five presbyters worked in the churches since there was a total number of about seventy at the beginning of the fifth century. They cele-

brated the eucharist, with the help of ostiaries, lectors, and acolytes, attended to the needs of the faithful, and with the help of
the exorcists prepared the candidates for baptism. Donations made
to them were originally reserved for the bishop, but with an increasing number of adults wanting to be baptized and the gradual
implementation of baptism for children, the bishop had to delegate his authority. Therefore, bapistries were built from the end
of the fourth century in several titular churches as well as in
cemetery basilicas outside the city such as St. Peter's, S. Agnes, and
S. Lorenzo. It is probably due to the presbyters that the practical
consequences of Christianization, such as the making holy of Sundays and marriage before a priest, were already established in
Rome by the end of the fourth century.

Another task for both bishop and presbyter in making Rome
Christian was the Christianization of the burial ceremony. As their
ancestors had done, the Christian Romans celebrated the memory
of their dead with *refrigeria*. The habit of enjoying wine just a bit
too much on these occasions provoked indignation in the leaders
of the congregation. From the end of the fourth century, this kind
of commemoration in the cemeteries was gradually displaced by a
veneration of the martyrs who were buried there. Except for the
times when Constantine and his family arranged for the construction of expensive buildings, bishops, other clerics and lay persons
had small memorials built to honor martyrs, or bigger basilicas for
their own burials. These were built in and near the mostly under-
ground catacombs.

The increasing number of church structures indicates that the
new religion in Rome was rapidly winning converts. By the middle
of the fourth century the number of believers was so large and
their activity on behalf of the community so much that many
Christians after the death of Bishop Liberius in 366 took to the
streets as supporters for one of the two factions competing for the
episcopate. The victorius candidate Damasus had on his side a
strange mixture of average community members, artists, and grave
diggers who worked in the cemeteries as *fossores* (from *fossa*, i.e.,
graves), as well as gladiators. The power of this coalition had quite
an effect, for over one hundred supporters of the opposing candidate Ursinus had to pay for their support with their lives. They
were burned to death by Damasus' supporters in a basilica that
Liberius had built on the Esquiline. Intervention by the imperial
court and its representative in Rome settled the dispute. The

nickname of Damasus, the victorious pope and former deacon, was "auriscalpius" (from *auriscalpium*, i.e., earwig), which, along with the charge against his predecessor Liberius that he collaborated with members of the Senate against the Arian emperor, indicates that in the middle of the century Christians were already present in the upper class. They were eagerly supported by deacons in the drawing up of wills in favor of the church. It is hardly surprising, then, that under Damasus women from these classes wore the veil to devote themselves to God alone and formed pious groups, mostly on the Aventine, under the leadership of presbyters such as Jerome. They also donated their wealth to the church, and, becaue of this and an asceticism that was sometimes too strict, they drew the ire of their families. It must be stressed, however, that all the bishops up to Damasus and his successor, Siricius, took care not to force a Christianization of the Senate, even if the emperor himself wanted it. Only with their successors was this reluctance given up. This change, in particular along with the failure of any *Oppositionspolitik* based on maxims from Roman antiquity, including the launching of rival emperors, brought about, from the time of Innocent I, the Christianization of even such conservative senatorial families as the Symmachi and Nicomachi. A sign of the Christianization of the upper class is still visible today in a mosaic in the apse of S. Pudenziana completed in 400, which shows Peter and Paul dressed as senators. From this it can be assumed that by the year 410 Rome had been, at least superficially, Christianized. This is the same period in which the upper class exercised increasing influence over the appointment to the bishop's throne and the bishops intensified their attempt to broaden their legitimization outside Italy, as we shall see later.

But first, it was necessary for the bishops to put the form of worship and ecclesiastical organizations under their supervision and at their service. The birth of Christ on December 25, the former festival of the *Sol invictus* (the invincible sun), was celebrated in the West even before the middle of the fourth century in honor of Christ, "the new sun." In the same period, in the eastern part of the empire, the birth was mostly celebrated on January 6 with emphasis on the epiphany (Christ's appearance on earth). Both dates were observed in Rome at this time, probably because of the heterogeneous nature of the Roman congregation. And with this there arose a ritual balance to the importance of Easter, which also became clear locally in that the bishop celebrated the Christmas festivities in St. Peter's. And the third great festival, Pentecost, was probably already being celebrated in St. Peter's in the fifth century. St. Peter's soon became the second main church and a rival to the Basilica of the Holy Savior in the Lateran. It is unknown to what extent other churches were included in the episcopal worship services, churches such as the first one dedicated to Mary (Santa Maria Maggiore), built by Sixtus III after the Council of Ephesus (431), and the other great basilicas located outside the city walls. Equally uncertain is whether the bishop held his *statio* (i.e., episcopal worship service) on certain days, such as during the pre-Easter period, in one of the titular churches. It is more likely that he celebrated these days, if at all, like he did Sundays in his episcopal church. To keep in contact with the various congregations, however, acolytes in the late fourth century started bringing to the individual titular churches the *fermentum*, a part of the bread consecrated by the bishop which the officiating presbyters immersed in consecrated wine. Two developments in the fifth and sixth centuries were important for the link between bishops and titular churches and at the same time the first steps toward the formation of the college of cardinal priests. One of these developments was that presbyters of certain titular churches could assist with the services in basilicas at cemeteries. The first instance of this took place under Innocent I. Simplicius ordered that presbyters of certain, probably ecclesiastical regions were to hold weekly services in St. Peter's, St. Paul's, and S. Lorenzo. The goal most likely was to better care for the souls of pilgrims and of the people who lived outside of the city walls. (Probably for the same reasons the first monasteries were built at these churches in the fifth century.) The second development was that, from the beginning of the sixth century, presbyters who worked in titular churches were divided into a hierarchy. The *presbyteri priores*, predecessors to the cardinals, differentiated themselves from the other presbyters, especially in the administration of church property.

Another way of generating ritual unity was the effort to institute a common language of worship. Latin names for presbyters and letters of the third century lead to the assumption that not all members of the community spoke Greek. The trend in favor of Latin grew stronger in the following century, especially under Damasus. The continued use of Greek phrases during this period, however, indicates that the Latinization process was quite protracted. Probably only at the end of the fifth century was it completed. After that the chief elements of the Latin mass were fixed. In regard to the Latinization of the liturgy, it is often noted that Damasus promoted a new translation of the Bible by Jerome, his secretary for several years. From this it has been concluded that this translation, the so-called Vulgate, was used very early in Rome. This is a false assumption, however. Since the Latinization of Rome was by and large complete before Jerome had finished his new version, and since he was held in little esteem by Damasus' successor, Rome continued using older translations longer than other congregations. This is seen most clearly in the Psalms—the most used text in the liturgy—as the Vulgate had been withdrawn from use for readings from the Old and New Testaments probably in the seventh century. Only in the fourteenth century did Jerome's Psalms finally gain use in the papal court.

Equally as important as the unification of a language for worship was the standardization of celebrations for days commemorating martyrs. To understand this, it must be taken into consideration that, according to Roman sacred law, which for the time being was official law in Rome, the translation of remains was considered a desecration of the dead and therefore sacreligious. Thus the martyrs had to be venerated where they were buried. For the same reason, only things which the martyr had touched (cloth, lamp oil, etc.) could be officially exported, although this did not prevent the *fossores* working in the cemeteries from selling a bone or two on the sly. This only became worthwhile, however, after a specific martyr had been officially recognized by the congregation leadership, with attempts to do so beginning in the middle of the fourth century. Under Liberius, an almanac was made up in 354 in which the commemorative days having the blessing of the bishop were presented month by month. Most of these days fell between Pentecost and October. With this, the bishop had the opportunity to establish a definite liturgical year in connection with the three other great festivals of Christmas/Epiphany, Easter, and Pentecost. This tendency was further advanced when the following pope, Damasus, honored and officially recognized many of these martyrs by having epitaphs in verse inscribed on their tombstones. Damasus' epigrams show not only the relatively high cultural standards of the board of deacons, but also show the disinclination on the part of the church leadership to let the creating of legends get out of hand. This rational bent can also be recognized in the prayers and sermons handed down by bishops (Leo I, Gelasius I) from the fifth century. However, the cataloging of martyrs did not remain within this restricted range; in fact, in the fifth and early sixth centuries, there was an expansion that reflected the political changes in the empire, as can be seen in the naming of saints in Ravenna (Chrysogonus) and in the East (John and Paul, Cosmas and Damian, *quattro coronati*, etc.). Several saints received even more emphasis in the episcopal liturgy when, in the year 500, they were included in the canon of the mass. In addition, the number of saints—initially only fourteen names (Mary, Peter and Paul, Clement I, Sixtus II, Cornelius, Cyprian, Lawrence, John the Baptist, Stephen, Marcellinus and Peter, Perpetua, Agnes)—was later expanded to thirty-nine. The original list of names shows clearly that, except for a few saints (Mary, John, Stephen), for the most part, only those saints were honored who had some significance for the founding of the Roman congregation or who, like Cyprian, had close ties with the Roman congregation. With the spread in the number of Roman names in particular from the seventh century, this Rome-oriented selection would also shape the veneration of saints in Italy, Gaul, and England. Though not surprising, it must be emphasized that, from the beginning of this development, Peter was particularly honored in that he had two commemorative days: June 29 as the day of his death, February 22 as the day he supposedly took office as first bishop of Rome (the festival of *cathedra petri*). Since February 22 was the old Roman day of the dead, this second festival meant that, at least in the eyes of the bishops, Peter had become the forefather of the Roman community. If one keeps in mind that at the same time the basilica St. Peter's had become the second most important church for the episcopal liturgy, it is clear that, at this time, the cult of Peter had already far surpassed all other cults in Rome.

The veneration of Peter in Rome—and with it the basis for papal claims outside Rome—can also be seen in the iconography. For example, Peter was compared to Moses, for just as Moses received the laws of the Old Testament from God, so Peter received those of the New Testament from Christ. For this reason, the *traditio legis* (the handing down of the law) became a favorite theme in pictorial representations, as did the the *traditio clavium* (the handing over of the key), a reference to Matthew 16:18.

All that was necessary now to guarantee episcopal claims was to make a clear connection between Peter and the succession of the

Roman bishops. As mentioned in the first chapter, a line of succession for the Roman bishops had already been laid down in the second century, first outside Rome, then in the city. Beginning in the third century, the Callistus catacombs on Via Appia contained a vault for bishops which, like the graves of other saints, was decorated by Damasus and given prominence with epigrams. There already existed at the time of Damasus a list of Roman bishops that stated exact, if fictitious, dates for the periods of time which particular bishops held office. Moreover, Peter was listed as the first bishop of Rome (the papacy beginning in the year of Christ's death!), while the non-Roman line usually started with Linus or Clement. It was pure good fortune that, at the end of the fourth century, Rufinus of Aquileia, who had close ties to Rome, translated into Latin parts of the *Clementine Homilies* and *Recognitions,* a novel-like legend of the life of Clement I. Written in the East in the third century by Jewish Christians to support the Jerusalem tradition, the collection contains a letter allegedly written by Clement to James, the brother of Christ, in which James, as leader of the Jerusalem congregation, is called the "bishop of bishops," in other words, the supreme leader of the Christians. What was important for Rome, however, was Clement's description of how Peter had consigned to him as his successor the power of binding and loosing. The letter, considered genuine, was proof for the Roman bishops that they possessed the full powers of Peter, just as Clement did. At the end of the fourth century the doctrine was put forward that every Roman bishop possessed the *cathedra petri.* Out of a combination of these various elements arose the doctrine of *sedes apostolica* (apostolic see), which stated that every Roman bishop, as Peter's successor, possessed the full power of authority granted to this position. Because this was not bound to the person of the individual bishop, but rather was transpersonal and had been established by God himself, the bishops were considered invioable. Leo I solidified this doctrine with the help of Roman law by making the Roman bishop the valid heir of Peter. From now on, the Roman bishop, by his own understanding, was the vicar (i.e., representative) of Peter, and through Peter, also the vicar of Christ for the entire church.

The position of the Roman bishop received further support in the latter part of the fourth century, when an increased emphasis was placed on Paul in both worship and teaching. At the time of Damasus, the so-called Ambrosiaster in Rome annotated thirteen of Paul's letters. During the latter part of Damasus' rule as bishop, a basilica worthy of St. Peter's was built over Paul's grave, and this with imperial backing. Thus a local and cultic parallel was established between the two saints. From now on there were pictorial representations featuring both apostles, such as on glasses (for private worship) or the aforementioned mosaics in S. Pudenziana. The images of the two apostles were meant to make clear that they had received their authority from Christ: Peter the power of binding and loosing, and Paul the instruction of the people. As a result of a further unfolding of older traditions recognized in Rome since the first century, both apostles were now considered to be the forefathers of the bishop of Rome, the bishops inheriting from one the position of chief shepherd, from the other supreme authority on doctrine. Thus the festival on June 29, when both apostles were commemorated, grew in significance for the solidification of the episcopate. The disappearance of the ancient Roman cult as a consequence of Rome's Christianization, along with the downfall of the Roman empire through Germanic invasions, moved Leo I in a sermon on June 29 to glorify the two apostles as the true patrons of Rome instead of Romulus and Remus. The same pope showed that Peter, however, was the most important of the two— as Romulus was in the legends of ancient Rome—when he had medallions painted in St. Paul's, and probably also in St. Peter's, in which the bishops of Rome were portrayed, beginning with Peter. In this way, he made the basis and the claims of the Roman bishop clearly visible to every visitor or pilgrim at both churches. Leo was also the first bishop who had himself buried in St. Peter's. Most of his successors followed this custom and were buried near the forefather of their episcopate. Out of this custom also arose, in circa 500, the tradition of usually burying bishops of the first and second centuries until the time of Victor in or near St. Peter's. The graves of Victor's successors were known to be in other cemeteries.

The ritual prominence given to Peter and Paul was only possible, as were other liturgical changes, because the bishop was able to bring the clerics and the various parishes of the city under his undisputed supervision. The Roman clergy can be categorized in two divisions based on the developments of the second and third centuries: the clergy of the bishop's churches and those of the titular churches. Since communion and baptisms could take place in both the episcopal churches as well as the titular churches, the necessary clerics—ostiaries, lectors, exorcists, but not the presbyters—worked in both churches. Quite a few details are known about the lectors in particular. They had to be able to read and, because of the way the Psalms were presented, also sing; in other words, they had to have a certain minimum level of education. Since these tasks could be carried out by children, the usual way to begin a career in the clergy was through the office of lectors. Those who wanted to continue being active in a titular church could then become acolytes and presbyters, while those interested in working for the bishop could become deacons and subdeacons. Thus the offices of presbyter and deacon were the final stage in two different careers. The bishop could be chosen from either group. If the new bishop had previously been a deacon, then he received the authority to celebrate communion as a presbyter upon taking office. In contrast to the regulations that evolved at the same time in Spain and Gaul, it was not necessary in Rome before becoming bishop to have held in succession the five lower positions (ostiary, lector, exorcist, acolyte, subdeacon) or the two higher ones (deacon and presbyter). In general, a cleric could keep a lower position for his whole life.

It is not known whether at this time the lower clerics working in the titular churches were trained in their office by the bishop. Nevertheless, the bishops tried to regulate the entrance age and the length of time for holding office. Both Siricius and Zosimus made statements that were at odds with each other regarding this, showing that the matter was not undisputed. After the pontificate of Zosimus, a cleric had to be 25 or 30 years old to become a deacon or presbyter respectively. Since the deacons served the bishop directly and their numbers were few, it was probably easy for the bishop to check their work and apply his rule. That the bishop would get his way with the presbyters was more or less guaranteed inasmuch as before the ordination of presbyters the deacons obtained information about the candidates and made it known to the bishop. And, unlike the lower clerics, it is known that the bishop ordained higher clerics, usually in December. The bishop could use this opportunity to check the candidates' life-styles, especially as regards celibacy, to which both groups—though not the lower clergy—had been bound since the late fourth century. Of course, because of all this checking, the ordination of clerics who held unaccepted doctrinal opinions could be impeded. This scrutinizing also served to exclude morally unworthy candidates, or ones who were unsuitable because of previous work. In the first category were, besides penitents, men who had married a second time or who had married widows. The second group consisted of those whose earlier jobs had involved the spilling of blood—soldiers, judges, etc.—or those who were dependent on others. Not only were slaves, tenant farmers, and freedmen considered dependent, but also members of compulsory guilds, and decurions. The latter were members of city councils and were personally responsible for the collection of taxes.

As the initial exclusion of the decurions shows, these guidelines were not meant so much to raise the level of social prestige of the clerics as to guarantee their independence. Since even at that time, however, it was possible to admit decurions by making exceptions while other groups remained excluded, the Roman clergy usually was recruited out of the upper middle class, and finally out of the senatorial upper class. Thus, even in this period, there was a social distance between the clergy and ordinary churchgoers, which was usually also a determinative factor in the Middle Ages. The largely tax-exempt status of clerics attracted many to the clergy. And because only clerics who were presbyters and deacons were bound to celibacy—whether Leo I's attempt to force the subdeacons to celibacy was successful is not known—there were several clerics of the same generation in one family or clerical dynasty. Even bishops sometimes came from the same family: Damasus' father had been a bishop, though not in Rome; Silverius was the son of the Roman bishop Hormisdas; in addition to other clerics, the bishops Felix III, Agapitus, and Gregory I all belonged to senatorial families. This goes to show how much family connections prevailed in the clergy, especially from the fifth century, and how they determined an ecclesiastical career.

Over time, the proximity to the bishop, especially the work as deacon, shaped the career of many bishops in addition to family affiliation. Nevertheless, within the local congregation the presbyters and the deacons at least were on equal terms. As their advanced age when entering office and the occasional apologetic statements by the Roman bishops indicate, the presbyters were accorded the highest level after the bishop. This was based on their status of being the only ones besides the bishop who baptized new Christians, that is, received them into the community. They also celebrated communion and were active in caring for souls. In these matters they were considered equal to the bishop, who exceeded them only by virtue of his office and the powers that went with it. Therefore, it was also the presbyters who together with the bishop decided on questions of faith for Rome at synods, and with him constituted the ecclesiastical court. Though the bishop may have previously been a deacon, the presbyters exceeded him in experience even with affairs of worship and ministry. Thus presbyters often acted as legates of the Roman bishop at synods or councils that were not held in Rome. They could even become bishops in places other than Rome. In Rome itself, however, the chance to become bishop was greater for deacons, especially in the epoch we are now discussing. Of sixteen bishops and rival candidates between 352 and 526, about whose careers few details are known, only three had previously been presbyters (Boniface I, Sixtus III, Lawrence), while the others had been deacons.

The deacons' standing was no doubt rooted in the closed nature of their group and the small number of board members, only seven, in addition to their being close to the bishop. In contrast to the presbyters, who were spread all over the city, the deacons were always centrally located as they carried out their duties for the bishop; therefore, they knew each other well and were perforce known to the heads of government administration. Their good contacts resulted from their on the job activity. They collected the donations—also stemming from this was their aforementioned function at the episcopal eucharist celebrations. They administered monies, episcopal valuables, and property; they saw to it that the needy were provided for; and they were responsible for the archives of episcopal writings, perhaps even taking part in composing them. In contrast to the presbyters, they were joined together in a college under the direction of the archdeacon in the fourth century, which must have increased their effectiveness. And finally, in circa 501, a constitution supposedly made up by Sylvester was ratified under Symmachus, which gave the deacons control over all the lower clerics, from lectors to subdeacons. And because of their proximity to the bishop, the *cardo* (i.e., the hinge) of the community, the text of the constitution described them as "cardinal deacons" (*diaconi cardinales*). This is not to say that they were loved by everyone, however. In fact, already by the fourth century they were considered arrogant. And since nearly every bishop until the time of Zosimus had previously been a deacon, the presbyters attempted to make one of their own bishop in 418. The government administration and the imperial court initially favored the rival candidate, the archdeacon Eulalius, to maintain the status quo. After he had ignored an imperial prohibition, however, the secular leadership also came out in favor of the presbyter, Boniface. This was the first schism in Rome that arose solely from the rivalry between presbyters and deacons, that is, not from political, doctrinal, or disciplinary differences.

As they did in 366 after Liberius' death and would do later, in 498, after the death of Anastasius II, the secular authorities in 418 also decided who was to be regarded as the rightful bishop after a disputed election. This de facto influence on the election of popes by nonclerical powers would continue in the future, even into the early twentieth century. The bishops took great pains, however, as early as the fifth century, through their own decrees or through decrees of Roman synods, to develop criteria that would make such interference unnecessary. The Roman bishop was elected by the "clergy and people," in conformity with the ongoing and valid legal pretense. Reports from the fifth century indicate, however, that what was meant by clergy was mostly deacons and presbyters, and by people was the *meliores civitatis*, members of the upper class. There are also signs that the election itself was reserved for the upper echelons of the clergy, while the leading lay persons were granted merely the right of assent. In disputed elections, the winner was the one to whom the majority of the clergy remained faithful and the one who was consecrated first. Because of this, the bishops from the area around Rome—the bishop of Ostia and his colleagues—also had a potential influence on the designation of the better candidate in that, according to a resolution of the Council of Nicea (325), the new bishop of Rome had to be consecrated by one of them. In addition, the synod of 499, which backed Symmachus, prohibited monetary donations and sworn promises, thereby admitting that even at this time simonistic practices were not unknown in Rome. To what extent these resolutions were adhered to in undisputed elections, the usual case, is unknown. In any case, they were not enough when there was dissent among the voters. There was continuous disagreement in the clergy and the upper class—a schism in the Senate erupted over the election of 498—leading to mostly bloody consequences and the intervention of the ruler at the time or his representative.

The bishops' upper-class origins in Roman society created, as mentioned, a social distance between them and the majority of the people. And yet there were also positive aspects for most of the people since in the early fifth century the bishops took on new, principally social duties, which required large amounts of money. To accomplish this, however, it was usually propitious for the bishop to come from wealthy families and have good contacts with others of similar status. After the interruption of the regulated supply of grain from abroad for Rome's inhabitants at the end of the fourth century and during the Visigothic threat (408–410), it was evident that the imperial government was no longer capable of supplying for the daily needs and security of the Roman people. With this came a deterioration in the effectiveness of the secular administration led by the city prefects. This situation not only offered the bishops the chance, but even made them duty bound, to take over the position of the failing governmental authorities through the expansion of their charitable activities. This new type of engagement was to some extent evident when Innocent I and Leo I interceded, later embellished to legendary proportions, on behalf of Roman interests in confrontations with the Visigoths, Huns, and Vandals. But in these instances the bishops were merely members of a greater delegation also comprised of representatives from the upper class and the secular administration. Far more important, however, was the social activitiy in Rome itself. A reflection of this activity was the praise given to Gelasius I in the *Liber pontificalis,* a book written in the sixth century and about which more will be said later: "He loved the poor and expanded the clergy. He freed the city of Rome from the fear of hunger." One of his successors, Symmachus, built shelters for the poor near St. Peter's, St. Paul's, and S. Lorenzo and bought the release of prisoners. Also under Gelasius, the quartering of the church's assests, which later became canonical, was recognized. One quarter of the assests went to the bishop, one quarter to the clergy, one quarter to the poor, and the remaining quarter to maintaining church buildings. This presupposed, however, an effective administration and augmentation of church income. For this reason, Gelasius had a list drawn up for the first time of all ecclesiastical possessions (*polyptichum*).

The church's wealth probably increased through donations and through assets left in the wills of the faithful. It is not known for this period in Rome whether the church received money from the estates of deceased clerics, or whether the bishop received a general tribute upon taking office—the *cathedraticum* . What was important, however, was that after the Christianization of the upper class a part of their wealth came into the hands of the church, and that property, once gained, was not allowed to be immediately sold off or alienated. Even the bishop, who by the late fourth century was in supervision of the church's overall assests, held to this prohibition. As a result, the church's property diminished chiefly through plunder (Visigoths in 410, Vandals in 455) or through the hostile takeover of agricultural estates. Moreover, revenue from these estates depended on how well agriculture was faring economically.

If the numerous churches and the sporadic information about the social concern of the bishops are any indication, the wealth of the Roman church in the fifth century was probably not seriously impaired. Though precise information is unavailable, the landholdings were so extensive that in the middle of the fourth century an administration was set up modeled after the state. The bishop and his deacons were responsible for general supervision. For practical matters, however, lay persons were needed who knew something about economics and law, the so-called *defensores* (i.e., defenders, lawyers). Probably as early as the fifth century, these were brought together in a *schola* (i.e., corporation) under the direction of a *primicerius* (i.e., the first person). They represented their ecclesiastical clients in legal actions and tried to maximize profits on the assets, which for the most part were probably made up of real estate in the city and the country estates. And, since the church's properties reflected the prevailing economic system, the labor on church lands came mostly from slaves and tenant farmers. Thus the *defensores* not only dealt with donations, bequests, deposits or trade, but also with the freeing (*emancipatio*) of dependent persons.

Since Roman law required all legal matters to be written down, the church administration employed literate persons—notaries (*notaria*, i.e., shorthand)—who knew the abbreviation system in use. In addition, the notaries, under episcopal order and supervised by the deacons, wrote documents on martyrdom, so that the cult of saints could be standardized and controlled. They also prepared the minutes of Roman synods. Belonging in part to the lower clergy, the notaries by the fifth century were also organized in a *schola* under a *primicerius*. There were secretaries for composing episcopal letters, although a differentiation between the secretaries and the notaries is not always possible. All documents were kept in a *scrinium* (i.e., "shrine," archive), the founding of which was later attributed to Julius I. The keeping of archives is therefore of general importance for the history of the papacy because early on it guaranteed continuity in the representation of papal claims outside Rome.

Here it might be worth while to examine these claims more closely. In so doing, the position the bishops of Rome held toward the emperor or his representatives must be distinguished from the one held toward other church institutions. As emperor, Constantine the Great was, as were his predecessors, the *pontifex maximus*, the chief custodian of all recognized cults, with supervision over the maintenance of sacred rights. In this capacity and for political reasons, he was interested in guaranteeing the unity of the new religion by supressing teachings and movements which were not considered orthodox or which threatened religious peace and, by extension, the social order. If not, the political unity of the empire could be put in jeopardy. His successors continued this outlook, even though they no longer carried the title *pontifex maximus*, which was considered pagan. Thus the emperors strived to show their pious disposition through bequests or donations or by raising the status of the Christian clergy to that of other religious officials by giving them the same privileges. But more than that, the emperors appointed bishops as judges to preserve the faith and control discipline, convened and directed local synods and state councils, or saw to it that certain doctrines were implemented, which even went so far as to their formulating new dogma.

The imperial policy on religion had undoubtedly solidified the church at that time. Had emperors not convened them, the four great councils of Nicea (325), Constantinople (381), Ephesus (431), and Chalcedon (451) would not have taken place since an ecclesiastical authority responsible for the whole "oecumene" (i.e., inhabited world, thus the Roman empire) did not exist. And it was these four councils that established the dogma that even today is recognized by both Catholics and Orthodox. At the same time, however, the ecclesiastical authorities, especially in the Eastern part of the empire, fell into an often detrimental dependency on the political designs and private religious opinions of the emperor. The spiritual and secular leaders were almost continually in conflict with each other. The teachings in the West that grew out of this conflict have in part shaped the relationship between church and state even to the present. The bishops of Rome played a decisive role in the formation of the church's views, especially in the fifth century. This sketch of the ecclesiastico-historical background of the church must always be kept in mind, if the position of the Roman bishops regarding state power is to be understood. Above all, it is worth bearing in mind that it simply is not true that the popes were the only and most important defenders of the church's freedom. What distinguished the Roman bishops in this regard from their other important colleagues—Hosias of Cordova, Athanasius of Alexandria, Hilary of Poitiers, Ambrose of Milan, Augustine of Hippo, John Chrysostom of Constantinople—is the established continuity of doctrine in fifth-century Rome. This was not only shaped by the personalities of individual popes—Innocent I, Leo I, Gelasius I. Equally important were Rome's reputation as the theoretical center of the empire, the fact that the ruler's residence was far away, and the stability of the church's political policies, vouchsafed by the college of deacons and the keeping of archives, within the leading strata of the Roman congregation.

In the first half of the fourth century, the only difference between the Roman congregation and others was the strong support it received from Constantine and his immediate successors. Besides the construction of churches, as mentioned previously, the emperor showed his favor by granting privileges. The Roman bishop received, as did his colleagues, the right to act as judge in legal cases that affected Christian discipline. And the clergy in Rome, much more so than elsewhere, was for the most part placed beyond the legal jurisdiction of the state, and the church's property was freed from numerous taxes and services. Though to be sure, by the second half of the century, various emperors had limited these special rights because of acute financial emergencies in the empire, so that the state's heed for these privileges was subject to change. To what extent the Roman bishop, through title and rank, was considered equal to the upper ranks of the imperial administration is, in the face of older assertions, extremely uncertain. The only certain fact is that from the time of Damasus bishops were allowed, as were high state officials, to ride in carriages through the streets of Rome.

The emperor's use of the bishops of Rome was in keeping with this granting of privileges. The oldest example of this—often wrongly interpreted in favor of a special position of the bishop of Rome—is the Lateran synod of 313, convoked by the emperor and presided over by the Roman bishop Miltiades, which was to straighten out a disagreement between the bishop of Carthage and a group of rigoristic Donatists. But since no one recognized the synod's decision, the emperor had another synod in Arles reconsider the matter. Hence, it follows that Miltiades was of significance for Constantine only as bishop of his empire's capital, but was not considered the highest judge in matters concerning the Christian congregations in the West. Even more important were the opinions of the Roman bishops in the dispute over the teachings of Arius. Julius I and Liberius courageously supported the resolutions reached in Nicea against Arius. Liberius paid for his decision by being exiled for a time. Yet the bishops' leading position in the church as a whole was as tenuous as their position vis-à-vis the emperor.

It must be stressed, however, that Rome at this time had reached a prominent position within the Western empire, initially based on its political importance, but soon thereafter on apostolic succession. That the beliefs of the Roman congregation should serve as the guiding principle of other congregations was emphasized by Western synods such as the one held in Sardica (today Sofia) in 343—one of the canons appointed the bishop of Rome as appellate judge in questions of discipline and doctrine—and was recognized in the year 380 by the Western emperors Gratian and Valentinian II, and later by the emperor of the Eastern empire, Theodosius. As a reflection of Rome's special position in the West, in the following year the Council of Constantinople, long unrecognized by Rome, granted Constantinople, as the "new Rome," the same hierarchical rank that the "old Rome" had. This resolution, renewed in 451 in Chalcedon—Theodosius demanded it at the time with his capital city in mind—shows that, in the eyes of the emperor and the council fathers, Rome's importance was still based chiefly on its political position. Such a linkage reflected the common parallel at that time between the importance and prestige of secular and religious centers. Thus, in addition to Rome and Constantinople, capitals or administrative centers such as Alexandria, Antioch, and Carthage—and to a lesser extent Thessalonica, Arles, Milan, and Ravenna—rose to be the centerpoints of ecclesiastical regions. For this same reason, Jerusalem stood in the shadow of the city of Caesarea, the government's administrative center, until well into the fifth century. And just how much the Roman congregation was actually ruled by the emperor is seen not only in state intervention in disputed elections, but also in a canon of the Roman synod of 378, which designated the emperor as the highest judicial authority for cases which involved a Roman bishop.

Not long after, however, the way the relationship between church and state was viewed began to change, first outside Rome, and later in Rome itself. Ambrose of Milan thoroughly convinced Emperor Theodosius that, as a Christian, he had to obey the bishops. As a result of the Visigoth's sacking of Rome in 410, Augustine of Hippo, in his work *De civitate dei,* reflected upon the foundation of the earthly and heavenly kingdoms and from this developed a doctrine that would be authoritative for centuries in the West. In this doctrine he also emphasized that the earthly ruler was obliged to help the servants of the heavenly kingdom. This view was also circulating in Rome at this same time, as a letter in 420 from Boniface I to the Western emperor shows. Reflecting this tendency, Leo I, in a conflict with the bishop of Arles in 445, had Emperor Valentinian III sanction the authority of the bishop of Rome over the churches in the Western empire. This same pope wrote to the Eastern Roman emperor, Leo, that his authoritative power had been entrusted to him "chiefly for the protection of the church." Felix III expanded on this doctrine when he wrote to Emperor Zeno that he was obliged to obey God's laws and the church in matters of faith, for he was a son, not a bishop, of the church.

When he was still a deacon, Gelasius I had perhaps helped compose Felix III's letters. As bishop, he formulated the doctrine that would shape, especially from the eleventh century, the relationship between church and state: the so-called "doctrine of the two powers," as it was stated in a letter to Emperor Anastasius in 494. The most important passage for later times defined the various functions of secular and church power and of those who held the power: "the holy authority of the bishops and the sovereign power." "Of these is the burden of the priests that much heavier in that they have to submit before the heavenly judge the account of the kings of men." Based on this, even the emperor was to obey them in matters of faith and church discipline. And Gelasius also claimed, humbly yet unequivocally, the highest authority in the church for the bishop of Rome, "whom the highest deity chose to stand above all priests." Different from his medieval successors, however, he emphasized the principle of noninterference. This becomes clear in another text, Timothy II 2:4: "the servant of God does not entangle himself with the affairs of this life."

This rejection of state influence in church affairs was strengthened under Symmachus, who had become bishop with the help of secular powers, in this case the Ostrogoth king Theodoric; yet, when Symmachus was accused of moral lapses by his adversaries, he and his followers rejected a decision of a synod convened by Theodoric in 501, though the proceedings were in full accord with valid judicial practices of that time. To ensure this new position, various texts were drawn up and dated during the rule of Sylvester, who was given legendary status in approximately 500. On the grounds that no lesser person may judge his superior, it was stated succinctly: "No one may judge the first see" (*Nemo iudicabit primam sedem*), not even the emperor. Like the doctrine of Gelasius, this sentence, later formed in a different language, would achieve its full effect only in the eleventh century.

It is clear, nevertheless, that the Roman bishops ascribed to themselves a position equal to that of the emperor's ever since the end of the fifth century, that is, after the end of the Roman empire in the West. This they also showed in their public appearances, clear for all believers to see. Probably even at this time, and certainly in the sixth century, they wore the pallium (a narrow band of white material worn over the shoulders) and then bestowed it upon bishops associated with them, such as those from Ostia, an act that was usually the duty of the emperor. Until at least the twelfth century, the pallium was the symbol of authority of the bishop of Rome. And probably also from the fifth century, the Roman bishops imitated the emperor by having candles and incense carried at the front of processions.

Reality, however, was not always what they imagined it to be. It was difficult to make the claim of being guardian of the true faith, especially when in approximately 470 Ricimer, commander of the army, built a church for his Arian soldiers near the most important garrison in Rome. The church was also used by Gothic troops, and like other Arian churches in Rome was first Catholicized by Gregory I (S. Agata dei Goti). This dependence on rulers who did not even possess the true faith had to be tolerated to an even greater extent by John I, twenty years after the Symmachan Forgeries. Though John I was the first Roman bishop to travel to Constantinople, where he was welcomed with honor, his mission was anything but favorable to papal dignity, for by order of Theodoric he was supposed to give his support to the toleration of the persecuted Arian Goths in the East. Not surprisingly, his mission was unsuccessful. After returning to Italy, John died, perhaps in a Gothic prison and, in Rome, was then considered a martyr, helping Theodoric to gain the reputation of being a heretical tyrant. For this reason, John's pontificate is an especially good example of the discrepancy between Roman fiction and reality at the end of this epoch.

This discrepancy also characterized, for the time being, the position of the bishop of Rome within the church itself. To discern this position more clearly, it might be useful to keep in mind three geopolitical spheres: Italy, the Western empire, the Eastern empire.

Emperor Diocletian had subdivided the empire, for the purposes of more efficient management, into bigger administrative areas (diocese), which were usually made up of several smaller areas (provinces). Constantine and his successors changed this subdivision for the same reason. One of these changes concerned the diocese of Italy. The northern half of the diocese, which stretched from the Alps to the Apennines south of Florence, was to supply the imperial court in Milan (*Italia annonaria*) with provisions. The southern half, including the islands of Sicily, Sardinia, and Corsica, supplied Rome and was called *Italia suburbicaria* (*urbs* meaning "city," i.e., Rome). The two provinces were governed from Milan and Rome. And true to the usual assimilation of a secular and ecclesiastical midpoint, the bishops of Milan and Rome respectively supervised the Christian congregations of their provinces. Because of political changes, the bishopric of the bishop of Milan grew smaller to the advantage of Ravenna and Aquileia, especially from the beginning of the fifth century, while the Roman bishop's remained fairly constant until the Gothic wars. The bishop of Rome wrote instructions to the bishops of the diocese of Milan for observing the liturgy and discipline. Bishops of the same region were ordained by the Roman bishop, they attended synods held in Rome, and some presbyters of the Roman congregation were appointed bishops of this province. A letter in 416 from Innocent I to Bishop Decentius of Gubbio shows how subordination was established in Rome: since according to tradition Peter was the only apostle to have worked in the West—Paul is completely overlooked here—the only persons to have founded Christian communities in Italy, Gaul, Spain, Africa, Sicily, and the western islands were bishops appointed by Peter or his successors. Therefore, all these congregations had to abide by the regulations from Rome. The letter is one of the first examples of what in the future would be a preferred tactic of the Roman bishops, namely, the basing of claims on very questionable historical evidence. Nevertheless, these anachronisms, though recognizable back then, did not stop later popes and their partisans from turning assertions into historical fact, with the growing distance in time from the original date of the letter increasing the certainty of the "proof."

Geopolitical events, which had determined the extent of the early Roman republic in the pre-Christian era and had been of significance in the Middle Ages, led to the province of *Italia suburbicaria* having one smaller region of greater importance for the Roman community, namely, the lower reaches of the Tiber, the Alban Hills, and southern Tuscany. If the popes were not from Rome itself, then they usually came from this small area. From Albano came Innocent I; from Campagna, Celestine I, and Hormisdas; from Tuscany, Leo I and John I; and from Tivoli, Simplicius. At the same time, the bishops in this area, who from the fourth century consecrated the pope, were active: the bishops of Albano (first ordination prayer), Porto (second ordination prayer) and Ostia (third ordination prayer). The most important of these bishops was the bishop of Ostia, which is why he was granted the pallium by the Roman bishop, probably in the fifth century. The *Liber Pontificalis* of the sixth century ascribes the bestowal anachronistically to Bishop Mark. And participation by the Ostians was seen even at that time as so fundamental that, as the next epoch began, Pelagius I was ordained by a presbyter from Ostia (the bishop's see was probably vacant at the time, a precedent for similar regulations in the twelfth century).

If, as already mentioned, the subjugation of suburbicarian Italy to Rome remained unchanged during the whole epoch, then the influence of the bishop of Rome in areas of the Western empire outside this province largely depended on political changes. Since the position of the bishop of Rome beyond Italy achieved significance only from the time of Damasus, and since Britain, the lower Rhine, and the area north of the Danube were, from about 400, by and large no longer subject to imperial authority, the importance grew of Spain, Gaul, Northern Italy including the Alps, the western Balkans including Greece, and North Africa except for Egypt. If one took literally the decree of the synod of Sardica (343), then Rome would have already had at this time the appellate authority for all communities in the Western empire. On the other hand, synods organized by Ambrose show, for example, that under his pontificate Milan was much more important for southern

Gallic and Illyric bishops than Rome. In contrast to historians of dogma and law, who like to consider synodal decrees as perpetually valid, one must proceed with the idea that such decrees as well as decisions of the Roman bishops were often for specific situations and merely restated the views of specific groups within the church, so that nothing of general and permanent validity can be deduced from these decrees.

In view of its geographical proximity, Northern Italy might be assumed to have been an important goal of papal integration policies. This is not the case, however. The mere fact that the imperial capital was established first in Milan, and from the end of the fourth century in Ravenna, led to considerable autonomy for the church in this province. Along with that there were strong personalities such as Ambrose of Milan. Hence, it follows that there were personal contacts between North Italian bishops and Rome as well as an exchange of liturgical forms or in the veneration of saints. Furthermore, Gelasius I gave his support to buying of freedom for prisoners in northwest Italy, and from time to time Roman presbyters even became bishops in Northern Italy. But, until the middle of the sixth century, not all parties recognized Rome's direct authority to supervise congregations in Northen Italy.

The influence of the bishop of Rome appeared for awhile to have been stronger in Illyricum and in southeast Gaul, as indicated by the bishops of Thessalonica and Arles functioning as the Roman bishop's vicar. Here, too, the position of these two cities in terms of the state is significant: Thessalonica was the administrative center for the Macedonian diocese (the west Balkans, i.e., Illyricum to the Danube and Greece), while Arles was the imperial capital for a time in the fourth century and, from the beginning of the fifth century, a refuge and center for Roman citizens who had remained in Gaul.

The first contacts between Rome and Macedonia were made under Damasus. In the Western part, the pope battled against the Arian bishops with the help of Roman synods. Success came not to Damasus, however, but to Ambrose of Milan, who together with Emperor Gratian, who was residing in Ambrose's episcopal city, was able to appoint orthodox bishops. The situation was different in the Eastern part, especially Macedonia, which from time to time was subject to the authority of the Eastern emperor, Theodosius. To avoid being under the influence of the bishop of Constantinople, the bishop of Thessalonica tried to secure his independence by turning to Rome. The turmoil which broke out shortly thereafter in the Balkans—especially the plundering by the Visigoths—and Macedonia's renewed subordination to the ruler of the Eastern empire, which resulted from this, temporarily impeded what little contact there was with Rome. Despite all obstacles, Siricius tried to set up an orthodox hierarchy in Illyricum. To this end he used, above all, the metropolitan of Thessalonica, to whom Siricius awarded a position within the metropolitan's bishopric like the one he himself had in suburbicarian Italy. With this power, the metropolitan was then to put the ideas of the pope into effect as his vicar. This effort was unsuccessful, though it was a model for similar attempts by later popes, among them Innocent I and, in particular, Leo I. Occasionally more successful than Siricius, they were unable, however, over the long run to turn their designs into deeds. Innocent saw the attempts by the Eastern emperors and the patriarch of Constantinople to expand their authority to Macedonia as running contrary to Rome's ideas. For Leo, the metropolitans of Thessalonica used the preeminence Rome had given them to control and govern their territory without Rome's consent, which led to conflicts with Rome. In the end it was the Ostrogoth's war machine and the so-called Acacian schism between Rome and Constantinople at the end of the fifth century that led to the breakdown of Rome's efforts. This was not without consequences, however. Until the eighth century, Rome claimed religious supervision over the Illyrian region, and with the western portion of Illyricum at least maintained correspondence and liturgical contacts. A letter that Leo I wrote in 446 to Anastasius of Thessalonica, who had ideas of autonomy, was destined in Carolingian times to become more important, however. In this letter, the pope emphasized that Anastasius had only a share of responsibilty, not, like the pope, full power of authority (*ut in partem sis vocatus sollicitudinis, non in plenitudinem potestatis*). To be sure, the letter referred only to the function of the bishop as the pope's vicar, and not to the bishop as metropolitan. Yet this letter—its wording somewhat changed—has served since the ninth century as the basis for the subordination of the bishops to the absolute power (*plenitudo potestatis*) of the pope.

Rome's policies toward Arles sometimes met with greater success. As mentioned, this city at the beginning of the fifth century was the center of military and political resistance to the Germanic "barbarians." The bishop of the city, Patroclus, exploited this situation to expand his authority over the bishops of Marseille and Vienne, who appealed to older privileges. To this end, he quite adeptly made use of the bishop of Rome at that time, Zosimus, who wanted to secure his own authority in Roman Gaul and, at the same time, to improve the rather desolate state of the church there. In this regard, the fictitious historical basis of Rome's intervention is once again instructive. Stirred on by Patroclus, and in similar fashion to Innocent I in his letter to Decentius of Gubbio, Zosimus asserted that Arles and its territory had been missionized by Saint Trophimus on behalf of the bishops of Rome. In this way, a direct connection was constructed between the cult of local saints and the vicar of Peter, a model for similar attempts by later popes, especially in Gaul and the Rhineland. Since Zosimus had clearly come down on the side of Patroclus' faction, he only managed to increase the confusion in South Gaul. And his immediate successors had great difficulty in restoring respect, which they tried to do by distancing themselves from Zosimus' policies. But for these successors, too, Arles remained the bishop's see with whose help they wanted to increase their influence on the church in South Gaul.

Leo I had great success in South Gaul just as he had had in Macedonia. Patroclus' successors, Honoratus and Hilary (from 430), were monks at the island cloister Lérins (near Cannes), and they tried whenever possible to appoint bishops in Gaul who had the same ideals they had. As a result, they did not justify their actions on the grounds of being vicars of Rome, but rather, on the grounds of realizing their intention of a Christian, ascetic way of life. This must have provoked oppostion in Rome, however. Innocent I had already decreed, in connection with the difficulties with Arles, that all *causae maiores* (major legal cases) of bishops should fall under the general competence of the bishop of Rome. Which cases were meant by this remained undefined until the High Middle Ages. It was precisely this uncertainty which offered later popes the chance to intervene in the affairs of other bishoprics by citing this decretal. Leo I was successful at a Roman synod in divesting Hilary of all functions that went beyond the normal duties of a bishop. Church law and Roman discipline won out over a theologically and socially engaged discipleship based on other motives. Soon after, Ostrogothic rule, and later Frankish rule, made it impossible in both the eastern area and in South Gaul to continue either the

Roman policies or those of Arles. Yet both sides continued their claims, as the relatively lively exchange of letters between Roman and South Gallic bishops shows.

Political and, with that, social upheaval frustrated any hope of a lasting success for the papacy in what was later known as "Provence," and even more so in greater Gaul, despite the long legacy of Roman institutions and ideas. Of course, in the second century, Irenaeus of Lyon kept up ties with Rome, and, in the fourth century, bishops such as Hilary collaborated with Roman bishops against the Arians and other heretics. But the barbarians who had swept through or settled down in Gaul since the fourth century—Alans, Vandals, Sueves, Visigoths, Burgundians, Franks, Alemanni—temporarily impeded an expansion of a church structure based on the Roman provincial model, even if most of the bishoprics stayed in place. Unstable conditions also hindered a successful subordination of Gaul to Rome, although even Gallic bishops tried, with Rome's help, to overcome the instability through the use of decrees from Rome on questions of liturgy, organization, and discipline. There are quite a number of extant letters from the end of the fourth century and the first half of the fifth—from the time of Siricius to Leo I—which were addressed to the whole episcopate of Gaul or to individual bishops (of Narbonne, Toulouse, Rouen) and in which solutions were sought for the problems just mentioned. And even in the most turbulent times regional synods tried to follow Roman guidelines. They were helped by the fact that in the fifth century, Gaul was, along with Italy, the country from which many pilgrims, both lay and clerical, went to Rome to pay their respects at St. Peter's grave. They then founded many churches in Gaul in honor of Peter and Paul. And even earlier than in Rome itself, the faithful in Gaul celebrated the *conversio Pauli* on January 25, as well as the *cathedra Petri* (though, different from Rome, on January 18). Nevertheless, the effects of the political and ethnic upheavals were such that the ties with Rome were not institutionally solidified and, by the end of the fifth century, had nearly been severed altogether. Just how little contact there was at the time between the Franks and Rome is shown by the lack of any response on Rome's part to the baptism of Choldwig (circa 498), although this was the first time a Germanic ruler, together with the leading circles in that society, embraced Catholicism. The only recognition given in Rome was the donation of a consecration crown at St. Peter's after Choldwig's death. Thus there was no contact between the synods that were held in Gaul from the time of Choldwig and the popes who were in power during that same time. Nevertheless, these assemblies laid the basis for further Roman influence in that they used letters of earlier popes as guides for certain decisions. As a result, some papal letters were kept in the canon law collections of Gaul. The head of the Frankish church, however, was the king.

The situation of the Spanish church matched that of the Gallic. As early as the third century, Spanish bishops turned to Rome in the contest over doctrine and discipline. Under Constantine and his sons, the leading figure of the Spanish church, Bishop Hosius of Cordova, was a defender of Roman authority, as the synod of Sardica in 343 shows. The Spanish bishops continued to ask the bishops of Rome for advice and instructions. The most famous example of this is a letter from Bishop Siricius in 385 to Himerus of Tarragona, considered to be the first papal "decretal." (More about this concept later.) In his letter, Siricius declared that Roman rules of discipline, such as in the question of celibacy, were binding for all the Christian communities of Spain. To what extent the Roman directives were actually acknowledged in Spain, however, is not known. Similarly, information is lacking about the outcome of Roman efforts against heretics who had stirred up agitation in Spain, of whom the Priscillianists were especially widespread. It should also be kept in mind that Spain had even less of a centrally organized church than Gaul had. And because of the political situation in the Western empire, many bishops preferred dealing with Milan, with whose liturgy they had more in common, than with Rome. A synod held in Toledo in 400 sent an envoy to Innocent I, who answered, as had Siricius, with rules of discipline, but what effect this had is also unknown, as is the outcome of a letter from Pope Zosimus in 417. The barbarian invasions underway at this time, and which finally ended in 507 with the establishment of Visigoth rule over all of Spain—while Roman generals added to the confusion with separatist aspirations—prevented any intensive contact between Spain and Rome until the end of this epoch, even though popes such as Hilarus and Simplicius continued sending letters to individual Spanish bishops.

If Roman influence in Gaul and Spain foundered because of the organizational weakness of the church there and the bellicose times, then in North Africa, it was a strong organization that proved to be a drawback. The writings and actions of North African bishops such as Cyprian of Carthage in the third century and Aurelian of Carthage and Augustine of Hippo at the beginning of the fifth century, along with those of their Roman partners and adversaries, are famous examples of the ties between Rome and North Africa. Because Cyprian and Augustine were both famous theologians and were cited as authorities even by opponents of church power from the late Middle Ages, many Catholic historians of the church, not to mention historians of dogma, were and still are tempted to present both figures as especially impressive and early witnesses of papal primacy. But this position is untenable. Cyprian praised Peter as the origin of all Christendom; in saying that, however, he did not want to postulate a preeminent postion for the Roman congregation. Augustine's position was by and large the same. To be sure, he venerated Peter and attached importance to keeping the church in Rome with Peter's successors. But, in conflicts with Rome, he also defended the independence of the North African church under the direction of Carthage. In addition to Donatists, Augustine and his colleagues fought against the Pelagianists (chief dissent: the doctrine of grace and of original sin), who had been tolerated for a long time by Roman bishops and circles of the upper class there, even though North African synods had approved resolutions against them many times and had called on Rome for solidarity. In protest against Rome's attitude, a council in Carthage in 418, in which Augustine took part, prohibited all North African clerics against whom their bishops had made a judgment from appealing to Rome. Instead, highest authority was to be reserved for the primate in Carthage or a universal council. Soon after, Zosimus gave in and condemned Pelagianism. With the preceeding synodal decrees behind him, Augustine considered the case closed (*sermo* 131: *Causa finita est, utinam aliquando finiatur error!*). Later apologists for Rome turned this sentence around, Augustine's words becoming instead: "Rome has spoken, the matter is thus decided" (*Roma locuta, causa finita*). And, with that, they made him a supporter of Rome's claims. During Augustine's lifetime, the Vandals conquered North Africa, killing or dispersing most of the bishops and thereby destroying the North African church organization. Rome lost a troublesome opponent.

In glancing over Rome's relationship to the various areas of the Western empire, we can see that the popes were unsuccessful in this epoch, except for suburbicarian Italy, in obtaining a lasting supervision and jurisdiction that was recognized by all parties. Nevertheless, attempts to do so in later epochs were significant inasmuch as the letters written for this purpose were collected in Gaul and Spain, as well as in Rome, and thus handed down to later users. In the right situation, the letters could then be pulled out as ecclesiastical law secured by historical precedent. The writings collected in Rome, beginning with Gelasius I, were especially important, in particular, the collection of the Scythian monk Dionysius Exiguus. Most likely during the pontificate of Symmachus, he organized according to their systematic aspects some of the decretals, which had been written from the time of Siricius to Anastasius II. Other compilations had usually been chronologically ordered. *of letters* Because of their practical utility, it was not long before the "Dionysiana" played a major role, especially after the eighth century, as the authoritative collection of old decretal laws.

These letters have usually been called "decretals" since the time of Siricius. Among these are included written opinions which, like imperial rescripts, refer to particular cases, but which also define general guidelines that are to be followed. This is true for the letters from the time of Siricius until the time of Leo I, as can be seen in the phraseology of decisions and orders (*decernimus, iussimus, prohibemur*) and ironic reproaches (especially Innocent I: *miramur*). Even more so in later generations, these could be acknowledged as valid laws. It was this attempt to implement the authority of the bishop of Rome, or at least the claim of authority, to lands outside Italy, which allows us to use the word "pope" for bishops starting with Damasus or Siricius.

The attempts by Roman bishops to gain something more than a vague preeminence over the clergy of the Eastern empire was successfully rejected in this epoch, and, even today, this preeminence has not been recognized by all sides. From the time of Constantine's reign, Roman bishops were wrapped up in the affairs of the Eastern church that related to matters of orthodoxy, chiefly the questions of Christology, Arianism, Nestorianism, Monophysitism. Two factors led to the popes having little say in matters of faith, compared to later local interpretations. First, Roman bishops, except for Leo I, were usually bad theologians in comparison to representatives of the Eastern church; second, important decisions were made at councils at which few representatives (Nicea 325, Ephesus 431, Chalcedon 451) or none at all (Constantinople 381) from the West took part—an example of how little prominence the West held at that time in theological questions. Leo I was a famous exception. As a result of the Robber Synod of Ephesus in 499, he occupied himself intensively with monophysitic teachings about the divine nature of Christ, ordering Emperor Leo to convoke a new council, which met two years later in Chalcedon. With the help of the imperial policy on the summoning of councils, the majority of that council's participants was, like the pope, unfavorably disposed toward the Monophysites. When Leo's legate read the pope's position, which also conformed to the intentions of the members of the synod, they were happy to have found a speaker who was neutral on the internal bickerings in the East, and they applauded him, exclaiming: "Peter has spoken through Leo." From this Leo derived the magisterium for all Christians, as did later popes to an even greater degree. But the council fathers also showed that they would only accept the Roman line if it corresponded to their own views. They did so by granting the patriarch of Constantinople the same position in the Eastern empire that the patriarch in Rome held in the West, just as their predecessors had done in 381. Little wonder that both of the decrees drawn up in Chalcedon on this point were not accepted in Rome. Nevertheless, later popes maintained the position held by Leo. And because of a favorable ecclesiastico-political situation, Hormisdas and Agatho especially were able to get, for a short time, a verbal recognition of papal authority on doctrine over the emperor. The Gothic wars and the changes which came about in their aftermath, however, meant that even in Rome these successes were soon forgotten.

The reason for the decrees of 381 and 451 in favor of the "new Rome" was the importance of Constantinople in the Eastern empire. The position of Alexandria and Antioch was presented in a similar way in 325 in Nicea and by later synods. The decrees reflected the aforementioned principle of adapting the church organization to that of the state. This was resisted in Rome by negating the corresponding decrees or by the adoption of their own way of doing things through arbitrary changes in the Latin translation of the canons, as in the case of Nicea. Only because of these changes were most of the decrees of the four great councils admitted by Rome and, from the time of Gregory I, their validity made equal to the four gospels. This meant, however, that the basis for discussion in negotiations or conflicts, in which the four councils were quoted by both sides, was different for Rome than for the East due to the varied interpretations of the decrees.

The negation of Rome's secular origins and the emphasis on the apostolic succession, which the Romans had been arguing since the middle of the fourth century, had many repercussions on the relationship between the Eastern and Western church. This argument was quite sensible for Damasus and his successors in that, for them, the position of Peter as the first bishop of Rome was obvious in view of the cult and the doctrine of succession that had already developed. On the one hand, the East did have a close connection with the cult of Peter: many legends about Peter ("Quo vadis," the crucifixion, the *Clementine Homilies*) came from the East and spread there. Communities such as Antioch and Alexandria perceived themselves as having been founded by Peter (Antioch) or his pupil Mark (Alexandria). On the other hand, because no Eastern community claimed to be the site of Peter's grave, nothing of similar worth could be set against the Petrine doctrine of Rome. Since the fifth century, Constantinople had been claiming Andrew as its founder, though by doing so it became at most an apostolic foundation as in Ephesus and Corinth, even if later in Constantinople some preeminence over Rome was derived out of this since Andrew had supposedly been called by Jesus to be a disciple before Peter. The new doctrine established that, for the time being, Rome only recognized as patriarchial sees, in addition to but subjugated to Rome, the communities of Antioch and Alexandria (the so-called Petrine trias), both of which originated directly or indirectly from Peter. It was not until the fifth century that Constantinople and Jerusalem were regarded as secondary partriarchates. The four Eastern patriarchates also believed in the ministry and death of Peter in Rome and in the apostolic succession of the Roman bishops. But this meant for these four that the Roman bishops merely had a higher rank, not a higher authority in doctrine and dogma. They considered themselves the highest authority in their own spheres. The turning to Rome for support by the patriarchs of Antioch and Alexandria in conflicts with the East does not change this fact since, in emergencies, they also sought help from other communities, such as Carthage and Milan, that had a lot of influence in their territories. Therefore, it is wrong to read into the phraseology of such written petitions a general recognition of Rome's primacy. But it was not only the varied reception and interpretation of council decrees and imperial or episcopal writings that hindered the implementation of papal claims in the Eastern empire. The political division of the empire was not very conducive for Roman intentions, either, nor was the different liturgy, the language barrier between Greek and Latin, the varied church discipline, nor finally, the superiority of the Eastern theologians.

Just how limited the popes' sphere of influence was beginning in the late fifth century is shown in what is left of their correspondence. Because the letters were often responses to questions, we not only get an idea of Rome's interests, but also the area in which bishops and other office holders found it necessary or purposeful to turn to the Roman bishop. And, in contrast to the geographic expanse of the correspondence of, for example, Innocent I and Leo I, the correspondence of Gelasius I was astonishingly limited. He addressed most of his letters to bishops in suburbicarian Italy, with clerics in Illyricum forming the next largest group. Letters to Constantinople (emperor or patriarch), Syria, North Africa, or South Gaul were few in number, while there are none at all to Northern Italy, Spain, Egypt, or the Franks. This range of letter writing was reduced even more under his successors. Except for suburbicarian Italy, other regions were given more consideration only by certain popes: Provence under Symmachus, Illyricum and Constantinople under Hormisdas.

Even in the circle of the Roman bishops, the mental horizon was extremely limited, according to another source we have already mentioned, the *Liber pontificalis*, i.e., the book of popes. This book, which probably came about as a result of the Symmachan schism and was written before Felix IV, contains "short biographies" of Roman bishops since Peter. The authors most likely came from the inner circle of the episcopal court. Models for the book included old catalogs of bishops, records of church property and legends. The Roman see stands at the center of the commentary. Consequently, the stereotypical name, place of origin, and length of time in office of each pope are noted, in addition to the number of presbyters, deacons, and suburbicarian bishops ordained by him. Reports about the decoration of new or renovated Roman churches take up ample space, as do new regulations for the liturgy. Reports about events outside Italy take second place, the conflicts with Byzantium being the only exception, even if they are somewhat fancifully reported. Thus it is hardly surprising that an important pope like Leo I received less description than his successor Hilarus since during Leo's time there was little to report about church construction. For Choldwig, the only entry is the donation of a coronation crown for St. Peter's. And yet, with these limitations, the *Liber pontificalis* shows quite impressively how the circle around the Roman bishops at the end of this epoch viewed itself. It was continued until the end of the ninth century, the individual biographies usually being finished immediately after the death of each pope. The book continued to offer important information about the prevailing mentality in the papal circle.

In conclusion, let us say that by the end of this epoch the popes had fully Christianized and integrated Rome, and had even won some influence over the government administration. Beyond the city, they had some say only in suburbicarian Italy, for the most part in matters of worship, discipline, and jurisdiction. As for the other areas of the Western empire, whenever there were far-reaching objectives, they could not be realized, but which nevertheless created the written basis for more successful political policies in later times. The distance to the East was soon so great that even today it cannot be spanned. Yet, beginning in the fifth century, pontiffs claimed in the East the same supreme authority over doctrine they have in the West. Moreover, they ascribed to themselves—Gelasius I made it especially clear—the same position within the church as a whole that the emperor held in the secular world. Because these claims were continued into the following epoch, conflicts between the papacy and the Byzantine imperial court were inevitable.

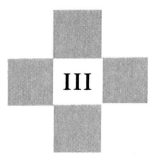

III

The Papacy Under Byzantine Rule (until 774)

Disputes over the successor to the Ostrogoth king, Theodoric the Great, who died in 526, led to an intervention in Italian affairs by the emperors Justin and Justinian. And after the latter had freed North Africa from the Vandals and had reconquered parts of Spain from the Visigoths, his army commanders Belisarius and Narses managed to liquidate fully the rule of the Ostrogoths in long, bloody battles from 535 to 553. The whole western Mediterranean belonged once again to the Roman empire. Justinian's success was short-lived, however, at least in Italy, for in 568 the Lombards invaded. Though they never came as close to ruling all of Italy as the Ostrogoths had, they did succeed through vicissitudinous battles in securing their rule in Northern Italy, including Tuscany and parts of Central and Southern Italy (the duchies of Spoleto and Benevento). In the seventh and eighth centuries, such kings as Rothari, Liutprand, or Aistulf, and various dukes tried to expand the territory under Lombard rule. Thus the rest of the Byzantine part of Italy, including Rome, remained exposed to the Lombard threat. This continued until the Frankish king Charlemagne declared himself king of the Lombards after conquering the Lombard capital of Pavia, thereby ushering in a new epoch for Italy and the papacy.

Preparations had been underway since the time of Gregory II, however, for Rome to break away from the Byzantine federation. Since the papacy was also starting to win influence also in that part of the West that had remained Christian, it seems useful to divide the epoch into two sections.

The Papacy Until the Time of Constantine I (715)

The Lombard invasion caused not only a division of Italy—which, politically at least, lasted until the nineteenth century—but also a reorganization of that part which remained Byzantine. Henceforth, an exarch acted as representative of the emperor, with his residence in the former capital at Ravenna. Under him were several *duces* (meaning literally "leaders") who controlled the army and also part of administration in their "duchies." Except for the Veneto—where the title (doge) continued until the Napoleonic era—Naples and Ravenna as well as probably Rome were the centers of duchies (Sicily was directly under the emperor's control). The only tie Rome had to Ravenna was by the Via Flaminia, which was increasingly threatened by the Lombards. Consequently, Rome was now the center of a rather small and isolated area—Lombard strongholds were barely sixty kilometers away—and for the first time lay on the extreme periphery of the Roman empire. Thus, for the emperor, Rome now had more the significance of a border town than of a center of an empire.

Before depicting the integration of Rome and its bishops into the Byzantine empire, let us look for a moment at the demographic, economic, and social consequences of the Gothic and Lombard wars. Even though it is impossible to fix the exact number of inhabitants in Italy either before or after the wars, it is probably safe to say that at least one third of the population lost their lives in military campaigns. Agriculture was largely ruined as most of the farmers were either dead or refugees in the cities and cultivated plants that need great care, such as olive trees and grapevines were destroyed nearly everywhere. Thus a new prosperity was long in coming to the Byzantine territories, and not only because of the Lombard threat. The cities, too, had suffered greatly. Rome had been completely depopulated for a short time under Totila. The returning inhabitants, accompanied by refugees, found life to be quite miserable. There were perhaps 30,000 altogether. On a positive note, they were now able to plant within the walled enclosure grapes and grain in areas where villas and palaces had previously stood. What few inhabitants there were settled for the most part in the lowlands (Suburba and Campo di Marzo). The surviving members of the upper class had either fled to Constantinople or joined the clergy in greater numbers than before. This meant, at the same time, that those who had previously been a link to Roman culture and tradition no longer existed or their inherited ideals were exchanged for those of asceticism, escapism or the belief in miracles, all of which gained in popularity because of the war. While Theodoric and his Roman collaborators such as Cassiodor had wanted to maintain the old traditions through a symbiosis of Romans and Goths, Justinian's efforts in reviving the empire had the effect of ruining Roman architecture and the economy and making old traditions seem antiquated. From now on that which bore witness to the signs of Rome's former greatness would hardly be noticed, while the churches were greatly admired.

Justinian's most significant accomplishment for the following age was not his conquests; it was the compilation of laws he initiated, later called the *Corpus iuris civilis*. This collection contained, in additon to a textbook (*Institutiones*), opinions of earlier jurists (*Digesten*) and older laws (*Codex*), new laws made by the emperor himself (*Novellae*). The laws were binding for the whole empire, which included Italy during the Byzantine epoch. Even under Frankish and German rule (eighth to eleventh century), civil cases, at least in Rome, were handled according to rules set down in this corpus. The *Novellae*, as laws of the land at that time, offer much information about the position of the Roman and other bishops in the Byzantine empire. Recalling Gelasius I, Justinian emphasized the duties of the priests for the caring of souls and the duties of the emperor for the civil welfare (*novella* 6). But unlike the pope, he deduced from this a leading responsibility for the keeping of the faith and the church doctrine, thereby assuring himself control of the church. As a result, he was the person responsible for getting rid of heretics (*novella* 132). And it was Justinian who, before Gregory I, decreed the four ecumenical councils equal to the Gospels (*novella* 131). In the same *Novella* he stated that the

bishop of old Rome was the first among all priests, with the bishop
of new Rome following directly behind him in rank. In so doing,
the authority of the pope was limited de facto to the territory of
the earlier Western empire. In other laws the emperor determined
that bishops were to participate in the civil life of their cities by
carrying out functions on behalf of the secular ruler. And Italian
bishops were authorized, from the time of the Pragmatic Sanction
of 554, to take part in the installation of local government officials.
If during this epoch the popes had an increasing say in the administration in Rome, then this was in full accord, at least initially, with
the intent of Justinian law.

One result of the emperor's responsibility for the church and of
the civil duties of the bishops was that the government had to have
and wanted to have more influence in the filling of the most
important bishoprics in particular. Therefore, every new pope was
obliged to have his election confirmed by the emperor or his
exarch. And only after a successful approbation was he allowed to
be consecrated. The fate of Martin I shows how serious the imperial court took this duty. Because he had himself ordained in 649
without imperial approbation, the exarch at the time, Olympios,
was supposed to have him arrested. But Olympios himself had
intentions of becoming emperor and of doing battle against the
Muslims in Sicily. Martin was therefore charged with collaborating
with Olympios. After being imprisoned and then dethroned, he
was put on trial in Constantinople by Constance II in 653 for
having been consecrated without imperial permission. He was sentenced to death as a traitor, which was later reduced to banishment. He died in 655 in the Crimea. The popes Silverius and
Vigilius had already suffered similar fates in the sixth century.
And yet, as we shall see, the following decades were a turning
point for Rome. Starting with the late seventh century, similar
attempts by emperors or exarchs to intervene could no longer be
implemented because of the changed situation.

The popes needed a permanent representative at the imperial
court because of their largely subordinate position to the emperor.
This became the role of the apocrisiarius. He represented papal
interests, but at the same time he passed on imperial instructions
to Rome. And just like in earlier times when it was the archdeacon
who had the greatest chance to become pope, so now did the
apocrisiarius. Gregory I is the most famous example of this. In this

way, conformity with imperial interests on the part of the papal government was guaranteed. Yet this too would soon change after Martin I.

Rome's incorporation into the Byzantine empire was evident principally in the ceremonial, although it was also seen in the garrisoning of a militia (in Trastevere and above the Trajan market near what was later called the *Torre delle Milizie*) and the activity of Byzantine officials and judges, who were subordinate to the *praefectus urbi*. During every papal mass the emperor was prayed for, and on Good Friday the faithful asked God to provide for the stability of the empire. What is more, at this time the custom arose of the pope celebrating a second mass at Christmas in the church of S. Anastasia, which stood on the Palatine hill, the nominal imperial residence. S. Anastasia was therefore a kind of church of the imperial court. A portrait of every new emperor was ceremoniously received outside the city by the pope and his court and then brought in a procession to the Palatine. And on the Forum Romanum, for the time being still the center of public life, monuments to the new emperors were occasionally erected. The last visible column today was dedicated by Gregory I to the emperor, Phocas, even though he had his predecessor and Gregory's friend Maurice and his family murdered. This shows, as do Gregory's troubles with the equally bloodthristy Frankish queen Brunichildis, that this holy pope knew how to adapt to the political realities. Because Rome was part of the imperial church, some popes supported—partly for political reasons (Vigilius, Pelagius I), partly because of a lack of expert knowledge (Honorius I)—theological doctrines from the East that otherwise were not accepted in the West.

The emperor's lack of interest in the city stood in direct contrast to the efforts of Gregory and other popes to develop goodwill. Not one Byzantine emperor ordered the construction or renovation of structures in Rome. And when Constance II visited Rome, the last Byzantine emperor for many centuries to do so, his single great deed was to have sculptures and roofs (for example, the Pantheon) stripped of their metal in order to sell it and then buy weapons with the profits. And yet the next few popes remained faithful to Constantinople. In 688, Vitalian prevented the success of a usurper after the murder of Constance; Leo II sustained the conviction of Honorius I as a heretic by the Third Council of Constantinople

(680–681), and propagated an even harsher condemnation in the West.

That Constantinople's influence on Rome and the papacy had diminished by the end of the seventh century was due to the threat to the empire in the East, to the weakness or petty political policies of the exarchs in Italy, and to the changed mentality of Byzantine troops and administrative personnel in Italy.

For centuries, the Persians had been threatening the eastern border of the Roman empire. At the beginning of the seventh century, they succeeded in conquering the Middle East and Egypt. Although Phocas' successor, Heraclius, was able to defeat the Persians and reestablish the old borders, peace did not last long. Heraclius himself lived to see Mohammed's followers conquer Syria and Palestine and invade Egypt starting in 633. By the end of the seventh century, they ruled all of formerly Roman North Africa as well as important islands such as Cyprus and Crete and threatened the capital itself several times before and after 700. Their expansion was made easier because of the religious schisms in the empire. The Syrians and Egyptians were predominantly Monophysites, with liturgies in their own languages. With the unity of the empire in mind, rulers and patriarchs tried to reach out to them with compromise doctrines (Monotheletism, Monoenergism), and in doing so irritated the West. Other emperors advocated the orthodox doctrine, partly on account of the inhabitants in the West and in North Africa, but in so doing, and because of high taxes, increased the objection to Byzantine rule among Syrians and Egyptians, who were still suffering from the effects of the Persian wars. In this same time period, the Avars and Slavs, and later Bulgarians, occupied most of the Balkans and Greece. The Visigoths conquered the Byzantine territory in Spain during the seventh century. Thus the Byzantine empire by 700 had shrunk, excluding Italy, to a part of Thrace (Constantinople) and Asia Minor. And even these remaining areas were constantly threatened, especially by the Arabs. Consequently, the Byzantine emperor's main consideration was to secure the remaining territories and, in Greece at least, to gain a stronger foothold. In the eighth century Leo III and his son Constantine V were successful on both accounts. A consequence of this desperate situation, however, was that military intervention in Italy became almost impossible.

This stationing of Byzantian troops in the East also had conse-

quences for the exarchs. Whenever they were strong and successful, they then tried to become independent of the emperor, or
perhaps even become emperor themselves. Whenever they were
weak, they could not get their way with the army or the civil
administration, nor could they offer any resistance to the Lombards. In any case, the exarchs were dependent on their troops,
who only fought when they were paid. This had been a stumbling
block from the beginning for the exarchates. Even Gregory I paid
the Roman garrison to keep them from rebelling, as did some of
his successors. To solve the problem, soldiers in the seventh century were increasingly compensated with land. A result of this,
however, was that they and their descendants became more reluctant to follow orders from far away Constantinople. Like the soldiers, government administrators had also settled in or were recruited from the local population. And the same process held true
for the militia. From this resulted a new bureaucratic and military
aristocracy that by the late seventh century tended to support the
local bishop rather than the foreign exarch or emperor. Sympto-
matic of this is a well-known incident that took place under Sergius
I. The militia refused to obey a deputy of the exarch who had
come to arrest him. Threatened by the locals, the deputy fled to
the Lateran Palace, where he hid under the pope's bed, begging
him for protection. A short while later a Roman bishop with the
splendid name of Constantine I traveled to Constantinople, the
last pope to do so. With his successor Gregory II a new era of
"Roman nationalism" began for the papacy that eventually led to a
complete break from Byzantium.

The latter half of the seventh and the first half of the eighth
centuries is often called the period of the Greek popes. And yet it
would be a mistake to conclude from their origins that these popes
were especially dependent on Byzantium. In fact, quite the opposite! Popes who hailed from Rome or Central Italy such as Vigilius,
Gregory I, Honorius I, or Vitalian were much more dependent on
Constantinople than many of these "Greeks." Conon was the son
of a militia officer, John VII the son of the Palatine overseer. They
represented the upwardly mobile social groups of Rome during
Byzantine rule. Other popes had fled—as earlier ones had done
(Theodore, for example)—from former Byzantine territory, especially from Syria and Palestine or were descendants of refugees
from these areas. Among them were such energetic popes as Agatho,
Sergius I, Gregory III, or Zacharius. Their origins led them to

resist the expansionistic policies of the patriarch of Constantinople and to introduce variant usages into the liturgy. In any case, these "Greek" popes were not usually the emperor's handymen. Nevertheless, they contributed as much as their Latin predecessors or successors had to the increasing Greek influence on the papacy and Rome beginning in the late sixth century.

This becomes apparent in the papal administration. As mentioned, many members of the upper class died or fled during the disturbances of the sixth century. As a result, the papacy became the greatest landowner in Italy since its earlier possessions remained, nominally at least, in its hands. And the lands left by deceased popes and clerics, as well as donations made by the former upper class and by the important new social groups, led to an increase in property. This property was divided into patrimonies of greater administrative units in which individual properties (called *massa, fundus, villa*) were regionally combined. Originally, the patrimonial property was dispersed throughout the Roman empire, but the difficult sea routes as well as conquests by Arabs, Slavs, and Franks caused the controlled areas to be reduced in the long run to Central and Southern Italy and Sicily, except for small holdings in Provence or in Istria and Dalmatia. And since Sicily remained for the most part untouched by the Gothic and Lombard wars, it had been the bread basket for Rome and its bishops since the late sixth century. On the remaining lands farming had to be restabilized. For example, the output of the estate in Picenum on the Adriatic had been reduced by one quarter because of the wars.

A major portion of the landed property was leased out. There were two methods for doing so, and their application offers information on papal social history and the pontiffs' ability to have their way: the libellar lease and emphyteusis. The former consisted of leasing a usually small plot of land to an individual for 19 or 29 years, which prevented alienation by inheritance and an accumulation of property. In contrast to that, a larger property (often entire *massae, fundi* or *villae*) was ceded to a family for two or three generations in exchange for the payment of tribute. This was called emphyteusis (i.e., copyhold). This practice encouraged, of course, the alienation of church property by those receiving the land. It is important to note that the libellar lease predominated from the late sixth to the late seventh century, and emphyteusis after that. From this it can be concluded that the revitilization of landed estates came about with the help of small leaseholders who later became dependent on the members of the new bureaucratic and military aristocracy. At the same time, this change is an indication of the growing dependence of the papacy on these new groups.

The managers (*rectores*) of the estates were sometimes local people, but usually they were Roman clerics. According to statements in letters of Gregory I, they also made sure that the output from the land reached Rome. At least at the time of Gregory there must have been very close contact between Rome and the Italian estates. Occasionally, the administrators of the estates were also papal representatives for the local communities, and so had control over who became bishop. They were in turn controlled by Roman emissaries. In Rome itself, the deacons supervised the emissaries and property managers. In addition to them there were also papal advisers (*consiliarii*), some of whom were lay persons, whose main duty was correspondence with the estates. It is obvious, then, that the earlier dominating position of the deacons had been reduced in this epoch.

Ever since the late sixth century the difference between members of the papal court, who were more or less dependent on the pope, and members of the traditional groups had been getting more and more distinct. The traditional groups consisted of the upper clergy, the notaries, and the *defensores*. As the deacons had been earlier, the presbyters were now loosely joined together in a college under the direction of an archpresbyter. Archdeacons as well as archpresbyters represented the Roman clergy before the pope. They ruled the bishophric together with the *primicerius* of the notaries during a vacancy of the see, which sometimes lasted several months; in addition, they supervised the papal election. The notaries were also responsible for a portion of the correspondence and the filing of it in archives. And probably because their *primicerius* often had to deal with "greater policies," he now had a deputy (*secundicerius*). The college of *defensores*, in contrast, remained as it had been. To be sure, now all notaries and *defensores* had to be clerics, a sign of the increasing clericalization of the Roman administration. Yet this offered chances for certain families since usually the notaries and *defensores* were minor clerics, who were able to marry and perhaps pass on their position. In accordance with Eastern customs—and a point that is not always clear in modern historical research—the wives of deacons and presbyters who had married before their ordination were also integrated in church society, as is evident in their designation as *diaconissae* and *presbyterissae*. There were also a few *episcopissae* in the following epoch, as an inscription in S. Prassede from the beginning of the ninth century shows. This no doubt made the keeping of celibacy that much more difficult.

Because the members of these groups held these positions on a lifetime basis, and even bequeathed them to the following generation, they were a danger for popes who wanted to govern independently. Gregory I tried to expel them by entrusting administrative duties to monks and to the *consiliarii* he had appointed. The result was that deacons and presbyters, as the most important electors, prevented the election of a monk for the next seventy years. In general, recognition for Gregory's legacy in Rome was slight until the middle of the eighth century. For this reason, the pontiffs who followed him had to apply other methods. The most successful possibility was the expansion of the court personnel. Even before Gregory there was a deputy for the pope (*vicedominus*). And though information about this office is scanty, it appears that the holder of this office had, apart from the archdeacon, the greatest influence on the papal government. Moreover, in the seventh century, the court was remodeled after the imperial administration. There was now a *vestiarius* for the vestments and the valuable utensils, an *arcarius* for controlling income and a *sacellarius* for expenditures. In addition, the pope personally ordered the *nomenculator*, who accepted and took care of petitions. The differences among the new officeholders were visible in the ceremonial. The members of the traditional bodies walked in front of the pope, thereby outwardly showing their rank, while the occupants of the newly created offices went directly behind the pope, forming then the closer papal retinue. This pattern of precedence (placement before or after the pope) remained throughout the Middle Ages a significant indication of the changing importance of certain official positions.

Access to the positions also changed as a result of the new structure. Even before Gregory I there was a *cubiculum* (literally: sleeping chamber) for the pope. This represented the persons who were closest to the pope—in other words, a circle of advisers who served him without control from the outside. Gregory had tried to oust lay persons from this inner circle and replace them with clercis or monks. His successors, however, gave up this attempt, so that lay persons continued to serve as cubiculars along with clerics. Usually children from respected families—and also orphans, especially in the eighth century—were taken into the *cubicilum* and given training. Well versed in papal opinions, they could later build a career in the papal household as a *sacellarius*, notary, *defensor* or, though more seldom, as a deacon or presbyter. The *cubiculum* was a sort of hinge between the upper class and a high post in the church. Another possibility was the *schola cantorum* (i.e., union of singers), supposedly founded by Gregory I, but most likely stemming from the middle of the seventh century. As the name indicates, young boys were trained for chanting, the setting down of rules for which was also erroneously attributed to Gregory I. In contrast to the *cubiculum*, however, the *cantores* were able to become deacons and presbyters. Until the middle of the eighth century it was actually quite rare for a pope to have taken this career track; instead, they were usually "Greeks" who often joined the Roman clergy only later as adults. This was due to the influence the Greek colony—not to be confused with the representatives of the Byzantine emperors—had in Rome.

Their influence can be seen, apart from their holding the position of pope, in the liturgy, in the cloisters and diaconates, among business people and laborers, and finally among members of the militia or public administration. The latter two groups were, as already indicated, orginally from the East, but had soon assimilated themselves and, after the elimination of most of the senatorial families, formed the new upper class. Later names such as Theophylact or Christopher indicate that families who had a say in papal history from the eighth century came from these groups. Already by the seventh century they had given themselves empty titles such as "counsul" or later "dux" to point out their position in society. Even if there is hardly any information about their wealth or their function, they are still recognized as significant groups in politics and society, especially because of the *Liber pontificalis* and the *Liber diurnus* (daybook, or diary). The *Liber diurnus* is a collection of formulae for papal correspondence, the first edition of which probably came after the Third Council of Constantinople in 680–681. Expanded and altered, the collection served as a model for papal collaborators in the composing of important letters until well into the eleventh century. It can be concluded from formulae 60–63 of the *Liber diurnus* that, in theory at least, these groups participated in papal elections. And disputed elections at the end of the seventh century show that at that time reality conformed with this theory. Moreover, public administrators are called by

Greek words such as "axiomatici" (officeholder) or "iudices" (literally: judge, but meaning here: officeholder). There were two different military groups: the Byzantine forces, or the militia, commanded by tribunes, and the *exercitus Romanus* (i.e., Roman army), the troops of the citizens of Rome under the command of "consuls." The participation in elections by these groups shows how much the papacy had integrated the leading secular classes into its power, but that it was also dependent on them because of this.

In one of his letters, Gregory I complained that even the last remaining money changer finally had to close up shop. It seems speculative to conclude from this that foreign exchange offices in Rome had closed down, since pilgrims most probably brought foreign coins to Rome. This does indicate, however, that there hardly could have been a brisk foreign trade. Most imports came initially from Constantinople or other areas of the empire, and since the Arab invasions from the papal lands in Southern Italy and Sicily in particular. It was mostly Greeks who managed transportation and sales, Greeks who lived near markets and ports on the Tiber and were joined together in a guild (*schola Graeca*). Their prinicipal churches were also there: S. Giorgio in Velabro near the ancient arch of the money changers and later S. Maria in Cosmedin, which appropriately enough had the nickname of "*in schola Graeca.*" In addition to trade, the Greeks were also master craftsmen, as evinced in frescoes, mosaics, and architecture.

Since the Greeks most likely dominated trade, the providing of food to the Roman population also went through an institution that was already in existence in the East from the sixth century: the diaconates (social charity institutions). These could be set up in churches—for example, SS. Cosma e Damiano on the Forum Romanum—or in buildings that in ancient times were used for the same purpose. Later the diaconates were converted into churches. Thus there were diaconates in the old annona (the collection point for grain, and today S. Maria in Cosmedin), and two others in ancient *horreae* (granary, today S. Teodoro and S. Maria in Via Lata). Like these, most other diaconates were dedicated to Greek saints. Most were built in the seventh and early eighth centuries, though new ones were still being founded into the ninth century. They were usually run by a patron (*pater diaconiae, dispensator,* and others). If they included a church, then they had one or more presbyters as well.

As in the diaconates, the Greek influence can also be seen in many cloisters. After a slow start in the fifth and sixth centuries, by the seventh century there were twenty-four cloisters in Rome, six of them with Greek monks. The most important was S. Saba on the Aventine. As so-called basilica cloisters (approximately eight altogether), the Latin cloisters attended to the hourly prayers in the papal basilicas (particularly at the Lateran, St. Peter's, and Santa Maria Maggiore), each one also entrusted with caring for the basilicas of S. Lorenzo and St. Paul's. The eight "normal" Latin cloisters were only slightly more numerous than the Greek ones. And even if most of the Greek monks, like their brothers in the East, could hardly have been very educated, those few in these cloisters who were educated had an even greater importance for the papacy. A certain Abbot John is a good case in point, who as a letter writer for popes Honorius I and John IV played an ambiguous role in the dispute over Monotheletism. And the Roman synod of 649 was organized and directed by Greeks, a not unusual occurrence for that time.

And finally, the Greek influence is also evident in the liturgy. In the previous chapter it was mentioned that during the Byzantine epoch saints who were venerated in the East were brought into the canon of the Roman mass. Furthermore, the Roman Christian community now observed feasts of the Lord brought from the East, such as the dedication in the temple on February 2, or the conception on March 25, as well as the triumph of regaining the holy cross from the Persians by Emperor Heraclius (September 14). There were also several Marian feasts, such as the assumption into heaven on August 15, and her birthday on September 8. Sergius I, from Syria, introduced into the mass the reference to Christ as "Agnus Dei," or the Lamb of God. This also showed, however, that the liturgical innovations could also indicate an estrangement from the imperial captial, since the new usages in Rome were also common in Syria, but prohibited in Constantinople. For Rome this meant that for the first time Christ himself— previously only an intercessor between mankind and God the Father—was included in the mass, the *adoratio.*

At the same time, Rome was becoming more Christian than ever before, and was also being included in the liturgy that was fixed by the pope. And while the buildings of the old Roman religion were falling into disrepair, Christian ones were being built, restored or installed in earlier pagan structures, such as the Pantheon. The Eastern influence dominated in architecture, as indicated by the numerous Eastern church patrons, the frescoes, the mosaics, and the oriental architecture such as buildings in the round and women's galleries. Not only earlier pagan temples, but also Roman government buildings were being turned into places of worship. This showed particularly clearly who was master in Rome. At the end of the previous epoch, Hormisdas had changed the supposed former headquarters of the city prefect on the Forum Romanum into a church (SS. Cosma e Damiano). In the seventh century, the curia and the secretariat of the Senate, damaged during the Gothic wars, became churches (S. Adriano and Santa Martina). The huge imperial palace on the Palatine began to fall apart—the representatives of the exarch who lived there could not or did not want to prevent this—or was transformed into cloisters and churches. Of great significance there was the church Santa Maria Antiqua, particularly under John VII, who as the son of the former palace administrator, Platon, even installed his episcopate there. His predecessors and successors—Vigilius, Theodore, and Honorius I, for example—preferred the Lateran, which they, with the construction of basilicas (oratories and reception rooms), built into a vast complex. The Lateran was considered the center of the Western church, and from about 700 had the title, as did Constantinople, of "patriarchium."

The Roman churches can be placed in three categories according to their privileges and functions: the basilicas (Lateran, St. Peter's, Santa Maria Maggiore, St. Paul's, S. Lorenzo), which the pope directly controlled, and then the titular churches and the diaconates. All three were included in the papal liturgy through the so-called "stational mass." Tradition called for the pope to celebrate his *statio* in the basilicas on the main holidays, although Sundays and weekdays, particularly during Lent, were celebrated in the titular churches and diaconates. Since representatives of secular society (the *iudices* as well as the commanders of the militia and the army of the city of Rome) had to attend these services, at least on the most important days, along with the inhabitants of the region, papal dominance over Roman society was also found in the liturgy. This was also important for the Christianization of whatever remained of pre-Christian cults. The popes were unsuccessful at this whenever they tried to eliminate pagan usages without offering a substitute, as the continued celebration of New Year's Day attests. For this reason, strong measures were taken to transform pagan customs into Christian ones. Processions were particularly useful for accomplishing this. Just as earlier the *pontifex maximus* tried with a torchlight procession to drive the demons from the city with the *amburbium,* so did the pope as *summus pontifex* lead a new fesitval on February 2 in a candlelight procession, beginning from the same spot, the former curia of the Senate with the arch of Janus, and ending at Santa Maria Maggiore (hence the German designation *Mariä Lichtmess,* or Candlemas in English). The robigalia, an ancient festival for the safeguarding of grain, was replaced by a procession on the feast day of St. Mark (April 25), which the pope, clergy, and community led from the Lateran through the entire city and over the Milvian Bridge to the new patron of the city, St. Peter's. Similarly, an old fertility rite was replaced by a procession on the day of Mary's assumption, August 15. For the same reason the quatember days (Wednesday, Friday, and Saturday at the beginning of every new season; "quatember" means *quatuor tempora,* i.e., four seasons) took the place of the ancient festivals of the seasons, though they are also a continuation from those ancient beginnings. It was on the quatember days that the pope ordained new clerics. Whether the popes also instructed the people in matters of faith while they preached is unknown, except for the case of Gregory I.

Since most of the new customs and festivals were exported to other areas, particularly after the eighth century, the changes are significant as an indicator of the spread of the Roman liturgy. This exportation was made easier in that in the seventh century the most important parts of the worship service were no longer improvised, but were now established and compiled into collections. Of these, the collection of prayers, the sacramentary, which the pope or priest spoke, and the hymns, have become especially important. These collections were supplemented in the eighth century by the *Ordines Romani* in which the appropriate rituals were described (mass, baptism, consecration of churches, etc.).

Disputes over dogma were very significant for the papacy's position in the empire as well as for its recognition in the West. In fact, most papal histories give preeminence to this question. Disputes usually flared up over the interpretation of the doctrine on the two natures of Christ, which in 451, with the help of the papacy, the Council of Chalcedon had defined. Emperors since the fifth century, and even more so after Justinian, decreed new interpretations and new formulae or they convened councils, whether out of their own theological interests or to maintain the unity of the empire. Justinian—educated in theology but unstable in his beliefs—condemned three deceased theologians because their teachings were suspect to the Monophysites, touching off the long-lasting Three Chapters controversy, which damaged church organization in Italy by dividing the so-called patriarchate of Aquileia into the separate bishoprics of Aquileia and Grado. Justinian's successors or their patriarchs tried in the seventh century to gain a compromise with the Syrian and Egyptian Monophysites by emphasizing only one energy (Monoenergism) or one will (Monotheletism) in Christ, thereby reducing the significance of Christ's humanity. The West, less educated in theological matters, usually rejected these attempts at compromise because the Council of Chalcedon supposedly had given the final word in establishing Christian beliefs. Moreover, the West lacked understanding for the domestic political problems of the Byzantine empire.

These conflicts put the papacy in a difficult situation. Toward the usually indifferent bishops of Gaul, Spain, and North Africa, the papacy had to submit a proof of its orthodoxy, i.e., its keeping of the Chalcedon Creed. The emperor was considered to be an ordinary member of the imperial church, and thereby subject to its orders. All of this was in view of the church's own understanding, as emphasized by pontiffs such as Hormisdas or Agatho, that the Roman church was infallible in matters of faith. The tough situation in which the papacy found itself is expressed clearly in the behavior of the popes Vigilius and Pelagius I. Under pressure from the emperor, Vigilius, in Constantinople at the time, finally agreed to the decrees of the Second Council of Constantinople in 553 in which the Three Chapters were condemned. For this action, his apocrisiarius, Pelagius, reviled him, though Pelagius himself also stood behind the Council's doctrines, and even became pope through the influence of the emperor and his exarch Narses. The Roman clergy accused him of having had a hand in the death of Vigilius and of having betrayed the Chalcedon Creed. Therefore Pelagius had to confess publicly his faith in conformity with the Council of Chalcedon—unheard of in papal history. When dealing with the imperial court, however, he continued to support the decree of the Second Council of 553. Even his successors maintained this murky position. The result was that every pope up to Gregory I, who was later venerated as a father of the church, was accused by Western bishops of not teaching the proper faith. And because of political changes in the church in the seventh century, both Vigilius and Pelagius were seen in the East as holding wrong beliefs. An irony of history is that because both agreed with the Second Council of Constantinople, this Council even nowadays is considered an ecumenical council, although its decrees contradict the main doctrines which are held in the West.

The posture of Honorius I toward Monotheletism was even graver for the papacy, as mentioned briefly earlier. In two missives to the patriarch of Constantinople, he expressed his opposition to new trivialities, which problematized the teachings of Chalcedon, but approved of the patriarch's newly proposed teaching on the one will in Christ. Heraclius then declared in his Ecthesis in 638 that the new teaching was binding on the whole empire. This Ecthesis did not contribute to peace in the kingdom, however, for not only supporters of Chalcedon (Patriarch Sophronius of Jerusalem) rejected it, but also the radical Monophysites. The Ecthesis was also condemned in the West in 649 at the Lateran Synod, which was prepared by Pope Theodore and Maximus the Confessor, and eventually realized by Martin I. Another interesting point about this synod is that Maximus and Martin wanted to help it get ecumenical recognition. Their plan was not even successful in the West, however, which shows what little respect the papacy had at that time when it came to questions of the faith. One result of this synod was that both of Honorius' letters were removed from the papal archives. And even earlier, under John IV, the man who composed these letters, Abbot John, wrote an interpretation that deviated from the content of the letters, making Honorius' conduct in Rome look less insidious than it was. The legates of Pope Agatho to the Third Council of Constantinople (the so-called Trullan Council of 680–681) were surprised, therefore, when they were shown the authentic version of the letters. Honorius was anathematized at the council as were other champions of Monotheletism. Agatho's successor, Leo II, accepted the verdict, though Agatho insisted that the Roman church and its flock had never strayed from the true faith. Because of this condemnation, henceforth every new pope before taking office had to acknowledge solemnly—as stated in the *Liber diurnus*—the true faith inclusive of the condemnation of Honorius. Because sources in the West soon merely mentioned that Honorius was an insignificant heretic, his standing as a pope thus falling into obscurity, he was no obstacle to later papal pretentions, though the East kept up the tradition. From the Reformation until the First Vatican Council, the "Honorius question" was taken up again by both opponents and defenders of papal doctrinal primacy. In the seventeenth century, the papal curia even banned an edition of the *Liber diurnus* because it contained the aforementioned oath of faith. There seems to be no doubt, however, that to the supporters of the Chalcedon Creed in the seventh century, Honorius was the perfect example of a heretical pope.

The disputes over Monotheletism also had positive consequences for the development of papal primacy. Greek popes such as Theodore and Agatho or influential Eastern theologians in Rome such as Maximus the Confessor emphasized in these conflicts that when Christ ordered Peter to tend his sheep and to strengthen the faith of his brothers, he also entrusted Peter with preserving the one true faith. Together with this and the conviction that the Roman church had never strayed from the true faith, the popes now formulated even more strongly than their predecessors their claim of supervision in matters of doctrine over all Christians. Earlier popes had based their claims more on jurisdiction and discipline. And since for them the former Roman empire was still the ecumene, the inhabited world, even though imperial power was recognized in only a few areas, Peter was now considered the guarantor of the faith taught by his successors and as the bond in what was now seen as a spiritual unity. With this, another stone was added to the foundation on which the religious as well as political ambitions of the papacy from the eighth century could be built.

As the final relic of the Byzantine epoch we should mention the official title still used by popes today: *servus servorum dei* (servant of God's servants). Initiated by Gregory I, this title has often been interpreted that Gregory wanted to emphasize his modesty—he was a monk, after all. This does not correspond completely to reality, however. Gregory's adversary in Constantinople referred to himself as well as his predecessors as an "ecumenical patriarch," an idea which, so far, nobody in the West had taken exception to since it merely meant that the patriarch belonged to the ecumene, that is, the empire, though of course possessing a special position. Even Roman bishops since Leo I had given themselves such a title. Gregory took great pains to battle against this title, though not even in the West did he receive any recognition for his efforts. And so to counter that title, he created his own one of modesty which has stayed with the papacy, even though the office holders

were not always worthy of the content of the title, and that goes
for Gregory himself, not to mention many of his successors. That
Gregory wanted to indicate a superiority can most likely be in-
ferred from the Bible passage on which the title is based, Mark
10:44: "And whoever will be first among you, shall be servant of
all."

Justinian's conquests brought North Africa, the islands of the
western Mediterranean, and parts of the Spanish Mediterranean
coast back to the empire, and thus to orthodoxy. At the end of the
same century, the Visigoth king, Reccared, his nobles, and his
people converted to the Catholic faith. In the course of the seventh
century, the Lombards gave up their Arianism. With this, all
Christian realms within the Roman empire were now united in
one faith. And the pilgrims from all these lands streaming to Rome
attested to the general veneration of Peter. This did not mean,
however, that Peter's successors were recognized everywhere as
guardians of the faith and doctrine. The political situation prevented this; Rome was, after all, a part of the Byzantine empire.
The unstable or erroneous behavior of a Vigilius, a Pelagius I, or
a Honorius I in questions of faith called for prudence. More than
anything else, however, it was the church structure in most of the
Western areas that prevented the papacy from having a more
profound influence.

In Italy, pontiffs from the time of Gregory I tried to bring the
royal Lombard house to the true faith, but also tried to prevent an
expansion of Lombard rule by demanding tribute, which did not
sit well with the emperors and exarchs intent on reconquering
these lands. This was one of the reasons why papal claims were not
fully recognized in Byzantine Italy. In addition, there was the
bishop of Ravenna's aspirations for autonomy. One of the bishops
was finally successful in having Emperor Constance II declare
Ravenna the see of an independent metropolitan in 666, which, as
in Rome, had to be consecrated by three provincial bishops without the need for confirmation by the pope. Constance II's son,
Constantine IV, revoked this privilege twenty years later, but Ravenna continued its push for autonomy. In Istria and Venetia,
Viligius' conduct led to a division in the church. And even when
this dispute ended in the late seventh century, Rome could get its
way in these areas only when it suited the bishops. As a result, the
papacy retained its predominance only in the Byzantine part of

Central and Southern Italy and in Sicily. To put it succinctly, the papacy had power where it had territory.

The situation in Lombard Italy was even more difficult inasmuch as it depended so much on the political constellation. The preeminence of the pope was undisputed despite the traditional self-government sentiments in the ecclesiastical province of Milan. Attendance at Roman synods and the implementation of Roman directives were usually only possible, however, if the kings and dukes allowed them. Since the supreme sovereignty of kings in the duchies of Friuli, Spoleto, and Benevento was not permanently recognized, papal negotiations with dukes over Rome's prominence in the inner kingdom could have negative effects—especially in Lombardy. And finally, let us look at what is often in historical literature referred to as the exemption for Bobbio granted by Honorius I. This cloister was founded by the Irishman Columba and was to have been autonomous in accordance with Irish tradition. Thus the abbot obtained a privilege from the pope in which the power of the bishop responsible for this area, the bishop of Piacenza, was limited, and the cloister was put under the protection of Saint Peter. How much success this granting of exemptions had is unknown for this early period.

Since the time of Justinian, North Africa was, like Italy, a part of the Byzantine empire under the direction of an exarch who resided in Carthage. Though the political ties to Constantinople were close—for example, the father of Emperor Heraclius' exarch was from Carthage—integrating the North African bishoprics into the imperial church was even less successful than integrating the Italian ones. In fact, old aspirations for independence stemming from the pre-Vandal period came back to life. And in contrast to Rome, North Africa had a number of fine theologians, particularly in the sixth century, who courageously fought against the condemnation of the Three Chapters. Thus in light of the conduct of Vigilius and his successors, there was little respect for Rome, despite the veneration of Peter. Independence was further encouraged by the fact that according to imperial church law the North African church was not considered to be subordinate to the pope. Thus during the North African conflict Gregory I was forced to correspond with the exarch as representative of the emperor, and not with the primate of Carthage. Only in Numidia did he directly intervene, and this because he had a bishop whom he could trust there, though for this reason the bishop was either attacked or avoided by his colleagues. Gregory's interventions in other areas under the exarch's rule, such as Corsica, Sardinia—there is no information available about the Balearic islands—and Baetica (southern Spain) were hardly more successful. The Roman church could only forcefully intervene in spiritual matters in those areas where it possessed territory. The ties between Rome and North Africa were somewhat closer in the conflict over Monotheletism. For example, several North African synods at the time of Pope Theodore acknowledged his preeminence and authority in matters of faith. How far this recognition went in actual practice is not known for certain. And the Arab invasions, which put all of North Africa in Arab hands by the latter part of the seventh century, signaled the end of an openly Christian way of life. Christians were allowed to continue their worship practices and keep their church organization, though contact with the non-Islamic world was hardly possible.

Not much later, in the years 711–712, the Muslims conquered most of Visigothic Spain, of which former Byzantine lands were a part from the second half of the seventh century. The loss for Christendom was greater than in North Africa, for in the seventh century the Spanish church stood preeminent over all other Western lands in matters of church law, doctrine and, to a certain extent, even in theology. This loss was no gain for the papacy, however. Gregory I had praised the conversion of King Reccared, but its significance he little understood. The Spanish church's development was principally a gain for the king and the two episcopal brothers Leander and Isidore of Seville. Though both had become good friends with Gregory as apocrisiarii in Constantinople, they did not allow the pope to interfere in their work. They began the tradition, which lasted until the end of the empire, of holding imperial councils at the royal residence in Toledo under the chairmanship of the primate of Toledo at which questions of faith, doctrine, and organization were declared binding for the whole realm. The ordo drafted for this purpose was often imitated outside of Spain and formed the model for most synod agendas in Christian Europe until late into the Middle Ages. Also of great importance was the collection of ecclesiastical law compiled in Spain. And the Spanish liturgy had a major influence on the liturgy of Frankish Gaul until into the eighth century.

As noted, the imperial councils met in Toledo, the royal residence, resulting in the king having some influence over the church. Just as in Constantinople, the bishop of Toledo, as the highest ranking member in the church, was designated by the king, and often had previous experience as a royal officeholder. Other indications of the close ties between king and church are the bishop's position as the highest appellate judge and the role of imperial councils as the decision-making body for new imperial laws. This meant that, with the decreasing importance of the king in the second half of the seventh century, the bishop along with the higher nobles dictated the affairs of the empire. Thus the Spanish church was the most complete example of a national church in the early Middle Ages. From this it followed, however, that there was no room in Spain for a supranational institution such as the papacy. Instructions from the papacy were accepted by the Spanish only if they accorded with their own views. For example, at the fourth Toledo Council in 633, Isidore of Seville put through as a council resolution a letter Gregory had sent to Isidore's brother Leander regarding baptism. But if the pontiffs insisted upon their superiority and discriminated against the Spanish bishops—Honorius I called them, in the words of the prophets, "mute dogs who know not know how to bark"—then the persons under attack maintained their dignity and received much pleasure in making light of how little their papal adversaries knew about the Bible and other specialized subjects. A final example of this is the controversy between Pope Benedict II and Julian of Toledo. Thirty years later, the Arab conquest made further contacts impossible, aside from a few exceptions.

Just as the Arabs had reduced the territory for papal activities in the West and South, so did the Avars and the Slavs in the East. The see of the metropolitan and the Roman vicar in Thessalonica had become an enclave in hostile territory, as had the cities in Illyria. As the memorial chapel to martyrs of Dalmatian Salona in the Lateran bapistry and the sporadic traces of correspondence show, contact was not cut off altogether, though church policies like those of the fifth century were no longer possible.

Somewhat more intensive for the time being were Rome's contacts with Arles. Provence as well as the early Burgundian empire had belonged to the Franks since the Gothic wars. In contrast to Spain, however, Frankish territories after Clovis' death in 511 were rarely united under one king. And even when they were united, the king was not able to prevail everywhere. From the early seventh century, the tripartite division of the empire along the old basis of Neustria, Austrasia, and Aquitaine was solidified. This did not mean, however, that these individual regions were in themselves homogeneous. In particular, Aquitaine was, along with Provence, fragmented into areas that were mostly oriented to a city and rarely under direct royal influence. Moreover, in the seventh century the Gallo-Roman senatorial families, which had transmitted culture and tradition to the society, either adapted to the lower Germanic cultural level or died out. One of their last great representatives in the late sixth century was Gregory of Tours, both history writer and bishop of Tours. His lively books show clearly how confusing the church's situation was even at his time, only to grow worse in the following century. Bishoprics and monasteries were often in the hands of the nobility, who desired them more for their property than for their spirituality. There still were synods, particularly in the north (Paris, Orleans) and Lyon, but whether their decrees were implemented everywhere is an open question. The situation was even more dismal for those areas east of the Rhine which were only loosely associated with the empire, such as Alamanni and Bavaria. Thus, the popes usually lacked a competent partner, which would have been necessary had they decided to intervene.

Tradition and his property in Provence, reduced though it was, made the bishop of Arles the most important papal contact for the time being. His duty was to organize the collection and delivery of the revenue from the patrimonies. Various popes also wanted to grant him supervision over the Gallic bishoprics, though except for a few letters this project never amounted to anything. Attempts to elevate the bishop's position to that of papal vicar also failed. Because Arles was situated on the southern periphery, Lyon, and Autun for a time, were much more important for the Frankish church. Gregory I must have learned just how desperate the conditions were in the Frankish empire when in 599 he wrote the first of many letters to Queen Brunichildis, her grandchildren, and several bishops, vainly trying to convene a synod that would prohibit widespread simony and the ownership of church property by lay persons. When an empire-wide synod finally met in Paris in 614 under Chlothar II, it regulated in particular the organization of the Frankish church and the relationship among king, nobility, and episcopate. Rome played no role in this, nor would it in the following hundred years. Had it not been for Frankish pilgrims going to Peter's tomb, or the handing down of old papal letters to Frankish synods, Rome would have been forgotten by the Franks.

All in all, in the first phase of the Byzantine epoch the papacy had direct influence only over Central and Southern Italy and its patrimony. That the papacy in the eighth century still rose to become the head of the Western church was due chiefly to the new church in England.

The honor of having started the Christian mission in England is usually awarded to Gregory I, though this is only partly correct. Even before Gregory Irish monks had successfully missionized in the north of the Anglo-Saxon realm. Gregory I was the first pope, however, who consciously and out of his own initiative sent missionaries to areas that lay outside of the traditional ecumene. It was evident that Gregory was not thinking of expanding the Roman sphere of influence inasmuch as the abbot he sent, Augustine, was ordained bishop in Gaul on Gregory's orders and made subordinate to the metropolitan of Arles. Both the mission bishop's ineptitude in treating the converted and the political situation on the island hindered Gregory in implementing his organizational plans of having an archbishop in York and London, each with twelve suffragan bishoprics. Instead, the Roman mission was limited for the time being to the small kingdom of Kent. Since that time the bishop of Kent's "capital," Canterbury, has been the archbishop of the English church. That the English church was able to expand at all and gradually turn more toward Rome is due to Gregory's successors and especially due to first the foreign and then local missionaries and bishops. Still long after Augustine's death—he died in 604 as did his employer, Gregory—the Irish mission was dominant in England. But the English church finally succumbed to Rome, thanks to the Northumbrian Wilfrid, who as a young man in Rome became a zealous champion of the papacy. In 664, he "proved" to King Oswy at a synod in Whitby, which dealt with the disputed question of the date of Easter, that Peter was a stronger saint than the Irish saint Columba because Peter could open or close heaven. With the acknowledgment of Peter's magic powers, Rome won in England. In 699, a monk named Theodore, who was banished from Tarsus in Asia Minor and later appointed archbishop of Canterbury by Pope Vitalian, began forming the church's organizational structure. To be sure, the opinions of the kings in England, especially the ruler of Northumbria, remained decisive, as Wilfrid's life of wandering shows.

Nevertheless, England was the first area outside of Italy in which church law and liturgy were patterned after Rome and whose bishops and monks turned to Rome more than those of other regions did for moral edification and justice. The Celtic element survived above all in the major role of the monasteries, in the penitentials, which are extremely informative about pastoral duties or daily customs, and in the urge to missionize. This combination of Roman and Irish traditions shaped the missionaries, who looked to expand their activities to the continent: first Wilfrid himself, then Willibrord, who was closely tied to Wilfrid, and the greatest of them all, Winfrid/Boniface. And since Rome was the model for organization, church law, and liturgy for these missionaries, their activity was most important in paving the way for the expansion of Rome's authority east of the Rhine and in the kingdom of the Franks. Thus the papacy's future success was principally due to the one country from which even Gregory I had probably expected the least because of its low cultural level.

From Gregory II to the End of the Lombard Kingdom (715–774)

Even during the pontificate of Gregory II, tendencies can be isolated that shaped the history of the papacy until the time of Adrian I: conflicts with the emperors, which gradually led to the withdrawl from the Byzantine empire; the leadership of the pope also in the secular concerns of Rome, the duchies and finally in a major portion of Italy; the struggle against Lombard expansion; and religious, then later, political contacts with missionaries, bishops, and rulers beyond the Alps, which led to the epoch-making alliance between the papacy and the Frankish rulers. As dim and as poor in source material as the history of the eighth century is, it was also fundamental for the following centuries, for many of the papacy's characteristic problems since then—the relationship to the Frankish or German rulers, the establishing and securing of the Papal States, dependence on the Roman nobility and its society—are a product of this era. And yet, in view of these changes, it must not be overlooked that one consequence of the previous period was that Rome and the papacy considered itself until the end of the century as belonging to the Byzantine empire, and the Byzantine or Greek influence on law, liturgy, art and administration continued for centuries. Thus, for the time being, the new political establishment did not bring about any changes in Rome's church organization and for this reason should not be overestimated.

Papal disputes with Constantinople began over taxes and culminated in a controversy over worship practices. In the years 717–718, Leo III successfully repulsed the Arab attempt to conquer Constantinople, an event that was just as momentous for the East as Charles Martel's victory over the Saracens in 732 was for the West. Both victories prevented the spread of Islam to Europe for centuries, except for some islands and coastal areas. The emperor reformed the army and the government administration in order to drive the Arabs out of Asia Minor and reconquer Greece and parts of the Balkan. One result of this was that he collected more taxes than his predecessors, taxing even church properties. Papal property lying within the imperial sphere of influence was also affected by these measures. Gregory II refused to give his approval to this encroachment on his income and, for this reason, was supposed to have been arrested, but the attempt failed. Soon after, in circa 725, the emperor tried to prevent the veneration of religious images. This was preceded by a prohibition of images for Christians in Islamic territories which the Caliph Yazid II instituted in 723, as well as by polemics by bishops in Asia Minor against the worship of images, and similar agitation on the part of the Syrian Pauline sects. Because the emperor himself came from the Euphrates region, his measures were perhaps influenced by these oriental examples. The patriarch of Constantinople opposed him, so Leo tried to win the pope over to his side, but Gregory II refused to support him. This did not prevent Leo from having images destroyed and having his political opponents persecuted, until finally his son Constantine V, at a council in 754, had iconolatry prohibited in the entire empire. And since the prohibition stirred up the average churchgoer with his relatively primitive beliefs much more than earlier conflicts over dogma, internal warfare broke out in the East, although most of the monks were on the side of the iconolaters. In Italy, the implementation of the prohibition brought about rebellions that hastened the breaking away from the East as well as the immigration of persecuted monks. The consequences were especially grave for the papacy. Leo took away papal jurisdiction over the vicariate of Thessalonica as well as that of Sicily and Southern Italy in favor of the patriarch of

Constantinople; from then on, all areas of the empire, except for the exarchate, were now united ecclesiastically. In addition, the emperor confiscated papal property in Southern Italy and Sicily. Both measures meant a catastrophe for the papacy as it lost the biggest portion of its land, and its ecclesiastical power was now limited to Central and Northern Italy, though it was exactly this contraction that brought about an intensification of papal influence in Italy and a new orientation toward the West.

The rebellions in Italy led to cities in the exarchate joining together for the first time against their ruler and getting rid of the heads of the army and administration whom the emperor had set up. Though the exarch, Eutychius, was able, with the help of the Lombard king Liutprand, to tighten his hold in part of Northern Italy, in the Roman duchy the exarch no longer personally chose the *dux.* From now on, it was the nobility and the pope who decided the new leadership of the army and government administration. The government of Rome and the duchy was now effectively in the hands of the pope, even though the emperor was still the sovereign. The pope's new position manifested itself in concrete measures. The planned restoration of the Roman city walls under Gregory II was completed under his successor, Gregory III, as were the walls of the port of Centumcellae, known today as Civitavecchia. That it was now Peter and Paul, the princes of the apostles, and their representatives, who governed the duchy is clearly evident by the fact that the popes now negotiated with the Lombard rulers, kings or dukes, for the return of conquered territory. The oldest example of this, again under Gregory II, is the Sutri castle, returned to the two apostles by King Liutprand. Gregory III acquired territory from the duke of Spoleto, Trasamund Gallese, for "the holy state and the Roman army." Zacharius proved to be the cleverest and most successful in obtaining land. From the time of his pontificate, the pope held the highest authority, even in Northern Italy, and for this reason the exarch, archbishop, and people of Ravenna asked Zacharius to intercede for them before Liutprand on behalf of the exarchate's continued existence.

Though Liutprand, who was devoted to St. Peter, for the most part complied with the requests Peter's vicar on earth had asked of him, his successor, Aistulf, carried out his political plans without religious scruples. In 751, he conquered the rest of the exarchate, subdued reluctant duchies in Central Italy and, ultimately, threatened Rome itself. Thus the new pope, Stephen II, traveled first to Pavia, where he urged Aistulf in vain to restore the conquered territory, and then to the Frankish kingdom, the first pope to go there, where he concluded an alliance with King Pepin in 754, about which we shall have more to say later. As part of the alliance, Pepin promised St. Peter and his vicar a piece of Italy, and with this he laid the cornerstone of the so-called Papal States. And then later in Pavia the Franks, Romans (led by the pope), and the Lombards concluded a treaty guaranteeing the integrity of their respective territories. This did not, however, prevent Aistulf from continuing with the same policies. This caused Stephen to write several letters to the Frankish king and his vassals, in one of which he even suggested that Peter was a partner of the Franks. Yet it was only when the Lombard king in 756 once again conquered part of the Roman duchy and threatened Rome that the Franks went into battle against Aistulf and forced him to relinquish to Peter's representative a part of the exarchate and Ravenna itself. The keys of the cities were deposited at Peter's tomb by Pepin's emissary, Abbot Fulrad. When King Desiderius, who promised the pope more cities for his help in making him king in 757, renewed Aistulf's policies in 771, Charlemagne conquered his kingdom and reaffirmed and expanded Pepin's promise in 774.

What Stephen II's motives were in the negotiations with Pepin has been much disputed. An envoy of the emperor accompanied him to the court at Pavia. And the pope himself bestowed the title of *patricius Romanorum* on Pepin and his sons. At that time, the representative of the emperor, that is, the exarch, carried the title of *patricius*, though ususally without the suffix *Romanorum*. It is a much discussed controversy among researchers whether Stephen granted the title on his own or as a representative of the emperor. Among other evidence, a letter from Adrian I in 785 to Emperor Constantine VI in which Charlemagne is referred to as *patricius Romanorum* has been cited in favor of the second thesis. This presupposes that Constantinople had approved of the bestowal, since otherwise it would have been a snub on the pope's part to the imperial court. Other papal letters, however, show that pontiffs did not always express themselves tactfully if they wanted something. Moreover, the concept *"Romani"* could have had various interpretations at that time. And the so-called Donation of Constantine (more about this later) shows that, precisely in this period, opinion was strong inside the papal court to rule Italy without and instead of the emperor. It must be emphasized, however, that it was on the title of *patricius* in particular that pontiffs since Stephen II based Pepin's and Charlemagne's intervention in Italy. The Frankish kings saw the situation differently. Pepin, at least, never actually had the title of *patricius,* justifying his invasion with his promise to St. Peter. Thus, in 756, he rejected demands by the Byzantine envoy that he surrender to the emperor the parts of the exarchate which he had conquered. For Pepin, the new master was the prince of apostles.

The popes were still nominally subordinate to the emperor, but the extent of the Donation of Pepin shows that they were probably thinking about a territory of their own to rule. First of all, the Donation of Pepin affected the Roman duchy, which was to be placed completely under the rule of St. Peter and his successors. And then portions of Byzantine Italy that were conquered by the Lombards in the eighth century were put under Frankish protection. This included the area around the port of Luni in the west, Ravenna and its environs in the east, including the cities of the Pentapolis south of Ravenna, and the roads which connected these regions. In addition, the Byzantine portion of Northern Italy, Venetia, and Benevento were to be removed from Aistulf's control. These regions roughly corresponded to the ones from which attendees at the Roman synods after 731 hailed. If one keeps in mind that since this same period the popes had been emphasizing their care for the "sheep" entrusted to them as the work of a "shepherd," basing their negotiations with the Lombard kings for regions beyond the duchy on this principle, then the conclusion is not hard to reach that the popes now wanted to govern as secular rulers all bishoprics that remained under the papacy after Emperor Leo III's reduction, or at the very least, wanted to incorporate them in their sphere of influence. Such attempts were not unusual at that time in Italy, so that in Naples, for example, the offices of duke and archbishop were combined for a short time. And the archbishops of Ravenna tried more than once to become the legal successors to the exarch over their Roman rivals.

The political conditions in Italy prevented the papacy from realizing its territorial ambitions. Nevertheless, because of these conditions, henceforth the papacy was very much influenced by politics in Italy, and secular power brokers were interested more than ever in making sure that whoever held the papal office worked in their favor. This became clear for the first time with the dramatic events after the death of Paul I in 767. At the time, there were three power groups in Rome: the administrative leaders preferred by the deceased pope or his brother and predecessors; the property owners of the area around Rome, who were pressed hard by Paul in particular; and a Lombard party. Initially, the pretender of the second group, Constantine II, was successful. But the united efforts of the other two groups succeeded in having him deposed. The Lombard friends were then thrown out, and finally the victor, the Sicilian Stephen III, removed the far too powerful leaders of his own party. These events of 767–768, in their abundance of treachery, cruelty—the mutilation of noses, the putting out of eyes, or torture—and murder, show just how Byzantine Rome still was and what the city would become were it left to itself. This type of "politics" continued to an excess in the ninth and particularly in the tenth century. And it is characteristic of the situation that even in the eighth century popes were busy taking part in these intrigues.

Before the chaos of 767, and even more so afterward, there were two groups in Rome that had influence on both secular and ecclesiastical power: the *iudices de militia* and the *iudices de clero*. The word *iudex* in this case does not mean judge; rather, more broadly, it means dignitary. Thus, in Roman sources, Frankish counts or royal emissaries are noted as *iudices*. Members of the first group were made up of the heads of the secular administration and army, in other words, the representatives of the leading lay persons of both Rome and its environs, who were often referrred to as "dux" or "consul." Leading members of the papal administration belonged to the second group, the *primicerius* and *secundicerius* of the notaries, the *primicerius* of the *defensores*, the *acarius, sacellarius, nomenculator, vestiarius, vice-dominus* and the head (*superista*) of the cubiculars. They could therefore be regarded as belonging to the clergy because, as noted previously, they often had received a lower ordination. They were first and foremost, however, representatives of the leading Roman families and thus made sure, just as much as the other *iudcies* did, and with the help of the papacy, that the interest, prestige and wealth of their own families were ever increasing. Thus a new pope usually could successfully govern only if he came from an important Roman family that could outmanuever the supporters of the predecessor and promote his family and his friends instead. Nepotism from now on became an important, albeit problematic means of personal papal politics, and remained so until the nineteenth century.

It was in this political atmosphere that an attempt was made by Stephen III to increase the influence of the higher clergy, the presbyters and deacons, but it met with only partial success. With the events surrounding the death of Paul I still on his mind, the new pope convened a synod in 769 at which a new decree regarding papal elections was promulgated. It stated that only the Roman clergy was allowed to elect a pope, and cardinal priests and deacons were the only eligible electors. After the election, the new pope was to be brought to the residence, the *patriarchium Lateranense,* where he would receive an oath of allegiance as lord of all (*omnium dominus*) from the leaders as well as the rest of the army, upper-class citizens and the community of the Roman people. During these proceedings, no one was allowed to enter the city from the outlying areas. The clergy, at least, now saw the pope as the clear ruler of the city, but managed to exclude lay persons from influencing his appointment. The clergy thus distanced itself from those events which had created Stephen himself, for under the guidance of the *primicerius* Christopher, the clergy, army, and people all united behind him at an assembly that took place at the Forum on the site of the old Roman assemblies. As the *Liber Pontificalis* suggests, the decree was followed at the next election. And yet, the decree did not curb the influence of the families since the second group of *iudices* also belonged to the clergy.

In the decree, one group of presbyters was referred to as "cardinales," that is, especially tied to the pope (who was the *cardo,* the door hinge). This indicates that in the eighth century representatives of the titular churches—probably one per church—had a major say in papal government. The selection of these few from the whole host of presbyters is an important step in the development of the cardinalate. And so, in the future the title of "cardinal" was to be reserved principally for this group. Besides them, the decree also speaks of a renewed importance for the deacons. The first reference to a group of cardinal bishops also comes from Stephen III's pontificate. As the *Liber pontificalis* reports, the pope, while in the process of reforming the clergy, ordered that the seven cardinal bishops who held services during the week in the Lateran basilica should celebrate mass at the main altar of St. Peter's on Sundays. Contrary to the traditional interpretations, this regulation does not mean that from the time of Stephen seven cardinal bishops were attached to the Lateran basilica; in fact, this activity is described as having already been in existence. What is new in this is the service in St. Peter's. Perhaps they were to act as representatives of the pope, while he kept for himself the Sunday mass in the Lateran. Whatever the case may be, the one certain fact is that in the eighth century, of all the bishops in the duchy, seven had a closer relationship to the papal court. It was not firmly established until the twelfth century, however, which bishops belonged to this seven. The bishops who were most likely to have continuously been part of the seven were the ones from Ostia, Porto, and Albano, since they were involved in the consecration of new Roman bishops.

Stephen III's two regulations, as well as other information, show that the pope and the heads of the Roman clergy tried to limit as much as possible the influence of the Roman noble families. A reorganization of church properties by setting up so-called *"domus-cultae"* (literally "cultivated house") was helpful in this effort and in balancing the losses at the hands of Leo III. Zacharius had first laid out an agricultural operation of this kind, and Adrian I continued the policy. Similar to the Frankish royal demesne, this operation took in larger units—*fundi, massae, casalia* (isolated farms) with water mills, vineyards, olive groves, pastures, and fields—which were exclusively for supplying food to the Roman church, and thus were controlled by the church and were not allowed to be alienated. These agricultural operations were located not far from Rome, and they had the effect of partially curtailing the expansion of property held by the nobility.

⌈ The extent to which the developments since Gregory II—the distancing from Constantinople, the accentuation of the papal clergy, and the economic and political consolidation of Rome— had increased clerical self-assurance is evident in a text which probably comes from papal circles of the second half of the eighth century: the *Constitutum Constantini*, usually rendered in English as the Donation of Constantine. In the first part, based on the Sylves- ter legend which had evolved from the late fifth century, Constantine the Great portrays his conversion to Christianity as it was brought about by the princes of the apostles and Sylvester. The second part gives reasons for making Constantinople the capital—the earthly emperor should not reside where the representative of the heavenly emperor has his capital—and contains

donations and privileges for the Roman church. As a result of
these privileges, the pope, as supreme head of the universal church,
possesses the rank of emperor—thus the emperor performs the
"stirrup service" for him, presents him with the so-called tiara
along with other honors, and grants him the right to ride on a
white horse just like the emperor; the papal clergy is placed on an
equal footing with the imperial senate; the pope resides in the
Lateran, for the first time referred to as *"palatium"* and which
earlier was supposedly an imperial palace. And finally, the emperor transfers to the pope sovereignty over the western lands and
islands, never exactly defined. To what extent the text was known
and used in Rome cannot be established until the middle of the
tenth century. Therefore, the writer of the text and his motives
are uncertain. The text became even more important after the so-
called Investiture Contest as a justification for papal claims. And,
at least as a testament to the independence of the Roman church,
the text is also very informative for the papacy of the early Carolingian period.

The *Constitutum* shows how strongly the papacy was fixed on
Constantinople even in the late eighth century. Its main theme
seems to have been the legitimization of or justification for papal
claims to Italy and the inevitable breaking away from the Byzantine empire that this required. Accordingly, it characterized that
phase in papal history when Byzantine influence was already waning, but the growing power of the Franks in Italy was still not very
noticeable. And it shows clearly that the alliance with King Pepin
did not bring about any changes in the Roman mentality—a fact
which must not be undervalued for later governments such as
Charlemagne's, Otto the Great's, Otto III's, and Henry III's.
Nevertheless, it would of course be wrong to deny the objective
significance of the alliance between the papacy and the Franks, for
it determined, to a large extent, the political and ecclesiastical
orientation of Rome for the next centuries. Thus, in closing, let us
take a closer look at this alliance and its premises.

Probably the most important premise was the influence of the
papacy on the churches beyond the Alps. Gregory II had already
tried to intensify the Christianization of the inhabited parts of
Bavaria and to form its church organization on the Roman model.
His plans were frustrated, however, by the opposition of the dukes
there and by most of the missionaries. The "Romanization" of
Christianity north of the Alps did not take place under the initia-

tive of popes, but was the work of Anglo-Saxon missionaries, particularly Boniface. Like Willibrord before him, Boniface wanted to
missionize the Frisians first, but he soon found himself active in
the tribal areas of Thuringia, Hessen, and Bavaria. Often dependent on Frankish troops to carry out this work, he founded in the
three regions new monasteries and bishoprics, which functioned
as mission centers. A large part of the ecclesiastical organization of
Bavaria today can be traced back to Boniface. Also of note is that
he was ordained as a bishop in Rome in 722, taking on the name
of Boniface after the saint whose day it was. Furthermore, he took
an oath of obedience to the pope, which heretofore only the suburbicarian bishops had been required to do, and he also requested
Rome to instruct him on mission work and church organization.
In 733, he acted in the name of the popes as "archbishop of
Germania." This did not by any means make him the "apostle of
Germany," as has been claimed since the nineteenth century, but
rather the first successful promoter of Roman maxims north of
Italy. It is all the more astonishing, therefore, that his name never
comes up in the contemporary Roman historiography except for
his position in the biography of Gregory II in the *Liber pontificalis*.
This is yet another example of the how dominating the papal
fixation was on internal Roman and Italian affairs.

Boniface received a letter of introduction to the Frankish seneschal Charles Martel from Gregory III, and Boniface himself tried
to get Charles' backing, though to a large extent the protection of
the Frankish ruler only became decisive under Charles' son, Carloman, after Charles' death in 741. This is evident in the synods of
743 to 745, which Boniface wanted to use to reform the church in
the territories controlled by Carloman (the larger areas of the
eastern Frankish lands). In the sphere of Carloman's brother
Pepin, however, Boniface carried no influence. For this reason, he
had to reduce his activity when, in 747, Carloman renounced his
rule to become a monk in Rome. Even earlier, there had been
opposition to Boniface, including death threats, on the part of
Frankish bishops, and this opposition now increased, even though
both Pepin and his brother took up the reform of the Frankish
church, not with the help of Boniface, but with that of the Frankish bishops. These bishops were influenced by reform ideas which
had spread mostly from Lyon since the early eighth century. All in
all, however, it was Boniface's missionary, organizational, and ref-
ormational activity that brought about an increase in contact be-

tween Rome and the Frankish kingdom, of which Bavaria in 745 was again a major part. And the beginnings of internal Frankish reform were also often based on the decretals of earlier popes. Moreover, if one considers that the traditional Frankish veneration of Peter was intensifying at the same time, it becomes clear that there was an emotional and organizational basis for a close collaboration between the papacy and the Franks.

This collaboration was touched off by Pepin's ambitions to make himself king of the Franks over the powerless Merovingian, Childeric III. To ensure his claims, he asked for Pope Zacharias' opinion through an envoy. The answer came back that whoever has the power should also wear the crown. Upon hearing this, and of course after gaining the support of the Frankish magnates, his former peers and his rivals, Pepin was anointed Frankish king in 751 (perhaps by Boniface), while the former king was hidden away in a monastery. From then on, Frankish kings needed, in addition to being elected by the magnates, an anointing by the church, which of course led to increased church influence on the crown. Roman sources do not mention these events. The probable reason is that the significance of Zacharias' answer was not recognized, and the position of the major-domo as equal to the king was not doubted, as the *vita* of Zacharias shows. In this biography, Charles Martel is referred to as king of the Franks (the passage was written before 750).

In contrast to this, and understandable from the Roman point of view, the events of 754 were emphasized. As mentioned, in 753 Stephen II traveled together with the Byzantine envoy to Pavia to ask for the restitution of the exarchate from Aistulf. But since the Lombard king behaved rather unconciliatory, the pope continued his journey to the Frankish ruler Pepin, whom he met at the imperial palace in Ponthion. In St. Denis, the burial site of most Frankish rulers, he anointed Pepin once again as king of the Franks, as well as his sons Charles and Carloman. What else actually happened in Ponthion, St. Denis, and Quierzy is a source of dispute. It is possible that in Ponthion, Pepin and Stephen, in the manner of a Frankish oath of friendship, agreed to an alliance of mutual support. What is certain is that Pepin subordinated himself to St. Peter, promising to protect Peter's vicar, while Stephen designated Pepin as *patricius Romanorum*. Later the emphasis changed, however, and the alliance was no longer based on an oath of friendship, but became a spiritual alliance since the pope was godfather of both sons and therefore spiritual father (*compater*) of Pepin. Proof for either of these assertions is scanty. In Quierzy Pepin promised, as mentioned, portions of Central and Northern Italy to St. Peter and his successors. If one considers that the contracts (no longer extant) were written in Latin, which the king probably did not understand, Frankish terms thus also having to be Latinized, then it is clear that, later, the contents of the contract were able to be interpreted differently by the Roman and Frankish sides. Both sides recognized the duties of the king toward St. Peter. Pepin fulfilled this duty in 756 when he defeated Aistulf and placed portions of the promised areas under papal control. In contrast to Pepin, the popes played up his obligation as *patricius Romanorum*, that is, protector of Italy, while both sides recognized the contract of mutual friendship. Because the contract was made between two living persons, and thus after their deaths expired, it was renewed in writing by later popes. And when Charles visited Rome in 774 during his military campaign, he and the pope at that time, Adrian I, made a vow of mutual friendship at the tomb of Peter. Charles' title of *patricius Romanorum* was renewed by the pope as was Pepin's promise, by Charles himself. Compared with those made in 754, papal claims had swollen to include areas outside the duchy, which the pope wanted to subject to his rule. It appears doubtful, however, that Charles approved of all the claims, especially those regarding Venetia, Istria, and the Lombard duchies. Moreover, in 774, papal and Frankish interests were probably not identical. And as a result of the conquest of Lombard lands, which came a short while later, the relationship of relative equality between the two partners gradually changed into one of papal dependency on the king, even more so than it had been with Constantine earlier. To be sure, this dependence did not prevent the papacy from gaining, first during Pepin's reign, and later even stronger during Charles', a great influence on the liturgy, laws, and organization of the Frankish church.

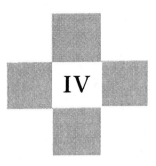

The Papacy Under Carolingian Rule (774–904)

The outstanding event of this epoch was the crowning of Charlemagne as emperor on Christmas Day of the year 800. With this act, a tradition was founded that was to last for a thousand years, until Napoleon's empire. For Rome, this meant that, for the next three hundred years, the emperor would be overlord of Roman territory and, with that, of the pope. So first, let us examine the events which led up to the coronation, the coronation itself, and then, the relationship between emperor and pope in the ninth century.

As mentioned previously, during the occupation of Pavia in 774, Charlemagne renewed his father's promise to St. Peter. In connection with this, however, he did not make any effort to realize Adrian's claims to greater Ravenna and the duchies of Spoleto and Benevento, the latter still ruled by the Lombards, which were based on that promise. In fact, the pope, powerless as he was, had to tolerate encroachments from the new Frankish territories of Spoleto and Tuscany. And when the king met with the pope again in Rome in 781, he did not fulfill the pope's request; instead, in his capacity as the new king of the Lombards, he reduced the lands claimed by the pope: he retained for himself, as king of all Lombards, the conquest of Benevento, and Spoleto remained a part of his kingdom under the government of a marquis. Moreover, the border betwen Spoleto and Roman territory in the Sabine was accurately measured, a first in medieval history. The territory reconquered from the Lombards in the eighth century was the only area nominally placed under the pope, specifically, Ravenna and the Pentapolis to the south of it. In addition, as a concession, Charlemagne entrusted to the pope some cities in southern Tuscany, among them Orvieto and Viterbo, which later were to be of great importance to the papacy. And so, for the time being, the pope's aspirations for territorial expansion came to an end. He possessed direct power of authority only in the Roman duchy and in what was left of the Patrimonium Petri.

⌈Charlemagne described in general terms how he envisaged the collaboration with the pope in a famous letter he wrote in 796 to Adrian's successor, Leo III: "It is our duty, with God's help, to protect from without the holy church of Christ from invasion by heathens and from destruction by unbelievers, and to secure it from within by recognition of the Catholic faith. Your work, most Holy Father, is to raise your hands together with Moses to God, and in so doing help our struggle, so that with your prayers, under the leadership of God, Christians everywhere may gain the victory over enemies of His holy name." Though the pope's responsibility as the most important person for the saying of prayers must not be discounted, Charlemagne kept control of the church here on earth for himself. ⌉

Charlemagne had earlier proven to Adrian that he took this claim seriously. In 787, a council in Nicea, with papal representatives present, once again allowed iconolatry in accordance with Adrian's wishes. When the pope then asked Charlemagne and his bishops for their consent to the council's decrees, the king refused. True to tradition, the pope, as member of the imperial church, had been invited to the council, but no Frankish bishop had been, which was the reason why Charlemagne did not acknowledge the validity of the decrees for his kingdom. What is more, the Latin translation that Charlemagne received of the council's acts had many errors and increased the suspicion among Frankish bishops that in the Greek East, as well as in Rome, religious icons were actually being prayed to. The upshot was that, in the *Libri Carolini*, perhaps written by Theodulf, one of Charlemagne's most important theologians, the pope and Constantinople were attacked, and a synod in Frankfurt in 794 which Charlemagne had convoked condemned the decrees of 787 and the pope as well, though indirectly. The synod turned out to be an embarrassment for the pope inasmuch as he had sent representatives to Frankfurt who, in the end, had to consent to the condemnation of their boss. The extent to which Charlemagne by now felt himself to be head of the entire Western church is evident in the fact that English bishops also came out against the decrees, and the doctrine of adoptionism developed in Muslim Spain was condemned as heretical. Upon orders from Charlemagne, Adrian had to repeat the condemnation at a Roman synod. Accordingly, the pope was not much more than the highest bishop in Charlemagne's empire, while Charlemagne himself was equal to emperor. Little wonder, then, that Adrian exalted him as the new Constantine.

Despite all this, the idea persisted in Rome at this time that St. Peter, and through him the pope, had a special position. In fact, Adrian had silver images displayed in St. Peter's upon which Peter was portrayed as patron of the pope as well as of the Frankish king. Leo III acted similarly, as can be seen in the mosaics he had commissioned between 795 and 800 in his former titular church, Santa Susanna, and in particular in one of the triclinia he had built in the Lateran as reception rooms. The triclinium mosaic, though altered in the Baroque era, still exists. In the apse itself—at least in its eighteenth-century form—the mosaic portrays Christ sending out the apostles to missionize the world, while to the right of the apse he is presenting the keys to Peter, representing spiritual power, and to Constantine a flag, representing secular power. To the left, Peter himself discharges his power by handing the pallium to Leo, and to Charlemagne, as king, a flag. In the pope's mind, Charlemagne was not only Constantine's successor, but also Peter's deputy, from whom he received his legitimation. The ground was now prepared for a new Western empire in Rome—by the grace of Peter, however. The final push to the creation of this empire set off some turbulent events in the year 799.

Leo III was elected in 795, probably with the help of Adrian's relatives, though he seems later to have lost their respect. Charlemagne's adviser, Alcuin, already knew in 798 of the pope's difficulties in Rome. The pope's opponents wanted to declare him unfit for office according to Byzantine custom and to remove him. They decided, therefore, to maim him during the Greater Litany (penitential procession) on St. Mark's Day in 799 and have him confined to a monastery. Their plan failed. Leo was indeed taken, though his eyes were not gouged out nor his tongue cut off as the conspirators, high-ranking officials in the Lateran palace, had foreseen. A short while later, the pope was able to flee. Under Frankish escort he fled to Charlemagne, who received him in Paderborn. Leo's opponents also sent representatives, and it was probably in Paderborn that further proceedings were planned. Leo returned to Rome along with emissaries of the king. In one of Leo's new triclinia, they investigated the charges of his opponents, who accused the pope of adultery and perjury. The accusations proved to be unfounded, though the investigating judges seem to have discovered other transgressions by the pope. These must have been so grave that Alcuin, full of disgust, burned a letter of Archbishop Arn of Salzburg, who was one of the judges, because, out of his repsect for the papacy, he did not want to believe that the charges were true.

Charlemagne himself came to Rome toward the end of the year 800. On November 23, he was received as an emperor by the pope, the clergy, and the people. The conspirators were considered traitors. According to a law proclaimed in 740 by Leo III and his son Constantine V, traitors were only allowed to be sentenced by the emperor. Because Rome was becoming more and more estranged from Constantinople, and because the empress at the time, Irene, was considered a usurper on account of the murder of her son, the rightful emperor Constantine VI, there was no legitimate judge. But in any case, Leo could not be judged, he himself as well as the Suburbicarian and Frankish bishops referring to the Symmachan Forgeries, which stated that the pope could not be tried by anyone. Both of these conditions determined the events that followed. On December 23, the pope cleared himself of the accusations against him by taking an oath in St. Peter's— as Pelagius had done in the sixth century. Two days later, at the third Christmas mass, Leo crowned Charlemagne, and the Romans who were present acclaimed him emperor according to Byzantine custom. In the days that followed, the new emperor sat as judge over the conspirators, condemning them to death as criminals against the crown, but later pardoned them at the pope's request and banished them to Frankland.

Charlemagne's later biographer, Einhard, reports that Charlemagne knew nothing in advance of an imperial coronation, nor that he wanted it. This is, however, most likely a later interpretation, perhaps coming from Charlemagne himself, meant to reduce the influence of the Romans and the pope. The coronation was, of course, interpreted differently from the papal point of view than it was from the Frankish. The *Liber pontificalis* clearly emphasized the initiative of the pope and the Romans. Frankish sources justify the empire by saying that Charlemagne ruled over several lands, and that all capitals of the former western Roman empire—Trier, Arles, Milan, Ravenna, and Rome—and the Byzantine throne were abandoned. An interpretation that was initially neglected was Alcuin's, who saw the empire as a protectorate for all Christians.

Charlemagne himself used the new title mostly to unify the secular and relgious sphere in the heterogeneous areas of his realm and to complete the tribal laws which until then had remained untouched. The new title also offered him the opportunity, more than ever before, to govern the Roman territory as overlord. After a three-month stay at St. Peter's, he appointed permanent representatives to remain there and defend his interests. As a result, the pope was temporarily under the control of the emperor.

Charlemagne's strong hand was also evident in religious questions. Under Visigothic influence, it had long been common in the Frankish liturgy to emphasize in the creed that the Holy Ghost proceeded not only from the father but also from the son by inserting the word *Filioque.* Though the theological value of this word in the Byzantine church was not denied, the imperial church, including Rome, had so far refused to alter any of the contents of the creed, which was first drawn up in the fourth and fifth centuries. Then, when a dispute broke out at the beginning of the ninth century in Jerusalem between Frankish and Greek monks over the *Filioque,* Charlemagne called upon Leo III to take a position. Leo III stuck with the traditional form. The dispute was not so important for Leo, since in Rome the creed was recited only as part of the baptismal liturgy, while in the Frankish lands it was common at every Sunday and holiday mass. And to strengthen his position, Leo had the traditional creed in Latin and Greek made part of the mass at St. Peter's. However, a national synod convoked by Charlemagne, at which the Frankish usage was restipulated, proved how little weight Leo III had in Frankish lands.

The pope's subordination was also evident in Charlemagne's policies toward Constantinople. Irene was overthrown in 802. Her successors considered the pope to be a schismatic who had seceded from the imperial church, and Charlemagne was a usurper. Only after Charlemagne gave up his designs of conquering Byzantine Venetian, and Constantinople needed help against the Bulgarians, could negotiations begin in 811. After a change of power in Constantinople, the talks led to a mutual recognition in 815. The pope, however, like other Frankish magnates, was merely allowed to sign the agreement. And in 813, Charlemagne, after successful negotiations with the envoy of Michael I, crowned his son Louis as co-emperor in the Byzantine tradition, without any papal involvement. In so doing, he denied any claims of the pope or Rome to the bestowing of the imperial crown. Louis the Pious acted likewise when a few years later, in 817, he crowned his oldest son Lothair I as co-emperor.

But already during Louis' reign the development had begun that eventually led to the pope having the exclusive right to confer the imperial crown. In 823, Paschal I crowned Lothair emperor once again, this time in Rome. His son, Louis II, by that time king of Italy, received the crown in 850 from Leo IV. After Louis' death in 875, John VIII showed, by preferring Charles the Bald in 875 and Charles III in 881 over other candidates, that it was the pope who was empowered to bestow the imperial title. At the same time, however, respect for the empire outside Italy had declined considerably. Although Louis the Pious, with the help of imperial prestige, wanted to maintain unity within the empire, and wanted, even more than his father did, to reform the church, his weak rule led to a division in the empire in 830, which only grew stronger under his sons and grandsons after his death in 840. Possession of the imperial title did not bring any additional dignity to its holder among the Frankish nobility and upper clergy. As a result, from the time of Louis the Pious the empire more and more served the purpose that Leo III had wanted it to back in 800: the protection of Rome and of former Byzantine lands in Central Italy. Therefore, it was understandable that the popes also tried to accommodate the views of whomever was emperor.

Paschal I followed this maxim in 817. Like his predecessors, he concluded an alliance of friendship and a pact with Louis in which Louis supported the territorial claims of the pope. But in contrast to the policies of his father pursued since 800, Louis did not interfere in the government of the Papal States. Rome was once again governed by the pope. This went so far as to Paschal turning a blind eye to the murdering in the Lateran of two Roman pro-Frankish partisans. As revenge for these murders, papal legates in the Frankish kingdom were held prisoner until the new pope, Eugene II, singed a new agreement with the Franks. However, this new agreement, the so-called *Constitutio Romana* of 824, and an oath by the pope and the Romans that was linked to it, together with some energetic policies vis-à-vis Italy on the part of Lothair I and Louis II, led in 875 to the papacy being more strongly controlled by the emperor than it had even been under Charles. As in Byzantine times, a newly elected pope was only allowed to be consecrated if the emperor had confirmed the election in advance. And imperial interests were maintained by two permanent representatives (*missi*), of which one was designated by the emperor and the other by the pope. The system only functioned, however, when the Roman nobility—the *iudices de clero* and the *iudices de militia*—acted in concert with the imperial representatives. Otherwise, conflicts arose, as with the election of Benedict III in 855. Moreover, the new system did even less to help arouse any sympathy for the Franks in Rome.

Charlemagne's deeds did not lead to his glorification as a legend in Rome as they did north of the Alps. In the *vita* of the short-lived pope Valentine, Rome is praised as the city "that has the honor of having the highest clergy and royal (ruling) authority." And when the Franks and the Spoletians ravaged the countryside around Rome once again in 844 during Sergius II's pontificate because Sergius had been consecrated without imperial confirmation, the author of the *vita* expressed his disgust after their retreat. He wrote: "And therefore everyone, the Senate and the people of Rome, together with the women and children, happy to be freed from this monstrous pest and to be saved from the yoke of tyrannical brutality, venerated the holy Bishop Sergius as the bringer of salvation and the restorer of peace." It became clear to the Romans a short while later in 846, however, when the Saracens plundered St. Peter's and St. Paul's and continued stirring up troubles along the coasts, that the pope could not guarantee peace without the emperor's energetic protection. This fact was driven home even more so after 875, when the autonomous marquis of Spoleto harassed Rome. Thus it was precisely those emperors who are otherwise little esteemed in Frankish history, Lothair I and Louis II, who for decades guaranteed a relative stability in Rome. After Louis' death, there was little the popes could do in the long run except crown the Spoletian rulers as emperors, and later the Tuscan and Northern Italian princes, instead of the powerless and distant Carolingians. Though this may have been understandable on Rome's part, by the end of the ninth century it led to imperial dignity temporarily sinking to a *quantité négligeable* beyond the Alps.

The compact between the papacy and the Franks had consequences for the Frankish church's liturgy, organization, and laws. There were also continued papal contacts with Constantinople. Both of these trends will be discussed later. It appears even more astonishing, then, that the relatively close relationship between Rome and England in the seventh and early eighth centuries took a major step backward in the Carolingian era. At the end of the eighth century, King Offa of Mercia not only visited the apostles' graves, he also took up a collection for St. Peter in his kingdom. Other Anglo-Saxon rulers of this period undertook similar actions. The so-called Peter penny was supposedly developed later from these payments. But it seems that, as early as the ninth century, the payments were no longer collected, even though Anglo-Saxons continued to make pilgrimages to Rome, including such kings as Alfred the Great, some of them staying there the rest of their lives as members of the Anglo-Saxon colony (*schola Saxonum*). There is no evidence of an increased papal influence over the Anglo-Saxon church. One of the reasons was probably the Vikings and their invasion and eventual rule over most of the island. Another reason was the cultural decline of the Anglo-Saxon church, which hardly produced another important scholar after Alcuin. Only the Irish monastic church continued to flower for some time, producing a theologian like John Scotus Eriugena, but the church's ties to Rome were as weak as ever.

The papacy had even less contact to the churches in Islamic and Christian Spain. The condemnation of adoptionism by Adrian I and Leo III had been recommended to them by Charlemagne. None of the popes put forth his own initiatives. The Mozarabs (Christians under Arab government) more or less submitted to Muslim rule; and when Christians consciously martyred themselves, as some did in Toledo in the middle of the ninth century, Rome showed absolutely no interest. In Christian Spain, the church flourished in the Kingdom of Asturias, principally under Alfonso II (791–842) and Alfonso III (866–909), which laid the cornerstone for the later so important cult of Santiago de Compostela.

But the church was modeled, in both religious and secular affairs, on the earlier Visigothic system, which from the beginning hindered close ties with Rome. The churches of the other regions—Navarre, the valleys of the Pyrenees, and even in the Spanish Marches (later Catalonia), which were ruled for a time by the Franks—were still too concerned with their own limited regional development to concentrate on nurturing contacts with Rome. Also of note at this time was an inquiry of the bishop of Tripoli to Leo IV, which Leo answered by urging a return to the early church practice of penitence. Further contacts with North Africa failed to materialize, however, so that the brief correspondence merely attests to the continued existence of Christian communities south of the Mediterranean. Equally scanty were papal contacts with Scandanavia, which, under Charlemagne and Louis the Pious, were directed toward supporting the Frankish mission. At the end of the ninth century, however, it became impossible to carry out this evangelical mission.

Thus only the Frankish kingdom, Constantinople, and the territories of the Slavs and Bulgarians remained within the range of papal church policies. Regular contacts between Rome and Constantinople at first were impeded by the iconolatry dispute, since the veneration of icons, which was decreed in 787, was again prohibited after the ouster of Irene in 802. On top of that came the short-lived schism over the imperial coronation of 800. There was, however, no lack of opposition to the church in the Byzantine empire, especially among the monks, whose spokesman at the time was Abbot Theodore of Studios. He was not only against iconolatry, but also against the preference for profane science over theology. To strengthen his position, he heavily emphasized the preeminence of Rome over Constantinople. Of course, this had more to do with tactics on his part, and cannot be seen as a sign of a general acknowledgment of papal supremacy in the East.

The dispute between the two patriarchs of Constantinople, Ignatius, and Photius, which lasted for decades in the middle of the ninth century, must be looked at in a similar vein. Ignatius, of an imperial family, belonged to the monastic party. Photius was a brilliant scholar and theologian. The political situation at any given time determined which of the two was patriarch. For this reason, there were continuous changes on the patriarchal throne. Important in all this for Rome was the fact that over the course of the conflict Ignatius, in contrast to his earlier position, sought the support of the pope, thus emphasizing the papacy's position vis-à-vis the Eastern church; Photius, with the backing of other Eastern patriarchs, countered by emphasizing the autonomy of the East. The pontificate of Nicholas I shows just how quickly the constellations could change. A spring synod in 863, which he headed, deposed Photius. Later, the pope successfully called upon the Frankish episcopate for solidarity. Thus, in May 868, a synod in Worms condemned "the stupidity of the Greeks." Photius countered in the summer of 867 by having the pope deposed through a decision of a synod convoked by Emperor Michael III. But in September of the same year, Michael was overthrown, and with him Photius, and the new emperor, Basil I, as his first act, returned Ignatius to his position. Roman success at the Fourth Council of Constantinople (869–871) was similarly short-lived as Photius won in the end by outliving his opponent. The whole so-called Photian Schism is important not because of the supposed supremacy of the pope over the East, but because of the resentments and liturgical/theological differences which became apparent out of it and which differentiated the Western church from the Eastern. A mutual understanding was hardly possible anymore, particularly between the Frankish and Byzantine clergy.

The mission to Bulgaria also played an important role in forming Photius' posture, as did the internal Byzantine squabbles and the ongoing dispute over the *Filioque*. The Bulgarians, settled in the southern Balkans and south of the Danube, had been threatening Constantinople since the eighth century. When one of their princes, Boris, had himself baptized and his people converted by Byzantine missionaries, the securing and expansion of Byzantine rule was expected. The shock was even greater, therefore, when Boris sent an emmisary to Pope Nicholas I, asking to have Roman missionaries sent. Nicholas sent the bishops Paul of Populonia and Formosus of Porto, who later became pope, and promised, in addition, the establishment of an archbishopric. This meant that the Bulgarians were to receive their own church organization, though under Roman influence, which led to a considerable reduction of the patriarchate, and what is more, with the Bulgarians moving closer to the West politically, endangered the capital Constantinople. Photius, therefore, strongly attacked the papal policies. Both popes Nicholas I and Adrian II involuntarily helped Photius by rejecting the two Romans whom the Bulgarian ruler wanted as archbishop, first Formosus of Porto, then the deacon

Marinus, so by 871 the Bulgarian prince was leaning again toward Byzantium. Despite the efforts of Adrian II, and later of John VIII, the Bulgarians have remained separated from the West to this day.

The popes were more successful with the Slavic Moravians. To obtain independence from Austrasia, their ruler, Rastislav, requested missionaries from Constantinople in 863, receiving them in the form of the brothers Cyril and Methodius, both from Thessalonica. Both spoke Slavic, and for their mission they translated the Eastern liturgy into Slavic by using an alphabet (*glagolica*) they had developed for this purpose. They ran into opposition, however, from the Eastern Franks and in Rome. Only the three languages that were on Christ's cross—Hebrew, Greek, and Latin— were allowed in the liturgy. They were called to Rome in 867 by Nicholas, bringing with them the supposed remains of Clement I, one of Peter's successors, which they had found. While in Rome, they acknowledged the authority of the pope, and for doing so they received permission to continue using the Slavic liturgy. Adrian II consecrated Methodius as archbishop for Pannonia and Moravia, thereby securing the Moravian mission for the West. Since that time, the border between the Western and the Eastern church has run through the Balkans. John VIII, however, through a legate of Methodius, prohibited the use of Slavic as a church language. Soon after Methodius' death in 885, the missionaries from Austrasia held the field, especially those operating out of Salzburg and Passau. The students of Methodius were driven out by Prince Sviatopluk, and they later turned to the mission of the Southern and Eastern Slavs (Croatians, Serbs, later Russians) and Bulgarians, where the new alphabet was used as a model for the later Cyrillic script.

It was evident from the Moravian mission that papal and Frankish interests did not always coincide, a difference in interests that had also been evident earlier. But first, let us examine to what extent Roman exports and papal prestige changed the Frankish church.

As mentioned in the preceding chapter, Boniface and Frankish bishops had already attempted, during Charles Martel's reign, to reform the Frankish national church. In doing so, Boniface relied heavily on the Roman model, and even the Frankish bishops preferred the older canons of church law which contained papal decretals from the fourth and fifth centuries. Pepin, and to a greater extent Charlemagne, devoted much attention to reforming the church, with an eye toward stabilizing unity within the empire also in spiritual matters, and to this end they sought Rome's support. To promote a unified liturgy, they or their assistants imported collections of Roman prayers for mass—first the *Sacramentarium Gelasianum,* and in particular the *Sacramentarium Gregorianum*—and instructions for carrying out liturgical acts (*Ordines Romani*). In contrast to the later Romanization of the liturgy in the sixteenth century, however, the Roman prayers and instructions were not blindly accepted by the Carolingians; rather, they were made to fit Frankish needs. Thus there arose a Romano-Frankish blend in the liturgy. This mixture also extended to the construction of churches. With St. Peter's and the Lateran basilica as models, the important churches of the Frankish kingdom (Fulda, Cologne, etc.) were built with the apse toward the west—analogously to St. Peter's, Fulda held the tomb of Boniface—though the liturgical center usually remained the eastern apse. From this time until the eleventh century, the double apse construction was the standard for cathedrals and monastery churches, with the west apse often reserved for the ruler. The most important architectural example from the Charlemagne era, the villa at Aix-la-Chapelle, was in part a Roman imitation. While the architecture of Ravenna and Constantinople served as models for the rotunda of the villa's church, the sacristy was called the "Lateran" because in it, as in the papal palace, the precious liturgical vestments and vessels were kept.

A similar mixture can be observed in church law. Charlemagne requested Dionysius Exiguus' collection of canon law from Adrian I. Henceforth, the so-called Dionysio-Hadriana became one of the important cornerstones of church law. Of course, other collections, such as the ones from the earlier Visigothic kingdom, had an influence, so that Frankish canon law was not exclusively Roman. It should also be mentioned that Charlemagne requested the Benedictine rules from Adrian for the monasteries. From that point on, the Frankish monasteries adapted more and more to this system, until finally, in 816–817, Louis the Pious at synods in Aix-la-Chapelle directed all monasteries to follow the Benedictine rules. Only beginning from this date can it be assumed that Frankish monasteries were chiefly Benedictine.

The collaboration between the papacy and the Frankish rulers also brought about some changes in Rome, though not to such an extent. For example, the monasteries in Rome likewise gradually became Benedictine, while until this time the Benedictine rules had probably not been followed exclusively in a single monastery. Leo III took the idea of having a penitential procession on the three days before the Ascension from the Frankish liturgy. He also made such Frankish holy festivals as All Saints' Day on November 1 a part of the Roman tradition. And perhaps beginning as early as the time of Pepin, the Frankish rulers held the patronage of the Petronilla Rotunda south of St. Peter's basilica as a sign of their special ties to St. Peter. Roman synods, under pressure from the emperor, even came out in favor of reforming the Roman clergy, such as doing away with simony. The synods also recognized for the first time in Central Italy the Frankish institution of the "proprietary church," that is, the control of a church, its officials and its property by its founder or lord.

Apart from the flourishing export of relics and the active pilgrim traffic, the collaboration had its biggest consequences in the organization of the church. From the time of Charlemagne, it was customary that new archbishoprics were to be established solely by the pope, because when Charlemagne divided the Frankish church into provinces headed by archbishops, using the metropolitan constitution of late antiquity as a model, he acknowledged the pope's right to determine the size of the ecclesiastical provinces and the see of the archbishop. Only after receiving the pallium consecrated on Peter's tomb could the archbishop take office. With this, the early church principle of an *espirit de corps* among bishops was given up in favor of a hierarchial system with the pope at the top. Of course, ecclesiastical real estate was controlled by the ruler, though formally the pope had gained a definite influence on the Frankish church. To build and transform it into an actual influence was only natural whenever the position of the secular ruler was diminished.

Gregory IV availed himself of this chance. When the elder sons of Louis the Pious rebelled against their father in 830 because Louis, at the urging of his second wife, Judith, had also bequeathed a portion of the kingdom to their son Charles the Bald, the pope traveled over the Alps to represent the interests of Lothair I and his bishops against Louis. Of course, the older bishops who were still attached to the emperor opposed the pope, and the pope had to recognize that he was being exploited by the Lothair party for their purposes; nevertheless, in the course of the negotiations, he issued a decretal that would have importance for the future. In this decretal, by excessively interpreting instructions Leo I had given to his vicar in Thessalonica, Gregory emphasized that only the pope possessed full powers (*plenitudo potestatis*), while the bishops had received merely a partial responsibility (*pars sollicitudinis*) from Christ. Since the end of the eleventh century, this has served as the basis of papal supremacy, and has seldom been challenged. But thanks to a major legal forgery, the "Pseudo-Isidorean Decretals" (or the False Decretals), this was spread far and wide, from the middle of the ninth century, as a legal text.

The occasion that brought about this forged collection was probably the conflict in circa 850 between Archbishop Hincmar of Reims and some of his suffragan bishops who had been consecrated by his deposed predecessor Ebbo and who wanted to prevent their rights and functions from being curtailed. For this reason, Hincmar or the forger stressed the independent authority of each bishop and assigned only to the distant pope full powers of supervision, but not to the archbishops. To secure this position legally, a cutoff point was placed on early canon law: decrees of early synods, particularly those of the fourth and fifth centuries, were altered in their texts, with statements of theologians now being issued as decretals of the bishops of Rome of the pre-Constantine era, and recent Roman claims being issued as laws of earlier popes. For example, the promulgation of Gregory IV was suddenly considered to be a decretal of Vigilius, without taking into consideration that Vigilius was viewed as a heretic by his contemporaries. For the first time, there was a preponderance of papal decretals in canon law. The collection was soon copied in many areas, and with an added compendium was made easier to apply. In the middle of the century, the collection was already being used as the basis of church procedural law. More than this, it increasingly began to shape the religious and, because of the admittance of the Donation of Constantine, the secular position of the papacy.

As a result, much of that which was to bring the papacy to new heights starting in the eleventh century had its theoretical basis in the ninth century, similar to the hostile relations between the papacy and Constantinople. Practice deviated greatly from legal theory, however, with the pontificates of Nicholas I and his successors attesting to this fact. In the course of Lothair II's marriage affair, which cannot be described here in its complexity, Nicholas I removed the archbishops of Cologne and Trier because they had illegally divorced the king from his wife. The pope's action was supported by the majority of the Frankish episcopate, though it only led to success after the political situation had changed. The dispute between Nicholas and Hincmar of Reims was much the same. It centered around the removal from office of bishops by Hincmar and the synods under his direction. The bishops appealed to the pope, who annulled the decrees because the synods had been convened without papal representatives. The pope based his action on three points: on a historically mistaken interpretation of the synod of Sardica of 343; on papal privilege, which since Charlemagne came from the granting of the pallium; and probably also on the False Decretals. But even with this, he had success only after Hincmar lost the support of Charles the Bold.

Nicholas I is often thought of as the pope who successfully pursued his political policies, policies that are later found under other pontiffs such as Gregory VII. For example, Nicholas condoned opposition to a ruler if that ruler were to disregard church laws. He was the first pope who tried, and until the investiture controversy the only one who tried, by virtue of his authority, to hold Frankish imperial synods in Rome instead of the emperor holding them. However, the desperate efforts of Nicholas' successor, Adrian II, to prevent the condemnation of Nicholas' measures, show just how narrow the basis was for such policies. The sinking prestige of the imperial office in Frankland beginning in 875, as well as the desperate situation for the popes in Central Italy, prevented popes such as John VIII, when emulating Nicholas, from being successful. Nevertheless, as the first pope of the Middle Ages, Nicholas vigorously expounded the papal position. And later charters indicate that he was the founder of the legal tradition in many places. Thus, from the late ninth century, a general papal directive continued to be recognized in Frankish territories. Of course, it could only be implemented if the Frankish church had an interest in working together with the papacy. Since this kind of collaboration was usually lacking, the popes had no real influence for the time being.

To conclude, let us look at the situation in Rome itself. Accounts in the *Liber pontificalis* attest, as do ruins still visible today, to the building or restoration of numerous churches in Rome, which most of the popes from Adrian I to at least Leo IV undertook. They enriched these churches with paintings, stained glass windows, textiles, liturgical vessels, and books. The same holds true for cities within the papal sphere, from Fondi and Terracina in the south to Armeria in the north, and even to Ravenna. Usually this is the only kind of information about papal activities beyond Rome, that is, about the actual government of the Papal States. In contrast to later times, the popes also concerned themselves with the catacombs lying outside the city. Relics from the catacombs were transferred to Roman churches or exported. This demonstrates that there was a turning away from ancient sacred law— due to outward threats—and an increasing prestige for the Roman church and for saints in Rome and the Carolingian empire. Popes up until John VIII also looked out for civil safety in Rome. Aqueducts received the last refurbishing they would get for centuries, or new ones were built; the sewer system still worked. The Roman city wall was restored. And to counter the threat from Moorish pirates, the pontiffs fortified the Tiber ports of Ostia and Porto and settled refugees there, mostly from Corsica. Leo IV's building campaign is the most famous. After the Saracen invasion of 846, he built Leopolis, named after himself, near Centumcellae, which had been destroyed. The inhabitants soon returned to their old city, however, which since then has been called Civitavecchia (Old Town). It became the most important port of Rome due to the silting up of the mouth of the Tiber. The *Liber pontificalis* attributes to Leo, as does local tradition, the credit for the "City of Leo," the building of a wall around the borgo (borough) of St. Peter's. The initiative for protecting St. Peter's with a wall goes back to Emperor Lothair I, however, who not only raised an army after the Saracen invasion of 846, but also collected funds within his territory for the construction of a wall around the borgo of St. Peter's. Credit is due to the pope, however, for the construction of the walls, towers, and gates from 848 to 852, since he attracted workers from other cities, monasteries, and *domuscultae*. Leo made the Frankish assistance seem insignificant by appearing as the sole initiator of the construction and as ruler of the city in the prayers said at the consecration of the three gates; only those who were educated were able to read the inscriptions on the gates, which stated that the emperor also had a hand in the construction of the walls. Following Leo's example, John VIII had a wall built around St. Paul's, and S. Lorenzo was also secured in this way.

Rome was now clearly being governed by the pope. Charlemagne's envoys in the year 800 headed the investigation into the conspirators at the Lateran, but Charlemagne himself probably never went beyond St. Peter's during his long stay in Rome. Later emperors were also intentionally kept away from the city, of which the borgo of St. Peter's was not a part. For this reason, starting in the eighth century, popes allowed the imperial palaces on the Palatine to fall into disrepair; the new center of secular administration and justice was the Lateran, the symbol of which was the nearby equestrian statue of Marcus Aurelius until it was moved to its present location on the Campidoglio. Other symbols of authority from antiquity, such as the famous wolves, were probably set up at this time near the palace entrance as a sign of papal authority. That this was seen more than anything as a rivalry with Constantinople is evident both in the use of the concept *"palatium"* in the traditional texts, and in the triclinia of Leo II, which were built in a Byzantine style. The importance of the Lateran was also evident in the ceremonial. Both the oldest ordo for papal consecrations, drawn up under Leo III or Leo IV, and accounts in the *Liber Pontificalis*, report that a newly elected pope had to first take possession of his office from the Lateran, where the religious and secular heads of the city paid homage to him. Only later was the pope consecrated at St. Peter's, crowned on the steps of the church with the tiara as the symbol of secular rulership, and then led back to the Lateran with great solemnity. The enthroning in the Lateran, therefore, was a constitutive act of the taking of office. It is hardly surprising, then, that pontiffs from Leo III to Leo IV, as mentioned earlier, expanded the palace and refined the ceremonial there on the Byzantine model.

For this same reason the importance of the secular and religious palace officials grew. Because of the relatively low level of general education, it seems more than likely that most later pontiffs were reared and educated in the Lateran, usually called the *patriarchium*, though sometimes called the *palatium*. The popes' aides were usually the traditional *iudices*, while the presbyters and the deacons appeared to carry little weight. For this reason, it was irrelevant to which of the two clerical groups the pope belonged before his election. Perhaps already from the time of John VIII, the *iudices de clero* formed a consolidated group under the direction of the *primicerius* of the notaries, who, because of his high position, was now called *primicerius romanae ecclesiae*, "director of the Roman church," or given some other similar title. Whether the traditional colleges of notaries and *defensores* continued to exist after the eighth century is no longer known, as those who had heretofore been directors of these two colleges were in the future referred to as members of the new "college of judges." From the end of the eighth century, another official belonged to this group, the *biblothecarius*. As the name implies, he was in charge of the library and the archives. In addition, he managed the production of papal documents. In order to eliminate the influence of Roman families, the *biblothecarius* was usually, in contrast to the other *iudices de clero*, a bishop. Librarians working under popes from Nicholas I to John VIII demonstrably shaped the wording of papal documents. The most famous of them was Anastasius Bibliothecarius, the greatest Roman scholar of the ninth century, who had a profound knowledge not only of Greek, but also of papal archives going back to the fourth century.

Anastasius is a good case to see just how closely tied up with Roman family politics the popes and their governments were. Anastasius was deposed from his position of presbyter by Leo IV, and after Leo's death in 855 nearly became pope himself with the backing of the imperial party. His uncle, Arsenius, bishop of Orte, had a similar career in that he was alternately banished or made a papal legate. The strong position of his family became particularly evident under Adrian II when another relative, Eleutherius, kidnapped the pope's daughter and eventually murdered her and her mother; Anastasius, however, was able to stay in office. This episode is an example of the brutality common to Rome at this time. As the pontificates of Leo III and Paschal I show, murder itself did not stop with the pope or his palace, and *iudices de clero* or *iudices de militia* were usually involved as either victims or perpetrators. Their families also determined papal elections. For this reason, the *Liber pontificalis* names the nobility (*proceres, primates,* and others) as the most important, or even the only, electoral group for papal elections. The clearest example of this is the election of Gregory IV in 827, who was elected "so that under his doctrine and government the entire nobility of senators could live honorably." Thus sometimes the election of a new pontiff not only resulted in conflicts within the nobility and the exacting of revenge on former governing cliques, but also a plundering of the palace inventory. Stephen V complained about this in 885, as did John IX in 898, who described it as a "very criminal custom" (*scelestissima consuetudo*), attempting in vain to outlaw it.

Any attempt to judge individual popes objectively runs into difficulty because of the available sources. Letters tend to reflect the standpoint of the *bibliothecarius* or of other authors rather than an individual pope's. Adrian II, for example, after Frankish protest, distanced himself from the rather blunt stylistic practices of his librarian Anastasius. Frankish record keepers reported Roman events rather selectively, at times with an anti-Roman point of view. The *Liber Pontificalis*, on the other hand, leaves out all that is potentially damaging for the current hero. And different than in earlier *vitae*, there is almost no pope who is not praised in his *vita* as pious, educated, peace-loving, and charitable to the poor. That these characteristics were usually unrealistic is evident in the *vita* of Sergius II, which is swollen with these sorts of praises. Yet, at the end, it continues with a second *vita* which perhaps the same author, disgusted by the Saracen invasion of 846, had written, and in which the pope is described as incompetent and frail. The nobility considered Sergius a cipher (*adnullabant optimates Romanorum*), even though he came from the same family as Stephen IV before him and Adrian II later. Actual power was with Sergius' brother, Benedict, "dumb (or brutal) and doltish" (*brutus et stolidus*), who ran after prostitutes, exercised a reign of terror, and adhered to such simoniacal heresies as selling bishoprics for two thousand or more mancuses (the common gold coin of the time). Because of this, God punished Rome by sending the Saracens. Moral pictures of this kind are contrasted in other *vitae* with papal miracles. Leo IV, for example, not only conjured away a conflagration in the pilgrims' quarter of Rome (later the subject of a painting by Raphael), but he also drove the mythical cockatrice out of the city.

Conditions in Rome grew worse after John VIII. Though it is still not certain whether he really poisoned one of his relatives and beat in his skull, as reported in the Fulda Annals, it certainly was at any time within the realm of possibility. Threatened to the south by Saracen pirates or mercenaries, squeezed by independent marquises to the east and north, the papacy became more and more a plaything of Roman families. The situation became more difficult when, in 891, Formosus, a bishop, became pope. This was not, of course, the first time this had happened (Marinus had been a bishop before his election), though in general there was a prohibition on the translation of bishops since they were considered to be married to their home church. Thus the various rival power groups, which had been going at each other since 891, could very admirably apply the prohibition against their adversaries. At the infamous

"Cadaver Synod" of 896–897, Stephen VI had the partially decomposed body of Formosus clothed in papal vestments, degraded, mutilated, and then thrown into the Tiber. Henceforth, until John X, it was disputed whether Formosus had been a legal pope and whether the ordinations he had bestowed were legal. Writings made in his support clearly show the decades-long confusion as well as the crisis of conscience of the Formosians. The struggles between them and the anti-Formosians led to most pontiffs having a short stay in office, since frequently there was the danger of either imprisonment or murder. It was therefore fortunate nonetheless when, in 904, along with Sergius III, an aristocratic clique obtained outright power in Rome. *The Liber Pontificalis* likewise hints that a new era had come; the last, but incomplete, *vita* praised Stephen V. And with the coronation of Louis III in 901, even the title of Holy Roman Emperor, conferred by the pope, came to a pitiful end for the time being.

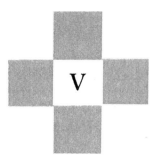

The Papacy Under the Influence
of the Roman Nobility
(904–1046)

W hen Cardinal Cesare Baronio wrote his church annals at
the end of the sixteenth century with a Catholic interpretation to counter the Magdeburg Centuriators' Protes-
tant church history, which in his eyes was distorted, he described
the tenth century as the *saeculum obscurum* (dark century). He came
to this conclusion not only because of the lack of written documen-
tation but also because of, in his opinion, the immoral conditions
in Rome at that time. This negative vision was later intensified, so
that since the eighteenth century some historians have been using
the rather unflattering term "pornocracy" for the type of government Rome had before the invasion of Otto the Great. Another
reason for the adverse judgment given to the epochs we will be
looking at was the clear efforts by contemporaries to do away with,
in a manner worthy of the previous era's alleged decadence, the
success the reform papacies achieved from the middle of the eleventh century. It is doubtful, however, whether these blanket ver-
dicts, which still shape historiography even today, are justified.

To be able to assess adequately the behavior of the Roman
bishops and the nobles, various political and social changes that

characterized the epoch must be taken into consideration. If we look to territories in the East such as Byzantium and Russia, the tenth century was the last period in the European Middle Ages in which a major portion of the population was threatened by foreign invaders. Only the turning back of these invaders and the political consolidation that went with it made the later developments possible, including the papacy's rise to international prominence. The biggest threat to Italy for the time being came from the Saracens, after 902 the undisputed masters of Sicily. From there, as well as from North Africa, Spain, and from a provincial base in Southern Italy, they threatened Italy's west coast. Important victories, in which the popes John X and Benedict VIII took part, such as on the River Garigliano in 915 and near Luni in 1016, as well as smaller ventures in Central Italy and the first signs of dissolution in the Islamic sphere, led to the Saracens giving up their aims at expansion in Europe, apart from Spain, at the beginning of the eleventh century. The Hungarian peril, which brought plunder to Central Europe and to parts of Italy, was put down as a result of victories by the German kings Henry I (933 at Riade) and Otto I (955 at Augsburg) as well as by similar successes for the Byzantine emperor and the Prince of Kiev. Consequently, individual families in Hungary itself as well as in Bohemia and Poland grew stronger, eventually seizing absolute power. Out of religious conviction, as well as to secure their position, these families encouraged the spread of Christianity from Germany, a development which gradually benefited the papacy due to the deepening ties between it and Otto I. In the same period, the situation in Northern Europe stabilized, though Viking raiders still plundered some areas. The integration of the Normans on the lower reaches of the Seine in Neustria from the beginning of the tenth century and the rise of a Danish, Norwegian, and Swedish dynasty brought about the establishment of the kingdoms in Scandinavia at the turn of the millennium that are still in existence today, with some changes of the actual borders. Because of this, Christianity was able to spread throughout the north much more easily than before.

German rulers from Henry I tried to protect the population from invaders, particularly in Saxony, by building fortified castles which served as residences for nobles and as shelters, while the peasants continued living on the land outside the fortifications. In Central Italy, on the other hand, the Saracen and Hungarian threats acclerated a process which had begun in the ninth century:

the *incastellamento*. As long as settlements on the land—*villae, fundi, massae, domuscultae*—could not be successfully fortified, people living there either moved voluntarily, were enticed to move, or were forced to move by the landlord to unpopulated highlands or to mountain settlments that once existed in antiquity and whose "Cyclops walls" were now being restored. Because of this, the landed population could henceforth live more securely, though the coastal lowlands north and south of the Tiber became even marshier than before—malaria was the worst enemy of the German army. In addition, the religious and secular leaders felt pressed to incorporate as many castles as possible within their realms. And just as these new castles and the resettled hill towns shaped an image of Central Italy that persists to this day, the conflicts of the popes with the nobles and the monasteries—particularly at the beginning with Farfa and Subiaco—over the possession of castles and their surroundings also characterized the history of the Papal States until the early modern era. Moreover, these conflicts frequently influenced the overall papal position and papal policies beyond Italy. This dependency of the papacy will become especially clear as we now examine local factors.

Though elected by the anti-Formosian party in 897, Sergius III was not able to occupy the Lateran see until 904. Above all, he had Theophylact to thank for his success. Theophylact and his successors ruled Rome in a direct line until 963, though most likely even the Crescentians and the Tusculans, the leading families until 1046, belonged to his lineage. As his Greek name leads one to believe, Theophylact perhaps came from a family that had achieved power and influence in and around Rome during the Byzantine era. He himself held the positions of vestiary and *magister militum*, giving him partial control over the papal treasury and direction over the Roman city militia. The tying together of papal positions with municipal functions would also be significant for his successors. Unfortunately, sources concerning government in Rome during the first half of the century are extremely sparse. Besides a few documents, we possess the accounts of the chronicler Benedict of S. Andrea at Soratte (north of Rome) and those of Liutprand of Cremona, the slanderer of the age, both of whom wrote under the influence of Otto the Great. Yet it is quite probable that Theophylact did not hold absolute power, but rather, had to take into consideration the interests of his compeers. Thus it was essential for him to place puppet candidates on the papal throne and to maintain good connections with the more influential neighbors. To this end, he had his elder daughter, Marozia I, marry the marquis of Spoleto, Alberic I. Liutprand, in particular, found Marozia to be abominable, while later male historians had even worse to say about her. Today she can be acknowledged as one of the not so rare examples of tenth-century women who were independent and who pursued their own political policies. It remains uncertain whether Marozia was the lover of Sergius II and the mother of John XI. It appears more certain, however, that she had the energetic John X imprisoned and then put to death when he wanted to form an alliance with the Northern Italian king, Berengar I, who in 915 was decorated with the imperial crown, though without doing much for Rome in return. Marozia herself was overthrown in 932 by a son from her first marriage, Alberic II, when, after a second marriage to Wido of Tuscany, she married Berengar's successor, Hugo of Vienne. The new husband was barely able to escape.

Under Alberic II (932–955), Rome experienced its most secure and prosperous period of the whole century. In contrast to his grandfather Theophylact, he ruled Rome with absolute power. Most of the pontiffs, with the exception of Agapitus II, probably fared like Marinus II, about whom the aforementioned chronicler Benedict, in an excellent Latin, had this to say: *Electus Marinus papa non audebat adtingere aliquis extra iussio Alberici principi* ("The elected Pope Marinus dares not touch anyone without the order of Prince Alberic"). Alberic's position is also clear from the title of prince, which he probably adopted using the model of the Lombard potentates of Southern Italy. His son and successor, who had the classical name of Octavian, would be even more independent. The leading representatives of Rome had to swear to Alberic in 954 that they would choose his son as pope at the earliest opportunity. Thus Octavian was not only secular ruler after the death of Alberic and Agapitus, but also bishop of Rome. As pope he called himself John XII. From this time on, it became increasingly common for the new pope to take on a new name, and by the end of the century this had become the norm. As a ruler, however, John apparently met with little success. With a policy toward the king of Northern Italy, Berengar II of Ivrea, that lacked focus and an opposition within the Roman nobility and clergy that put pressure on him, in 960 John summoned Otto I to an imperial coronation in Rome. Otto had already been wearing the the crown of the king of Italy since 951, but had been kept out of Rome by Alberic.

So from 962, Rome once again had a powerful patron, though like earlier under Charlemagne, who Otto emulated, this protection was soon to change into oppression. For Otto and his successor, the pope was the supreme spiritual leader of the church, though of course under imperial direction, while for the Roman nobility and a major portion of the clergy, he was the nominal guarantor of independence, however limited regionally. Because of these contrasts, the next forty years were ones of continuous conflict, heightened by the members of the leading noble families—especially the Crescentians, later the Tusculans—who, depending on their interests, supported the imperial pope one day, and his opponent the next. The same was true for many Roman clerics and bishops in the surrounding area. The last years of John XII offer the first evidence of this. For political reasons, which were anchored, however, with moral and theological arguments (reproaches for sexual misconduct, or apostasy), a synod which the emperor had convened in 963 deposed the pope, replacing him with the *protoscrinarius* Leo. After Otto's departure in 964, John was able to return to Rome. A synod under his direction, and attended by many of his former accusers and judges, then proceeded to depose Leo as a usurper. It became evident after the death of John XII, who allegedly died while committing adultery, that the emperor was interested in asserting his control over the papacy, not in finding the most suitable candidate. Because his successor, Benedict V, a pious man with the honorable name of "Grammaticus," was elected without the emperor's consent, he was deposed shortly after the election and banished to Hamburg. Few of the popes who followed died a natural death. There were now usually two competing popes, as there had been since 963. Though this may not present any problems to a historian, it certainly does to a dogmatist. Because there is a lack of criteria, it is difficult to decide who lawfully governed and, by extension, who carried on the apostolic succession. The most successful pontiff was John XIII, who was perhaps related to the Crescentians, or in any case supported by them, and also had the blessing of Otto the Great. Thus this pontificate was not only the longest of the second half of the century, but also the most peaceful.

The state of affairs became more complicated after Otto III

gained power. To the dissatisfaction of the German lords, and even more so to the Roman nobles, he wanted to make Rome the seat of his government to implement his program, the *renovatio imperii Romanorum* (revival of the Roman empire). It was his intention to be the first Western emperor to install his principal palace in Rome—where he installed it is a matter of dispute, perhaps on the Palatine among the ruins of earlier imperial palaces. He wanted to rule his empire and the church as *servus Jesu Christi* or *servus apostolorum* (servant of Christ or the apostles). With these titles he conformed to Eastern Romano-Byzantine custom; he was, after all, the son of a Byzantine princess. The pope was probably just as subordinate to him as the patriarch of Constantinople was to the Byzantine emperor. In support of this supposition is the fact that Otto was the first emperor to appoint non-Italian popes, and ones that were close to him. The first was his relative Bruno (Gregory V) in 996, and then his teacher Gerbert (Sylvester II) in 999, though out of consideration for the prevailing conditions in Rome, neither could accommodate their mentor's every wish, otherwise they would have received no support at all from the Roman population. With the death of the emperor in 1002, and Sylvester's about a year later, the dreams of empire had passed by, and the Crescentians were able to regain the power they had possessed before Otto's invasion.

Without imperial protection, Rome now experienced a relatively peaceful repose, even if it was determined by local interests. Like Theophylact and Alberic before them, the Crescentians who ruled both before and after Otto III strove to place candidates on the papal throne who were committed to maintaining their power. As a sign of their position, they gave themselves a title which until the coronation of Charlemagne had designated secular power: the title of *patricius*. They were able to maintain their rule until 1012. Later, however, the "counts" of Tusculum, who had been gaining power under Otto II and particularly under Otto III, used the death of the Crescentian pope Sergius IV—he had the lovely nickname of *os porci* (pig's snout) and was apparently the son of a cobbler—to put one of their own family members on the papal throne. In this they were successful because the rival candidate, the Crescentian Gregory VI, traveled in vain to the court of Henry II. And so, the pontificate of Benedict VIII ushered in the more than thirty-year period of the Tusculan papacy. In contrast to the usual custom, in this period the pope himself was ruler and not a lay member of the family. The relatives were there chiefly to secure the pope's secular authority. This system functioned until 1044, principally because of the good relationship with the German kings and emperors. Then, however, Benedict IX had to give way to a new candidate of the Crescentians, Sylvester III. A short while later he entered Rome, and then renounced his position in favor of his godfather, who called himself Gregory VI. Gregory paid his godchild some money—whether as compensation for his stepping down or as payment to Benedict's troops is unsure—and was soon considered a simonist. Be that as it may, there were now three popes whose legitimacy was in dispute. And when a short while later Henry III went to Rome for his long-planned coronation, he had all three pretenders deposed in 1046 in Sutri and Rome. Like Benedict V before him, Gregory VI had to go into exile in Germany, while the other two were able to retain, for the time being, the territories ruled by their families—Sylvester in the Sabine, Benedict in the Alban Mountains. Meanwhile, in Rome, the period of the "German popes" began and with it the period of the great reform.

The often muddled state of affairs directly contributed to the decline of long-standing institutions and customs. Apart from a restoration of the Lateran basilica by Sergius III and John X and a few new churches on the Aventine, the Palatine and the *isola tiberina* by Alberic, there are hardly any accounts of church construction. The convent of S. Ciriaco in the aristocratic area of Via Lata was an important stronghold for the nobility into the twelfth century. We know even less about whether the *statio* services were kept, or whether parts of the social infrastructure such as the aqueducts were still working. The papal administration also seems to have suffered in the general decline. The output of papal documents was so little that it was no longer necessary for the papacy to have its own college of scribes; instead, any work needed could be done by librarians or their deputies and by private scribes—known as *scrinaria*, notaries or tabellions—employed by others. Apart from the librarian, it is unknown to what extent the other six *iudices de clero* actually belonged to the clergy, even the lower clergy, and worked for the pope; only the dating and the signature on documents attest to their existence. This decline contributed to the creation of new institutions or the reform of existing ones.

Roman similarities to German administrative methods were recognizable perhaps as early as the pontificate of John XIV, who directed the royal chancery in Pavia before becoming pontiff. These methods were surely in use by the time of Sylvester II, and then fully developed in the following epoch. For the first time, pergament was used in addition to papayrus as the writing material for documents. Just as in Germany, there was a chancellor to direct the writing operations—known as *cancellarius* or even *archicancellarius*—so that the position of librarian gradually became an honorary post. For this reason, the position of librarian under the Tusculans could also be assigned to a foreign prelate, such as Archbishop Pilgrim of Cologne. Also stemming from the time of Sylvester II was the practice of having a few clerics in the papal circle who were especially trusted, and who, like in the court of a German lord, held the title of "chaplain."

German influence was also evident in the liturgy. German bishops brought a collection of liturgical texts to Italy and Rome for the coronation of Otto the Great which described the liturgy of a bishop and which had been put together only shortly before in Mainz; these texts are the so-called *Pontificale Romano-Germanicum.* A major portion of the texts were imported to the Frankish kingdom from Rome during the Carolingian era and were then altered. Some texts, such as the coronation ordo, were apparently completely unknown in Rome before 962. This transfer of texts shows clearly how much the Rome of the Ottonian period differed from the Rome of the Carolingian era. If it was Rome that in earlier epochs brought culture to regions that were still "barbarian," then Rome itself was now being stimulated by the higher culture that had developed in these areas. All important texts used at the ordination of the pope until the thirteenth century were derived from the new mixture of Roman and Frankish texts north of the Alps. Their origin in the seldom loved north was quickly forgotten, however. Under Gregory VIII the texts were already considered genuinely Roman.

This suppression of memory affected another liturgical text. As mentioned in the previous chapter, the Christian community in Rome pronounced the creed only in the baptisimal liturgy. And it was Leo III who successfully barred acceptance of the *Filioque.* This persistence of old traditions also characterized the tenth century. But on the occasion of his coronation in 1014, at a synod that had probably been prepared by a synod of Sergius IV in 1009, Henry II prevailed upon Benedict VIII to decree that in Rome the creed would henceforth also be sung at mass on Sundays and holidays as it was in Germany, including, of course, the *Filioque*. Soon this became so typically Roman, as well as liturgically and theologically correct, that pontiffs after Sergius IV considered the disregarding of the *Filioque* in Constantinople as a deviation from the true, Catholic faith. As a result, the dispute over the *Filioque* was one of the events that led to the break with the Eastern church in 1054. And the dispute over the *Filioque* has remained into modern times a stumbling block in unification negotiations.

Other evidence of the close liturgical connection between Germany and Rome at this time is the cult of St. Mauritius, chief saint of the Ottonian dynasty, and to whose honor an altar was erected at St. Peter's around the turn of the millennium. This altar played an important part at imperial coronations for many years to come. It should also be mentioned that perhaps from the time of Henry II the emperor was the honorary canon of St. Peter's, just as in Germany he was an honorary member of all important national religious establishments on the basis of the theocratic understanding of sovereignty.

Other liturgical acts, however, show that the German influence did not extend to all public functions of the pope; in fact, older traditions were being observed once again, especially after the period of the Tusculan popes. Among them were the proceedings for assuming papal office, with emphasis on the Lateran, the grand processions and popular festivities, which were celebrated together by the pope, the clergy and the people in the ancient Roman or Byzantine style. In Rome this took on a specific form: New Year's Day, spring festival—with the *laudes Cornomanniae* in a strange mixture of Latin and a partly corrupted Greek—and Carnival, which until modern times was begun under the pope's direction. The only exact information we have about these three festivals is from texts probably written in this epoch.

In the continuation of older traditions the Lateran complex became even more important as the center of episcopal government. This includes not only the palace but the basilica as well. Thus now, for the first time, deceased Roman bishops were interred not only at St. Peter's or the basilicas of other saints such as St. Paul's and S. Lorenzo, but also in the Lateran itself. This tradition was also continued in the following epoch. Even more remarkable was the emphasis on the palace as a center of government. The palace was being called *palatium* more often than before, in conjunction with the Donation of Constantine being cited in Rome as the historical proof for the secular position of the pope. In 962, a certain cardinal-deacon named John even produced a document that was supposedly Emperor Constantine's original draft. And just as the clergy of the Roman bishop had been placed on equal footing with the imperial Senate in the forgery, the cardinal clergy was now, in fact, assigned to the palace: beginning in the tenth century, the seven deacons, as well as parts of the lower clergy such as subdeacons and acolytes, were considered members of the palace staff (*diaconus sacri palatii*). Similarly, the *iudices de clero* were called "palace judges," and their number was now limited to seven. In several tracts—the older and the younger "Catalogues of Judges," the older written around 962 at the latest and the younger around 1030, as well as the *libellus de imperatoria potestate* (probably from the end of the ninth century)— they were assigned functions similar to those held by the high palace officials of the Byzantine emperor or of the royal palace in Pavia. Because of the prominence given to the Lateran palace, Roman regional synods took place there, at least under John XIX (Sylvester Chapel).

This centering of power on the bishop's palace reflected the new secular and ecclesiastical organization of Rome. The city now consisted of twelve regions, although the boundaries had still not been clearly fixed, an organization that in theory conformed to the Augustan age, but in practice emphasized the lowlands along the Tiber. In the secular realm, this plan called for the organizing of the municipal militia under the leadership of "counsuls" or *decarones* (standard-bearers). The regions received twelve new deacons (*diaconi regionarii*) for church administration, an important step in the formation of the College of Cardinals later. The leading clerics of the titular churches, the cardinal-priests, apparently were more explicitly assigned to the Lateran, as were the new twelve and the traditional seven deacons, both of which were under the direction of the archdeacon. This stems not only from their participation in palace synods and their subscription of papal documents, but also from the fact that they were only allowed to be ordained or judged by the pope. In other words, they were exempt from the authority of other bishops, even when their church did not lay within the Roman diocese. Further proof of the upper clergy's turning toward the Lateran is the *fraternitas Romana,* a fellowship among the rest of the clergy that had been in the making since the middle of the tenth century. Originally formed perhaps only for a communal participation at the funerals of members, this union was also to become important in other church matters, and a potential opposition to church government, particularly in the twelfth century. A more exact marcation of the bishopric's border under the Tuscalan popes followed the internal secular and religious organization of the city. Benedict VIII placed the *isola tiberina* and Trastevere under the bishop of Porto in 1018, except for the titular churches and two monasteries. Eight years later, John XIX granted to Silva Candida supervision over St. Peter's and the insitutions associated with it. For the time being, the city of Rome ended in both a religious and secular sense with the left bank of the Tiber, the secular intergration of the inhabitated areas beyond the Tiber only being completely finished in early modern times. The measures of both popes were probably meant to place the cardinal bishops more firmly under papal authority. Thus Peter of Silva Candida received his residence on the *isloa tiberina* in 1026, that is, in the diocese of his neighbor from Porto. In the following epoch another cardinal bishop, the bishop of Sabina, received his residence on the Roman forum (S. Lorenzo in Miranda).

The reshaping of ideology was to be just as significant for the future as the actual changes in papal rule and in the organization of Rome and its environs were. This consisted of a more intensive emphasis on institutions and ideals from antiquity, as they were understood. The impulse toward this end came from the emperor on the one side, and from Rome itself on the other.

For the emperors, Rome served as the legitimizing center of their power. Thus the city was called *caput mundi* (capital of the world), even under Conrad II, one of the emperors least interested in the city. Favorite cities in Germany of the rulers were beautified with the honored title of *Roma secunda* (e.g., Aix-la-Chapelle, Bamberg) and were even made similar to Rome in their design (Bamberg). The peak of this tendency came when Otto III tried to rule his empire from Rome. And, since some emperors or their assistants stressed the ancient roots of their authority, this perforce had to go back to Rome. The best example of this is the pontificate of Otto's teacher, Gerbert, who named himself Sylvester in memory of the supposed collaboration between pope and emperor in antiquity that was marked by the myth of the Donation of Constantine, even though the emperor himself was skeptical of the document.

Just as important, however, was the internal Roman impulse. In addition to the tracts already mentioned, as well as the ones alluding to Byzantium and Pavia, this impulse is evident in the new regions, even Trastevere, which, though not a part of the city, was referred to as a region according to the Augustan plan (*regio XIV* as it was in the Augustan age). Like in antiquity, the city itself, from the middle of the tenth century, was governed by a city prefect or *patricius*—as a parallel there was even an ominous "sea prefect." Alberic II probably had antiquity in mind when he named his son "Octavian," a name which then often came up again among the Crescentians. Furthermore, the appeal to the "Donation of Constantine" and the pope's claim to imperial rank and decoration were also a part of this revival of antiquity. The miter was also part of this rank and decoration, along with the pallium and tiara. In addition to the pallium, the pope now bestowed the miter on foreign prelates, particualrly abbots, as a sign of special favor. The other side of the coin was that abbeys and bishoprics with exemptions occasionally had to supply the pope with white horses, a sign of the emperor's rank that can be dated back to the "Donation of Constantine." If the white steeds, as well as the tiara, and probably the miter too, were signs of the pope's secular rank, then his ecclesiastical preeminence was evident, in addition to the pallium, in his carrying of the ferula (a staff that was probably decorated with a cross), and not the crosier, as the bishops did.

So far, the changes which took place in papal rule in Rome have been described in some detail. It should be clear, therefore, that even in this epoch the pope was, above all else, the bishop of Rome. At the same time, however, there were increasing signs of a gradual papal control of the universal church. Let us start with Italy.

Attempts from the time of Alberic II to bring important castles near Rome, especially in the Sabine and near the old consular roads heading south, under papal authority, and consequently under the control of the de facto ruler, strengthened the security of the city. Except for some narrative accounts and a few documents, about the only way to understand this process is by observing the estates of the Crescentians in the Sabine and the areas of Tivoli and Palestrina, and those of the Tusculans in the Alban Mountains. Important families such as the "counts" of Galeria and the Frangipani are also mentioned under the Tusculan popes of the following period. From this time on, the ring around the Roman countryside was decisive for the early development of the Papal States and the actual power or lack of it of the pope. Connected with this was the attempt to place under papal authority the monasteries of Farfa and Subiaco, both with affiliates in Rome, and both of which were struggling for autonomy and their own territory, and the attempt to reorganize to the pope's advantage what were later called cardinal bishoprics.

The policies toward Southern Italy were to be a signpost for the future. These policies not only served to repulse the Saracens, but also served to expand the territory actually ruled by the pope and his church authority. Thus attempts were made to secure rule over the areas of Fondi (old patrimony) and Terracina, and in this Sylvester II was the first pope, in the case of Terracina, who tried to combine the old method of conferring by emphyteusis with the transalpine feudalism entrusted to him. To the benefit of church authority, important monasteries such as Monte Cassino and S. Vicenzo al Volturno were placed directly under the pope by exemption in 944. And beginning in 960, places under Lombard rule, such as Benevento, Capua, and Salerno, and even cities in Byzantine-controlled areas such as Siponto and Bari, were transformed into archbishoprics with their own ecclesiastical province, although nominally under the supreme authority of the pope. For the time being, these attempts produced no real results, although they were the basis of successful ventures by popes in the epoch of reform which followed.

If one considers that important harbors such as Naples and Amalfi were still under Byzantine rule, and that from the second half of the century Byzantine emperors were expanding their dominion over Southern Italy, with even Rome at times being threatened, then it becomes clear that relations between the papacy and Constantinople were not only shaped by dogmatic or ecclesiastico-political problems, but also by regional problems. Not only was there a long Byzantine tradition in Rome, the Eastern empire was also in fact often closer to the popes than the empire of the German ruler. Marozia and her son, Alberic II, tried by friendly means, chiefly by marriage, to be on good terms with Constantinople. This also depended on the conduct of the popes they had put in office. But with Otto the Great's coronation, conflicts with Byzantium increased because Western rulers tried to bring Southern Italy under their control, as Charlemagne tried earlier. The founding of new, Latin archbishoprics mentioned earlier is directly related to these events. Only in the context of this new orientation of the papacy can John XIII's addressing of the Eastern emperor as *imperator Graecorum* instead of *imperator Romanorum*, much to the displeasure of the emperor, be understood. Even after the failure of Otto III, the papacy continued this policy. Benedict VIII supported rebellions in Byzantine Italy, for the first time bringing the papacy into contact with the Normans, who were becoming ever more important in the region. The pope also moved the German emperor Henry II into action in Southern Italy, though earlier the initiative had always come from the German rulers. Because of ecclesiastical policies on both sides and the regulation regarding the creed, the way was paved, even if unintentionally, for the conclusive split in the church. The frequenting of Greek monasteries in Rome by Latin monks was just one sign of this tendency. An exception to this was the influence of the Southern Italian hermit Nilus, who not only impressed Otto III but also founded, with the protection of Otto, the Greek abbey at Grottaferrata south of Rome, which became the family monastery for the Tusculans and for centuries supplied the "specialists" for the Greek readings in papal worship services.

Concurrent with the worsening relations with Byzantine was a strengthening of papal relations with Germany, the new political center in the West. There are two possible explanations for this and for the expanded contacts to other areas, both having their origins in the Carolingian era, but coming to the fore only in the tenth century: the control of regional synods by papal legates, and the special relationship church institutions—initially monasteries, later bishoprics—had to the papacy. This second explanation manifested itself in papal protection or in exemptions. This protection meant that, from the time a monastery had been granted this special right, it was guarded by St. Peter, with an attack on the monastery tantamount to an attack on Peter, the doorkeeper of heaven and the vicar of Christ. Often associated with such privileges was, among other rights, the right to elect freely the abbot or abbess. An extension of this protection was the exemption from episcopal power by being directly under papal control. Of course, this exemption was never total; rather, it usually only included freedom from the episcopal fiscal administration, which cut into a bishop's income, and from the bishop's disciplinary powers—supreme judge in these cases was the pope—and the right for abbots or, since the Tusculan period, bishops (the bishop of Bamberg was the first), to receive the necessary ordination directly from the pope, his representative, or from a bishop of choice. Those who received these privileges often had to pay a tribute to the pope, contributing to his income.

Because the German church at the end of the Carolingian era was still not completely developed and established, cooperation with the pope was deemed valuable even before Otto's coronation. This was evident in synods presided over by papal legates in Germany (Hohenaltheim in 916, Ingelheim in 948) and in Roman synods that took up German matters (in 921 and 949). Likewise, evidence of this cooperation is seen in charters granted to German monasteries and convents, as in Fulda in 917, St. Ursula in Cologne in 925–926, Gorze in 938 (very important for Germany), St. Moritz in Magdeburg from 939 to 941, Gandersheim in 948, Essen in 951, and Gernrode in 961. And further evidence is seen in important German pilgrims who went to Rome, such as Salomo of Constance and St. Gall in 904, Ulrich of Augsburg in 942, and Hadamar of Fulda in 955. However, papal charters for Germany should not be overestimated. Those who received the privileges were also under royal protection as members of imperial monasteries or convents, which meant the king could have more real influence than the pope. Monasteries and bishoprics that had been granted charters after 962 were also affected by this power structure. Nevertheless, the charters show that even before the first imperial coronation there was a strong interest in acknowledging the preeminence of the pope in the German ruler's realm, and through the privileges conferrred by the pope in securing a position against any possible rivals.

For European history as a whole, the coronation of 962 is therefore of significance because, from that year, the wearing of the imperial crown was limited more and more to the German kingdom, thus making German kings, as emperors, the supreme protectors of the church, a title which could only be received from the pope. During this period, this mutual dependency worked principally to the advantage of the German rulers, but from the time of the investiture controversy it offered the popes the opportunity to intervene more forcefully in German affairs than elsewhere and to trim the power of the ruler. The popes' temporary dependence on the emperors was evident, as mentioned, in Rome itself and in Southern Italy. However, this dependence also had positive consquences for the papacy. Just as they did during the height of Carolingian power, the synods, now convoked by the emperor and pope, united not only the usual representatives of Italic churches but also the German and even non-German prelates and rulers. These synods, especially under Otto III and Henry II, helped with the reorganization and internal reform of the church, the best example being the synod at Pavia in 1022. Although at the beginning the initiative clearly lay with the emperors, the publication of decrees in the name of the pope made clear, as did the legates' control over the synods, that discipline and organization within the church lay ultimately with the popes. This new position, based on events from the Carolingian era, could not be successfully challenged in the long run if in the collections of canon law—those of Bishop Burchard of Worms were the most influential—the independence of each bishop was stressed and individual prelates justifiably protested against exemptions or one-sided legal decisions by popes, as in questions of marriage.

Because the emperors were also the kings of Italy, the pope benefited from his connections with them in Northern Italy. Otto the Great in 962 and Henry II in 1020 once again asserted papal territorial claims in the former exarchate with the traditional *pacta*, though these ended with Henry II. Otto III, on the other hand, without recourse to the *pacta* or even to the Donation of Constantine and acting on his own authority, granted several regions south of Ravenna to Pope Sylvester II in 1001. The actual implementation of these rights remained problematic in the future. But the effect of the imperial policy was that henceforth, more than even before, the papacy was recognized as supreme head of the church by Ravenna, Aquileia/Grado, and even Milan, even if in individual cases some pontiffs were forced to make decisions that stood in opposition to previous policies, as John XIX was forced to do when Conrad II backed Aquileia's claims. At the request of Northern Italian prelates, the popes intervened as mediators to settle quarrels among bishops, and with emperors they presided over synods. And as the privileges granted to the reform monastery at Fruttuaria in 1006 show, the popes also encouraged movements which would later prove troublesome for German influence. Before 1046 there also existed connections between the Tusculan popes and other Northern Italian reform movements led by Romuald of Camaldoli, Peter Damiani, and Guido of Pomposa. It should be emphasized, however, that the initiative for contacts of this kind usually came from others, not from the popes. The same held true for the eastern Adriatic, where in 925 legates of John X presided over a synod in Split at the request of the Croatian king, out of which gradually developed a relationship in which the pope provided protection for the benefit of the kingdom there. And finally, it should be noted that, with the emperors playing a decisive role, new churches were founded in the East—Magdeburg in 968 by Otto I, later Gnesen for Poland by Otto III and under Henry II the organization of the Hungarian national church—which expanded papal authority since the new bishoprics had been nominally founded by the pope and thus subordinate to him. In Poland and Hungary, this even resulted in the paying of tribute to the pope via the ruler—the Peter penny. At the same time, this was meant to be a sign of subordination to papal protection, which had already been in place in Poland since 990 and soon after was also granted to Hungary.

In contrast to Germany, the king's sphere of influence in France, the former Neustria, was very limited for the time being. Royal prestige was weakened by frequent struggles among various pretenders to the crown all the way to the end of the Carolingian era in 987. The royal domain of the Capets, who ruled from 987, was centered around Paris and Orleans. The beneficiaries of this royal weakness were the dukes and counts, for whom the the king was usually just a nominal head. With this kind of power structure in place, many bishoprics and monasteries came under the influence of the nobility. To take steps against this, from the end of the tenth century in particular, the kings tried to expand their power base by determining appointments to abbeys and bishoprics that lay outside their domain, such as Reims and Bourges, though this did not always happen peacefully. On the other hand, the upper aristocracy and bishops did not always found new monasteries for religious reasons, but frequently to stabilize their power. The situation then became complicated when some monasteries, even more so than in Germany, tried to free themselves from the supervision of the appointed bishop or from the influence of the nobility by exploiting the balance of power. And because there were no courts in France authorized to act in these matters, the monasteries often turned to the pope for protection and support.

Thus, in the tenth century, France became the classic land of the exemption. The exemption of the monastery at Cluny, whose patron from the beginning was St. Peter, became the most famous and later, because of the development of monastic associations, the most successful example. In 909 and in 928, Cluny was placed under papal protection by both its founder and the pope. In 931, it received an exemption that was, with changes, continually confirmed and expanded by later popes up to the Tusculans. Only Benedict IX held out in confirming these privileges, which gave him no reason to expect support from the now very influential abbot of Cluny, Odilo, at the synod in Sutri in 1046. Even in its initial period, Cluny was therefore important for Rome because Alberic II and his popes, particularly Leo VII, with the help of Odo of Cluny, brought about reforms in Roman monasteries, such as St. Paul, and for this conferred privileges upon Odo's abbey. Cluny is a perfect example, however, of how the exemptions weakened the traditional church structure, and in so doing strengthened the position of the papacy. Thus, at the urging of the Bishop of Macon, whose bishopric included Cluny, a synod held in 1025 at Ansen near Lyon declared the papal privilege of exemption illegal and invalid because it ran counter to canon four of the Council of Chalcedon in 441, according to which monasteries were to be under the control of local bishops. Two years later, at the request of Odilo of Cluny, John XIX confirmed the privileges, admonishing the archbishop of Lyon and the bishop of Macon to be obedient and calling on King Robert of France to provide protection for Cluny. The pope claimed that these decrees possessed a binding validity under canon law, that is, ecclesiastical law. It thus became clear that the granting of privileges was now a successful instrument for the asserting of papal primacy. Consequently, most of the popes of the following epoch made good use of this system.

Let us look for a moment at other monasteries besides Cluny, since they not only contributed to the reform of the Benedictine system, but also served as the basis for future papal policies. St.-Pons-de-Thomières, under papal control since 937, played a significant role in papal policies in Aragon around 1100. Fleury, exempt since 938, was thought to be the burial site of St. Benedict and was important in the Loire region and for the reform of English monasteries. Féchamp, like Cluny exempt since 1016, was founded by the duke of Normandy and aided later popes in gaining influence there. And finally, there was the work of the reform abbot William of Volpiano, who in 1006 founded the monastery of Fruttuaria in Northern Italy, which was also exempt. Other monasteries that William directed and reformed included St. Bénigne in Dijon, Gorze, Moyenmoutier, and Fécamp. William's reforms, as well as those at Cluny, left a lasting impression on many of the assistants of future reform-minded popes or on these popes themselves.

Equally as important as the policy of privileges, and sometimes even more spectacular, were papal interventions in ecclesiastical conflicts in France. A synod in Ingelheim in 948, for example, presided over by a papal legate, and one in Rome in 949, settled a dispute in the archdiocese of Reims. Likewise, a synod at Aix-la-Chapelle in 991, again with a papal legate, dealt with a schism in Reims, as did one presided over by the pope and emperor in Rome in 996. Another synod, under Gregory V and Otto III in Rome in 999, took up the question of the marriage of the French king, Robert, to a relative of his. And finally, in 1007, John XVIII sent a legate to France because, once again—this time concerning Fleury—French bishops doubted the papal authority to grant exemption privileges. Some of these events show clearly how the collaboration between German rulers and the popes benefited the latter even outside Italy and Germany.

As in France, political and ecclesiastical relations were also complicated in another former area of the Carolingian empire, in Catalonia, the former Spanish mark. And again, just as in France, Catalan nobles founded monasteries and sought, as did the monks under their wing, protection in Rome. To this end, there were more Catalan than French petitioners, both laymen and clergy, at the papal court in the middle of the tenth century. As Cluny was for France, Cuxá near Prades was the exemplary monastery of papal exemption, which it had received in 950. Soon after, important abbeys gained exemption, such as Ripoll in 951, Rodas in 955, or Besalú in 977. Popes were also busy in Catalonia, even more so than in France, with the reorganization (Vich, Urgel) or establishment (Besalú, which failed) of new bishoprics. In the year 1000, Sylvester II invited the viscount of Barcelona before a Roman synod, though it must be stressed that in Catalonia, too, the initiative for such steps always came from the nobles and prelates there. The fact remains, however, that Catalonia became a springboard for later papal activity in Spain.

With the rest of Spain, on the other hand, the popes still had no contact. This can be seen clearly in the plans to reestablish the archdiocese at Tarragona, despite the fact that the city itself at this time was still under Islamic rule. It was probably in 955 when a

Spanish synod in Compostela entrusted the administration of the new church province to the abbot Caesarius of Montserrat. Because of internal difficulties, Caesarius turned to John XIII for help in 970, without success, however. Instead, the pope backed the plan of Catalan petitioners to move the archepiscopal see to Vich, but this also failed. Thus one must assume that the Catalan church existed separately from the kingdom of León, and that until the end of the eleventh century generally remained untouched by papal activity. And so, it was not the pope, but rather national synods and royal measures that guided the church.

In the Mozarabic part of Spain, it even seems that the caliph had taken on similar functions, such as the appointment of bishops, according to emissary reports from Abbot John of Gorze. The visit by a Mozarabic prince from Andalusia to Rome in circa 946–951 while on a pilgrimage to Jerusalem was, in the end, somewhat inconsequential. And yet, it would seem from this visit, as well as from that of Armenian Symoen in 981, and the visit by envoys from Egypt and Palestine in 922, that Peter's tomb also enjoyed great esteem even outside areas that had previously been part of the Carolingian empire. It was in the spirit of sentimentality toward late antiquity that in the period between 981 and 983 an envoy from Carthage complained to Benedict VII about the lack of priests back home and beseeched the pope for the ordination of an archbishop. Such sporadic reports show clearly to what extent papal influence was, for the time being, still limited to the territory of the earlier Carolingian empire.

This reduction is also evident in the relationship of the papacy to England. True to tradition, most of the archbishops of Canterbury, and some from York, made the pilgrimage to Rome to receive the pallium from the pope, and until the turn of the millennium paid a fee to the pope for this. These archbishops were eventually released from paying this, thanks to an annual tribute collected throughout England, the Peter penny. In addition, there was still the alliance (*schola*) near St. Peter's, made up of Anglo-Saxons, that paid a "protection fee" to the pope. In contrast to the continent, however, no synod, neither in Rome nor one headed by papal legates, dealt with ecclesiastical problems in England, nor did any Anglo-Saxon monastery receive any privileges. Rather, reforms came from the Anglo-Saxons themselves, under the influence especially of Fleury and Cluny. This meant that the papacy was unable to exert any real influence on the church in

England, and because of that, apparently had no interest in England, one sign of which was the almost complete nonexistence of correspondence between Rome and England. As a consequence, the increased missionary work among the Danes and Norwegians that the English undertook from the time of Canute the Great's reign did little to spread papal prestige for the time being. Canute's visit to Rome on occasion of the coronation of Conrad II in 1027 did nothing to change the situation.

Finally, another innovation should be mentioned, one that slowly hinted at the commanding position, now also theological, of the papacy: canonization, the right of the pope to declare Christians as saints. Until the end of the tenth century, the worship of a saint usually grew out of local veneration, but in 993, for the first time, a pope, John XV, upon German request, raised the former Bishop Ulrich of Augsburg to the honor of the altars and provided for him to be worshiped throughout the entire church. John XVIII granted the same rank to five Polish martyrs, as did Benedict VIII to the Armenian hermit Symeon. These canonizations actually proceeded rather formlessly, and there continued to be places where saints were worshiped locally, without papal regulation. These three precedents, however, gradually served to expand the papal prerogative in canonization as early as Leo IX's pontificate, but particularly from the twelfth century. With the Counterreformation, canonization by other prelates was excluded, as was the veneration of saints, which by then had become very popular.

From this discussion, it should probably be clear that this epoch was only in part the "dark century" that Cardinal Baronio described it to be. Not only were the changes in Rome itself—secular and ecclesiastical organization and the revival of antiquity—or in Central and Southern Italy fundamental for the future, but also the unabashed use of legates and the privilege of exemption. The areas that had belonged to the former Carolingian empire were the ones that were affected for the time being. This limitation would by and large characterize the following epoch, too. At the same time, the conduct of the popes—usually just reactions to foreign initiatives—vis-à-vis monasteries and the sending of legates made clear how much the political and ecclesiastical instability in lands such as France and Catalonia worked to the benefit of establishing papal primacy. In contrast, the German church, headed by the king, who from the time of Henry II, and even more so in the person of Henry III, proved to be a priestly king, was quite secure and homogeneously organized for the situation at that time. Therefore Germany was bound to become the touchstone of the papacy, beginning with the pontificate of Leo IX, as it gradually tried to free itself from the influence of the laity, including the king.

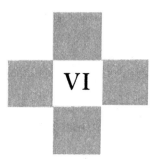

VI

The Papacy During the
Investiture Contest (1046–1123)

The German rulers Henry IV (1056–1106) and Henry V
(1106–1125) frequently found themselves at odds with popes
of that time. One of the points at issue was whether the
German king should be allowed to invest abbots and bishops in his
kingdom by bestowing the ring and staff. The one-sided weighting
of the issue, with its emphasis on national aspects and the rejection
of ultramontane influences, stirred authors of the twelfth century
like Gerhoh of Reichersberg, not to mention German historians of
the last century, into using the blanket term the "Age of the
Investiture Contest" to describe this fundamental epoch which
raised the papacy to universal prominence. Recent research has
shown that the conflict over the right to invest was just one aspect
of the upheavals of that age. Because other names, however, such
as the Age of Reform, also fail to include all the changes, the first
concept is internationally accepted and also implicitly indicates that
one of the most important consequences of the epoch was the
papacy's breaking away from the tutelage of kings. For these reasons, Investiture Contest is also used in this book.

In 1046, Henry III set the wheels in motion for the ensuing

changes with his synods in Sutri and Rome. His intervention was greeted unanimously by contemporaries, especially by those who backed reform. But the more the reforms were carried out and the conflicts with his successors increased, the more his reputation as a simonist grew. Thus the verdict on his deeds changed from acclamation to condemnation, until finally by 1200 he was seen as a heretic. This change of opinion clearly shows how much the texts which describe the upheavals could be tainted by subjectivity. Their value must therefore be viewed with some caution.

Henry III strived to reform the Roman church equally as much as the synodalists of 1046 did. However, because the first two popes whom he had placed in office in the Ottonian tradition, Clement II (1046–1047) and Damasus II (1047–1048), were able to spend only a few months or a few days of their short pontificates in Rome, activity in favor of reform got started only with Leo IX (1049–1054). This was due not only to the personality of the new pope and his longer stay in office, but also to the persons he had brought with him to Rome or who soon joined him. Among them were later popes such as Hildebrand (Gregory VII) and Frederick of Lorraine (Stephen IX), as well as Humbert of Moyenmoutier (the later bishop of Silva Candida) or Hugo Candidus (Hugo the White). At the same time, the pope was assisted by foreign reformers, including the Abbot Odilo of Cluny as well as the hermit Peter Damiani and Archbishop Halinard of Lyon. It must be stressed that they were all shaped by efforts to reform the monasteries, less by Cluny, however, and somewhat more by William of Volpiano. Because their places of education in the preceding epoch had been in close contact to the papacy, their efforts were now directed toward implementing their reform ideas throughout the entire church, beginning with a reformed and fortified papacy. Consequently, from the outset, reforming the church also meant strengthening the papacy. This does not mean, of course, that all attempts at reform after 1049 were worked out ahead of time in theoretical detail, nor that all popes and their assistants had the same reform goals. A historically exact analysis should investigate at least five successive periods: the age of Leo IX and Victor II (1049–1057); the period of Stephen IX to Alexander II (1057–1073); the pontificate of Gregory VII (1073–1085); the pontificate of Urban II (1088–1099); and the age from Paschal II to the First Lateran Council (1099–1123). In so doing, individual persons and groups should be differentiated. But due to space reasons, only a systematic summary is possible. Let us begin, then, with the attempts to reform the clergy.

One of the first goals was the extermination of Nicholaitism. Referring to the name of an early Christian sect, this term denoted the cohabitation of clergymen and women. From now on, celibacy (*caelebs,* i.e., unmarried) was to be a binding norm not only for monks and canons, but for all who were ordained into the higher orders, from subdeacon to bishop. This was to serve the goal, on the one hand, of allowing only worthy clergymen to celebrate mass—according to the ideals of the early church, celibacy, as a return to the supposed true nature of man, was preferred to marriage. On the other hand, celibacy was also supposed to prevent the children of clerics from inheriting the office of their fathers, which would lead to the danger of ecclesiastical offices primarily serving economic needs. Thus legislation favoring celibacy was soon expanded to include sanctions against the children of clerics. Both plans were based on similar attempts in late antiquity. There were better chances now, however, of implementing these two plans, at least as legal standards that were valid everywhere, because, in contrast to the fourth and fifth centuries, the papacy was also recognized at this time as the highest lawgiver of the Western church—but more on this later. Both plans also included measures against the wives of clerics, making the wives equal to concubines, regardless of whether they were legally married to their partners or not. Until the end of the eleventh century, most of the steps taken against them consisted of their having to work for the local church as dependent servants. And finally, another important point should be emphasized: breaking the law of celibacy was punished only when it became "notorious," i.e., made public. This perforce encouraged secret contraventions of the law, and with that a propensity to hypocrisy.

Beginning with the pontificate of Leo IX, a ban on simony was declared at Roman synods along with the ban on Nicholaitism. Since late antiquity, the obtaining of religious authority by material means had been known as simony, in reference to the narrative in the Acts of the Apostles by Simon Magus. Gregory the Great further defined the concept by differentiating among *simonia a manu* (buying), *simonia a lingua* (acquisition by promise), and *simonia ab obsequio* (obligations resulting from ordination). These broad definitions were taken over by the reformers. There were still differences among them, however, as seen in the increasingly radical position of Cardinal Humbert of Silva Candida (*Adversus simoniacos libri tres*) and the relatively moderate tract of Peter Damiani. Disputes included whether simonists had to be reordained, i.e., consecrated again—a theologically difficult problem that was solved by the scholastic theology of the thirteenth century. Also disputed was the question of who was to be considered a simonist. Participants at Leo IX's first Roman synod were terrified by this point, arguing that, with too broad a definition of the concept, they would all be simonists, and that the Roman dioceses would lose their entire clergy if the prohibition were implemented. In contrast to assertions that have been put forward in the past, Humbert's influence at the papal court was relatively slight. The popes usually shared Damiani's pragmatic outlook. And the papal practice of appointing bishops, particularly since Urban II, led to the gradual acceptance of the idea among radical reformers that the papacy was the chief simonist; consequently, as early as the twelfth century, as the fate of Arnold of Brescia shows, the papacy was attacked and accused of heresy. For the time being, however, the papacy was the biggest foe of simony.

If simony was to be effectively fought, then the way in which bishops and abbots could receive their offices in accordance with ecclesiastical law had to be regulated. For this reason, the Roman synod backed the idea of free elections—again with recourse to the ideals of the early church—which, in the case of the bishops, were to take place among "the clergy and the people," and in the case of the abbots, among the monks of the cloister. Similar regulations were in force for the papal election of 1059, about which more later. And to settle disputed elections, attempts were made to recognize only those elections in which the *maior et sanior pars,* the greatest and the "healthiest part," of the voters participated. All these regulations were so vague, however, that even the instalation or recognition of prelates remained material for dispute between religious and lay institutions, and the longer it did the more frequently it offered the papacy the pretext to intervene to regulate and decide the affairs of local churches.

The prohibition of investiture was connected with the attack on simony and the setting up of free elections. In the third book of his opus on the simonists, written from 1059 to 1061, Humbert condemned the investiture of prelates by laymen, but he found no support for this position. Even Gregory VII did not initially turn against the right of investiture. He and his retinue changed their minds, however, at a Roman synod in 1078. This synod was preceded by a resolution against investiture at a synod in Brittany, though it probably did not influence the Roman decree. Nevertheless, the simultaneous measures show that the time was ripe for this within the church. The final break between the reform papacy and Henry IV, which came shortly after in 1080 for other reasons, hindered for the time being an emphasis on the investiture prohibition because the most important person engaged in this dialogue was missing. Only under Urban II were increased steps taken against the investiture of prelates by rulers. This was directed initially and principally toward the kings of France and England. At the same time, there was some deliberation about how this conflict could be solved legally. Gregory VII and Urban II wanted to retain for church leaders the right to appoint prelates in all their functions, while other writers, among them Bishop Ivo of Chartres, who was usually devoted to his king, developed criteria that differentiated between spiritualities (purely religious functions) and temporalities (purely secular functions and property). On that basis, the dispute was settled in France and England around 1106. The bestowing of temporalities to the prelates was promised to the rulers. In addition, it was also decided, as a provisional compromise, that the election had to take place in the presence of the ruler or his representatives. Callistus II concluded a compromise to this effect with Henry V in 1122 after a long dispute with the emperor. This compromise, the Concordat of Worms, differentiated between the individual spheres of power of the emperor. In Germany, which now for the first time was defined by those outside Germany as an independent sovereign territory, the investiture with temporalities by bestowing the scepter was to take place between the election and the ordination, which ensured the continuation of the rulers' influence. In imperial Italy and Burgundy, it was to take place within six months after the ordination. This severely limited any opportunity for the ruler in Italy and Burgundy, since he was only able to exert his power after all constitutive acts had already been performed. That was one of the reasons why Burgundy in particular increasingly distanced itself from the emperor.

All reform plans sketched out so far could succeed only if the standing of the papacy was also elevated. The first written statements by those reformers who backed the pope, such as Humbert and Damiani, stressed the papacy's supremacy within Christendom. Papal decrees, of course, contained similar pronouncements, as did decrees of Roman synods. According to plan, Gregory VII finally proclaimed in approximately 1075, in guidelines—the *Dictatus pape*—which he had entered in his register, which rights the pope claimed for himself as the successor of Peter and vicar of Christ. He claimed to possess supreme control and supervision within the church, meaning only he was allowed to issue new laws, only he could appoint or remove prelates, and, on the basis of his position, he was to be considered as a saint on earth. Furthermore, only those who followed the teachings of the Roman church could be considered Catholic. Gregory also claimed that only the pope was allowed to wear imperial insignia and to appoint or, above all, depose secular rulers, basing this stand in part on the Donation of Constantine and probably also on the example of Nicholas I. This assessment of the world was based on a new interpretation of older texts, and from the time of Urban II was even more clearly emphasized. Thus, from the the papacy's point of view, the doctrine of the two powers proposed by Gelasius I was usually now interpreted in favor of an unequivocal supremacy of religious authority over secular authority. Furthermore, the original significance of Leo I's statement about his *plenitudo potestatis* was increasingly being abandoned in favor of the interpretation according to Gregory IX's letter and the False Decretals. Thus the papacy clearly defined its position within the church and its relations to secular rulers in a new way.

To adapt reality to the papacy's wishes, regulations had to first be laid down regarding how the pope was to obtain his office. A decree regarding papal elections from a Roman synod in 1059 served to this end. This was preceded by disturbances after the death of Stephen IX, during the course of which a part of the Roman clergy and nobility elected John of Velletri as the new pope. He belonged to the reform party, though he was close to the Tusculans, as his bishopric in the Alban Mountains would indicate, and called himself Benedict X after the last Tusculan pope. Soon after, a majority within the reform party, under the protection of the Marquis Godfrey of Tuscany, elected and consecrated Godfrey's protégé, Bishop Gerard of Florence (Nicholas II), as the new pope. Most of the cardinal bishops, but few members of the Roman clergy or ordinary citizens, took part in this action. For their own security, it was now necessary to legalize retroactively these proceedings that had gone against tradition. Thus it was decreed that papal elections could take place outside Rome and that they were to be executed by the cardinal bishops. In addition, the cardinals, as quasi-metropolitans, were to supervise the elections and to consecrate the newly elected pope, since only God was higher than the pope. The rest of the clergy and other Romans, if present, had to conform to the cardinals' vote. This was the first step toward the cardinals obtaining the exclusive right to elect the pope. The ensuing step came because of the special conditions surrounding the schism that had existed since 1080 as a result of the election of an imperial pope, Clement III (Guibert of Ravenna). Clement held his own in Rome as late as the time of Urban II, relying principally on the cardinal-priests, who, in a modified wording of the decree on papal elections, were considered the most important electors. Urban, therefore, had to meet this group halfway and acknowledge their demands in order to increase his own influence in Rome. From the same time or slightly later—the exact circumstances are unknown—the seven palace deacons and twelve regional deacons were counted as cardinals, with the total number, however, being reduced to eighteen. Thus, at the latest from the time of Callistus II, the three groups of cardinals were made up of six—instead of originally seven—bishops, whose locations were fixed, twenty-eight priests, and eighteen deacons. Fifty-two members only became the standard because from Callistus' time not all the positions were occupied. The consolidation of this group into a college came in the course of the twelfth century.

The prominence of the first two groups of cardinals was originally due to their liturgical service in the five episcopal basilicas—the Lateran, St. Peter's, St. Paul's, Santa Maria Maggiore, and S. Lorenzo fuori le mura. As a result of their increase in power from the time of Leo IX and Nicholas II respectively, they also received additional functions. The deacons' membership in the college was based on their traditional service to the papal court. The cardinals also gradually replaced—no doubt because of the frequently instable situation in Rome—the earlier synods that had convened during Lent and had included the pope, bishops, abbots, and the Roman clergy. They formed the most important board of advisers and assistants to the pope. Their nearly equal ranking with the pope was stressed under Leo IX in a tract ascribed to Humbert, called *De Romano pontifice*. While this was based on the position that some cardinals had reached in the preceding epoch, there was a continuity evident in the fact that from the time of Gregory VII, and even earlier in the ninth century, the cardinals visited other regions and presided over synods abroad in their capacity as the most important legates of the pope.

The cardinals received a further strengthening of their position when the Roman curia was established. Despite a dearth of information about the papal administration and its finances during this epoch, what emerges is that a change was taking place whose onset had been in preparation since the late tenth century. The writing of less important documents was probably taken over by the traditional *scrinarius* as long as the pope resided in Rome. The same persons who worked under Leo IX can be identified under Benedict IX and Gregory VI. And yet, it was clear that control was now in the hands of the chancellor instead of the librarian. Frederick of Lorraine was important in this position, not to mention John of Gaeta (later Pope Gelasius II), who under Urban II decisively fashioned the style and face (minuscule instead of curial) of papal writings. Beginning with him, it became common for the chancellor also to be a cardinal. While the chancellor replaced the librarian, from the time of Urban II the archdeacon was gradually relieved of his role as administrative head by a new official in the Cluny tradition, the chamberlain. Initially, the chamberlain was responsible for finances, perhaps also for the archives and the library, at the same time making the earlier functions of the *vestararius* and *arcarius* unnecessary. The office of the chamberlain corresponded to existing positions at secular courts, so, in a similar fashion, the papal court now also had a cupbearer, marshal, and seneschal. The latter two soon merged and replaced the traditional *sacellarius*. Another new post that emerged, at the latest from the time of Paschal II, was that of papal chaplain. Because all these newly created functions usually corresponded to functions at the courts of Western sovereigns, the main concept was also dervied from these courts, so that from the beginning of the twelfth century the papal court was called the "curia." Since then, the expression "curia" has been reserved for the papal bureaucracy. Urban charters in Rome also speak of the seven *iudices de clero*. With their offices at the Lateran Palace (*primicerius palatii*), they acted solely as judges. Moreover, it is uncertain whether they were appointed by the pope and whether they had any sway over the pope's government.

This effort by the papal court to approximate secular courts was also seen in the ceremonials. To install the newly elected pope, from now on it was necessary not only to have him take possession of the Lateran, to enthrone him at St. Peter's or some other church and to consecrate him there and present him the pallium and the ferula, but he also had to be immantated after the election. The mantle that went along with this immantation ceremony was made of purple material, thus signalizing the similarity to the imperial office since this color had always been reserved for the emperor. And accordingly, from the time of Paschal, an emphasis was placed on the new pope taking up his position in the Lateran on a seat made at least of fake porphyry, which was also reserved for the emperor. Similarly, bishop thrones built in Roman churches from the beginning of the twelfth century, as well as new floors, were inlaid with prophyry. Thus the competition with the imperial office, or even its replacement by the papacy, which was emphasized from the time of the Donation of Constantine and Leo III and given prominence once again by Gregory VII, was made conspicuously evident.

As previously indicated, reforms were to take in the entire Western church, which more and more was being understood as a uniformly structured universal church directed by the pope. To reach this goal, synods presided over by the pope himself (Leo IX, Urban II), or by papal legates, were held more frequently in places other than Rome—except for England, where royal influence remained strong. This helped make possible the handing down of papal directives. Trips made by papal legates to the areas assigned to them served the same purpose. The extent to which the papacy's position was consolidated was evident in France in particular, where legates removed or named some abbots or bishops—sometimes without papal instruction—and intervened in the church structure by dividing or merging bishoprics. And more frequently than in the two preceding epochs, popes rewarded their supporters with privileges—especially exemptions—and in so doing changed the structure of the church to their advantage.

The basis for these sorts of actions was the canonical law collection, though the numerous new collections make it clear that church law had still not been uniformly standardized. The foundations were usually the Pseudo-Isidorean Decretals. Whatever was added to this base depended on the goals of the individual compiler and the kind of documents he had to work with. For example, compilers who worked at the papal court, such as Deusdedit, Anselm of Lucca, Gregory of S. Grisogono, appropriated Roman texts (*Liber diurnus),* which are not found in French collections. What all collections had in common, however, was that decisions of contemporary popes were contained in them, in contrast to the traditional compilations. Noteworthy in this regard is that Gregory VII, in contrast to his political influence, was barely represented. His intransigent promulgations, in particular, are missing from later collections, as well as from the *Dictatus pape.* The papal texts can be divided into two groups, the first dealing with decisions made by papal synods, the other with promulgations of individual popes on specific issues. It should be pointed out that the second group included not only precepts and prohibitions but also dispensations, such as ones regarding the consequences of celibacy and the non-observance of it; in other words, these were decisions that regulated deviations from the norm. As the canonical collections of Ivo of Chartes show, dispensations could sometimes even exceed the number of authoritative texts. It is clear, then, that some compilers, with Ivo being one of the most influential, saw dispensations not so much as emergency measures for specific periods of time, but as important measures for mitigating for wider usage rules considered too harsh. Dispensation legislation and usage would retain its significance in the future for both the papacy and the church. The pope was not only the chief lawmaker of the church, but was also the person who deemed when and how much deviation from these rules was to be allowed.

Laws and dispensations, as well as the activities of synods and legates, could only be successful, however, if they were accepted by those whom they affected. Therefore, let us look at who supported the reforms the papacy was advocating.

As was evident with the assistants of Leo IX, the papacy found its biggest support among the various reform groups at the monasteries. While previous research had always given too much influence and importance to Cluny—so much so that the entire reform movement could actually be characterized as Cluniac—it has become clear in the last few decades that other monastic groups played at the least just as great a role. Among them were groups of hermits, especially in Italy, the most of important of whom was Peter Damiani. It would be wrong to imagine these hermits as persons who had completely turned their backs to the world. To the contrary, they were out gathering supporters, over whom they had influence, and corresponding with other like-minded persons. One result of this movement was the establishment of new monastic communities that combined the hermetic and Benedictine traditions, such as the Camaldoli. The hermetic ideal was closely observed by the Carthusians, founded by Bruno of Cologne, though for this reason they did not gain a wide influence.

More important for the papacy than the hermits were groups of monks in Italy, France, and Germany, which split from already existing reform movements or which were newly formed groups. This period saw the founding of many such communities. Depending on when they were established, their significance for this epoch varied. The Cistercians played an important role only after 1130. Communities that were established before the Cistercians, such as St. Victor near Marseille, La Chaise Dieu, Vallombrosa, or Hirsau, were important helpers for energetic popes like Gregory VII or Urban II. Some of the communities, such as Hirsau or Vallombrosa under John Gualberti, are even examples of early agitation aimed at defaming adversaries.

And finally, the communities of canons regular should be mentioned. These were clerics who lived together under the spiritual guidance of St. Augustine. They were first established in Italy around the middle of the century at places like San Frediano in Lucca, a monastery which also reformed the clergy attached to the Lateran basilica in Rome. Similar communities were also established in Germany, France, and on the Iberian peninsula, beginning with the pontificate of Gregory VII. They all held the ideal of the *vita apostolica* in common. This meant they followed the example of Jesus and the apostles by being poor and by wanting to strengthen the faith of the Christian laity. For this reason, they had a strong influence among the common people. They were encouraged by popes, especially from the time of Alexander II.

All groups, whether hermits, monks, or canons regular, because of their own ideals, participated in the fight against Nicholaitism and simony. As they joined this common struggle with the papacy, they requested exemption and other privileges from the pope. Consequently, they were, even more than their forerunners in the preceding epoch, trailblazers for the universal position of the papacy.

Papal support of the episcopates, on the other hand, was usually less forthcoming. To be sure, the efforts of various archbishops to expand older traditions indicate that the general preeminence of the papacy, despite all of the current divergences, was undisputed. From the middle of the eleventh century, the three archbishoprics of the Rhine—Mainz, Cologne, Trier—vied with each other to be the "special" daughter of Rome. In France and elswhere, individual archbishops in places like Lyon or Toledo tried to become primates for larger areas and, by so doing, to obtain a rank between the pope and the archbishops of those areas. And for the popes at least, it had been established that all prelates from bishops to patriarchs were their "assistants" (*opifices*), as Innocent II expressed it later to the patriarch of Aquileia, Peter. Thus it was clear for the papacy, from the time of Gregory VII, that all rights that had been granted could be lifted whenever it seemed expedient. The following provisio was therefore often inserted in charters granted in the reform epoch: *salva auctoritate sedis apostolice* ("saving the authority of the apostolic see"). It was on this statement that Urban II, for example, based his declaration that the Roman church as "the prince of all churches" (*ecclesiarum omnium princeps*) is "like a mother, befitting of respect from all" (*cui ut matri debet ab omnibus reverentia exhiberi*).

It is astonishing, and not completely explainable, why the reforms propagated by the papacy found a positive echo among various lay groups. Members of the upper and middle nobility founded family monasteries more frequently than before, which they filled with supporters of the new movements, or they endowed reform monasteries with property and privileges. The canons regular also received benefits from the nobility. However varied the motives of these donors and founders of monasteries may have been, through them papal aspirations were promoted. Church reform also found approval among the urban classes, especially in Italy. The *Pataria* in Milan is the most famous of these urban groups, its name probably being derived from the municipal secondhand market. Under the leadership of nobles and clerics in the city, they fought against simony and the breaking of celibacy by ecclesiastics, as well as against the archbishops appointed by Henry IV. Similar phenomena can be seen in other cities of Northern and Central Italy. Struggles of this kind were further encouraged by the fact that the popes—and in particular, Gregory VI—called on the laity to boycott the worship services of simonistic clergymen or of clergymen who did not lead a celibate life. This could also be dangerous for the papacy, however, since in this way the evaluation of the cleric was submitted to the judgment of the laity. Thus, from the early twelfth century, the papacy disavowed support of movements of this kind among the laity. Consequently, these

movements were increasingly dismissed as heretical since they presented a threat to the consolidated hierarchy which had placed the
pope at the top.

There is a close connection between the religiously motivated
lay movements and the crusades. As early as 1064, Alexander II
had promised his protection to the nobles who were fighting against
the still Islamic Barbastro in Aragon. Gregory VII wanted to establish a *militia sancti Petri*, troops that would use force to obtain his
goals. This led to success in 1095 in Clermont when Urban II
called for the retaking of the Holy Land. The first Crusade army,
made up of nobles coming mostly from French territory, set out in
1096 and three years later conquered Jerusalem after much blood-
shed. And, as the huge movements that were unchained by Peter
of Amiens and other preachers in Northern France and on the
Rhine showed, the call to arms was also fruitful among classes
other than the nobility. On account of the Jewish pogroms and the
massacre in Palestine, the crusade is now judged with much more
skepticism than it was earlier. Because the pope immediately lost
control, with an attempt being made to establish an independent
patriarch in Jerusalem in the early twelfth century, events did not
match the expectations of the initiators. Though seldom emphasized, the first crusade had some consequences on the relationship
of the papacy to the Eastern church. Since henceforth Antioch and
Jerusalem belonged to the Kingdom of Jerusalem, Western clerics
there acted as patriarchs. They were, like the Latin archbishops in
Europe, appointed to their post by the pope. Thus the actual
conditions now undermined the older pretense that the Eastern
churches were subordinate to the pope.

Not one king took part in the crusade. The sovereigns of France
and Germany had at that time been excommunicated, while others
had no interest, or had more important goals to work toward.
What is noteworthy here is that even in this epoch the papacy
could not always enforce its will.

As was to be expected from the events of 1046, relations between the papacy and Henry III were similar to papal relations at
the time of Otto I, and of Otto III in particular. Emperors and
popes worked in concert for ecclesiastical reform. The pontificates
of Leo IX and Victor II show, more than any others, that the
popes also looked after the affairs of the rulers in the empire.
These common interests were soon recognized abroad, causing
Henry I of France to forbid his prelates from taking part at a

synod held by Leo IX in Reims. Relations grew worse, however, during the regency of Empress Agnes after the death of Henry III. The reasons for this are many, among them was the fact that from the time of Stephen IX, who was a brother of Marquis Godfrey of Tuscany, Godfrey's protégés were elected pope without the prior consent of the German ruler's court. These protégés included Nicholas II and Alexander II, as well as Stephen. Godfrey, meanwhile, was considered an enemy of the state under Henry III. Another reason was the change in papal policy toward the Normans which had begun under Nicholas II. From the time Henry IV came of age in 1064, he endeavored, just as Alexander II and Gregory VII initially had tried, to continue the policies of his father. Internal German quarrels, however, as well as a dispute over the appointment to the archbishopric of Milan, led first to the excommunication of his advisers, and then to Henry's in 1076, with the pope also threatening to depose him. Though the excommunication was lifted in Canossa in 1077, the election of pretenders to the throne in Germany with the help of papal legates and the dispute over investiture, which began in 1078, caused Gregory VII to excommunicate Henry once again in 1080 in the name of Peter and to depose Henry from his throne as well as to proclaim his imminent death. Henry countered by occupying Rome and by having, in the person of his chancellor in Rome, Guibert of Ravenna (Clement III), a new pope elected and having himself crowned emperor by him. Gregory was isolated in Rome until freed in 1084 by the Normans, who in doing so destroyed major inhabited portions of the city, including the area between the Colosseum and the Lateran as well as Via Lata. Gregory died one year later in Salerno, cursed by many Romans but considered a martyr in the eyes of his supporters.

Urban II was able to regain parts of Rome only late in his pontificate. The emperor remained excommunicated until his death, which made a rebellion on the part of his sons, Conrad and Henry, easier. The latter tried to come to terms with Paschal II when he became the new sovereign in 1106, and eventually was crowned emperor by Paschal in 1111 as Henry V. Negotiations failed, however, due to Henry's obstinate and extortionate attitude (the "privilege" of Ponte Mammolo in 1111, revoked by Paschal in 1112). which was also rejected by many German princes, since success for Henry meant the temporalities of many German prelates would be rescinded. New negotiations under Callistus II finally led to the

Concordat of Worms in 1122 and to the resolution of the conflict in the German realm. In 1123, at the First Lateran Council, as it has been called since the sixteenth century, Callistus could celebrate the peace that had finally been achieved. And with this, the present epoch ended.

The conflicts that arose after 1076 did not mean that church reform in Germany had stagnated. To the contrary, Henry IV and the bishops and abbots who were on his side worked on behalf of the reforms as Henry III had envisioned them. Of course, they also tried to hold to a minimum the influence of hostile popes. To this end, they used all the means they had at their disposal. For example, Henry IV supported the citizens of Worms and Cologne, because the bishops of these two cities stood on the side of Gregory VII. Opponents of the king, as supporters of the pope, acted in just the opposite manner, insulting their rivals as enemies of reform, as seen in the fate of Bishop Hermann of Bamberg, who remained loyal to the king. The upshot was that hardly anyone, of course, denied church reform, but the prestige of the reform-minded popes depended on the domestic political situation at the time.

In France, just as in previous epochs, a differentiation must be made between two distinct areas: on the one hand, the crown lands and other territories more or less ruled by the king; and on the other, Central and Southern France as well as Burgandy, all far from the king. The latter regions were the more important ones for the papacy. Like their predecessors, the reform popes aided the established or newly formed communities of monks or canons regular. Such well-traveled popes as Urban II found support there, in exchange for which he consecrated churches or altars and distributed privileges. It was here, above all, that papal legates had their influence. For this reason, these areas, in addition to Italy, became extremely vital to the papacy, which later led to the close relationship between the papacy and France. Contacts with the royalty of France, in contrast, were not so close. Henry I already had quite a combatitive posture toward Leo IX, but relations cooled off even more by the end of the century when Philip I was excommunicated because of an extramarital affair. Moreover, he refused to acknowledge the prohibition of investiture. Only under the new king, Louis VI (from 1108), after the conflict over the right of investiture had been resolved in 1106, was the papacy able to apply its authority more vigorously in the areas ruled by the king of France.

England was even more estranged from the papacy. Though it was claimed in the years after the battle of Hastings in 1066 that William had conquered England with the backing of St. Peter and the blessing of the pope, it is doubtful whether this is anything more than historiographic fiction. Be that as it may, it is true that the reform of the English church, in conjunction with the replacement of Anglo-Saxon bishops with Norman ones, took place under the direction of the English kings. Thus the reform served, above all, to stabilize the new rule, though the papacy's leadership of the universal church was not disputed. Travel by English prelates to the papal curia, and the activities of papal legates in England, were possible only with permission from the king. For this reason, under Urban II the point of conflict was reached not only over the right of investiture, but also over the king's refusal to allow Archbishop Anselm of Canterbury to appeal to the pope. Even after the resolution of these conflicts in 1107, actual church power remained with the king. Perhaps this was connected with the fact that not long thereafter the archbishop of Canterbury was frequently considered a *legatus natus*, that is, the office of legate was tied to the episcopal see, making it seem unnecessary for the papacy to send its own legates.

The situation in Spain was complicated. The relationship with Catalonia, which went back to the tenth century, was strengthened. This can be seen not only in the newly distributed charters for monasteries and churches, or in the embracing of the reform movement which the papacy encouraged by St. Victor of Marseille in the Pyrenees, but also in the activities of papal legates. Aragon, however, would prove to be more important in the future. The rulers of Aragon had been trying since 1035 to establish a kingdom that would be independent from the powerful neighbor Leon-Castile. The second king, Sancho I Ramirez (1063–1094), more than others, exploited the papacy's desire for recognition for his own purposes. The aforementioned "crusade" of Barbastro in 1064 was an indication of the new policy. Soon thereafter, the king placed himself and his kingdom under St. Peter in Rome. Since then, the kingdom was considered a fief of the papacy, in the eyes of the papal court anyway. The new relationship took concrete form in that, from the time of Gregory VII, popes had influence

on the appointment to the one bishopric at Jaca. Other signs of
the new relationship included the operations in Aragon of papal
legates or special agents like the abbot Frotard of St.-Pons-de-
Thomières, as well as the decision by a synod there to accept, for
the first time in history, Roman canon law and the Roman liturgy
for the entire kingdom.

While Aragon was subordinate to St. Peter in Rome, Leon-
Castile from the time of Ferdinand I (1035–1064) had a special
relationship to St. Peter in Cluny and paid an annual tribute to the
monastery there. Cluny profited more than just financially, since
this also had an effect on monastic reform and on church administration. A good example of this is the monk Bernard, who came
from Cluny and was the first abbot of the important royal monastery at Sahagún, and who later became the archbishop of Toledo
after this city was obtained by Alfonso VI in 1086. As archbishop
of Toledo, Bernard sought, by harking back to the Visigothic
church organization, to become primate of the Spanish church
and thereby to expand his authority over the church as a whole.
In doing so, however, he gave his colleagues in Breda and Santiago
de Compostela grounds for protesting, since they were also trying
to establish an autonomous ecclesiastical province by referring
back to pre-Islamic times. Prospects looked brightest for Toledo as
long as Alfonso VI was in charge, but he died in 1109. Santiago's
situation then turned sour when it claimed, as the burial site of the
apostle James, to be the only *sedes apostolica* in the West besides
Rome, which was later rejected by both Leo IX and Urban II as
too dangerous for the papacy. After Alfonso's death, chaos broke
out in Castile as Alfonso's daughter Urraca, her second husband
Alfonso I of Aragon, and the supporters of her son Alfonso VII,
fought for control. Thus the competing bishops were without the
support of their own ruler, turning more submissively than ever
to the papacy for help. The dispute was destined to continue
throughout the twelfth century, though, from the time of Callistus
II, Braga and Santiago were allowed to form their own ecclesiastical provinces with suffragan bishoprics under them. The positive
element in all this for the papacy was that, for the first time, it was
able to intervene as the highest ecclesiastical court in the most
important kingdom of the peninsula, a kingdom that until then
had been inaccessible. Of course, Spanish petitioners recognized
that nothing was gained at the papal court for free. In a lovely
satire, probably written in Toledo during the pontificate of Urban

II, Albinus (silver) and Rufinus (gold) were portrayed as the supreme patron saints of popes. In other words, even during the struggle against simony, popes were ridiculed as simonists, their moral authority doubted.

While, on the one hand, the papacy's sphere of influence stretched all the way to the southwestern corner of Europe, in Scandinavia and Eastern Europe its prestige was relatively slight. Peter penny contributions by Denmark, Poland, and Hungary to the papacy, which wanted to interpret these payments as a recognition of papal protection or even of feudal suzerainity, do not refute the fact that papal prestige was low, for ecclesiastical organization in these areas was still quite underdeveloped and by no means corresponded to the ideas of the church reformers, especially as regards celibacy. For the time being, no pope intervened to regulate or reform these areas, revealing the papacy's de facto lack of power. Only in the following epochs, and then sporadically, were papal legates able to travel in these lands and to hold reform synods, most of which turned out unsuccessful anyway. Along with Hungary, Croatia formed the border to Byzantium, and was likewise viewed by the popes as a papal fief on the basis of an unhistorical interpretation of older texts.

The political border with the East was henceforth destined to cement strongly the division of the church, for in 1054 one of the most momentous events of this epoch took place: the splitting of the Western church from the Eastern, a division that continues to this day. With reference to the Donation of Constantine, the two legates of Leo IX, Frederick of Lorraine and Humbert of Silva Candida, excommunicated the patriarch and emperor in Constaninople, whereupon the patriarch pronounced an anathema against the pope. Though popes like Gregory VII tried from time to time to put an end to the schism, and even in the thirteenth and fifteenth centuries there would be no lack of such attempts, no pope had any lasting success. The papacy did get something positive out of this, namely, that from now on only those countries that recognized the supreme church authority of the papacy were counted as part of orthodox Christendom, with protests from the East dismissed as the opinions of schismatics or even heretics. A unification of the churches was only possible if the papacy was accepted as the highest ecclesiastical court.

The legates of 1054 were orignally supposed to reach an agreement with Constantinople over a common front to fight the Nor-

mans in Southern Italy. The break with the East was one of the
reasons why pontiffs since Nicholas II allied themselves with the
Normans. The Normans became vassals of the papacy, with whose
consent they subjected first all of Southern Italy, and, at the end
of the eleventh century, also Sicily, dealing a blow not only to the
Lombards and Saracens, but also to the Byzantines. After Benevento, Capua and Salerno, as well as Bari, and later Siponto, had
become, under Otto I, archbishoprics subordinated to the pope,
the newly conquered areas were placed under the papacy again,
doing away with the changes that had originated in the eighth
century. For the time being, however, this ecclesiastical authority
was mostly nominal as the real power was exercised by the the new
lords. Similar to the situation in Norman England, pontiffs could
only intervene with the consent of the Norman ruler. Yet the
papacy was content with this, its supreme secular authority still
acknowledged. Thus Pope Gregory VII at the end of his pontificate, as well as Urban II, were able to count on Norman protection
in times of need.

The more unstable the conditions were in Rome, the popes'
own bishopric, the more the Norman protection was needed—and
throughout almost this entire epoch conditions were unstable. This
can be seen in the constant nomination of antipopes, who often
had the support of part of the Roman population and the Roman
clergy. After the relatively limited success of Benedict IX at first,
who returned to Rome after 1046 despite having been deposed,
and then of Benedict X and Honorius II, Clement III in particular
governed Rome exceptionally well, though his various successors
were mostly marginal characters. The result of this, however, was—
and this can also be seen in the decree on papal elections of 1059—
that the papacy, the College of Cardinals, and the curia were
increasingly estranged from the city of Rome. In other words, the
more the popes became head of the universal church, the less
support they received in Rome itself. Nevertheless, the popes tried
once again to govern Rome, devoting much of their time to this
endeavor. As the Roman documents of that time and the so-called
Annales Romani show, a pope could seldom rule the city in its
entirety. Access to municipal housing estates was often forbidden;
even the Lateran and St. Peter's were usually extremely unsafe
places of residence. The popes were therefore often left to the
support of the Roman nobility. To have success, they promoted
new families, the most well known of which are the Pierleoni and

Frangipani. In turn, these families used the papacy for their own ascent, and soon were even dangerous for the papacy itself, as Gelasius II was to learn. And finally, it should be mentioned that the popes undertook their first attempts since Nicholas II to actually govern a part of the Papal States through a policy of controlling the castles in the Sabine and on the southern consular roads. But they had little successs at first, since they had to depend on the cooperation of the nobility and several monastaries, such as Farfa and Subiaco. More important, in the meantime, was the bequest by Marquise Mathilda of Tuscany to Paschalis II of the territory under her domain. Since these lands, however, were once a part of the old Kingdom of Italy, which the German kings were still trying to control, the struggle over the Mathildine lands became a constant of the following epoch, especially from the time of Barbarossa.

To sum up, the Western church, which now was understood as the universal church, was placed under the pope, at least in theory. The pope possessed the *plenitudo potestatis* and could not be deposed. Since he was the supreme judge and the only lawgiver, ecclesiastical law was changed by decrees of contemporary popes, and the popes were able to intervene in the structure of the church. The latter was evident not only in dispensations, or in the exemptions of monasteries, bishoprics, or churches, but also in the establishing, dividing, or merging of bishoprics or ecclesiastical provinces. As a result of this, the position of the archbishops, more than others, was weakened, not to mention what the ominous plans for establishing patriarchates and primates would have done to their position. Through their activities, the legates as well as the newly constituted College of Cardinals and the new curia, both of which were internationally staffed in contrast to the earlier almost exclusively Roman staff, helped the popes. This was, however, one of the reasons why the popes became estranged to their own episcopal city.

At the same time, the papacy, with the help of a new interpretation of Gelasius' doctrine of the two powers, reversed the relations of ecclesiastical and secular power with a strong appeal to the Donation of Constantine and anachronistic interpretations of charters dating from the beginning of the new millennium. If earlier it was secular rulers who were deposing popes, then it was now the pope's turn to claim the right to remove kings and emperors, and he did so, even with Henry IV. As a result of the new regulations regarding investiture, most rulers lost their sacred titles, making impossible a secular theocracy such as the one that existed for the last time under Henry III. Instead, the kings had to concern themselves with a new legitimization of their authority. Only since then has it been possible to speak of an opposition between "church and state." In addition, popes tried to become patrons or lords of secular domains, which initially they were able to do, especially in Aragon and in Norman Italy.

Whether and to what extent the church reforms were a success—whether celibacy actually prevailed, simony was successfully opposed, and church elections were actually free—is very much debatable. Legislation concerning these questions, however, was disputed less frequently over time, until they were considered, even among critics, as the yardstick for a Christian life of the clergy. In the twelfth century, this was to become dangerous not only for the organization of the church but also for the papacy, and much more so in the late Middle Ages, the less it corresponded to maxims that were propagated in the eleventh century. It was also dangerous because Gregory VII called on the laity to take a critical stance, thereby offering laymen the opportunity to react to the deplorable state of affairs in the clergy.

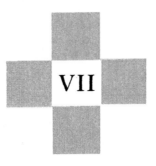

The Expansion of Papal Authority (1124–1198)

In contrast to such predecessors as Leo IX, Gregory VII, Urban II, and Callistus II, the pontiffs of the new epoch, apart from a few exceptions like Adrian IV, are often portrayed as having weak characters. Nevertheless, they were able to expand the foundation that had been laid in the eleventh century and to increase the real influence of the papacy to such an extent that Innocent III (1198–1216) could rule as *arbiter mundi* (arbiter of the world). This can only be understood if important changes of this period are taken into consideration.

The twelfth century is the period within the Middle Ages in which the greatest horizontal and vertical mobility can be observed in a broad spectrum of social classes. Without going into great detail, it should be emphasized that areas that had already been settled for a long time were now made more accessible, and previously uncultivated areas were opened up. This helped to improve the legal and social status of settlers. Freedoms were also expanded for those persons living in the growing or newly founded cities. This new mobility also included the aristocracy, as the ascendency of the ministerials with their new-found freedom shows. These same ministerials were the most important force in the new age of chivalry that was shaped by Christian values. The consequences for the church and the papacy were many. At times, new monastic orders such as the Cistercians played a decisive role in developing the new settlements. The intensification of settlements in the countryside as well as the expansion and increase of the cities required a futher development in the caring of souls and in the organization of the parish. Another consequence was the growing stream of pilgrims, which benefited, in particular, wellknown sites such as Jerusalem, Rome, and Santiago de Compostela. To handle these pilgrims, new bridges were constructed, roads improved, and hospitals built, mostly under the direction of canons regular. The pilgrims in Rome brought increased wealth and prestige to the papacy, though the papacy gained even more prominence by granting charters to hospitals, particularly the bigger ones, by granting dispensations, and by regulating, in its capacity as lawmaker, the life of the pilgrim and the pilgrim's family back home. The attitude of the papacy toward autonomy movements in the cities, however, was ambivalent. At times, the papacy exploited the cities, as in Northern Italy during the conflict with Frederick Barbarossa, while at other times it aided them. If in doing so, however, their own control or that of the obsequious episcopal rulers was jeopardized, then such autonomy movements were deemed heretical. Since this trend of declaring autonomy movements heretical was dominant after the Peace of Venice in 1177, it would leave its mark on ecclesiastical law, with effects that were to continue into modern times.

The intensification of settlements also contributed to the concentration of secular power. And since the hypothetical basis for this power had been removed as a result of the preceding conflicts, the actual extent and theoretical foundation of this power now changed. The new rulers, who were put in place to guarantee peace and the justice of God (*pax et iustitia*), intensified feudal law, cited Justinian law and often tried to subject the clergy to their legal authority. As we shall see later, this new way of doing things also provoked conflicts with the papacy. These differences were heightened when, in this same period, the clergy, as a unified class and the highest one in Christendom, was consolidated with its own ecclesiastical privileges (*privilegium ordinis*) and its own judicial administration (*privilegium fori*), which prohibited any intervention by secular courts. This meant that, in the eyes of clerical protagonists, the legal situation of late antiquity to which secular rulers made reference had become obsolete.

The theoretical basis for the legitimization of power was deepened on both the secular and clerical side. This process was made easier by the heavier emphasis on and idealization of phenomena of late antiquity as a result of the so-called twelfth-century renaissance, which was also marked by new developments in the schools of that time, leading to a new flowering in the spiritual as well as secular sciences. Though the rediscovery of Roman law may have benefited both sides, it was the clergy, all the way up to the papacy, who profited from the new scholasticism in theology and in church law.

It should also be noted that, by the middle of the twelfth century at the latest, reform fever had pretty much subsided, even though offenses such as simony and marriage of clergymen continued to be dealt with by synods. Popes were no longer at the front lines in implementing ecclesiastical reforms; rather, they were concerned with maintaining and expanding their own position. In so doing, they approved practices which would have been condemned earlier, and not just by radical reformers like Humbert of Silva Candida or Gregory VII. Consequently, criticism of the papacy and the church was on the upswing just at the time when understanding for criticism and interest in doing something about the sad state of affairs in the church were waning among those in power. It was Clement II who, in the end, formulated a decretal (X 5.26.1) stating that criticism of the papacy constituted a serious crime. But, since the religious impetus that had been unleashed, chiefly by Gregory VII, could not even restrain the laity any longer, the vacuity of the "official church" led in the twelfth century to the establishing of religious movements which, except for Catharism, initially demanded reforms. They were soon accused of heresy, however, approving practices that no longer coincided with official doctrine or liturgy. And it was after Lucius III met with Barbarossa in Verona in 1184 that the papacy strove to fight and wipe out, with the help of the "secular arms," all heresies. The lack of interest on the part of the pontiffs in meaningful reforms and a better religious instruction for the laity was one of the main reasons that from the twelfth century Latin Christendom was divided once again. At the same time, this meant that the basis for the historical legitimization of the papal position, namely, the implementation of ecclesiastical reform, could no longer be used. For this reason, it is understandable that henceforth opponents of the papacy used historical arguments, while the popes and their supporters preferred maxims of dogma and church law that were not bound to history.

Let us now examine some of the important events. After the death of Callistus II in 1124, the cardinals united behind the candidacy of Honorius II, not without some difficulty, however. Divergences continued after his death in 1130, when the chancellor, Aimeric, in breach of earlier agreements and with the protection of the Frangipani, had one of his supporters elected pope as Innocent II on February 14. The majority of the cardinals were not present, and on the same day they elected as pope a member of the competing noble family the Pierleoni, Anacletus II. It could not be decided who the proper pope was to be because there were no clear criteria. Consequently, both popes went about trying to gather as many influential supporters as possible. In the end, Innocent II was victorious, with his opponent since then being officially counted as one of the "antipopes." A hundred years earlier, just the opposite view would have held true since Anacletus was able to retain control of Rome while Innocent usually had to reside in Northern Italy or in France. This fact shows clearly just how much the situation had changed. Even though Rome continued to be the nominal residence, it was more important to be acknowledged outside Rome. The different programs of the two candidates did not play as great a role in the election as is often claimed; rather, it was personal connections, and partly the political constellation as well. Anacletus had supporters only in Rome, Southern Italy, Scotland (in opposition to England), and in parts of Southern France, while on Innocent's side stood all the important reform groups—Cluny, Cistercians, canons regular—and most of the bishops and rulers of Germany, France, and England. His most active supporter was Bernard of Clairvaux. Just how deep and lasting the gap was between Innocent and Anacletus is evident, in addition to the mutual invectives, in Innocent's insulting removal from office of Anacletus' cardinals—a move also criticized by Bernard—after his death in 1138. It was also evident in the fact, until 1154, that Innocent's successors were usually chosen from the circle of those who had elected him (Celestine II, Lucius II, Anastasius IV), and in the fact that Anacletus' brother (Giordano Pierleoni) initially headed the autonomous government that was formed in Rome after Innocent's death in 1144. But more about this later.

The influence of local rulers proved to be even stronger in the next schism (1159–1177), the last one for two hundred years, than it had been in this one. This was due in part to the changing situation in politics and within the church. Most of the protagonists of the older generation had recently died, such as Suger of St. Denis (the most important adviser of Louis VI and Louis VII) in 1151; Conrad III of Germany in 1152; Eugen III and Bernard of Clairvaux in 1153; Roger II of Sicily and Stephen of England in 1154; Peter Venerabilis of Cluny in 1156; Alfonso VII of Castile in 1157. New kings like Henry II of England (1154–1189) and Frederick Barbarossa (1152–1190) ushered in a new age, as did Pope Adrian IV (1154–1159). With the treaty of Benevento in 1156, Adrian completed the reorientation of his policies in favor of the Kingdom of Sicily, a move criticized by the cardinals, and one year later snubbed the emperor at a diet in Besançon. Both events led to an estrangement between emperor and pope. When, after Adrian's death in 1159, two popes were elected once again, both of whose legitimacy was disputed, Barbarossa backed the candidate of the minority, Victor IV, while the Sicilian king supported Alexander III since Alexander, as chancellor, had had a decisive hand in the new policies of Adrian IV. In contrast to the dispute in 1130, this time the monastic orders did not speak with one voice: Cluny stalled as long as possible, the main abbeys of the Cistercians voted for Alexander, while among the canons regular there often was great uncertainty. The episcopate was likewise divided over the issue. For these reasons, the heads of states ultimately carried the greatest weight. At first, Barbarossa believed he could convince Louis VII of France and Henry II of England to recognize his pope, though he failed because of his own mistakes. For this reason, Alexander was able to hold a well-attended synod in Tours in 1163. The German position was made more difficult after Victor's death in 1164. His successor, Paschal III, in the end also received help from Barbarossa, who even swore at a diet in Würzburg in 1165 that he and his princes would never acknowledge Alexander. Paschal had clearly become the German choice for pope, but he did not get any tangible support from Henry II, even though Henry was little inclined toward Alexander III on account of conflicts with Thomas Becket (1164–1170). The schism reached its end in 1168 after the death of Paschal, whose successors, Callistus III or even Innocent III, were merely peripheral players. The turning point was Barbarossa's efforts to bring under his rule once and for all the Northern Italian cities that were backed by Alexander III. These were the same cities that had dealt a decisive defeat to Barbarossa near Legnano in 1167. But he was unable to force the cities by military might alone after a major portion of his troops had succumbed to malaria near Rome, and the survivors were battle weary. After a secret preliminary accord in Anagni in 1176, pope and emperor made peace in Venice in 1177. The emperor made a pledge to the pope to retake Rome, in exchange receiving the usufruct of the Mathildine lands and a ceasefire with the Lombard cities, which acknowledged his suzerainity. And just as Innocent II had celebrated the end of the schism by holding a synod in the Lateran in 1139, Alexander III did the same in 1179 by convening the so-called Third Lateran Council. In contrast to 1139, however, the latter council was in fact a "general" one, bringing together around the pope representatives of all Western countries, showing once and for all that the pope was the head of the universal church in the West. Now all that was left to the pope was to regain control over Rome, his bishopric. In this, one of Alexander's short-lived successors, Clement III, was successful when in 1188 he came to terms with the Romans.

With this settlement, which returned control of the city to the pope while temporarily granting the de facto government to the Romans, a conflict was ended which had lasted for almost a half a century. Apart from Guibert (Clement III), even the popes of the investiture controversy and their successors were seldom able to live peacefully in Rome. Their stay in Rome was guaranteed only if the nobility, particularly the Pierleoni and Frangipani, offered protection. Both families were more or less supporters of Anacletus II and therefore opponents of Innocent II. Conflict with Innocent II broke out once again in 1143 as a result of an unsuccessful campaign against Tivoli. The situation intensified in 1144 when most of the nobles were driven out of Rome and a new municipal government was formed that was supported by the middle class and presided over by the Senate, while the militia continued under the leadership of the only nobleman deemed to be cooperative, Giordano Pierleoni. This was considered to be such a significant turning point that Roman documents were dated with a new chro-

nology, the *aera renovationis senatus* (the era of the Senate's renewal). The new authority in Rome was, in fact, purely middle
class, in contrast to Northern Italy. Harking back to antiquity, to
some extent erroneously, the Senate, backed by the radical church
reformer Arnold of Brescia who had been in Rome since 1147,
tried to govern the city, the *caput mundi,* as the sole legitimate
representative of the Roman people. The Senate even went so far
as to offer the imperial crown to Conrad III and Frederick Barbarossa, though these rulers rejected the crown since they were
emperors by the grace of God, not by grace of the people. Backed
by the successors or by the descendants of former officials of the
Lateran palace—such as *primicerius, secundicerius,* and *scrinarius*—
and by the *fraternitas Romana,* the regional union of the Roman
clergy, the Senate was able to exert its legal authority over most of
the Roman churches, which was unique for that time. The agreements with Eugene III and Adrian IV, which lasted only a short
time, did nothing to change the powerlessness of the pontiffs, nor
did the initial support of Victor IV. And in 1167, even the emperor came to terms with the government of the Senate in a treaty.

Roman documents dated after Alexander III—few persons dated
documents after Victor, most were in fact indifferent to him—
show him to have been acknowledged by many churches in Rome,
though he was usually prevented from residing in Rome. The
same held true for his first successor. Only over the Lateran, on
the city's edge, were they occasionally able to retain control. Nevertheless, a change in favor of the papacy gradually started to take
place. Toward the end of Alexander's pontificate, more and more
nobles were included in the Senate. This went so far that, from
time to time, one or two city nobles tried to gain absolute power.
And since members of the same families were also cardinals, there
was a partial overlapping of interests between the Senate and the
College of Cardinals. Therefore, an agreement was only natural
when Paolo Scolari, a Roman, became Pope Clement III. For
Rome's security, the College of Cardinals henceforth recruited
heavily from the nobility of Rome and its surroundings. They built
towers on the most important roads, some of which are still standing today. It was also with Rome's security in mind that, from
Clement II to Gregory IX (1187–1241), only members of such
noble families became popes, the most important of whom, Innocent III, even managed to make the Roman senator—usually there
was only one—a papal agent. Conflicts with the Roman people,

however, as we shall see in the next epoch, were not over. Much more than is often assumed, papal policies now and in the future were shaped by the struggle over getting and keeping power in Rome and the need to take Roman interests into consideration.

It was out of the same interests that pontiffs tried to convince the German emperors—Henry V, Lothair III, Frederick Barbarossa, and Henry VI—to give up the Mathildine lands, and made attempts, in competition with the Roman Senate, to control the castles and abbeys on the most important roads leading out of Rome. In both of these endeavors Innocent III was able to finish what his predecessors had begun.

This strong papal interest in Rome gave rise to criticism because the Romans were considered to be materialistic and deceitful— obviously a one-sided assessment since most of the critics (prelates and chroniclers) were of noble blood and showed little understanding for a municipal government and its economic problems. The policy on crusades of several popes also ran into some criticism. In 1146, at the urging of his mentor, Bernard of Clairvaux, Eugene III took over the spiritual leadership of a new crusade. Since kings and rulers also participated in this crusade, in contrast to the First Crusade, it was to be expected that this one would strengthen the preeminence of the papacy in Western Christendom. But it failed miserably. Though the pope was not to blame for its failure, both he and Bernard were held responsible. Forty years later another Crusade was ready to set out. In 1187, Saladin had wiped out the Christians near Hattin and then conquered Jerusalem. For the last time, there was an extensive mobilization in the West. The popes, and in particular the short-lived Gregory VIII, lent their support to a new Crusade. This one became famous because of the death of Barbarossa in Asia Minor and the conflict between Richard the Lionhearted and Philip Augustus of France. But success was slight compared to the expense that was incurred. Only coastal cities like Acre were reconquered, while Jerusalem remained in Muslim hands. After that, enthusiasm for the Crusades was by and large spent. With this Crusade, however, a development was set in motion that would be important in the following epochs not only for the papacy: the replacing of personal engagement with money. In England and France, the spiritual goodness of a crusade tax was extolled for the first time, the so-called Saladin tithe. Clement III also demanded a tribute from the prelates, though it was not fixed. Out of this came the crusade tithe, which, in the thirteenth century, contributed considerably to the papal budget, though not to the retaking of Jerusalem.

Let us now turn our attention to further institutional developments and the organization of the papal court. If in the "Donation of Constantine" the Roman clergy was compared to the imperial senate, and in the eleventh century the cardinals occasionally were referred to as "senate," by the twelfth century it was evident that the cardinals were active participants in government. Callistus II complained at the beginning of his pontificate that he was much too dependent on the cooperation of the cardinals. This dependence increased during the two schisms as papal opponents had to gain the backing of as many cardinals as possible. Even an energetic pope like Adrian IV had to rescind one of his decisions because the cardinals did not consent to it. One of the most important functions of the cardinals was to work with the papacy in handing down judgments in the *consistorium* (the court). Except in cases of *causae maiores* (jurisdiction over prelates), which popes, with Innocent I as precedent, reserved for themselves and were always expanding to new areas, cases of appeal and trials in which one of the parties overstepped the local court and went directly to the pope, were decided more and more frequently by both the pope and the cardinals. Even authors faithful to the pope such as Bernard of Clairvaux complained that the papal residence had become filled with the bustle of lawyers versed in Roman law, to the detriment of prayer and contemplation. Some popes, including Eugene III, complained about the great burden of dealing with so many trivial cases. Thus, in the second half of the century, the only cases that were allowed were those that dealt with a dispute valued at a minimum of twenty silver coins. And, from the time of Alexander III, it was common to let delegated judges decide regional cases. So, whether a case was decided at the papal court or locally, the avalanche of legal proceedings clearly indicates how much the prestige of the papacy had grown. This new development, heavily criticized by bishops, especially because it limited the traditional episcopal jurisdiction, pointed to a need at that time for fairer justice. Even if misuse is not discounted, the indications are that many plaintiffs and defendants expected a more objective judgment from the papal court than from their own bishop, at whose court local power groups were able to exert their influence. For the same reasons, the general chapter of the Cistercians was in demand as an interregional court. Similar trends were seen in the expansion of royal jurisdiction, especially in England and Sicily.

The cardinals continued to participate in the issuing of new privileges and the confirming of old ones, as seen from their subscriptions. Even though it is unsure to what extent the validity of privileges was dependent on this, it is nevertheless clear that at least the petitioners thought there was some value in having the cardinals involved. The importance of the cardinals was also seen at the Third Lateran Council in 1179. To avoid a future schism, the council decreed in its first canon that a legally elected pope was one who had received two-thirds of the cardinals' votes. Since then, the election of the pope has been an exclusive prerogative of the cardinals. And finally, the activity of the cardinals as legates should be mentioned. They were of particularly great importance during the schism, but also in conflicts with kings, and in deciding the frequently disputed episcopal elections. But even this system of legates provoked criticism as many cardinals traveled throughout the country with grand retinues, at considerable expense to the churches which had to provide for their food and lodging.

The increase in activity required an expansion of the curia. We have little information about this, however. If the traditional *scrinarius* in Rome was able to take over the work of copying and writing, then it must be assumed from the curia's frequent absence from the city that traveling scribes or ones recruited in the places where the curia stayed were employed. They were only responsible for the fair copy, however. The petitioner himself had to work out the content of such documents, especially charters. Papal notaries then composed the rough draft which the pope, and perhaps the cardinals, too, was to approve. Since many cases were the same, forms were drawn up, in particular at the time of Alexander III. Toward the end of his pontificate, a book of cursus (stylistic applications) was put together by the Chancellor Albert of Morra (later Gregory VIII). The book and the forms had to be kept secret to prevent forgeries. The notaries also seem to have held a position of confidence, so that with any change of pope they might be let go, which happened when Clement III began his pontificate. Despite all precautions, there were some forgeries of papal documents. Innocent III, for example, exposed a forgery operation that had flourished under Celestine III. Occasionally, a pope even retracted some decisions because they had been made without full knowledge of the actual circumstances. The chancery continued to be directed by the chancellor, though this function, perhaps for financial reasons, could also be carried out by the pope, particularly when he himself had once been chancellor, as was the case with Alexander III and Gregory VIII.

In this period, the position of chamberlain was of growing significance. Two cardinals in particular, Boso (1154–1159) and Cencius Savelli (1188–1197), should be mentioned in this regard. Beginning with Boso at the latest, the chamberlain was responsible for all the income and expenditures of the papal court and directly administered a few localities in the Papal States whenever the political situation allowed it. From the time of Boso, a tax roll and property register were made up for better control, the most famous of which is the *Liber censuum* of Cencius of 1192. From this, we learn that the chamberlain was allowed to excommunicate those unwilling to pay taxes and was, except for the chancery, head of all the curials, in other words, a sort of personnel director and disciplinary judge. Business had grown so much since the consolidation of Rome under Clement III and Celestine III that the chamberlain had his own scribes and assistants (*clerici camere*) at his disposal. The state of affairs must have often been catastrophic earlier, since traveling was often more like escaping, which made an orderly administration impossible. For example, during his stay in France, Alexander III did not know what regular revenue was due to him. As a result, he and his court lived from so-called "procurations," that is, at the expense of the host or the visitors to the curia.

There is not much information about the rest of the court officials. We know little, for example, about the papal chapel. Most likely, its members took part regularly in worship services at the palace and were entrusted with mostly work in the chancery. Since many of them were ordained only as subdeacons, the designations *subdiaconus* and *capellanus* were often synonymous. For the church as a whole, it was important that, from this time on, the pope ordained as subdeacons foreign clerics who would act as honorary papal chaplains once they returned home. This situation did not sit well with their bishops since such subdeacons were allowed to receive futher ordinations only from the pope or someone acting on his behalf, and even in the case of a serious crime they were exculsively under papal jurisdiction.

Exemptions of this kind, as well as the conditions at the papal court, were criticized. Only a few cardinals were felt to be incorrupt, not to mention the lower curials. Moreover, from the time of Innocent II's pontificate, some popes reclaimed foreign benefices for relatives and curials. Soon, the cry went up for a reform of the curia. Victor IV was the first pope who wanted to fulfill this wish by suggesting that cardinals and curials be given a fixed income from the cathedral churches and that all tribute and "gifts" to the curia be forbidden. The only person to react positively to this suggestion was the emperor. Since then, suggestions of this kind were part and parcel of the reform repertoire of rulers critical of the pope, and later also of councils. The only pope of this time period to develop similar ideas was Gregory VIII, and perhaps the chamberlain Cencius as well, though with no more success than Victor IV had. As a result, the curia remained an easy target for both honorable critics and wicked satirists.

If we consider that, despite all of his new duties, one of the most important tasks of the pope continued to be that of supreme liturgist of his episcopal city and his court, then the significance of the twelfth century for the papal liturgy and ceremonial may become clearer. With the pontificate of Innocent II, the noting of papal rituals was taken up again for the first time in a long time, similar to the court historiography that had ended in the late ninth century, only to be continued after the schism of 1130 by Anacletus' Cardinal Pandulf and Alexander III's Cardinal Boso. And, in contrast to the historiography that ended with Boso—later there were still *vitae* of just a few popes—the writing of liturgical ordos was on the rise from 1140 until the end of the Middle Ages, with twelfth-century texts often serving as examples for later authors, until the beginning of the Avignon epoch. Though the ordos of this epoch, without exception, had no official character, they nevertheless offered sufficient explanation of how the pope, as liturgist, was to act.

If one studies these texts, what is remarkable is that they all assume the presence of the pope in Rome. In the texts, the pope is considered first and foremost the bishop of Rome. These texts, then, were mostly written down for interested persons who were suitable as potential participants in the liturgy when the curia was in Rome—during the latter part of Innocent II's pontificate (1140–1143) and from the time of the Third Lateran Council in 1179. The ties of the pope with Rome also explain why what were typical conditions for the period of the Tusculan popes were presented as still existing and why, for example, in processions, the cardinal-deacons did not have a role as members of the College of Cardinals, but as officials of the Lateran Palace. And in spite of the internationalization of the papacy and curia, palace personnel held a higher rank than prelates, including cardinal-bishops and cardinal-priests, who were further removed from the pope. Only beginning with Innocent III would this change.

The ceremonial was also representative of some of the changes that had come about since the investiture controversy. This is not only visible in the use of concepts like "curia" in the texts, and in the fact that the chamberlain, from the time of Clement III, was responsible for the dispensation of the colleges of priests, for papal donations to cardinals and others on important feast days, and for expenses for such functions as processions. Even more so, it was seen, for the time being, in the immantation, as the most important constitutive act in the installation of a pope, as descriptions from the beginning of the pontificates of Victor IV and Alexander III show. In addition, the enthronement and the taking possession of the Lateran Palace were particularly significant acts. Perhaps it was precisely because Victor IV, in 1159, portrayed himself as the "legal" pope, basing his claim on the ceremonial, that at a council in 1179 Alexander III made sure that the various liturgical acts relating to a papal installation were reduced in their legal significance, making the election by two-thirds of the cardinals as the sole relative criterium for the future.

While the immantation was evidence of the pope's equal rank with the emperor, it was also in this period that the pope's aspect as the supreme ruler was emphasized. For this reason, there was an increase in the significance of the tiara in the ceremonial as the most important symbol of secular power; in churches utilized by the pope, the use of porphyry was on the rise. Moreover, two of the popes who were Romans by birth, Innocent II and Anastasius IV, had themselves buried in imperial sarcophagi, Innocent in Hadrian's, Anastasius in that of Constantine's mother, Helena, while in the Lateran Palace, Innocent II had Emperor Lothair depicted in a painting as papal vassal for the Mathildine lands, which made Barbarossa angry. What is more, Barbarossa himself was required to perform the ritual marshall duty of leading the papal horse by the reins, which emphasized the apparent subordination of the emperor to the pope. And finally, Clement III, once he had achieved supremacy over Rome, had the "Donation of Constantine" depicted in paintings in the newly constructed entrance hall to the Lateran basilica, thereby documenting his attitude toward the city of Rome.

The pope's connection with Rome is not only spoken of in the liturgical texts. It becomes much more obvious in such areas as architecture that the pontiffs were trying once again to unite Rome according to their directives. In particular , the two most important basilicas, Lateran and St. Peter's, whose canons were in stiff competition with each other at the time, began at that time to include elements of the papal liturgy for festivals at which the pope did not officiate. Other basilicas, too, like S. Lorenzo fuori le mura, began this practice. The pope's worship chambers were usually two chapels in the Lateran. There was the Nicholas chapel, perhaps built by Callistus II, where the papal chaplain worked, and the private chapel of S. Lorenzo, probably built by Leo III. The latter chapel was now elevated in importance inasmuch as only the pope was allowed to celebrate mass at its altar, with this exclusivity then carried over to the main altars in the Lateran basilica and in St. Peter's. The Lateran's supposed relics, including the rod of Aaron and the Ten Commandments of Moses, clearly symbolized that, in the papacy's eyes, Rome had replaced Jerusalem as the most holy site in Christendom. Thus this chapel was now called *sancta sanctorum* as the temple in Jerusalem once was.

If the spiritual preeminence of the papacy was evident in the liturgy, then its position as supreme lawmaker and judge was also evident in the expansion of canon law, which had been propagated by the papacy and its supporters from the time of Gregory VII in particular. To better understand this change, various internal changes in the church must be taken into consideration. Until the beginning of the twelfth century, the papacy largely depended on the various monastic and canonical movements, while from the time of Callistus II the epsicopate, in particular, was also included. This was made easier by the fact that new movements like the Cistercian and the Premonstratensian initially declined any exemptions. These new orders changed their minds, however, when their zest for reform began to fade around the middle of the century. Because, on the one hand, Alexander III was dependent on the support of the episcopate during the schism, without being able to renounce the support of the orders on the other hand, he pursued conflicting policies regarding privileges. His position, and that of his successors, was further complicated by the fact that the development of clerical privileges, which was encouraged by the papacy, ran into official opposition in important countries as the rulers themselves of these countries wanted to expand their control over the clergy. And, finally, it should be stressed that the ecclesiastical system of justice was, except for the False Decretals, very much shaped by Roman law, while the content and form of papal privileges and mandates often broke new ground. It was these privileges that influenced the new scientific discipline of ecclesiastical law, especially from the time of Alexander III.

Around 1140, a lawyer probably teaching in Bologna by the name of Gratian—whose name, contrary to earlier assertions, is the only thing certain we know about him—tried, with the help of the new scholastic method, to bring some conformity to the earlier, often contradictory church laws. For this reason, he named his work *Concordia discordantium canonum* (concordance of contradictory canons), though it was later referred to as the *Decretum Gratiani*. Although it was labored over privately, the work was soon used in law schools as an authoritative collection of traditional ecclesiastical law. Since it was incomplete, supplements (*paleae*), and later, appendixes, were added. What is more, collections of texts were produced that were handed down detached from the *Decretum* (extravagants). What is important for our theme is that, in the appendixes, and especially in the collections, the number of which increased in particular during the latter part of Alexander III's pontificate, the major portion of the texts were papal decretals that had been issued since the time of Leo IX, principally those of Alexander III. And since the collections were also compiled in Spain and England, which were outside Alexander's home territory of Italy and France, it can easily be surmised from them how far the validity of papal promulgations for the doctrine of canon law had reached. This can be seen in commentaries to the *Decretum*, which from circa 1160 were on the increase, and in which papal decretals are often cited as examples of current law. This compiling of laws was capped off in circa 1190 by the cathedral prior of Pavia, Bernardus Balbi, who systematically organized all the important extravagants in five books. He expressly mentioned that his intention was one of wanting to serve not only teachers of law but also judges. And since his collection—known as *Compilatio prima* (first collection)—soon gained a general recognition in law schools and in courts, he contributed enormously—he was himself active in the curia before 1187—as did many other commentators on the decrees, to the general recognition of papal texts as the valid legal norm. In other words, the actual implementation of papal law for all of Western Christendom was not so much due to the papacy itself but to the many compilers and commentators who formed a uniform law out of disparate texts. And since some cardinals and popes (Gregory VIII, perhaps Alexander III, too) were active as law teachers from the middle of the twelfth century, and in the following epoch from Innocent III on, almost every pope was educated as a lawyer, seldom as a theologian, the law schools made a considerable contribution to the lawyerization of the papacy and the curia.

Germany played only a small part initially in the compiling of laws that has just been described. This was partly because those persons wanting to study law usually went to Italy or France. Another reason, however, was probably the continuous conflict between the pope and the emperor. In this regard, it should be emphasized that, until 1197, the emperors, in particular Frederick Barbarossa and Henry VI, pretty much had control over the German church. Thus new theories that were developed during this period to clarify the relationship between the emperor and the pope still did not carry much weight. However, because they formed the basis of the policies pursued by Innocent III after 1198 and by his successor, they will be summarized as follows.

Apart from a few exceptions like Gregory VIII, the papacy and its adherents now interpreted Gelasius' doctrine of two powers to mean that spiritual power was above secular power. This interpretation, which had been championed since the investiture controversy, underwent an intensification with the so-called doctrine of the two swords, as it was put initially, not so much by the popes as by several of their supporters, such as Bernard of Clairvaux or John of Salisbury, as well as by canonists. Starting from the premise that the meaning of a passage from the Gospel of Luke—Luke 22:38: "Lord, behold, here are two swords. And he said unto them, it is enough"—was typological, the new theory, which was further developed in the thirteenth century and received a dogmatic form in Boniface VIII's infamous constitution of 1302, *Unam sanctam,* stated that Christ had entrusted two swords to Peter and, by extension, to the church headed by him. One sword symbolized spiritual jurisdiction and was administered by the church itself. The other was a symbol of criminal jurisdiction and was used on behalf of the church by the "secular arm," that is, by kings and rulers. The latter case meant that secular governments exercised their power merely on behalf of the church, and they could be replaced if they displeased the papacy. It must be stressed, however, that these conclusions were not approved by all ecclesiastical authors. And finally, the translation theory formulated at the time of Alexander III and Innocent III should be mentioned, for it states that Leo III took the imperial crown away from the Greeks and gave it to the Franks, whose successors were the Germans. This doctrine could also be used as a basis for deposing a ruler.

As already indicated, these doctrines were, more than anything, still theoretical speculation during the twelfth century. In countries like Germany, Sicily—in particular after the treaty of Benevento in 1156—and even Hungary, it was largely the rulers who controlled the local churches, held the power of judicial constraint even over the clergy, and thus usually determined for themselves how far the arm of the pope was to reach. For a long time this was also true of the church's position in England. Though the church was able to improve its position during the confusion after the death of Henry I (1137–1154), Henry II, from the beginning of his reign, won back the traditional control over the church, which was also advocated by the Anglo-Norman canonists. Thus, initially, Henry emerged unscathed from the dispute with the archbishop of Canterbury, Thomas Becket, who from the time of the constitutions of Clarendon in 1164 denied, among other things, that the king had jurisdiction over clerics who had committed crimes. Only after Becket's murder in 1170, for which the king was held partially to blame, did the page turn in favor of the church. It was from circa 1180, in particular, when Henry felt squeezed by the new French king Philip Augustus and by his own sons, requiring the intercession and help of the papacy, that he felt compelled to grant the church more freedom, in most cases by exempting it from secular jurisdiction and allowing appeals to be made to the pope as well as the entry of papal legates into the country. During the reign of Henry's sons, Richard and John, the papacy was finally able to expand its influence, so that England became an important address when papal decretals were sent out, decretals that were zealously collected in England.

The core of papal influence for the time being, however, was still France. This was due to the spiritual advisers of the king, such as Suger of St. Denis, as well as to the role of the reform orders and to the frequent visits of the popes to this country, where also many of the popes had studied and from among whose ecclesiastics they elected many cardinals. Even when Philip Augustus began to expand his royal authority to areas that had previously been mostly free of royal influence, and by doing so ran into conflict with Henry II, who ruled more than half of France, the alliance with the papacy held up since he was dependent on the papacy's help.

The position of the papacy on the Iberian peninsula was almost just as strong. Papal protection over Aragon continued, evident, for example, in the regulations concerning succession and the unification with Catalonia in 1151, as well as in the new ecclesiastical organization. The situation in the western part of the peninsula was more complicated. Through war and diplomacy Alfonso Henriquez gradually managed to create a Kingdom of Portugal independent of Catalonia, for which he had been requesting since 1143 not only the approval of the papacy but also, like Aragon, its protection. From time to time this rendered the relationship between the papacy and Castile more difficult. In conjunction with these desires for autonomy, efforts were also undertaken to achieve the independence of the Portuguese church, which ran counter to the claims of Toledo and Santiago, though relations between the primate of Toledo and the archbishop of Santiago were still unsettled. Because of this, representatives of the three competing archbishoprics traveled continuously to the pope and brought lawsuits before the curia, with the result that legates were frequently sent to their territories. Even though the conflict was not settled until 1215 at the Fourth Lateran Council, it set the stage for a lasting papal presence in Spain.

Areas on the northern and eastern frontiers of Europe also fell under the protection of the papacy. The church organization in Scandinavia was set up by legates, in particular Nicholas Breakspear, who later became Pope Adrian IV. In Slavic areas such as Bohemia, reform synods for the implementation of celibacy in particular took place under the chairmanship of papal legates. Even if their success was minimal at the beginning, it was nevertheless clear that the papacy was now acknowledged in all Catholic lands as the highest church authority in matters of law and doctrine.

It was all the more difficult, then, for the papacy to put up with the fact that it had a relatively weak position vis-à-vis the emperor, which meant not only in Germany but also in most of Northern and Central Italy. This condition grew even worse when Henry

VI—who Celestine III reluctantly crowned emperor in 1191—gained dominion over the lower Italian kingdom for his wife Constance, the daughter of Roger II, after the death of William II of Sicily in 1189 in a brutal battle. The popes, meanwhile, as liege lords over the Normans, advanced the claims of Tancred of Lecce. After Tancred's death in 1194, Henry was master of the situation, and in 1196 wanted to obtain from the pope succession to the crown for his son Frederick, not only in Sicily but in Germany as well. The methods he used to put pressure on the pope—occupation of the Mathildine lands and part of the Papal States by his brother Philip and ministerials like Markward of Annweiler—showed the curia how precarious their secular rule was, as well as perhaps even their ecclesiastical position, as a result of the German occupation of surrounding territories. It was therefore a gift from heaven when, in the autumn of 1197, Henry VI died, leading to chaos over the crown in both his kingdoms. Innocent III had the chance to use this opportunity for the papacy's benefit when he was elected on January 8, 1198, at the age of 37, as successor to Celestine III, who had died at 93. Not only did the "era of the hoary popes" come to an end, but the papacy was on its way to the peak of its power.

VIII

The Papacy at the Peak of Its Power (1198–1303)

The changes that occurred in the course of the thirteenth century are shown most clearly in the contrast between the first and last popes of this period. Innocent III and Boniface VIII represented largely the same position. Yet Innocent was highly successful in his politics, and is therefore much admired by historians of the papacy—he is considered the greatest pope of the Middle Ages—while Boniface was frustrated in almost every endeavor. This was not so much because of his overemphasis on the pretentions of the papacy—the traditional criticism—but because of a fundamental change underway in the relationship between church and state. Innocenct III had to check, above all, the expansionistic desires of secular rulers, and in so doing received the support of their respective rivals and of leading prelates. At the end of the thirteenth century, however, the rulers of France and England, the two most important countries for the papacy, were no longer quite as interested in expanding their kingdoms as they were in consolidating their rule at home. That consolidation included the desire to subjugate and tax the clergy under their jurisdiction. To this end, they were supported in part by ecclesiastics of their kingdoms, since many prelates, and especially the lower clerics, felt first and foremost a kinship to their native country and therefore wanted to reduce the possibility of papal interference—an important indication of the future collaboration between ruler and church. Another sign of the changes was the relationship of the papacy to Rome and the Papal States, often the center point of papal politics.

The basis of papal policies toward Rome remained the aforementioned agreement of 1188 between Clement III and the Senate. If at that time the interests of both sides were guaranteed, it was not long before Innocent III tried to place the municipal government more firmly under his control. He was so successful that henceforth usually only one senator ruled the city, and this as a papal agent. By way of some adept exploitation of Rome's desires for expansion, for example vis-à-vis Viterbo, the objectives of both Innocent III's papacy and the municipal government coincided. This was also true for the papacy of his successor, Honorius III. Signs of relative stability were everywhere, including the expansion of the Lateran, a new residence at St. Peter's and the construction, restoration, and embellishment of many churches in Rome. The construction of residential towers by the Conti and Savelli families and their close allies also served toward securing the papal position. By the time of Gregory IX, however, the situation for the papacy began to deteriorate. The Roman nobility as well as some ordinary citizens exploited Gregory's conflict with Frederick II to regain some autonomy. This tendency became even more pronounced after Gregory's death. His short-lived successor, Celestine IV, was elected under conditions that were ignominious for the cardinals as they succumbed to the power and influence of the Frangipani and Orsini. As a consequence, except for Adrian V and Nicholas IV, no more popes of that century were elected in Rome. The new site for papal elections as well as the preferred papal residence were such cities as Anagni and Viterbo as well as Orvieto and Rieti. Exploiting this opportune moment, the Romans built up municipal power once again during the pontificate of Innocent IV under the leadership of Senator Brancaleone degli Andalò, who had over one hundred aristocratic towers built. Nevertheless, the popes of the second half of the century were constantly striving, as had their predecessors a hundred years before, to win back control of Rome. The most successful were, above all, Nicholas III, who had himself named senator of Rome, and Boniface VIII, though neither was ever able to settle fully their differences with their adversaries in Rome.

From the time of Innocent III, the popes stepped up their efforts to realize their claim of dominion over Central Italy, a claim advanced since the Donation of Pepin. Innocent himself succeeded in establishing his control, especially around Rome (Campagna and Maritima) and in southern Tuscany (Patrimonium S. Petri in Tuscia). He ruled the areas which the Roman Senate had previously wanted to subjugate, and so is considered the founder of the Papal States. Visible signs nowadays of the papacy's early control are the works of Roman *cosmati*, artists who decorated churches and cloisters in Rome and its vicinity with mosaics and small sculptures. These artists were probably initially supporters of the city of Rome, many referring to themselves as "Roman citizens," and yet they received their commissions from popes and cardinals. It can be assumed, then, that their employers were in control of the place where the *cosmati* worked. The later popes were able, especially after Frederick II's death (1250), to expand their rule—at least nominally—to the duchy of Spoleto, the Marches and, after the abdication of Rudolf of Hapsburg in 1279, to Romagna, including Bologna. These regions were administered by rectors who were usually cardinals or papal curates.

The papal domination, however, was by no means total, especially in the areas which were added later. Usually, the pope was acknowledged as merely a nominal sovereign, while the traditional authority—part municipal government, part family dynasty—continued to exist. This was true even for the core area, since cities like Viterbo or Orvieto, sites of the new papal residences, kept their municipal governments, and the popes, while residing in these cities, had to come to contractual agreements with these local governments. Nevertheless, the papacy profited from its new power since not only ecclesiastical institutions such as bishophrics and abbeys had to pay tribute, but also secular powers, thereby contributing to the support of the curia.

The Papal States were already at that time, however, somewhat detrimental to the position of the papacy as a whole. Because of the many conflicts with Rome and with other local municipalities and rulers, the papacy's overall ecclesiastical policy became more and more driven by ambitions in Central Italy. Moreover, the political means which many popes used to obtain or expand their control provoked criticism. Nepotism was used as a personal political instrument, even more than it had been by many of their predecessors. In addition, they called for crusades to be able to do battle more successfully against personal opponents and ambitious cities, whom they denounced as heretics—a fusion of the church's leadership claim with its secular interests that was not exactly conducive to the Christianization of the world. The situation became complicated as some pontiffs, to secure the Mathildine lands and the southern Italian border, were continually running into conflict, first with the Hohenstaufen, and later with the Aragonese rulers, thereby allowing local objectives to dictate their overall policy toward Europe.

This mixture of church power, personal politics and a "grand foreign policy" for the implementation of local rule was evident as early as Innocent III. This pontiff understood much better, however, than most of his successors, how to base his intentions on, or even to conceal them in, arguments of theology and canon law. This can be seen clearly in the stand he took in favor of Otto IV over Philip of Swabia in the dispute over the German throne from 1198 to 1208. Because Philip, as representative of his brother Henry VI, ruled Tuscany and the Mathildine lands rather brutally and had already been excommunicated, and because barons in Sicily, under the leadership of Hohenstaufen ministers fought against the caretaker government of the pope—Innocent had been designated testamentarily as guardian of Frederick II by the emperor's widow, Constance—the pope refused to recognize Philip for fear that Rome and the Patrimonium Petri would again be surrounded and cut off. Thus before his coronation in 1209, Otto IV had to renounce claims to the Mathildine lands and promise not to attack Southern Italy. When the emperor then broke his promise and carried out the traditional imperial policy toward Southern Italy, he was excommunicated as an "enemy of the church." The pope then quickly crowned Frederick II as king of Sicily, and in 1212 as the German king. To avoid Rome's being cut off again, the pope made Frederick swear that he would have his son, Henry VII, crowned king of Sicily as soon as possible. However, the same game repeated itself, even though in Germany the emperor's sons, first Henry, and then Conrad IV, replaced their father as kings. Because Frederick, like his grandfather Barbaróssa, began to subjugate Lombardy while attacking the Papal States and backing the aspirations for autonomy in Rome, the secular power of the papacy was threatened with ruin. For this reason, Frederick was excommunicated again by Gregory IX and then, in 1245 at the First Council of Lyon, he was solemnly deposed as an enemy of the church and a heretic by Innocent IV, and a crusade was called for against him. This act, however, had little effect in Italy for the time being as Louis IX of France, who was later canonized, refused to cooperate with the pope. Only in Germany, where rival claimants to the throne were immediately chosen and where the so-called *interregnum* had been in effect since 1256, did papal policies, which were weighted in favor of Italian interests, contribute to a weakening of central authority.

To break the power of Frederick II in Sicily, where the pope himself was liege lord, Innocent IV looked for candidates from other ruling families. This was also meant to break the power of Frederick's energetic bastard son, Manfred (d. 1266), after Frederick's and Conrad IV's deaths in 1250 and 1254 respectively. Edmund, the son of Henry III of England, was the favorite candidate for a long time. But success came first to Charles I of Anjou, a brother of Louis IX of France, thanks especially to the fact that, at that time, two French popes followed in a row, Urban IV and Clement IV. Rewarded with Sicily in 1265 by Clement, Charles was the leader of a papal crusade, in the course of which he defeated first Manfred in 1266, and then Conradin in 1268, whom he then executed for treason in Naples. Even more unscrupulous than his Hohenstaufen predecessors, Charles strove for control over all of Italy, and to this end had himself elected as senator in Rome and to the *podestà* in Florence. The extent to which his drive for power unsettled the curia was evident in the papal election after the death of Clement IV. Depending on who held the majority in the College of Cardinals, either an Anjou rival (Gregory X, Nicholas III) or Anjou supporter (in particular Martin IV, a Frenchman) was elected.

The situation grew very murky after the Sicilian Vespers of 1282, in the aftermath of which Charles was limited to Naples and its surroundings, while on Sicily henceforth Aragonese kings ruled. Martin IV then wanted to see a crusade led against Aragon, for which he found little support, however. Recognition of the Sicilian kings was disputed for decades, supplying the source for new conflicts in the next epoch. Crafty diplomacy guaranteed the annexation of Corsica and Sardinia—both considered papal fiefs on the basis of the Donation of Constantine—for the Aragonese king, James II, who understandably distanced himself from his brother, the king of Sicily. The curia, on the other hand, oriented itself more toward Naples because of the ongoing "Sicilian question," the result being that the ruler of Naples continued to have a big influence on the election and the government of popes.

As mentioned, concern over the maintenance of secular power brought about increasing nepotism at the papal court. Innocent III preferred having his relatives in the College of Cardinals, in senatorial offices, and in the archpresbytery of important churches like St. Peter's. Meanwhile, members of rival families like the Savelli, to which the chamberlain and the chancellor of his predecessor, Cencio, belonged, were removed from office. The carousel turned when in 1216 Cencio became pope under the name Honorius III, and again, when Gregory, a relative of Innocent III, began his pontificate in 1227. Later pontiffs like Nicholas III (Orsini) and Boniface VIII (Caetani) successfully used nepotism. Ruling popes granted important cities in the Papal States to members of their own or friends' families. This meant that a change of popes promised to bring with it a saturation of the control of the favored clan, while threatening the group thrown out of power with losses that it was not at all willing to accept. Thus the thirteenth century is not only the age of ascendancy of new families—Conti, Annibaldi, Orsini, Colonna, Caetani—which to some extent have profited even into the present era from the increase in property they gained at this time, it is also a phase of continuous family power struggles in the Papal States, in Rome and in the College of Cardinals.

In addition to nepotism, there is another phenomenon to take into consideration that is not mentioned in many histories of the papacy: the *familia,* a personal clientele usually not based on a blood relationship. The most respected *familia* was of course the pope's, which at this time largely consisted of members of the papal *capella.* Not only every cardinal, however, but also every chaplain or high curial had his own *familia.* If one of these rose to the position of cardinal, then he could provide his familiars even better benefits than before, and even more so if he became pope, for in this case, his old *familia* would form the core of the papal chapel. As a result, belonging to certain *familiae* was not only important for a career in the curia or even for the papacy—little wonder that most curials were Italians—but also for the secular and religious policies of the popes since many nuncios and legates were chosen because, as former familiars, as chaplains or as cardinals, they were close to the pope. For the same reason, ambitious foreign clerics began their careers as familiars of cardinals, among them famous canonists like Godfrey of Trani or Raymond of Pennafort. Prospects were even better if, as a student, one befriended someone who was later to become a cardinal or pope, as the ascendancy of men like Robert Courçon or Stephen Langton under Innocent III shows.

A further consequence of the continuous struggles for Rome was the estrangement of the papacy from the city. The frequent necessity to stay in other residences because of this state of affairs caused officials such as *iudices, addextratores* (representatives of the nobility at ceremonies), *schola cantorum* and others, whose work was connected with Rome and who until now had managed to survive, to lose their rights. The once important *statio* services could only seldom be practiced as a sign of the liturgical collaboration of bishop, clergy, and people. The only exceptions were Innocent III, Nicholas III and, to some extent, Boniface VIII. And formerly constitutive ceremonies, like the enthronement in St. Peter's and the taking possession of the Lateran, were losing their significance. Henceforth, the most important act in the investiture of a new pope after his election was the crowning with the tiara, the symbol of secular power. That is why, from the end of the thirteenth century to present times, the act of investiture in general has been referred to as a coronation (*coronatio*). The new regulations under Innocent III regarding precedence in papal processions showed just how much Rome had to give in to represent the entire church: instead of members of the Lateran Palace and the Roman clergy, from now on it was cardinals as well as representatives of the universal church (patriarchs, archbishops, bishops) who walked directly in front of the pope. Thus, even more so than in the investiture controversy, the break with traditions became visible. In the following epoch, this break grew deeper because of the move to Avignon, even continuing into modern times after the return to Rome.

As mentioned previously, interests in Central Italy largely determined papal relations to secular rulers. This was especially evident in the policy toward Germany, which was co-ordinated with the security of Rome and the Papal States in mind and which also had far-reaching consequences for Germany itself. With this policy as a guideline, Innocent III, during the German dispute over the throne (1198–1208), defined the papal position regarding the election of German kings, in particular in his decretal of 1202 called the *Venerabilem*. He granted to the princes of the realm the sole right to choose the German king, although he reserved for the papacy the right to check their decision, which included the right to reject it. He based this on the fact that the reversion of every German king to the imperial throne depended on its being conferred by the pope. With this, the pope had enough possibilities at his disposal in any political configuration to intervene in the succession of German kings. The *Venerabilem* was quickly made part of the official collection of canon law and remained unchallenged even in Germany. It was observed well into the sixteenth century, remaining in force, theoretically at least, until 1917. And from the late thirteenth century, even the actual election of the kings was held more and more in the manner of church elections.

The papacy's interests in Central Italy brought about renewed struggles with the Hohenstaufen, with papal feelings of resentment continuing after Frederick II was deposed. After 1245, Innocent IV backed the rival claimants to the throne, Henry Raspe and William of Holland, with both money and legates, and his successors also let themselves be guided by anti-Hohenstaufen sentiments. Therefore, they not only rejected the candidacies for the crown of Conrad IV and Conradin, but during the interregnum they leaned more toward Richard of Cornwall, since his opponent, Alfonso X of Castile, was related to the Hohenstaufen. Relations with Rudolf of Hapsburg and Albrecht I were also frequently determined by the idea of not allowing the papacy's own power in Italy, or that of the Anjou's, to be endangered by German attacks. Only pontiffs such as Gregory X and Nichloas III tried to limit the power of Charles I in Italy and worked for a closer collaboration with the German king. These ventures did not last long, however. One of the consequences of this was that, after 1220 and until 1312, no more imperial coronations took place, and Italy, and with it the papacy, became increasingly estranged from Germany.

Ties with France were therefore strengthened all the more. France was where many curials and cardinals, and therefore popes, had studied. Those popes and cardinals who were not Italian were mostly French, among them several abbots of Cîteaux. A major portion of papal income in the thirteenth century probably came from France. The two important councils of 1245 and 1274 were held in Lyon, which, though theoretically a part of the Holy Roman Empire, was shaped by French culture. The French crown also profited from this connection. The wars of the first decades of the thirteenth century against the Cathars in Southern France, incited by the papacy, were just as profitable for the expansion of the crown's territory as was the inquisition that the papacy encouraged later. And the promotion of Charles of Anjou that began with Urban IV solidified French influence, not only on the papacy, but also in the Mediterranean area. It was directly due to these close mutual ties that the conflict between Philip the Fair and Boniface VIII, which I will go into later, deeply affected the position of the papacy.

Papal relations with England were more complicated. The fact alone that King John did not support Otto IV, who was backed by the pope and related to John, aroused the anger of the pope. The situation came to a head when, in 1207 in Rome, Innocent consecrated his old college friend and cardinal, Stephen Langton, as archbishop of Canterbury after a disputed episcopal election in Canterbury. The king, however, refused to acknowledge him. John's policy of leaving as many bishoprics and abbeys vacant for as long as possible to use their temporalities for himself during such vacancies heightened the conflict. The result was that in 1211 Innocent excommunicated the king and threatened to have him deposed. He also placed the country under an interdict, and encouraged an invasion of England, which he declared to be a crusade, by the successor to the French throne. Militarily weak, John gave in, declaring his kingdom a fief to the pope in 1213. The pope then became liege lord of England, and in this capacity received one thousand silver coins in annual tribute from the king. One of the first consequences of the new power structure was that Innocent did not acknowledge the Magna Carta, which had been wrung from the king in 1215 and in the writing of which Stephen Langton had participated. When, in 1216, John's rivals invited the successor to the French throne to cross the Channel and to take the English throne, the pope stood on John's side. After John's death in 1216, the cardinal legate in England, Guala, helped the young Henry III to the throne. For decades after that, relations between England and the papacy were especially close, outward evidence of which is still visible today in Westminster Abbey, where Roman *cosmati* worked on behalf of the king, the only example of their art outside Italy. Along with France, England was also, from 1213, a major contributor to papal income, and from the middle of the century meted out many benefices to curials and cardinals. Church law in England also bore the mark of the papacy. Just as in France, however, efforts were underway by the end of the century to reduce papal influence.

From the time of Innocent III, the papacy was able to intervene more intensively than ever in the internal affairs of Spain. In 1204, Peter II was the first Aragonese king who had himself crowned by the pope as his overlord. The actions taken against Peter III of Aragon and his successor after the Sicilian Vespers of 1282, and the deposing of Sancho II of Portugal in 1245, show that the papacy ascribed to itself, through its position as liege lord, a regulatory role that could go as far as the deposing of a king. Ecclesiastical affairs also were now more than ever adapted to the papal line. The long-standing dispute among Toledo, Santiago, and Braga was settled at the Fourth Lateran Council in 1215 to the detriment of Toledo. Henceforth the archbishop of Toledo enjoyed only an honorary preeminence; in reality, all three archbishoprics were on equal footing. Through legates such as the cardinal, Jean de Abbeville (1228–1230), this new papal right was asserted at synods. As a result, for the first time, the Cortes prohibited marriage for clergymen and papal dictums were included in the new Castilian statute book, Alfonso X's *Siete Partidas*. It is hardly surprising, then, that after the conquest of Estremadura and Andalusia, the reorganization of bishoprics was undertaken largely according to papal guidelines. The kings were not so eager to follow papal instructions, however, when their own personal advantage was at stake. For example, Sancho VII of Navarre concluded an alliance with the Moors over the protests of Innocent III. And when it came to royal divorce or marriage, the admonishments or prohibitions of the pope often fell on deaf ears.

The papal attitude toward Constantinople was ambivalent. After initial hesitation, Innocent III consented to the frightful conquest of Constantinople in 1204 by participants of the Fourth Crusade and to the establishment of a Latin empire there, although a crusade was only allowed to be led against enemies of the faith.But the consequences were too enticing for Innocent: for the first time, there was a patriarch of Constantinople who acknowledged the supremacy of the papacy. That the pope was hardly acknowledged at all among the Greek clergy and people was no bother to him. The triumph did not last long, however, for in 1261 Michael VIII Palaiologos reconquered Constantinople, resulting in the return to rule of a Greek patriarch who, of course, rejected the papal claims. Thus Urban IV and Clement IV, as Frenchmen, backed the attempts by Charles I of Anjou to gain, by way of Sicily, hegemony over Constantinople by force. The Italian Gregory X had other ideas. He planned a grand crusade to reconquer Jerusalem, for which he also sought support in Constantinople; for his part, Emperor Michael was interested in a settlement with the West. After lengthy preliminary discussions, and for the first time since the split in 1054, a union of churches between Greeks and Latins was concluded at the Second Council of Lyon in 1274. At first, even Gregory's successors held to this. The union did not last, however, as in the East the inflexible demands of the West for acknowledgment of the *Filioque* and of papal supremacy were rejected outright. The union ended with the death of the emperor in 1282.

In addition to the futile union with the Greeks, there was another spectacular event that came out of the Council of Lyon, and this in regard to a new crusade: the participation at the council of an embassy from the Great Khan of the Mongols. Innocent IV, impressed by the Mongol assault, had earlier sent representatives to Karakorum, the Mongolian capital. From the negotiations, Gregory X hoped to be able to attack the Palestinian Muslims from the East. This plan failed, though it resulted in the toleration of Franciscans as missionaries in Persia and China on the part of the Il-Khans, with the Franciscans later founding an archbishopric in Peking, and in so doing, contributing greatly to the expansion of the papal horizon.

In the end, however, it was Western and Southern Europe that remained the focal points for both the foreign policy and the ecclesiastical policy of the popes. The doctrine of the papal office, developed more forcefully than ever in this epoch, was applied to both of these usually closely bound thematic fields. Until the middle of the century, this was formulated principally in the arengas (prefaces) to papal promulgations and in the canonistic commentaries on decretals and constitutions. From the end of the thirteenth century, theologians in particular wrote tracts which, for the first time, systematically investigated problems of church government, from which a new theological discipline was created, ecclesiology (doctrines of the church). This new beginning is not only historiographically interesting, but it also informative about the situation of the church inasmuch as it shows that at least some scholars recognized that components of the church system of government, especially church-state relations, were problematic. And for the papacy itself, these new writings were important since they could serve as models for the papacy in formulating its own points of view. A famous example of this is the use of postulates from a tract of Aegidius Romanus in Boniface VIII's constitution, *Unam sanctam.*

Important in all this is that the popes and their supporters proposed hardly any new theories, instead deepening and expanding the initial formulations developed from the time of the investiture controversy. This can be clearly seen as early as Innocent III. Even more forcefully than his predecessors, he stressed his position as the *vicarius Christi* and, in conjunction with that, the extent of his power (*plenitudo potestatis*). With this as a base, Innocent and his successors intervened more forcefully in the affairs of local churches (more about this later). The function of the pope as the vicar of Christ had an effect on his relations with secular powers. As mentioned earlier, in the decretal *Venerabilem* of 1202, Innocent III did not dispute the right of the German princes to elect their king, and in the year before that, in another decretal (*Per venerabilem*), he stressed that the highest secular rulers within their kingdoms had received their power directly from God; in other words, Innocent had no secular authority over them. Nevertheless, he did ascribe to himself certain times when he could exert some influence. Vis-à-vis the German ruler this was based on the right to crown the emperor and on the theory of translation, vis-à-vis Portugal, Aragon, Sicily, and later also England or Hungary, on the pope's position as liege lord, and vis-à-vis all rulers in general on the doctrine of the two swords and the doctrine of original sin. The theological assertion of the latter was interpreted politically: because all humans are sinful and need the intercession of priests, the priests, and in particular the pope as the highest priest, could take disciplinary action against secular rulers who, because of their sinfulness (*ratione peccati*), have erred. Innocent advocated this idea, though in moderation, but with Gregory IX it received a major emphasis, and finally, together with Boniface VIII's doctrine of the two swords, was fixed dogmatically and intensified in the *Unam sanctam.* Thus the rulers were allowed less influence over ecclesiastical institutions within their sphere of power. The pope wanted to take their place.

To publicize and assert not only at law schools and universities, but also among judges and potential rivals, papal claims and the laws which the papacy had promulgated, Innocent III had the canonist and *familia* member Peter of Benevento compile the so-called *Compilatio tertia*, which he published in 1210 as the official collection of papal decretals. Innocent was the first pope to have his published texts compiled in this manner. Honorius III followed in 1226 with the *Compilatio quinta*. Both of these compilations, as well as unofficial ones, were surpassed in 1234 when Gregory IX published his *Liber Extra (vagantium)*, which was compiled by his penitentiary, Raymond of Pennafort and which, until 1917, was considered the official collection of ecclesiastical law, especially that law developed after Gratian and shaped by the papacy. Papal decretals and council decrees which came later were handed down in partly official (Innocentian, Gregorian), partly unofficial collections, and were finally published in 1298 by Boniface VIII (*Liber Sextus*) and in 1317 by John XXII (*Clementines*). These three collections—the *Liber Extra,* the *Liber Sextus* and the *Clementines*—from that time on not only shaped the practice of canon law, but were also often commented upon in critical apparatuses; systematically interpreted in summae; elaborated for use in confessional summae, sacramentals, and election tracts, among other things; summarized with key words in indices and registers; and accepted by synods. They also served as models for compilations of secular law, such as the *Siete partidas* of Castile or the legal collection of Bracton in England. It is clear from this broad distribution how papal law was, for the most part, implemented without any real challange in this epoch. This did not mean, however, that reality always corresponded with these laws, as is evident until the end of the Middle Ages in marriage ceremonies, which frequently ran contrary to the Fourth Lateran Council of 1215.

A problem that was often discussed in both law and practice was the question of how a bishop was to obtain his see. It was clear, in theory at least, that the election was the most important act. What was disputed, however, was who had the right to vote and how the voting was to be done. In regard to papal elections, the Third Lateran Council of 1179 had decreed that a two-thirds majority of the cardinals was needed to elect a pope. Gregory X then ruled, at the Second Lyon Council in 1274, that the election was to be done by conclave, which was later fine tuned by Clement V. Since that time until the most recent past, the method of electing the pope has been fixed. Episcopal elections became increasingly similar.

Not later than the Fourth Lateran Council, it was made clear that, like the College of Cardinals, the cathedral chapter was to act as the only electoral college. Though in contrast to a papal election, in an episcopal election a minority could oppose the majority as *sanior pars* (the healthier part), and in so doing reject the majority's candidate. For this reason, Innocent III and Gregory IX set up guidelines to regulate the form the voting should take and the claims of the various groups of voters. Because these criteria were not explicit, however, the curia was increasingly involved in disputed episcopal elections. This was even true from the time of Gregory X and Nicholas IV, when a vote of the majority was seen as decisive for episcopal elections, since due to the many legal cases which had been brought forward earlier, it was now custom that a bishop chosen in an undisputed election still had to be nominated by the pope. In this way, the papacy won a decisive influence over the filling of vacant bishoprics. The papacy continued to reserve for itself the right to appoint bishops in the case of disputed elections, or when the last officeholder died at the Roman curia. This provision, as well as the nomination, ensued after consultations among the pope and the cardinals in the consistory. There were also financial benefits in this. By the end of the thirteenth century, a tax had gradually developed out of what had initially been voluntary donations, a tax that every bishop as well as every abbot had to pay if he wanted to receive his post from the pope, known as the *servitium commune* (general service). It amounted to one-third of the first year's income. From the time of Boniface VIII, the tax obligations and the ensuing payments by bishops and abbots were written down in a register, with half of the money going to the pope, half to the cardinals. In addition, every candidate had to pay *servitia minuta* (reduced service), which altogether came to as much as the share of an individual cardinal and was to the benefit of certain curials. From the *servitia* register it can be seen how much wealthier England and France, and less so Spain and Germany, were in comparison with Italy. About one-third of the Italian bishops were exempted from the tax because their income was less than 100 florins, while the richest bishops, those of Rouen, Toulouse, and Winchester, each paid 12,000 florins. Just over thirty bishops paid from 5,000 to 10,000 florins, with only one of them being an Italian, the patriarch of Aquileia. Even clearer was the regional alignment among the abbots. The twenty abbots who paid between 4,000 and 8,000 florins held office exclusively in France or the Netherlands. To put it bluntly: the Italians, who dominated the positions of pope, cardinal, and curial, as well as at the councils, lived largely at the expense of transalpine local churches.

They were therefore also interested in minor benefices in these areas, especially in well-endowed cathedral benefices and other prebends. Twelfth-century popes provided relatives and close friends with ecclesiastical positions outside of Italy, as did their successors from the time of Innocent III. Until the middle of the thirteenth century, however, popes had to rely on the cooperation of local institutions. This all changed with Clement IV, who reserved for himself the right to confer all benefices whose incumbents had died at the curia. To be sure, the concept "curia" is somewhat ambiguous. Usually the pope did not reside in Rome, but in places that were often too small to be able to accommodate all the curials. As a result, any place where the curials were able to attend to their affairs was considered the see of the curia at that time. At the end of the thirteenth century, it was established that such places had to be within a two-day travel radius, a radius which at the same time was applied to the bestowal of benefices: all benefices whose incumbent died within this radius went to the pope. In this way, a useful instrument was created, and later perfected in the fourteenth century, to secure a good income for the curials. By 1300, the practice of the provision of benefices had overflowed its banks to such an extent that expectatives were conferred on benefices that were about to become free and claims were raised on the spoils (i.e., estate) of a deceased incumbent of a benefice. These practices could not be implemented everywhere, however. Probably only half of those who were given provisions got what they had hoped for. What is important, however, is that most of the benefices were in France, the Netherlands, and England.

The papacy was frequently called on by foreigners to intervene in the filling of bishoprics, and even more so in the conferring of benefices, because many of the candidates were stained with the stigma of having been born illegitimately. During Gregory IX's pontificate, approximately one-third of the clerics of several Iberian bishoprics were born out of wedlock, and a similar number must be assumed for other dioceses. And in Scandinavia, at the end of the thirteenth century, one-third of these illegitimate persons, in other words ten percent of the total clergy, were born of priests and other celibate persons. If the children of clerics did not enter a monastery or a chapter of canons regular in order to atone for the sins of their fathers, then they needed a dispensation. If they aspired to the priesthood, to a benefice connected with a ministry, or even to a bishopric, then only the pope could grant them a dispensation. Innocent IV alone granted dispensations to six persons who were the sons of priests, as well as to a bishop's son, to enable them to be consecrated as bishops. Apart from showing that celibacy laws of the eleventh century were little heeded, this granting of dispensations also makes it clear to what extent the pope had appropriated for himself the privileges of the bishops, and how deeply he intervened in the affairs of local dioceses. More often than in earlier times, the pope dispensed from other, early church or modern, ecclesiastical law norms. Dispensations now largely replaced exemptions, which had been common into the previous epoch. This alone makes it clear that not only did the often rigid legislation have to be studied, but also dispensations—which were of course only granted for a fee—if one wanted to understand the actual legal situation.

Papal legislation and governmental practice was often related to the Crusades. Protection of the Crusader and his kin at home was strongly regulated by canon law from the time of Innocent III. From papal decretals concerning the Crusades, commentators developed the early beginnings of international law. And popes such as Innocent III, Honorius III, Innocent IV, and Gregory X invested much effort in making the Crusades a reality, with the councils of 1215 and 1274 serving this purpose. For the same reason, the orders of knights were granted privileges, and more and more Crusade taxes were collected in the thirteenth century. Not even the Muslim conquest in 1291 of the last city of the Crusaders changed this situation, though enthusiasm for the Holy Land did start flagging. The reason for this was not just the lack of success of the Crusades, but also papal misuse of the idea of a crusade. As mentioned previously, pontiffs now were leading or backing crusades against political adversaries like the Hohenstaufen, the Aragonese, and the English; against personal opponents like the Colonna under Boniface VIII; as well as against real or imagined heretics like the Albigensians in Southern France and the Stedingeners on the lower Weser. The popes used the crusade tithe to finance their own wars, or to help rulers with whom they were on friendly terms.

There is still controversy nowadays over the crusades held against heretics. These crusades showed how little the church valued its own capacity to give instruction and how it instead resorted to violence. It must be taken into consideration, however, that at least those who formed the established powers on both the spiritual and secular sides saw the ecclesiastical and political order threatened by the heresies, and thus felt themselves justified in using force against the opponents of this order. And Innocent III tried, as Alexander III did before him, to reintegrate, through concessions, several groups, such as the "Lombard poor," despite criticism from his own ranks. And later still, attempts were sanctioned for bringing heretics back into the fold through discussions about the faith. However, this did not alter the fact that violence was the preferred method, at first in the form of crusades, and then the Inquisition, starting with Gregory IX. The Inquisition was based on decrees by Lucius III (*Ad abolendam*) and Innocent III (*Vergentis in senio*) as well as on royal decrees, such as Frederick II's coronation promise of 1220. But it was Gregory IX and Innocent IV who fully developed and perfected the Inquisition. Basing his decision on secular practices, Gregory decreed the burning at the stake for hardened heretics or ones who had had a relapse, and he assured anonymity for witnesses, making it much easier for informers. Innocent IV allowed the use of torture in investigations and designated the "wall," lifelong imprisonment, as punishment for penitent heretics. Papal legates, bishops, and their representatives acted as inquisitors, but the main corps of inquisitors came from members of the new mendicant orders, with the Dominicans being especially prominent, which is why the nickname *domini canes* (dogs of the lord, i.e., the pope) soon spread.

The pervasiveness of papal authority during this period cannot really be fully understood if one does not take into account the new monastic orders. Innocent III had tried to get the older reform orders, and in particular the Cistercians, to go along with his policies on heretics. He failed, however, because these orders were ill-suited for the caring of souls due to their monastic structure. The Benedictines, for example, at the Fourth Lateran Council, were only useful to Innocent as a model for regional organization. For missionary work, for the caring of souls, and for the struggle against heresy, he would need new helpers. From the middle of the century, there was a Franciscan legend going around about a dream that Innocent had in which the collapse of the

Lateran basilica—"a collapse of the mother and the head of all churches"—was prevented by St. Francis. The tale, which was soon depicted in paintings and later applied to Dominic, showed the high self-assessment the mendicant orders had of themselves as saviors of the church. But it was also a glorification of the past. It was the pope in the first place who, beginning in 1209 and in agreement with the bishop of Assisi, supported and encouraged St. Francis and his followers, though with the stipulation that they join the clergy. Likewise, he encouraged the work of the Castilian Dominic. His successors, and principally Gregory IX, who was related to Innocent, followed his example. Although the two orders had different regulations and internal structures, the heads of both orders were subordinate to the pope. In addition, the Franciscans at first, and then later the Dominicans, each had a cardinal as protector at the papal court who looked after their interests, but at the same time could pass along papal directives. And while it was the Dominicans in particular who served the papacy as inquisitors, the Franciscans helped to spread the Roman liturgy since Francis had integrated the customs of the Roman curia into the rites of his order, and in so doing prepared the way for the unification of the Catholic liturgy on the Roman model at the end of the sixteenth century. Communities that were similar to the Franciscans were organized by the papacy from the time of Alexander IV, including mendicant orders like the Augustine hermits, the Carmelites, and others. However, the close ties between the papacy and the mendicant orders did not prevent conflicts from arising in the second half of the century over the interpretation of claims of poverty, especially between Franciscan groups and individual popes. And because of the orders' many privileges and success at caring for souls, both priests and bishops opposed them because they were growing anxious about the rights and fees, such as for burials, that were due them. Only with great effort, and after many disputes, was Boniface VIII able, in 1300, to create a balance of interests with the constitution *Super cathedram.*

At this point, attention should also be given to the granting of papal charters to universities. Most of the universities were established without any papal influence. For a long time, some of the universities thought confirmation by the papacy was of no value, such as Oxford and Cambridge, or of little value, such as Bologna. Paris, on the other hand, did think it of value by having its organization and rights ratified by Honorius III (*Super speculam*) and by securing its position in later conflicts through a papal letter. Other French universities soon followed this example, and later Salamanca in Spain. It was common, then, at the end of the thirteenth century, for universities to have charters granted to them by the papacy, with Paris serving as the model. As a result, universities were bodies incorporated under papal law. The date of the granting of university charters should not be considered, as it often is, as the founding date, however, since the long development phase usually preceded the privilege. Innocent IV also followed the Parisian model when he founded a *studium generale* at the curia—Thomas Aquinas was one of the many who studied there. Boniface VIII also patterned a *studium generale* in Rome after Paris and granted it privileges. The teachers, however, were appointed by the rectors of the *fraternitas Romana*.

The diverse activities of the pontiffs required a reorganization and expansion of the Roman curia. Innocent III gave a tighter organization to the chancery, though some changes also took place under some of his successors in the development and functions of the chancery. There were similar changes in the *camera apostolica*. Along with the expansion of papal activities came new offices, such as the penitentiary. The transformation and the expansion of the curia lasted the entire thirteenth century. For the sake of simplicity, the curia will be described in the following passage as it was under Nicholas III and Boniface VIII. In so doing, it should be remembered that the importance of the various curials depended on what interests were being taken into consideration at a given time: for the foreign petitioner, the chancery and the penitentiary, as well as the courts were the most important, for it was there that he received the answers and favors he was looking for. In addition, there were the porters and the chamber attendants, whom he would not get past without some kind of greasing of the palms. The court offices probably would have seemed important to a curial, as long as he was not seeking a benefice or involved in a lawsuit, for it was from these offices that he received his daily rations for himself and the animal he used for transportation—there was no such thing as a salary paid in cash. The pope attached great importance to the *camera*, which administered income and expenditures, took care of political correspondence, and supervised a major portion of the curials.

From the time of Honorius III, the chancery consisted of the vice-chancellor, who in contrast to earlier chancellors was seldom a cardinal, the notaries together with *abbreviators,* the *auditor litterarum contradictarum,* the correctors, and the colleges of *scriptores* and proctors, which were supervised by the chancery. Usually, the *audientia sacri palatii* was also occupied with chancery business, and for this reason it was also under the vice chancellor. In order to get an idea of the work of individual persons, let us look in a simplified manner at the way a petitioner would approach the curia, at least as much as it can be reconstructed from the partly divergent sources.

The petitioner had to first search for a proctor—kings and rich ecclesiastical institutions often had their own—who formulated his request in a petition written in proper curial style. Once this work was paid for, the petitioner went to the chancery with his petition, where his proposal was dated (*data communis*) and then given over to a notary who either had been assigned to the petitioner or had been sought out by him. The notary then had one of his *abbreviators* work out a rough draft for the petition according to its wording. Once this was done and the text was approved and paid for, the petitioner or his proctor went with the rough draft to the distributor of the *scriptores.* (These were scribes organized in a guild, working under the vice-chancellor, to whom they had given an oath of service. At the head of these scribes stood a rescribendary and, from the time of Alexander IV, a distributor, who the scribes chose from their ranks. Their income went into a general fund, out of which the rescribendary paid them their alloted income.) The distributor then handed the rough draft over to one of the *scriptores* for the fair copy (*littera ingrossata*), and then, if needed, had it copied and assessed by other *scriptores.* And finally, the rough draft and the fair copy were brought back to the notary for comparison (*prima visio* and *auscultatio*). If major errors were found, the fair copy had to be rewritten. If the error was a fault of the *scriptor,* then he had to bear the cost of the revision. A second proofreading for form and content then followed, often done by the corrector. The corrector then sent this copy—as long as a new fair copy was not necessary—to the pope if the petition, because of its importance, had to be read aloud before him, or immediately to the *audientia sacri palatii* (also known as *audientia publica,* and later *rota*). In the second case, the fair copy was read in the presence of other petitioners and proctors. If one of these raised any objection to the text, then the case had to be deliberated before the *auditor litterarum contradictarum* (meaning literally the auditor/ judge of disputed letters). If the objection was overruled, then it was followed by the issuing of a bull by two *bullatores*, who usually were Cistercian conversi. If the document did not go through the *audientia* and was still not in the hands of the petitioner or his proctor, then there still could be an annulment (*revocatio*) before the vice chancellor. Usually, however, the petitioner received his document, which he could then enter (either the fair copy or the rough draft), if he thought it of great importance, in the papal register, which the vice chancellor was in charge of. The petitioner also paid the taxes due on it (fair copy, issuing of the bull, registration).

Benefice letters and various kinds of legal letters were usually written in the chancery; in addition, letters originating from the pope (*littere curiales*) that were not taken care of by the *camera* were also written there, as well as an occasional letter for the penitentiary when needed. The penitentiary, however, usually wrote its own letters, as did *scriptores* later. The Sacred Penitentiary was created in the thirteenth century—the name first appeared under Gregory IX—and only in the following epoch was it fully organized by Benedict XII. It was probably the most revealing "authority" of the papacy's ecclesiastical power. It was responsible for all favors the pope granted, unless he reserved the granting of certain ones for himself. Thus the Sacred Penitentiary's sphere of duties included the absolution of those who had been excommunicated, which was announced by the pope three times a year—especially on Maunday Thursday—in the so-called *processus generales*, as well as the absolution of spiritual crimes (heretics, forgerers of papal bulls). Other duties included the granting of the right to choose one's own father confessor, as well as the granting of indulgences and, above all, dispensations. Initially, there was only one penitentiary, who probably also served as father confessor for the pope and the cardinals. Later on, the penitentiary himself was often a cardinal, assisted by *poenitentiarii minores*, whose existence can be traced back to the pontificate of Honorius III, and some of whose distinguished personalities were the canonist Raymond of Pennafort and the chronicler Martin of Troppau. During visits to Rome they sometimes acted as father confessors at the Lateran or St. Peter's, and were usually chosen because of the need to have persons who knew the languages of various countries. From the second half of the century, they were recruited largely from the mendicant orders. From the time of Innocent IV, *scriptores* also helped them because of their constantly increasing workload. In Avignon, the *scriptores* joined together in a college on the model of the chancery scribes.

The *camera* retained its traditional duties, though it expanded its sphere of competence through the intensive control and exploitation of the Papal States, and through the increase in tributes paid by dependent feudal lords, one of whom was now the English king. Moreover, the duties of the *camera* also expanded due to the numerous crusade tithes and to the new *servitia*, which were now coming in. Therefore, the bureaucratic machinery grew larger. The chamberlain was aided by a maximum of seven *camera* clerics of the treasury. From the middle of the century the assets of the treasury and the library were administered by one or two *thesauraria* (treasurers), with the Papal States probably also having *thesauraria*. Outside the Papal States, there were collectors to take in the revenue. The *camera* also had notaries who were responsbile for the keeping of records and any other types of writing. As early as the second half of the century, money probably no longer circulated directly; rather, merchant bankers (*mercatores curiam sequentes*) were placed as go-betweens, their representatives collecting taxes locally from those obliged to pay, or from collectors. The merchant bankers also had representatives at the curia who managed the cash on hand, so that the chamberlain and the *camera* clerics retained only a supervisory role and determined the kinds of expenditures. There was a judge (*auditor camere*) and a lawyer (*advocatus fisci*) for judicial proceedings of a financial nature. As mentioned previously, the chamberlain was also responsible for political correspondence, both he and the pope receiving some assistance from private secretaries (*secretarii*). From about the time of Urban IV, a register was kept for this correspondence in particular, but also for administrative documents.

In contrast to the twelfth century, the organization of the curial system of justice was also now tightened up. For most cases, the existing *audientia sacri palatii* (also known as *audientia publica*, and later *rota*) was the competent court. If the auditors did not deal with the cases themselves, then they were passed on to delegated judges, a practice in use from the time of Alexander III. Usually the auditor consulted with his colleagues before passing judgment. The chamberlain, on the other hand, was usually responsible for curials who had violated disciplinary regulations, while criminal offenses by curials as well as crimes committed by laymen at the curia were judged by the marshal of justice, who was often also the papal commander-in-chief, and thus a nobleman or often a relative of the ruling pope.

The four court offices took care of provisions for the curials. They were the kitchen (*coquina*), the bread office (*panataria*), the wine office (*buticularia*), and the stables (*marescallia*), which, according to account books from the time of Boniface VIII, administered about sixty percent of curial expenditures. There was also the office for alms which, in addition to its contributions to the poor, also served the curia by covering the costs for processions as well as occasionally defraying the costs of building palaces or palace gardens.

The papal *capella* was not its own separate office, but, as mentioned previously, it was the heart of the papal *familia*, and in this capacity, reservoir for almost all important curial functions, even if its actual function remained the organizing of worship services in the papal palace. In regard to the *capella*, however, a distinction must be made between the numerous "honorary chaplains" and the chaplains who officiated in the curia and lived in the *capellania*—in the fourteenth century referred to as *capellani commensales* (chaplains who sat at the pope's table). To be such a chaplain was the surest way to a successful career. It is hardly surprising that the vice chancellor and chamberlain, as well as the *thesaurarius*, chancery notaries, penitentiary, and auditors, usually were once members of the *capella*, while the *scriptores* took steps to become a chaplain.

The importance of the chaplains is evident in the fact that, until the middle of the thirteenth century, they could not be distinguished from the cardinals in the way they dressed. It was Innocent IV who first allowed the cardinals to wear purple biretta to set them apart from the chaplains. Because until then, purple, the imperial color, had been reserved for the pope, it becomes obvious from this detail in the ranking of clothes that the importance of the College of Cardinals was on the rise. Soon after, the cardinals were referred to as successors to the apostle, as "part of the papal body" (*pars corporis pape*), similar to the imperial senate of late antiquity, and as "pillars of the church." The latter two titles were later applied to the electors in Germany. The second title also had a legal significance, for on the basis of this title an attack on a cardinal was considered an attack on the pope himself according to Roman law, and thus a crime against the sovereign. The increasing influence of the cardinals in the church can be seen in their taking over of functions usually performed by bishops, although they had never been ordained as bishops. During Martin IV's pontificate, for instance, the cardinal-priest Ancherus degraded heretical priests; and canonists discussed the question whether a cardinal priest was allowed to degrade ecclesiastics. At the same time, the cardinals were growing wealthy, since Nichloas IV promised them half of the revenue from the Papal States. And from the end of the century, they shared in half of the *servitia*. One example of just how strong their pressure on the pope could be was the lifting of Gregory X's strict regulations regarding conclaves by his successor. And even when Celestine V reinstated these regulations, and Boniface VIII put them in the *Liber Sextus*, the cardinals did not give up their opposition, leading in the following epoch to decrees by Clement V and Clement VI stating that papal elections should be made less complicated.

For the balance of power within the curia it is important to note that in Rome itself, and even more so outside Rome, most of the curials did not officiate from the papal palace. Besides the pope, permanent residents of the palace included the palace personnel such as the cubiculars, the doorkeeper, etc., as well as the chamberlain and the *thesaurarius*, and officials connected to the four court offices, which underscores the significance of these groups for the papacy. The chancery, however, in contrast to many secular monarchs' courts, was never housed in the papal palace. Instead, officials in the chancery usually handled their business in their own living quarters, which during their frequent trips might even be in a different city from the one in which the pope was staying. The relative unimportance of the chancery for the papacy can also be seen in that chancery officials usually served several popes without any express extension of their stay in office. Chamberlains and *thesauraria*, on the other hand, as well as penitentiaries, all confidants of the pope, lost their post with the death of their employer and had to be renominated.

The great increase in business made an expansion of the curia necessary. Early on, Innocent III recognized that abuses could take hold in the curia. Thus he and some of his successors tried to stamp out the worst abuses by clearly fixing emoluments and duties, unheard of among any secular administrations of that time. Despite this, in the thirteenth century voices of criticism grew over the corruptibility of the curia, especially the doorkeepers, chamber attendants, and officials of the chancery.

Even papal policies were not always free from criticism, however. Critics, for example, formulated a doctrine that today is the basis of the papal claim to be supreme keeper of the faith: the doctrine of papal infallibility. Based on older canonistic traditions, the doctrine was first formulated at the end of the thirteenth century by Franciscans critical of the pope. The Franciscans objected to Boniface VIII in particular, who they said wanted to revise the constitution *Exiit qui seminat,* which in 1279 Nicholas III proclaimed as an authentic interpretation of law, a constitution that was also favorable to the Franciscans. Initially then, the doctrine of papal infallibility was an attempt to limit the pope's jurisdictional competence by binding him to the decrees of his predecessors. Only from the time of John XXII were attempts made, at first by canonists like Guido Terreni, to interpret new teachings in favor of the doctrinal claims of the papacy.

Another point of contention was the subjugation of councils to the pope. It was the councils of this century (1215, 1245, 1274), and especially the Fourth Lateran Council, which in the end did not advise the papacy, but rather implemented his views in the church as a whole. There were, however, even then, the first stirrings of change. For example, the usual formulation of the Symmachan Forgery, *summa sedes* (or *papa*) *a nemine iudicetur, nisi a fide devius* (the pope cannot be judged by anyone unless he has deviated from the faith), included the possibility that the pope could become a heretic. Starting from this point, both canonists and theologians debated whether the pope, if he did become a heretic, could still be a pope at all, and if so, who was to judge him. During the thirteenth century, there was an increasing number of persons who saw a general council as the only possible way to judge. This rather academic doctrine became virulently political in that, from the time of the conflict between Gregory IX and Frederick II, rulers appealed to these kinds of general councils to have papal rivals condemned.

The criticism became a crisis under Boniface VIII. Fueled by millenarian expectations of various Christian groups that were partly heretical (Apostolics, among others) and partly orthodox (as were most Spirituals), the hope was increasing that the church symbolized by Christ and presided over by a secularized papacy would be dissolved by the kingdom of the Holy Spirit. The transition was to be carried out by a so-called angel pope. When the elderly hermit Peter of Morrone was elected pope on July 5, 1294, after a year-long conclave, taking on the promising name of Celestine V, many saw in him the awaited angel pope. But their hopes ended in delusion. The pope was a complete failure, unexperienced in political and administrative affairs and clearly influenced by the Neapolitan king, Charles II, and members of his own new order, the so-called Celestines. His pontificate made clear that a man "poor of mind" was not fit to be the vicar of Christ. After consulting with several cardinals, principally with Benedetto Caetani, Celestine abdicated on December 13, the first pope to do so voluntarily. This gave rise to rumination among canonists at that time since it was unclear whether a pope was allowed to resign. Eleven days later, the Caetani cardinal was elected pope as Boniface VIII. Many of Celestine's supporters believed that he was forced to resign by his successor and that therefore Boniface was not the lawful pope. Because of this, the new pope had his hoary predecessor interned in the isolated Castel Fumone, which lay within the Caetani sphere of influence, to prevent Celestine from being freed. Celestine died there in 1296. But doubts over the legality of Boniface did not.

Attacks multiplied as Boniface annuled programs of his predecessor and had statues of himself erected at the city gates and in churches, probably even on altars, thereby making himself susceptible to accusations of idolatry. He was also attacked for the aggrandization of his family's power at the expense of the Colonna as he took steps against them by such ecclesiastical means as excommunication, deposition, and crusade. But above all, he was attacked becuase of his conflicts with Philip the Fair of France and Edward I of England. Both kings imposed an unauthorized tax on the clergy of their lands in their war against each other during the vacancy in the papacy from 1292 to 1294, and once again, without papal consent, in 1296. The latter step contravened the Fourth Lateran Council. To counteract these measures, and after protests by some of the clergy, Boniface issued the papal bull *Clericis laicos.* In it, Boniface stressed the suffering of the clerics at the hands of the laity. He also strengthened the canon of the Fourth Lateran Council and made any contravention of it a crime. On the strength of this, the English clergy as well as the barons refused to pay further taxes to their king, as did the French episcopate. In reaction, Philip prohibited the exportation of precious metals, gold, and money, which cut into papal revenue considerably. After further accusations from both sides, the pope yielded in 1297 in order to gain a free hand against the Colonna. He even saw himself forced to void *Clericis laicos* for France. In conjunction with this, the pope canonized, in the same year, Philip's grandfather, Louis IX.

Nevertheless, conflicts with France began once again in the year following the first Jubilee Year in 1300, which Boniface used in an impressive manner to demonstrate the prestige of the papacy. Hundreds of thousands of pilgrims supposedly traveled to Rome that year. The conflict was triggered by events surrounding the first bishop of the new diocese at Pamiers, Bernard Saisset, who butted heads with Philip over the patronage of his episcopal see. The king then had him tried and convicted as a traitor and heretic and then incarcerated in Narbonne. This clearly did some damage to the clerical *privilegium fori*. Boniface countered by demanding Saisset's release, withdrawing all papal privileges from the king, putting *Clericis laicos* in force again, and summoning the king, his episcopate as well as cathedral chapters and university teachers to a synod in Rome for the end of 1302. In the bull *Ausculta fili* of December 5, 1301, he accused Philip not only of having suppressed the clergy and cheated his people, but he also emphasized how God wanted Christian kings to be placed under the pope. In so doing, he made the conflict the principal controversy regarding the rights of church and state. *Ausculta fili* was burned in the king's presence, and through a fake bull called *Deum time*, written in farcical form, its general assertions were made known in France. On April 4, 1302, the king then convened the Estates General, which for the first time included representatives of French towns. This assembly gave its support to Philip. As the conflict progressed, Boniface issued on November 8, 1302, after the sparsely attended French synod in Rome, the constitution *Unam sanctam*. Using the papal explanation of the doctrine of the two swords, and with his own peculiar interpretation of Bible passages, Boniface emphasized stronger than ever the papal position. He then decreed that "it is necessary for the salvation of every human creature to be subject to the pope" (*Porro subesse Romano pontifici omni humanae creaturae declaramus . . . omnino esse de necessitate salutis*). Though this statement had something in common with several theses of Thomas Aquinas and Aegidius Romanus, it was now no longer mere doctrinal opinion, but—supposedly—dogma. Nevertheless, the constitution continued to be disputed. Until the end of the Middle Ages it was not part of official canon law, even though it was commented upon. Only after it was confirmed by the Fifth Lateran Council in 1516, after renewed conflict with France, did the constitution gain general recognition in the Catholic church.

In spite of renewed negotiations between the pope and king the conflict grew sharper. Philip's chancellor at the time, Guillaume Nogaret, allied himself with the Colonna, adopting their reproaches against Boniface, while Boniface planned to excommunicate Philip and to release the king's subjects from their oath of fealty. This was to have taken place September 8,1303. But on the day before, Nogaret stormed the pope's palace in Anagni along with Sciarra Colonna, demanding his resignation. When Boniface refused, he was taken captive to be brought back to France to stand trial. He was rescued by the citizens of Anagni, formerly Colonna supporters, but he died in Rome a month later a broken man.

With the failure of his ecclesiastico-political designs, Boniface was to be a considerable burden on the papacy in the periods to follow. The high position the papacy had reached, mostly thanks to Innocent III, was now shaken with Boniface's fall. And at the same time, his conflicts with Philip of France were an indication of what would characterize the next centuries: the rolling back of the international papacy by the two new allies, the national ruler and the national church. Because of these far-reaching and important consequences for the future, the controversy depicted at the end of this chapter was described in more detail than other events.

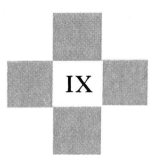

The Papacy in Avignon
(1303–1378)

Benedict XI, elected as Boniface's successor, had a heavy burden to take over. The attempted assassination at Anagni and the death of Benedict's predecessor gave new life to the feud between the Caetani and Colonna, as well as to the revolts in the Papal States. Benedict was supported by the Bonifacian party in the College of Cardinals under the leadership of the elderly Matteo Rosso Orsini. He also enjoyed the help of Charles II of Naples; however, the French king was against him because the king's chancellor, Nogaret, continued to support the Colonna and, together with the king, called for a general council at which Boniface was to be condemned as a heretic. In this difficult situation, the pope met the king halfway, though he excommunicated Nogaret and his aides as soon as he had absconded from Rome for the safer confines of Perugia. Boniface died there after only an eight-month pontificate.

The conclave that followed his death lasted eleven months because both cardinal factions—Matteo Rosso Orsini and the Bonificians, his nephew Napoleone Orsini and the pro-French line—took a long time to find a candidate they could agree upon. Thanks to some clever diplomacy on the part of Napoleone, the call finally went out to the archbishop of Bordeaux, Bertrand de Got, whom the Bonifacians mistakenly thought to be one of their own. He accepted the election and took the name Clement V. He did not travel to Rome, however, but rather directed the cardinals to Lyon for the coronation, which at that time was under French influence, although nominally it was still part of the Holy Roman Empire. There, under circumstances that foretold of the troubles to come, Clement was crowned pope. He then expressed his intention to go to Italy, though in fact he stayed in Central and Southern France for health and political reasons.

Since Clement had placed many of his nephews as well as other of his countrymen in the College of Cardinals and was heavily influenced by the French king (more about both of these points later), after his death the Italian cardinals found themselves in a minority. Therefore, when his death came in 1314, the election of a successor was made even more difficult than it had been in 1304. Under pressure from the Clementine partisans, the Italians walked out on the conclave in Carpentras, boycotting it for two years. The troubles did not end, though, when all the cardinals met again in 1316 in Lyon, for the brother of the French king, the future Philip V, going against his promises, put renewed pressure on the college. An agreement was only reached when the former popemaker Napoleone Orsini convinced three of his countrymen to come to terms with the Southern French. Their agreed upon candidate, whom Philip also accepted, was the 72–year-old Jacques Duèze from Cahors, who took the name John XXII after his election. Bishop of Avignon from 1310 to 1312, John moved to his former episcopal see after his pompous coronation in Lyon. He elevated the ruling bishop of Avignon, one of his *nipoti,* to cardinal, named him administrator of the diocese, and turned the bishop's palace into his residence. For the next six decades, Avignon became the site of the papal see.

This epoch has long been known as the "Babylonian Captivity" of the popes, especially to nationalistic Italians beginning with the time of Petrarch. (That from now on the word "Italian" instead of "Italic" is used for the inhabitants of Italy is based on their viewing of themselves, beginning in the fourteenth century, more and more as "Italian" through a common vernacular, as Dante and Petrarch attest to. In addition, there was Cola di Rienzo's attempt at political unification.) Avignon did have many advantages over

Rome, however. There were no factions among the nobility as potential opposition parties; the city was situated in an area of more efficient transport, the Rhone being one of the most important north-south connections, while an important east-west road crossed the river at the Pont St. Bénézet ("Pont d'Avignon"); theoretically, the city still belonged to the empire, though de facto to the Angevin sphere of power—John was chancellor of the kings of Naples from 1308 to 1310—until Clement VI in 1348 bought the city with the consent of Charles IV of Germany from Queen Joanna; the city was surrounded by the earldom of Venaissin, which from the second half of the thirteenth century was under the papal control. On the other hand, French territory began just beyond the aforementioned bridge, which made help readily available. If one considers that, since the investiture controversy, the pontiffs were more often away from Rome than actually in the traditional episcopal see, which made it considerably more difficult to establish an administrative continuity, then it was in Avignon where the papacy finally had the chance to create an effective and locally constant administration—and, of course, with all the disadvantages that go with that, too, which I will discuss later.

The center of papal government was the papal palace. John expanded the episcopal palace (a hall for *audientia,* for example), while Benedict XII started with a new structure in 1335. The earlier parish church of the cathedral became the palace chapel. It was closed off to the south by three wings, making the palace look like a cloister, which was no surprise since the builder in charge was a Cistercian. In the eastern palace wing extension were the reception rooms and the papal residential tower. Clement VI made a beautiful expansion of the compound by adding another residential tower and a new wing to the south, which contained a second chapel and a new hall for *audientia.* He also added an extension to the western wing, through which one entered the palace. Later expansions were done principally under Innocent VI and Urban V. Despite damage incurred during the French Revolution, the papal palace is the most comprehensive and imposing example of extant medieval architecture.

Papal life centered on the palace, especially from the middle of the century on. While previously the election and coronation of a pope had taken place in the Dominican monastery or in the cathedral, both constitutive acts—contrary to Roman tradition—were carried out exclusively in the palace. The liturgy, previously conceived for the bishop, clergy, and people of Rome, likewise was centered on the palace, which led to the exclusion of a major portion of the clergy and people. This change from a municipal liturgy into a palace ceremonial was to leave its mark for over five hundred years on the papacy's conception of itself and on the form in which it was represented. Henceforth the pope was a ruler removed from the people; the average cleric and pilgrim got a glimpse of him in Avignon only when he went—surrounded by bodyguards—to a cardinal's residence as an honored guest, when he took in the fresh summer air at Chateauneuf-du-Pape, among other places, or when he was transported to the cathedral as a corpse. That Rome had been replaced by the palace also became evident at the consecration of altars and through the use of several terms: true to the already well-known motto *ubi papa, ibi Roma* (where the pope is, there is Rome), Benedict's chapel, with its dedication to St. John, replaced the Lateran basilica, and Clement's new structure stood in for St. Peter's. The main entrance to the palace was named after both of the princely apostles, and an eastern wing, built by Urban V, was later called, during the period of the schisms, simply "Roma."

Just like the ceremonial, all important governmental functions were now concentrated in the palace: directly north of the residential towers the popes held the consistories and organized—graded according to the rank of the guests—receptions. The two ecclesiastical law courts—the *rota* and the *auditor litterarum contradictarum*—met in Clement VI's new building. The courts' central importance for the papacy was already well known under Clement V, for he had decreed, basing his action on the splintering of the curia because of constant travel, that a papal election should take place wherever the two audiences might be at the time of the pope's death. It was also this concentration of adminstrative functions that led to the most important papal assistants being housed in the palace. In addition to the usual palace personnel—the *magister domus* (palace supervisor), the cubiculars, Benedict XII's newly founded *capella,* and the doorkeepers, who were arranged in three ranks—the chamberlain and the *thesaurarius* lived and worked directly in the pope's residential tower, and later in an entry wing. The same was true for confidants such as the *confessor* or cardinals who were especially close to the pope. This in itself shows that the *camera* was still the most important "administrative authority," whose overseer the pope constantly wanted to have near him. The offices of the chancery and the Sacred Penitentiary, on the other hand, continued to be there where the individual officials—from the vice chancellor and the grand penitentiary down to the *scriptores* and proctors—lived, whether in Avignon itself or in its suburbs beyond the Rhone (Villeneuve-lès-Avignon). Even today, the appearance of both cities is dominated by the houses of the curials, and in particular the cardinals' livery, as well as the churches that were built or embellished back then.

If the palace compound was an expression of the new life-style and governing style of the popes, then the expansion of the curia reflected the increase in business which had occurred in the meantime. The new surroundings and the political constraints also raised the importance of the cardinals. To overcome the Italian faction in the College of Cardinals, as well as for his own security, Clement V placed mostly persons from Southern France in the college (seventeen), among them numerous *nipoti* (seven). The creation of cardinals under his successors generally followed the same principle. And because other relatives were promoted to the retinue of the cardinals as members of the *familia* in curial functions, *nipoti* of a previous pope or of a cardinal who had been created earlier were placed in the college by a later pope, or even became popes themselves—Benedict XII was a *nipote* of Clement V's vice chancellor Arnaud Nouvel, Gregory XI was a *nipote* of Clement VI. Earlier it had been members of the Roman noble families who largely made up the college and often dominated its policies, but now it was clerics from Southern and Central France, from the time of Clement VI clerics from Limousin in particular, who formed the majority of the cardinals. In addition to them, there were quite a few northern Frenchmen and Italians, several Spaniards, an Englishman under both Clement V and Urban V, though not a single German, let alone other nationalities. The changing regional origins of the cardinals led not only to rivalries during papal elections, but also to attempts to exert stronger influence on the papacy in order to increase the strength of one's own group. Accordingly, the college tried to cooperate in the accepting of new cardinals and in the limiting of the total number, for too great a number would have reduced the influence and income of the individual cardinals. This can be seen clearly in the electoral capitulation—the first known one in papal history—after the death of Clement VI in 1352. Though the newly elected pope, Innocent VI, revoked the capitulation after the election, the tendencies of the college in this direction remained intact. And finally, it should be pointed out that *nipoti* or compatriots of the pope often were in charge of the most important administrative offices: the chancery and the Sacred Penitentiary as well as the *camera*.

The organization of the individual administrative offices was an extension of the developments of the previous century, but was expanded even further in Avignon. The pontificate of John XXII was of special significance for the two offices under the vice chancellor, the chancery and the *rota*. In the reorganization of the chancery carried out in 1331, he arranged, most likely on the initiative of his vice chancellor, Pierre des Prés, the way in which business was to be conducted, and in particular the fees, for the chancery, the *auditor litterarum contradictarum* and for the *rota*. This set-up remained, along with a few additions, the model that was followed into the next century, though it was not able to remedy all abuses. Benedict XII recognized, for example, that many supplications were not processed because the petitioner had not thought of greasing the palms of the doorkeeper and the *cubicularum*. He ordered, therefore, the petitions to be registered. These petition registers have been preserved since the pontificate of Benedict's successor, and are one of the most important sources for the history of the curia.

More disposed to the spiritual life than his predecessors, Benedict XII introduced an examination for benefice seekers. The low educational level of the seekers became evident from the examination since it merely required the ability to read and write (Latin) and to have an agreeable voice. For the same reason, Benedict organized—which was fundamental for the period to come—the penitentiary: it was given a strictly defined field of action and a book of formularies. The increase in work also led the *scriptores* to organize themselves in a college. The longest lasting fixture that Benedict founded, however, was the *capella*—originally *capella intrinseca* (inner chapel), later called *capella papalis* or *pontificia*. It still exists today as the "Sistine Chapel." It was the duty of the *cantores* (singers) who belonged to it to devise the worship service held in the papal palace, a job done previously by the chaplain. And the more these *cantores* designed the entire ceremonial, the more functionaries that were added: ceremonial clerics, acolytes, subdeacons, sacristans. They were all, to some extent, confidants of the pope, but it was another functionary who, from the time of John XXII, played a greater role than before, the *confessor*. The *confessor* supervised the papal rooms, but because of his position of confidence with the pope his other activities can seldom be exactly identified. As a person holding the pope's highest trust, he initially directed the secretaries for political correspondence and the referendaries, who presented important writings to the pope and were gradually integrated into the chancery.

And finally, let us look at the *camera*, in which now the *camera* clerks responsible for the keeping of minutes joined together in a college, usually of seven members. If, in so doing, the work of the central bureaucracy was more strictly organized, then the dividing of the entire church in regional fiscal zones served the same purpose. Within these zones, collectors and their assistants were responsible for exacting revenue. It was the *familia* that in previous epochs acted as the most important springboard to a career. This opportunity was also institutionalized in Avignon by the fact that certain positions—*camera* clerics, chancery *scriptores*, and others—belonged to the papal *familia* because of their position, and thereby automatically had a share in the *servitia minuta* and enjoyed better chances when benefices were bestowed.

In contrast to the thirteenth century, most curials were now no longer paid in food but in money. This led to an increase in the curia's need for money; in addition, there was an expansion of personnel and a more luxurious way of life for the popes and cardinals. Thus the Avignon epoch is the period of the most effective fiscal control—one could also say exploitation—of the church as a whole by the papacy.

The basis for this was set down in administrative orders and legislative decrees, which were concerned first of all with the reservation of benefices. Clement V expanded reservations to all bishoprics whose bishop had been consecrated at the curia, or had resigned there, or to bishoprics which, through translation, had been newly occupied or exchanged. With his consitution *Ex debito* of 1316, John XXII further expanded reservations. They were now binding in cases when an election was declared invalid or when a postulation was rejected. In addition, reservations included all the benefices of both cardinals and curials. All reservations to this point in time were combined by Benedict XII in 1335, and then expanded once again, until finally, under Urban V, the filling of vacancies at all bishoprics and, up to a certain level of income, all monasteries and nunneries, was reserved for the pope. In this same period, the papacy was also gaining increasing influence over the filling of top posts in the mendicant orders, with practically all top ecclesiastical officials now dependent on the pope.

In addition, minor benefices were also more frequently loaned to the curia and put to use financially. From this practice there arose the danger of an accumulation of benefices, which John XXII tried to ban in 1317 with the constitution *Execrabilis*. In it, he complained that a shocking number of diocesan priests as well as priests from the orders were collecting benefices out of greed. The benefices were then neglected, to the detriment of the caring of souls. He therefore limited the ownership of benefices: henceforth the owner of a benefice that was connected with the caring of souls (*beneficium cum cura*) would be allowed to own only one other benefice that was not connected with pastoral duties (*beneficium sine cura*, thus the word "sinecure"). John himself, however, not to mention the benefice seekers, seldom heeded his regulations or his *Ex debito*. He worsened the situation himself by bestowing numerous expectatives. John's attempt on his deathbed, and attempts by his successor during his pontificate, to retract or at least to limit these expectatives was not very useful in the long run. As a result, sometimes as many as six persons owned expectatives to a benefice, bringing litigation about ownership before the curia. The accumulation of benefices was especially pronounced among the cardinals; Napoleone Orsini, for example, owned about one hundred of them. But even an average curial, such as a *camera* cleric, thought nothing of owning at least several prebends as sinecures. It was Benedict XII who tried to put an end to the worst abuses by ordering that payments be made from the estate of a deceased cardinal as compensation for benefices he had neglected. In the case of one Dominican monk, a "mendicant monk," Guillaume de Peire de Godin, compensations amounted to approximately 8,430 florins, about one thousand florins more than the annual income of the archbishop of Magdeburg. The conferring of benefices lured thousands of persons to the curia, especially when it concerned a little endowed benefice (*in forma pauperum*, up to twenty-four florins annual income). Though the number of such benefices cannot be checked since they usually were not registered, perhaps as many as 40,000 clerics in Avignon applied for this kind of benefice in the first months after the election of Clement VI.

Pontiffs from the time of Clement V were determined to exploit the benefices financially, beyond just the fees earned in the conferring of them. In 1306, for the first time, Clement V requested annates, the first year's revenue of a benefice, from all free benefices or those that were about to be free in England, Ireland and Scotland. Though a parliament in Carlisle protested in 1307, as did the Council of Vienne, they had minimal success. John XXII raised annates once again in all of Europe, and in individual regions as well. Starting in 1326, annates had to be paid for all benefices that were vacant at the curia. The amount to be paid fluctuated. Starting at the end of this epoch in particular, the annates were usually half of the first year's revenue. Included in this were all benefices that had been conferred at the papal court with a minimum annual income of twenty-five florins.

Until the pontificate of Urban V there was a system in place, similar to the collecting of *servitia* and annates, whereby the pope reserved for himself the estate (spoils) of all bishops, abbots, priors, deacons, and rectors (the heads of parishes) as well as cardinals and curials, in this way maintaining the usufruct during their vacancy of all benefices that had become free at the curia, the so-called intercalary profit.

The four methods of gaining revenue mentioned so far—*servitia*, annates, spoils, intercalary profit—formed the major portion of papal revenue. These sources of income were on the rise, while the amounts brought in through crusade tithes grew less because these, if paid at all, had to be divided with the respective kings. Income from feudal tributes was also down. England, for example, did not pay any tribute after 1365. To cover increasing expenditures, therefore, the popes turned voluntary donations (*subsidium caritativum*, that is, support out of Christian love) into forced tributes. One subsidy alone that John XXII raised in France for a military campaign in Italy brought in over 200,000 florins, an amount equal to the average annual income of the curia during his pontificate. Other revenue included criminal fines (raised by the justice marshal), taxes from the Papal States and the Earldom of Venaissin, as well as the so-called compositions (agreements, usually compensations, made after peace treaties). Clement VI opened up a new source in 1350 with the Holy Year. He allowed, for example, the inhabitants of Mallorca to acquire indulgences at home—in other words, without having to make a pilgrimage to Rome—in exchange for a payment of 30,000 florins, which set a precedent for Boniface IX and the popes of the fifteenth century. And finally, there is one more method of raising funds that should be mentioned, one that brought forth especially bad blood: procurations. These were originally used for travel expenses to cover visitations by bishops, archdeacons, or decaons, and were thus payable for visitations that had actually been performed. By about 1300, such procurations had to be paid even if no visitation had been made. The final step in this process took place in the fourteenth century when pontiffs reserved these procurations for themselves, of course without any visitation being made on their behalf. In this case, too, an instrument that was intended for the improvement of pastoral duties and discipline remained purely a fiscal product.

Financial pressure grew even heavier—as regards the *servitia* in particular—in that those who were slow in paying were excommunicated, which made it impossible to carry out ecclesiastical duties, while the *servitia* became more synonymous than ever with simony. In 1328, John XXII excommunicated more than thirty bishops and more than forty abbots, and his successor also resorted to such measures.

As mentioned previously, the various monies were brought in by collectors. The transferring of the money to the curia, however, and the actual payments, were mostly handled by Florentine banks. Since the amount of revenue fluctuated owing to the different number of vacancies at any given time, and since, by the middle of the century, expenditures exceeded revenue, the banks also acted as creditors. It was precisely this supranational banking activity in service of the popes that made a considerable contribution to the expansion of the use of money and bank credits, and which led more than fifty years ago to the assertion that the fiscal policy at Avignon was one of the most important steps in the establishment of early capitalism.

The money taken in was then spent according to the personal philosophy and political goals of each pontiff. John XXII, for instance, used most of the money for wars (annual average: sixty-three percent) and relatives and friends (about four percent). His successor, Benedict XII, concentrated on alms (twenty percent) and buildings and real estate (twenty-five percent). Under Clement VI the costs for ceremonials increased—the coronation in 1342 alone cost 15,000 florins—while under Innocent VI the expenditures for the reconquest of the Papal States made up the major portion of expenses (altogether circa one million, or about forty-five percent of the expenditures of the entire pontificate). The ways in which the individual popes managed their household budget likewise varied. John XXII and Benedict XII took in more than they spent. Clement VI and Innocent VI lived off of their reserve funds until this money was exhausted. Urban V and Gregory XI so enlarged on the deficit that their predecessors had left behind that with increasing frequency they had to obtain loans from the papal bankers, which was a heavy mortgage for the epochs to come.

Approximately fifty percent of the *servitia* and other income usually came from France, from where most of the cardinals and curials came, too. This alone shows the close ties the papacy had with France. It is understandable that the popes took great pains to remain on good terms with the French kings. Initially, however, this was problematic due to Boniface VIII's government and the assassination attempt at Anagni. Philip IV blackmailed Clement V in particular by threatening to have Boniface condemned as a heretic—on the charge of idolatry and other offenses—at a general council that he wanted to convene in Lyon. Under pressure from the king, Clement had important texts like the *Clericis laicos* erased from the papal register, an event that had never before occurred. To what extent the king was serious in threatening legal action is uncertain since he also needed the pope. Even before 1305, Philip had plans to unite under his leadership as a so-called "Grand Master" all the existing orders of knights in France (the Knights of St. John, the Knights Templar, Knights of the Holy Sepulchre). At the papal coronation in Lyon in 1305, he complained to Clement about the Templars. Two years later he had all French Templars arrested, tortured, and interrogated. Inquisitors continued the interrogations. The confessions, obtained by force, acknowledged anti-Christian habits and sexual misconduct. Whether the king believed that such misconduct had occurred cannot be proved. Probably more important for Philip was that he, like Edward I of England, was greatly in debt to the Templars, which gave him a great interest in seeing the Templars wiped out. Beginning with a meeting in Poitiers in 1308, he put increasing pressure on the pope. Finally, the pope summoned a council to Vienne in 1311. This council was to have addressed the questions of a new crusade and the ecclesiastical reforms, but the Templar issue dominated the proceedings. Despite the opposition of numerous participants at the council, Clement administratively abolished the order; in return, the king did not press for a trial of Boniface, though in 1313 he did have Boniface's predecessor, Celestine V, canonized by Clement. Except on the Iberian peninsula the Knights of St. John were theoretically the heirs of the Templars, though in reality the king, in France anyway, took over most of the Templars' property. The king died in the same year that Clement did.

Because Philip's sons ruled for only a short time, the papacy, in the person of the politically well-versed John XXII, became the stronger power at first. Only from 1328 could the kings of the new Valois dynasty, in particular Philip VI (1328–1350) and Charles V (1364–1380), again have a stronger influence on the papacy. In this respect it was to their advantage that two of the popes, Clement VI and Innocent VI, had served for a time as royal chancellor or adviser. The two main political problems of that time for the papacy were the Hundred Years War (1338–1453) and the conflict of the curia with the German king, Louis of Bavaria. But first, to the great Anglo-French dispute: the war was initiated by England because Edward III, as grandson (on his mother's side) of Philip the IV of Valois, claimed the French throne. In reality, however, the war served to maintain and regain English territory on the mainland as patrimony of the Plantagenets. One of the consequences of the war was the devastation of the French countryside, from which several areas, Quercy and Auvergne, did not recover for centuries. Numerous churches and cloisters were also hit by this impoverishing disaster, with the Black Death following behind in 1348. It must also be taken into consideration that many curials, cardinals, and popes, from the time of Clement VI, came from these devasted areas. It is only obvious that the popes would have no great sympathy for the English invaders and would back the French kings politically. To what extent the papacy also helped them financially—possibly even with revenues from England—cannot, despite all the accusations made in England, be settled beyond all doubt. What is clear is that the French kings, more than ever before, and probably with papal consent, provided their own clerics with productive benefices; in other words, they claimed the papal right of appointment for themselves. In addition, from the time of Clement VI, the crusade tithe from the French kings' territory was placed at their disposal without any obligation to repay it.

These papal measures were enough, however, to increase the number of anti-curia voices in England. Originally, this did not mean that the English clergy necessarily stood on the side of the king; rather, it had more to do with the maintaining of the clergy's own interests. To this end, Boniface VIII's edicts guaranteeing the clergy's freedom from taxation as clerics were used. For the same reason, in the first years of Edward III's reign the lower clergy managed to avoid being summoned by Parliament so they would not have to commit themselves to paying any taxes under pressure from Parliament. On the other hand, Parliament and king were also allies of the clergy when their interests coincided. This is evident in the protest by the Parliament of Carlisle in 1307 against the annates raised by Clement V, and in the government's support of the clergy in its refusual to observe the constitutions of John XXII, the *Ex debito* of 1316 and the *Execrabilis* of 1317. This similarity of interests between the clergy and the crown (and the landed nobility) also became clear in the middle of the century. Possessed by the fear that the English benefices would be overly exploited by foreigners via papal conferments, and that the English payments would be used to the benefit of their French adversary, Parliament, in two resolutions, the Statute of Provisors of 1351 and the Statute of Praemunire of 1353, limited the papal right of appointment in favor of the English patrons and the crown and prohibited the exportation of English money to the curia. However, Edward III seldom observed these statutes, though later Parliaments ratified them. But these statutes did help English efforts to become independent of the pope, which in the long run strengthened the position of the king vis-à-vis the national church in particular. Also assisting in this process were, by the end of Edward III's reign, lower clergymen active in royal service, such as John Wycliffe, who later during the schism was a prominent critic of the papacy.

The war between England and France also encumbered the papacy's relations with Germany to a certain extent. More important for relations, however, was both powers' policy toward Italy. The papacy was most concerned with securing Rome and the Papal States and with not imperiling the Anjou kingdom in Naples. Clement V had a good relationship with Albert I of Germany because Clement wanted to stem the enormous influence of France. For this reason, he welcomed the election of the Luxembourger Henry VII after the murder of Albert. Philip had hoped to obtain the German crown for Charles of Valois. Clement changed his mind, however, when, in 1312, earlier than planned, Henry— greeted joyfully by opponents of the Anjou such as Dante—came to Rome for the imperial coronation and brushed against the power interests of the new king of Naples, Robert (1309–1343).

Because Robert's troops had occupied St. Peter's, Henry had to be crowned in the Lateran by three cardinals. When the new emperor then took steps against Robert, accusing him of lese majesty, the pope stood on Robert's side. In the dispute that broke out as a result of this, which continued after Henry's early death in 1313, the position and right of the imperial office was thoroughly debated on both sides. It was Dante, for example, who in his *Monarchia* placed the imperial office directly under God, while the pope maintained that the emperor was not independent from the pope. Clement formulated his opinion after Henry's death in two decretals, which, as part of the *Clementines* published by John XXII, also formed the legal basis for the papacy later on. In the first one (*Romani principes*), Clement stressed that whoever was elected (*Electi*) by the German princes needed to get papal approbation, and as emperor was bound to the pope by an oath of allegiance to protect the church. In the second decretal (*Pastoralis cura*), he defended Robert against the accusation of lese majesty by stating that Robert's kingdom did not belong to the empire, but rather, that the king was a vassal (*homo ligius et vasallus*) of the pope. Clement repealed Henry's judgment of Robert by declaring it void, basing this decision on the fact that the pope stood above the emperor, that in cases of a vacancy in the imperial throne the pope had such authority, and on papal *plenitudo potestatis*. Soon after, by virtue of the power ascribed to him, Clement named Robert as imperial vicar in Italy during the vacancy in the imperial throne. The seeds of later conflicts with Louis of Bavaria were planted in both of these decretals.

Beginning in 1314, two candidates fought over the royal crown in Germany—the Hapsburg Frederick and the Wittelsbacher Louis—until Louis won out over his rival in 1322, forcing him to give up. John XXII dealt with both pretenders only as "elected" (*Electi*), that is, he recognized neither one. Instead, he used the situation to confirm Robert of Naples as imperial vicar in Italy and to fight in a new crusade against any opponent of the Anjou, labeling them all tyrants, heretics, and rebels, especially the Visconti of Milan. Louis invaded Upper Italy in 1323 at the request of the Visconti. Consequently, the pope still refused to recognize Louis and, more importantly, now sought a French candidate for the German throne. Louis defended himself at diets in Nuremberg and Frankfurt in 1323–1324, attacking the pope as a heretic in the Appellation of Sachsenhausen in particular. There was continuous conflict, interrupted by negotiations at the curia, all the way up to 1346 between the popes and Louis, whom John referred to contemptuously as "the Bavarian." These conflicts were to be the last great battle between the Holy Roman Empire and the papacy. Louis made his own situation more difficult by having himself crowned emperor in 1328—the only imperial coronation since the Carolingian period performed by a layman—by the elderly Sciarra Colonna, one of the assassins of Anagni, and by propping up Nicholas V, an impotent antipope. Negotiations with Benedict XII, which seemed to hold out some hope for success, failed in 1337 because Louis would not renounce claims based on his imperial coronation, nor would he recognize the papal claim of approbation, and because he formed an alliance with England. In the end, Clement VI was less ready to negotiate than his predecessor, setting up Charles IV as a rival claimant to the throne, who in 1346 was elected by a majority of the electors and after Louis' death in 1347 was gradually acknowledged in all of Germany. Louis' shortcomings do not mean the curia's position went unchallenged. The papal claim of approbation was never recognized in Germany, not even by Charles IV, ending up as a sort of unilateral party manifesto. And the largely pro-French and pro-Anjou position of the three popes made any objectivity on their part impossible. More politically astute than Louis, Charles IV met the pope halfway verbally, though in reality he obtained a growing independence from the papacy for Germany. Both Italy and Burgundy, on the other hand, he abandoned.

During Louis' conflict with the curia it became evident to what extent Germany had become estranged from the papacy. John XXII and his successors reimposed the interdict on areas whose inhabitants supported Louis, and in so doing banned all ritual practices. If this prohibition was observed—as it was in particular among the Dominicans—then many cities had no baptisms, church weddings, or burials, and no worship services for decades; if the prohibition was not observed, then papal prestige sank. In either case, aversion toward the papacy grew, as did the influence of municipal authority, in particular on the clergy, Strasbourg being a prime example. And as the *Planctus ecclesiae in Germania* (Elegy for the Church in Germany), written in 1338 by Conrad of Megenberg, shows without a doubt, thoughts of separating the German church from the papacy were not unknown. Without any cardinal presence at all in the curia, the German hierarchy was also estranged from the papacy. A clear example of this is the pontifical compiled on behalf of Archbishop Baldwin of Trier, the brother of Henry VII and grandson of Charles IV. Until the early sixteenth century it was more widespread in Germany than Roman pontificals, and it contained no ordo for either the imperial coronation nor the papal coronation. In the same way that Charles IV rejected the continuation of the principles of Otto I in his political policies, it was also necessary to break from the Ottonian age in the liturgy.

Contacts with Constantinople were intensified, in particular from the time of Urban V, a development important for the later epoch of councils. For the first time in more than seven hundred years, a Byzantine emperor, John V, visited Rome in 1369. He came with the idea of seeking Western aid to battle the Turks, who had already pushed into Asia Minor and Greece. Though he came away empty-handed, the threat to the Eastern empire and the attempts to reunite the two churches continued to be opportunities for renewed contacts between East and West, which eventually led to the works of Western theologians like Thomas Aquinas being accepted more than ever in the East.

Beyond Byzantium, however, the Latin church suffered heavy losses as the Ming dynasty, which ruled China from 1368, ended the Latin mission there and the ecclesiastical organization. The military expedition of the Mongol leader Timur Lenk, which began soon after, also contributed to the downfall of Christendom in Central Asia. The only positive element in this for Byzantium and the West was that the Mongol leader's campaign also threatened the Turks, thereby temporarily preventing any further penetration on their part in the West.

Criticism of the papacy was on the rise, not only in Germany but elsewhere, because of the fiscally oriented policy on benefices, the increased use of ecclesiastic punishments, the political exploitation of church marriage laws—especially by John XXII—as well as the jealous exploitation of crusade indulgences and crusade tithes. At least equally as grave were the doubts over the orthodoxy of the popes, especially John XXII's. Such doubts were raised during the so-called poverty controversy. From the beginning of the century, strict Spirituals in the Franciscan order reproached their community more than ever for not fulfilling the precept of poverty required of Franciscans. Their spokesman at the curia was Ubertino of Casale, who had been promoted by Clement V. The

Council of Vienne also accepted the complaint. For his part, John XXII backed the upper echelon of the order under the leadership of Michael of Cesena, elected in 1316, and had unruly Spirituals persecuted. But the leaders of the order also estranged themselves from the pope when, during the "theoretical poverty controversy," disputes arose whether Christ and the apostles had been poor, that is, whether they had owned any possessions or not. A general chapter in Perugia in 1322 answered by saying that they were indeed poor, installing this as orthodox doctrine. For the pope, as the successor of Christ, this was bound to have far-reaching consequences, namely, the renunciation of any possessions. With this in mind, John once again allowed discussion of Nicholas III's constitution *Exiit,* any word of which had until then been banned, and gave up all claim to the property of the Franciscan order, which popes from the time of Innocent IV and Nicholas III had taken over to preserve the order's "poverty." In so doing, he exposed the fiction of the order's alleged poverty. And finally, in 1323, he characterized as heretical the claim brought forward in Perugia regarding Christ's poverty. Several Franciscans countered by accusing him of heresy, an accusation Louis of Bavaria was only too happy to take up. Thus, in 1328, the general of the order, Michael, as well as his fellow members Bonagratia of Bergamo and William Occam, all of whom were being detained at the curia, fled to Louis, supporting him ideologically in his battle against the curia—especially in the latter part of John XXII's pontificate and after the failure of negotiations in 1337—together with another refugee, Marsiglio of Padua. Even part of the College of Cardinals, led by Napoleone Orsini, turned to Louis to obtain a condemnation of the pope by a general council. Robert of Naples and his consort Sanica likewise expressed their disapproval of John's theological ideas on poverty.

John supplied his critics with new ammunition in discourses he gave on the *visio beatifica* (beatific vision) in the years 1332 and 1333. With reference to early Christian views, the pope held the opinion that the souls of the righteous fully beheld God only after the last judgment, while the doctrinal opinion of the day said this vision came immediately upon death. In the opinion of most theologians, the pope had erred dogmatically. In Paris, the government came out against him, and Robert of Naples likewise wrote a tract refuting the pope's assertion. It is quite understandable that Louis and his assistants would make the most of this opportunity.

To stem the criticism, and out of his own conviction, Benedict XII established the traditional teaching as dogma in 1336. Because Benedict did not condemn his predecessor, however, and because he also—understandably—held the same opinion John did on the poverty of Christ, he was considered a heretic by Occam and others. It was due to this mixture of political, ecclesiastico-legal, and dogmatic elements that the conflict between Louis and the curia had such explosive power. The conflict weakened the position of the papacy in the areas of jurisdiction and doctrine.

Adding to the difficulties was the fact that many held the papacy principally to blame for the downfall of the church, no longer viewing the papacy as capable of reforming the church. The only Avignon pontiff to attempt a reform of the church on his own initiative was Benedict XII. He was, in fact, the last pope at all for two hundred years to try any reforms. His changes in the curia and in the bestowing of benefices have been briefly mentioned already. Even more consequential were his constitutions for the reform of several orders—1335 for the Cistercians (his own order), 1336 for the Benedictines and the Franciscans, 1339 for the canons regular—which remained in use, as guidelines at least, into the fifteenth century, some of them even to the seventeenth century. Although these constitutions very much reflected the monastic ideal, they did not take into account the strength of Franciscan regulations in particular. Benedict's pontificate does show, however, that a far-reaching reform of the papacy was not possible at this time, for not only was Benedict shaped by regionally and monastically limited ideas, but he also excluded any reform of his own office.

Yet from the beginning of the century, and especially after the Council of Vienne, reform of the papacy and the curia was being demanded. Bishops like the younger William Duranti of Mende envisioned a strengthening of the episcopates and through that the councils; representatives of the crown, like Jean Quidort of Paris, wanted equal footing for church and state; precursors of later doctrine, like Marsiglio of Padua, even postulated the placing of the clergy under state authority. Initially, these ideas were merely toys for theoretical speculation, useful in political conflicts with individual popes; but they soon gained in influence, especially with the papacy relying on the help of secular powers as it was after the beginning of the schism of 1378. The papacy's return to Rome was preceded by this schism.

Living beyond the Alps in Avignon did not deter the popes from striving to secure their rule over Rome and the Papal States. And just as it did their predecessors in the thirteenth century, this intention strongly influenced the popes' policy toward Germany, as the conflicts with Henry VII and Louis the Bavarian showed. They also frequently expressed the intention of having the curia returned to Rome. Their efforts failed, however, at least for the first few decades, due to the opposition of the upwardly moving Signori in the Papal States and because of the communes, which were often torn apart by party conflicts, as evinced by the long-standing legation of John XXII's nephew Bertrand de Poujet. It was only the Roman cardinals, and especially Giacomo Caetani Stefaneschi, who kept close contact with their home city, as can still be seen today in the works commissioned by Stefaneschi in St. Peter's (by Giotto and other artists). Benedict XII was somewhat more successful. He not only had the Lateran basilica and St. Peter's restored, but he also tried in 1338 to settle a dispute in Rome. His legate, Bertrand de Déaux, issued statutes for several communes that remained in force for years.

Clement VI was able to build on Benedict's success. At the beginning of his pontificate, a Roman legation appeared in Avignon which, following a tradition from the time of Nicholas III, proclaimed Clement senator of Rome, asking him to return to Rome and to proclaim a new Holy Year for the benefit of the Roman church as well as local innkeepers. The pope granted the second wish by proclaiming 1350 a Holy Year, going against Boniface VIII's instruction to declare such a jubilee only every hundred years. Preparations were disrupted in 1347 by a man who five years earlier had been a part of the legation: Cola di Rienzo, one of the most bizarre figures of the time. A friend of Petrarch's, he portrayed himself as successor to Constantine, knight of the Holy Spirit, and tribune, with the idea of freeing Rome from the control of the nobility and unifying Italy under Rome's leadership. This also jeopardized papal authority. As a sign of his intent, he had a stone slab with the *lex regia* of Vespasian on it brought to the conservatory palace on the Capitoline. This stone, still there today, had originally been built into the altar of the Lateran basilica at the end of the thirteenth century, and had as its main theme the transfer of power by the people to the emperor. After seven months, Rienzo's dream had temporarily run its course, the hero escaping to the mountains. The jubilee prepartions then began in grand style, directed in Rome by the legate Annibaldo of Ceccano, a *nipote* of Stefaneschi's. In spite of the difficult times of the Black Death, which the populace had just gone through, the Holy Year was a financial success; even an assassination attempt on the legate did not stop the bonds to the papacy from growing closer.

Under the new pope, Innocent VI, the most important preparations for the return to Rome ensued: the military subjection of a major portion of the Papal States by the Spanish cardinal, Gil Albornoz, an operation that lasted, with interruptions, from 1353 to 1365. His *rocche* (fortresses) are still standing in many cities today. He immortalized himself with his constitutions, which were built on those of Bertrand de Déaux and local statutes (Perugia's, for example) and which, until the Napoleonic Age, formed the constitutional basis of the Papal States. For this reason, the cardinal is considered to be the second founder of the Papal States, after Innocent III. The Spanish College he founded in Bologna still lives to this day from his endowment. But Cardinal Albornoz never made it to Rome. Initially, he depended on Cola di Rienzo in Rome, who had returned there in 1354 on behalf of the pope in his capacity as senator in an attempt to pacify the city. But after nine weeks he failed due to the opposition of the Roman nobility (Savelli and Orsini); he was eventually killed and mutilated by their agents. Yet his actions were not without success. In 1358, a new municipal government came to power—ratified by Albornoz—whose statutes of 1363 were similar to those of other communes in Central Italy (with a corresponding *podestà*, called "senator") and which ruled the life of the city for the next few decades. And just like earlier city governments, the new one also claimed that its sovereignty stretched from Montalto in the north to Terracina in the south.

With new ideas of autonomy in mind, the Roman government was bound to run into conflict with the papacy as soon as it was reestablished in Rome. The first step in this direction was undertaken by Urban V. The pope, greeted by Albornoz in Coroneto (today known as Tarquinia), entered Rome on October 16, 1365; Cardinal Albornoz had died two months earlier. Urban restored the great churches, in particular St. Peter's, where he lived and which he expanded. Both of these actions were based on the Avignon model. The Lateran lay "outside the city," as account books of the *camera* put it. It was Urban's wish to weaken the rising powers in Italy, and especially the Visconti of Milan, in order to be the most important political player on the Apennine peninsula. His plan did not succeed, however, as Florence held back and military success remained elusive. It took a peace settlement arranged by Charles IV to guarantee the status quo. In 1368, the pope left Rome, probably weary of the unrest there, henceforth staying in Viterbo and Montefiascone, which he built up as his residence. Disappointed by his political failures and under pressure from the cardinals—in creating two cardinals in Montefiascone he preferred Frenchmen—he returned to Avignon in 1370 against the advice of the highly esteemed nuns Catherine of Siena and Bridget of Sweden. Two months after returning to Avignon he died.

His successor, Gregory XI, created cardinal by his uncle Clement VI at barely eighteen years of age, soon planned a second return to Rome. In preparation, he called together in 1371 a new league against the Visconti. To put an end once and for all to Visconti power, he prepared the trip to Rome in 1375, this time with the backing of many cardinals. Deserted by several of his allies, he ended up, however, having to make peace with the Visconti on rather unfavorable terms. The situation grew worse when Milan and Florence formed an alliance, with other cities of Tuscany and the Papal States also joining in, which was brought about by the papacy's extreme demands for subsidies. After recruiting soldiers, and vehemently threatening Florence, Gregory left Avignon for good on September 13, 1376, supported in his plans by Catherine of Siena. At the beginning of 1377, the pope was in Rome, only to find that almost all the Papal States were in tumult. But since Florence was also inclined to a reconciliation because of its business interests, a congress took place in Sarzana in February 1378, under mediation of the Visconti, of all people, at which peace was to be restored. Before the negotiations could be completed, however, Gregory died March 27 in Rome.

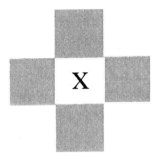

Schism and Reform (1378–1447)

Like Urban V, Gregory XI had probably planned to return to Avignon at the end of his pontificate, and specifically, by the summer of 1378. Supporting this assumption is the fact that Gregory issued a constitution a week before his death in which he repealed the decrees on papal elections of Alexander III and Gregory X if he were to die before September, which would necessitate a new election in Rome. In so doing, he wanted to reduce the pressure from the Romans and make a quick succession possible. Whoever of their circle received a simple majority—that is, the Limousin cardinals in particular—was to be elected. The pope's plan was not implemented, however, because the chamberlain, his cousin Pierre de Gros, did not release the text, so that none of the cardinals was aware of Gregory's stipulations. Thus the election took place April 7 in conformity with the usual formalities.

The claim cannot be made, however, that the cardinals were able to deliberate without outside pressure. The pressure to elect a Roman, or at least an Italian, came from all sides, first from deputies of the militia and the city of Rome, and then by the crowds themselves that had gathered in front of St. Peter's, all using threats. After discussing several candidates, most of the cardinals agreed upon Bartolomeo Prignano, the archbishop of Bari and head of the chancery in place of the vice chancellor, who had stayed behind in Avignon. Crowds then stormed the palace in protest, demanding a Roman pope, leaving the cardinals to enthrone hurriedly the aged Francesco de' Tebaldeschi in the chapel before they fled the palace. The next day, after Prignano had called upon them to do so, most of the cardinals came back to the palace and enthroned him. Prignano gave himself the name of Urban VI. The cardinals presented him with the customary petitions, and then took part in worship services being held not for the new pope but in celebration of Holy Week, before the new pontiff was crowned on Easter Sunday, April 18. The cardinals stayed at his court for the next three months, assisting him with liturgical functions. The curia that had remained in Rome likewise seemed to have acknowledged him. Nevertheless, doubts about the legitimacy of the election were soon expressed, as in the sermon of a Franciscan in the church Ara Coeli two days after Urban's election, and in a secret letter from cardinals to foreign princes. Urban himself did nothing to endear himself. In the eyes of the wealthy cardinals a mere archbishop (*archiepiscopellus*) whose episcopate numbered only 1,500 florins in *servitia*, he was blinded by his meteoric rise to power, believing that he had the right to depose of cardinals and kings at his discretion. Prolix and imprudent, he even offended his own supporters. He repeatedly stressed his having been elected by the Holy Spirit, which only fed the doubts about his election. He made a complete fool of himself when he claimed that portraits of the princely apostles in the Lateran palace used to have a sad look on their faces, but were smiling now that he held the papal office.

The situation came to a head in the summer. The cardinals met mostly in Anagni, where the curia had been sent in June, while Urban moved to Tivoli. The cardinals sent a legate to Tivoli who notified the pope in the name of the cardinals that he had no right to the papal office, though perhaps in a new election he would be reelected. Acting as go-betweens were the Italian cardinals who had stayed in Rome—Orsini, Corsini, and de Borsano. They tried early on to convene a general council that could serve to mediate the issue. But these efforts failed, and on July 20 the French cardinals declared the election invalid. They then moved to Frondi in Neapolitan territory and elected on September 20, in the presence of their Italian colleagues, Cardinal Robert of Geneva as the new pope, who took on the name Clement VII and was crowned October 31. As a final act, the chamberlain brought the insignia of the tiara to the new Pope Clement. For the next few decades there would now be two popes.

The question of who was the legal successor to Peter caused difficulties not only for the non-French cardinals—the three Italians (Tebaldeschi was now dead) and the Aragonese Pedro de Luna—but also for contemporary rulers, prelates, and theologians or jurists. Even today, the matter is still disputed; only to Catholic church historians who are influenced by the first Vaticanum and shaped by modes of perception that have come along since the fifteenth century is it clear that Urban and his successors are the legitimate popes. In Urban's favor was the fact that he was elected formally and in conformity with the traditional laws and that the cardinals who were in Rome had served him for three months. The charge of incapacity had not been clearly defined in church law, though the moral integrity of many French cardinals as nepotists, simonists, and benefice hunters was not beyond all doubt, either. And Clement VII did not exactly correspond to the ideal image of a pope. Moreover, there had also been secular pressure in earlier elections, as in the election of John XXII in 1316. Owing to the contested legal situation, the historian can merely confirm that from the end of 1378 there were two popes, each of whom had supporters who were morally irreproachable and versed in canon law. As it did in 1130 and 1159, the situation lay in the hands of the leading prelates and heads of the orders, in particular, however, with the secular rulers. These rulers were by no means unified, exploiting the situation to their own advantage—but more about this later. The result was that the obediences (spheres of jurisdiction) of both popes were consolidated on the basis of ecclesiastico-political points of view.

In addition to the old cardinals, most of the curials also supported Clement VII, who from 1381 resided in Avignon. Both of these circumstances guaranteed the normal routine at his curia. The countries which lined up on Clement's side after 1380 were France, the most important source of revenue up to now, Castile, Scotland (against England), and finally Aragon and Navarre. Urban VI had to first form a new curia. Already in 1378 he was able to count on Germany (except for the upper Rhine), its northern and eastern neighbors, as well as on most of the Italian power brokers and England. After much vacillating, Portugal also came out on Urban's side—because of competition with Castile and in alliance with England. Many of the great orders—the Cistercians, the mendicant orders—were divided, and now had two boards in charge of them. And owing to fights over jurisdiction, cathedral chapters and monasteries joined with Clement if their bishop or abbot was a supporter of Urban—and vice versa. Greedy benefice seekers petitioned both popes. But even the cardinals themselves oscillated in their support; the best-known example is that of Pileus de Prata, created cardinal by Urban in 1378, and who in 1387 moved to Avignon after Urban had five cardinals executed the year before as alleged conspirators. In 1391 he returned to Rome, and thus he is called the "cardinal with the three hats." It goes without saying that the doubling of pope and curia because of the claims made by both sides was a burden on the faithful, who were caught in the middle. There was also a stagnation of papal prestige, and as the split dragged on, a widespread insecurity regarding the validity of ordinations and sacraments. The division grew even deeper in that Clement VII's claims continued through his successor, Benedict XIII, while Urban VI's claims carried on through Boniface IX, Innocent VII, and Gregory XII, all of whom were convinced of their legitimacy and none of whom seriously considered stepping aside. For this reason, another method had to be found to end the schism.

The popes themselves—especially the experienced war commander Clement VII and his personally upright, still politically versed successor, Benedict XIII—followed the *via facti;* in other words, they tried to reestablish unity by defeating their opponent. Meanwhile, the French government and the University of Paris decided in 1395 after fruitless negotiations to renounce their allegiance (*via cessionis*) to their pope. The decree was formed at a spring synod in Paris over the opposition of the university chancellor, Pierre d'Ailly, who previously had been a member of Benedict's *familia* and quickly had received the episcopate of Le Puy from him. Benedict rejected the demands of the first synod as well as the second synod held in the summer. The third synod of 1398 had far more important consequences for Benedict. Since, in the meantime, both France and England had joined together after their cease-fire in support of the *via cessionis,* as did the French ally Castile, Aragon was the only kingdom that remained loyal to Benedict. On July 28, Charles VI solemnly proclaimed France's withdrawl from its obedience to Benedict. Eighteen cardinals followed this example by moving to Villeneuve-lès-Avignon in France and by trying to hinder Benedict from performing his official duties. The papal palace was bombarded by cannon; even after a cease-fire in 1399, the pope remained confined to the palace. But a turning point came in 1403: Benedict escaped and soon obtained the backing once again of the cardinals and the French government. This was due above all to the fact that the duke of Orleans, who looked favorably upon Benedict, was now the guiding hand behind French policies, and by extension, the force behind the cardinals. Benedict then attempted, over the course of several years, both through negotiations and through political and military pressure, to come to terms with the Roman popes, whose regime was in extreme jeopardy due to power struggles in the Kingdom of Naples in particular. First in September 1407, and then in the spring of 1408, Benedict and Gregory were supposed to meet in Savona, and then at a location in Tuscany, to bring about a solution to the schism. As the attempts to meet failed, principally because of Gregory XII, most of Gregory's cardinals deserted him, appealing to a general council and strengthening their ties to Benedict's cardinals. In 1408, France once again withdrew its obedience to Benedict after earlier in the year Benedict's most important supporter, Duke Louis of Orleans, was murdered at the instigation of the duke of Burgundy. In danger of being taken into custody by a French legation under the direction of the patriarch of Alexandria, Simon de Cramaud, Benedict called a council to the Aragonese city of Perpignan and headed there by sea. But most of his cardinals were now united with their Roman colleagues and soon called a council of their own to Pisa. Gregory XII also called for a council, which he decided would be held in Cividale and thus under the influence of his home base of Venice. Few prelates ended up coming, however. Thus there were now three councils taking place more or less simultaneously.

That all interested parties hoped a council could put an end to the schism shows clearly just how far the "conciliar idea" had spread. Canonists as early as the twelfth and thirteenth centuries had viewed a general council as a possible corrective power vis-à-vis the papacy, while such rulers as Frederick II, Philip the Fair, and Louis the Bavarian all had made appeals to a general council in conflicts with the papacy. And likewise during the preparations of the Second Council of Lyon in 1274 and the Council of Vienne in 1311–1312, the council was propagated as the highest board for church reforms. In light of the Avignon papacy, the number of supporters for councils increased, supporters who attributed in part a higher position to councils as a representation of the entire church than they did to the papacy. It thus becomes clear why there were scattered references made by persons like Marsiglio of Padua to councils convened in late antiquity by the emperor.

In view of this tradition, it is hardly surprising that already in 1378 the three Italian cardinals proposed a council, as did Parisian professors like Henry of Langenstein or the cathedral prior of Worms, Conrad of Gelnhausen, at which an end was to be put to the schism. This possibility must have been looked at even more favorably after other methods—*via facti* and *via cessionis*—did not get anywhere. Of course, there was still dispute over who could legally convene a council, since from the twelfth century this was considered a papal privilege. And both Benedict XIII and Gregory XII showed that they were abiding by tradition with their council plans, though relatively few prelates took part in their councils. It was important for the legitimization of the Pisa council that respect had risen for the College of Cardinals in the course of the fourteenth century; some even viewed the cardinals, not the bishops, as successors to the apostle. Clement VII's cardinals emphasized in detailed tracts their position as judge over papal elections. In addition to the cardinals, princes were also granted the right, and in particular the Roman king or emperor, to force the church to convene a council in an emergency. The question of whom the council was to be composed, like the question of who was to convene it, was answered in various ways: there were those who supported having a council in each obedience, such as the councils of Perpignan and Pisa. It was also thought to have a council made up of both cardinals and princes, or a council strictly of cardinals. Equally as controversial was whether the council stood over the pope as the representative organ of the Universal Church, and whether it alone was infallible. This diversity of opinion was to carry on in the future, so that in later conflicts between the papacy and the council, supporters of both parties were able to make appeals to precedence.

The councils of Perpignan and Cividale were meant to undermine the claims of the ruling pope at the time. Gregory XII had little success, in the end having to flee. Benedict XIII retained the continued support of Aragon and a part of the clergy of Provence, although he rejected the idea of resigning. Despite all that, the Council of Perpignan still sent a legation to Pisa. And not only members of this legation, but also other council participants and curials, turned away from Benedict to embrace the new Pisan pope, Alexander V.

Numerous abbots and many emmisaries from bishops, princes, and universities, mostly from Italy and France, were gathered in Pisa, in addition to twenty-four cardinals and over eighty bishops. Presided over by cardinals and dominated by Simon de Cramaud as leader of the French, the Council of Pisa sat for twenty-two sessions, which in turn were prepared for in the so-called nations (French, Italian, German, English, Provencal) and in the College of Cardinals. The main goal was the removal from office of both popes and the election of a new one; in addition, questions regarding reform of the church were discussed. On June 5, 1409, Benedict XIII and Gregory XII were excommunicated as schismatics, heretics, and perjurers and obedience withdrawn from them. The conclave was then prepared. The archbishop of Milan, Peter Philarghi, a native of Crete who had gained ascendancy in service to the Visconti, emerged victorious on June 26 from the election, becoming Alexander V in a coronation on July 7. He ratified for his supporters the benefices they had gained during the schism and convened a new council for 1412 that was to deal with the matter of church reform.

Even though Pisa was an important turing point on the way to church unity, the direct result was, however, that there were now three popes, since the Spanish rulers and the national churches did not recognize Alexander V, while the German king Rupert held to his Roman pope. This changed when the Hungarian king Sigismund, a son of Charles IV and a supporter of Pisa from early on, was elected German king in 1411. Alexander's successor, John XXIII, in accordance with the Pisan resolution, opened a council on reforms in Rome in 1412, which accomplished little except that upon adjourning it announced a new council for 1413. Soon after, John was driven out of Rome by Ladislas of Naples, who threatened the entire Papal States. John then had two cardinals meet with Sigismund to negotiate over the council that had been planned. One of the negotiators was the canonist and council supporter, Francesco Zabarella. The negotiations resulted in Sigismund announcing a council to be held in Constance on November 1, 1414, and the publishing of a bull of convocation by the pope at the end of 1413. This was followed by extensive negotiations on the part of Sigismund with Castile, and Aragon especially, to convince the supporters of Benedict XIII to attend the council. Another potential difficulty was the conflict between England and France, in which Burgundy was also involved. Sigismund succeeded in preventing the outbreak of war until after the council had begun, and in so doing assured the presence of French, English, and Burgundian participants. For the first time since late antiquity, it was a secular ruler who had assembled together the entire church, though of course only the Western church. But this alone clearly shows that the Council of Constance was heavily dependent on political factors.

The council was opened by John XXIII on November 5, 1414, and was to address not only matters of church reform and faith (which we will deal with later), but was, above all, to serve church unity as its forerunner the Council of Pisa had done. It soon became clear that it was necessary for John to step down to achieve unity. John seemed to have acquiesced, but on March 21, 1415, he escaped from the city under the protection of the duke of Austria and wanted to dissolve the council. In opposing him, the council decreed on April 6 that a general council had a higher authority than the pope (the decree *Haec sancta*). With this, the trial against John began. On May 29, the pope, who had been brought back a prisoner, was deposed, accused of being a simonist, a supporter of the schism, and a poor leader of the church. Soon after, on July 4, Carlo Malatesta announced the resignation of Gregory XII. The efforts by Sigismund and the council to force Benedict XIII to resign took longer, and in the end were unsuccessful. Nevertheless, the Spanish empire was won over to participate in the council by the Treaty of Narbonne of December 13, 1415, although it was two years before their representative actually attended the council as the fifth "nation" and the obedience was withdrawn from Benedict. On July 26, 1417, Benedict was finally deposed. This did not prevent him, however, from viewing himself as the lawful pope until his death in 1423 in the Aragonese Peñiscola. Of all the popes during the period of the schism, he was the best; under more favorable circumstances he probably would have become a significant pope.

In contrast to 1409, from 1415 to 1417 all rulers and national churches supported the proceedings against the popes. Because of this, all parties could expect that after Benedict's removal from office the new pontiff would be acknowledged everywhere. After several votes, a Roman, Oddo Colonna, was elected on November 11, taking the name of Martin V in honor of the saint whose day it was. He was crowned on November 21 and from then on presided over the council. On March 21, 1418, he proclaimed in his name seven reform decrees that had been worked out before his election, and concluded separate concordats with the five council nations which were to be valid—except for England—for five years until the next council and which were to assure the realization of the reform decrees, in particular a curtailing of the papal right to fill vacant positions.

Martin V had to accept cardinals and assistants of all three obediences, while for its part, the council limited the number of curials as well as papal income. Therefore, Martin desired to return to Rome as soon as possible and make use of the Papal States. He left Constance on May 16, 1418, though it was not until September 28, 1420, that he was able to make his ceremonial entry into Rome. His situation was made more difficult by the first great Italian *condottiere,* Braccio da Montone, who ruled most of Central Italy and with it the Papal States. On top of this was the confusing state of affairs in the Kingdom of Naples. Martin invested Louis III of Anjou with the crown, designating him as successor to Queen Joanna II. Joanna took revenge by adopting the young and energetic Alfonso V of Aragon, already ruler of Sicily, who entered Naples in 1421 and used the claims of Benedict XIII, who was still alive, as a means of exerting pressure. After a cease-fire in the autumn of 1421, and after further negotiations, Alfonso finally left Naples in 1424. In the same year, Braccio was killed in the siege of L'Aquila. In 1420 papal troops had already defeated a rebellion in Bologna. After 1424, the pope was therefore able to devote all his attention to the reconstruction of the Papal States; in fact, he is considered their third founder. Since by this time most of the concordats made in Constance had expired, there was from now on more revenue at Martin's disposition from the conferment of benefices. Yet it goes without saying that in this tense situation he did not expend much effort on the new council in Pavia/Siena of 1423–1424, soon dissolving it. His efforts were not directed toward restoring the churches but toward restoring the papacy along the lines of the papacy of the thirteenth and fourteenth centuries. In this regard, Martin accomplished a great feat, leaving his mark on the age to come.

He held to his promises made in Constance, however, if at times not voluntarily. On October 1, 1417, shortly before the papal election, it was decided at the council (in the *Frequens* decree) that regular councils should meet: the first one after five years, the second seven years later, and after that every ten years. A pope was allowed to shorten the frequency, but not extend it. Martin satisfied this requirement by calling together to Basle, shortly before his death, a new council over which the cardinal Giuliano Cesarini was to preside with the full power of authority to dissolve it immediately. The new pope, Eugene IV, confirmed Cesarini's mandate. Cesarini had the council opened July 23, 1431, by his representative since he himself was still battling the Hussites. A few months later, on November 12, Eugene dissolved the council, patterning his action on that of his predecessor in Siena. He had less success than they did, however, as Cesarini rejected Eugene IV's order with the backing of a majority of the cardinals (15 of 21). Henceforth the council and the pope were adversaries, even though the pope withdrew his bull of dissolution on December 15, 1433, his hand forced by the situation in the Papal States.

Eugene IV had the Greeks to thank for his eventual victory. Beginning in 1433, the council and the pope undertook negotiations with Constantinople to work out a union with the Eastern church as a basis for a crusade against the Turks. The main point of contention was where such a unity council should take place. Because both Eugene and the Greeks were interested in a location in Italy, which most of the delegates at the Council of Basle rejected, Eugene succeeded, partly by dint of some questionable means, in transferring the council from Basle to Ferrara on September 18, 1437, and then managed to direct the Greek emissaries to meet there. Since most of the participants at the council remained in Basle, however, there were now two councils—in other words, a new schism. The situation was aggravated by the Council of Basle's decision on June 25, 1439, to depose Eugene IV and to elect the widowed Duke Amadeus VIII as the new pope, the last antipope. He called himself Felix V. During this period, Eugene's council, which in the meantime had moved to Florence, formed a union with the Greeks on July 6, 1439 (the decree *Laetentur coeli*), followed by additional agreements with Armenians, Copts, Maronites, and others. Even though these various unifications were barely taken notice of in the East, they did increase the prestige of the pope in the West. His position further improved by the fact that even France did not acknowledge his removal from office, Castile stood by him from 1439, England was indifferent, and Alfonso V changed his mind in favor of Eugene in 1443 after the conquest of Naples and great concessions on Eugene's part. And the German king, Frederick III, also embraced Eugene IV because he wanted to receive the imperial crown from him. There was even an agreement made in 1447 with the German electors, though the archbishops of Cologne and Mainz had been deposed by Eugene in 1446. Thus Nicholas V, as the new pope, was soon able to unify the church and then to achieve both the resignation of Felix V and the dissolution of the Council of Basle in 1449 (it had moved to Lausanne in 1447). With that behind him, he was then able to undertake a vigorous drive for the restoration of papal power.

From the beginning of the schism, it became evident how much the prestige of the antipopes depended on the goodwill of secular powers. It is only logical that these rulers would exploit the opportunity to increase their influence on the clergy of their lands. The most successful rulers were those who belonged to the Roman obedience, since the position of the Roman popes was usually weaker than that of their competitors in Avignon. The kings of England were especially successful at taking away the papal right to fill vacancies and making use of this right themselves, resulting in the higher clergy becoming more and more dependent on royal power, an important prerequisite for the Anglican church constitution of the sixteenth century. The lack of interest in reform efforts on the part of English participants at the councils of Constance and Basle was due to these changes, since the curtailments in papal rights and revenue that were demanded at the councils had for the most part already been realized in England. What may seem surprising at first glance is that Italian princes and communes—Milan, Venice, Florence—also brought the clergy more firmly under their control. Working to their advantage was the fact that the Roman popes were dependent on their support, due to frequent threats by Naples and the uncertainty in the Papal States stemming from these threats. The situation in Germany was more complicated. Apart from Italians, Germans formed the major part of the curials in Rome, as far as is known. The German rulers relied more heavily on cooperation with the popes either because of domestic German poltical squabbles (Wenzel, Rupert), or out of conviction, or for the purpose of obtaining the imperial crown. On the other hand, individual princes or city officials were able to place more than ever before the national clergy and the city clergy under their own "government" by founding universities or by promoting and controlling reforms, in particular among the Benedictines and the mendicant orders. To be able to continue these policies on an even more intensive scale, and urged on by the grievances of disappointed former curials such as Dietrich of Niem, German participants of both secular and clerical standing at the council supported reforms of the papacy and the curia to reduce papal privileges and revenue for their regions. The German king also profited from this, in particular during the latter part of Eugene IV's pontificate and under Nicholas V, but more on this later.

Within the Avignon obedience, it was Aragon, in particular, that exploited this favorable opportunity. Just as his Castilian colleague did, Peter IV, "el ceremonioso" (1336–1387), had the controversial papal election of 1378 investigated, including an examination of witnesses, though in the end he remained indifferent, acknowledging neither of the two popes. He founded a *"camera apostolica"* for his own territory which adminstered the revenue from the benefices through a trust, though in case of need the funds were made available to the king, which of course encouraged royal influence in the filling of ecclesiastical posts. Peter's successor, John I (1387–1395), came out in favor of Clement VII. From that time on, the Aragonese kings up to Alfonso V (1416–1458) were the most consistent supporters of the Avignon obedience, the reason for this being that, from 1394 to the end of the schism, the Aragonese aristocrat Pedro de Luna, whose relatives often held important government posts, ruled as Benedict XIII. Yet the more uncertain French help for Avignon became, the more Benedict fell into dependency on Aragon. This was also evident in the fact that from 1408 he resided only in Aragonese cities (Perpignan, Peñiscola) and appointed almost all Aragonese curials. Benedict became a total political puppet when, in 1416 and 1417, most of the curials left him and the new ruler, Alfonso V, also backed the Council of Constance. Whenever it was useful for his efforts to obtain Naples, then Alfonso threatened to renew his support of Benedict. For the same reason, Alfonso tolerated the election of a new pope in Peñiscola in 1423, Clement VIII, who finally stepped down in 1429 before Martin V's legate Pierre de Foix. In the following period, Alfonso was able to blackmail the papacy with Naples, until he came to terms with Eugene IV in 1443. In addition, his political dominance in Southern Italy and in the western Mediterranean brought about a further dependence on royal power among the clergy under him—in the crown lands as well as in Sicily—and a degeneration to mere fiction of the feudal dependence on the papacy.

The kings of Castile were less successful. Beginning with the power struggles of 1369, the new dynasty of the Trastamara relied on the backing of the higher clergy. Initially an enemy of both Portugal and England because of conflicts involving hereditary succession, Castile associated more closely with France, which influenced Castile's position vis-à-vis the councils of Pisa and Constance. The assembly held in Medina del Campo showed that also in Castile the king had a strong grip on the church. After the first king of the new dynasty, Henry II (d. 1379), carefully reviewed the information from his envoys in Rome regarding the two papal elections, his successor, John I (1379–1390), sent representatives to Avignon and Rome in 1380 who, as witnesses, listened to the supporters of both popes. The statements made at this time served as the basis for royal consultations with prelates and confidants in Medina del Campo, which were supplemented there by additional documents and further hearings. On the basis of over one hundred statements, and after lengthy discourses—from November 1380 until May 1381—the king finally decided, and with him the Castilian clergy, for Clement VII. Medina del Campo was the biggest legal proceeding regarding a single ecclesiastical problem ever held up until that time. Documents from the proceedings are extant, and they clearly show the dominance of the king over his clergy. The next two kings—Henry III (1390–1406) and John II (1406–1454), who was dependent on the nobility—associated more closely with France after 1396, though they still favored Benedict XIII for a long time. For this reason they did not send any emissaries to Pisa in 1409; Castilian participants were present only at Constance from 1417. From that time on, Castile gave even firmer support to Martin V than Aragon, although there continued to be numerous supporters of the conciliar idea. Their chief spokesman was at that time in Basle, the renowned theologian and council chronicler Juan de Segovia.

However much the kings of Aragon and Castile, and to a lesser extent those of Navarre and Portugal, exploited the schism to guarantee their authority over the church, and however much

Aragon used Benedict XIII as a means of applying political pressure, it was France that was decisive for the continued existence of the Avignon obedience. As before, most of the cardinals and curials until 1408 came from this area, and the papal budget was largely dependent on French tribute monies. Thus France's recognition of Clement VII was fundamentally important for the existence of the Avignon obedience. The withdrawl of obedience in 1398, therefore, for which the royal government had the support of the University of Paris and the higher clergy, must have been that much graver. The prelates must have soon found to their disappointment, however, that in France, too, the king wanted to take the place of the pope by intensifying the royal system of provision. The king at that time, Charles VI (1380–1422), was under the care of a guardian until 1382 and again after 1392; thus the predominance of one of his relatives in the crown council was decisive. Of these relatives, it was Charles' brother, Duke Louis of Orleans, who promoted Benedict XIII, which is the reason for the government's support of Benedict until 1398, and again from 1403 until Louis' murder. Opponents of Louis found help at the University of Paris, whose professors, with increasing urgency, demanded a conciliar solution. The next king, Charles VII (1422–1461), also relied on the university, and for this reason French prelates and professors played a big role in Pisa and Constance as well as in Basle. Charles VII also made use of the Council of Basle to guarantee his dominion. After he had concluded peace with Philip the Good of Burgundy in Arras in 1435, thereby giving him a free hand to drive out the English, he adpoted in the Pragmatic Sanction of Bourges, at the urging of his prelates in his kingdom, the numerous decrees of the Council of Basle to limit the papal right of appointment, which automatically put him against Eugene IV. The pope found support in Southern France since prelates there wanted to prevent the use of the royal system of provisions in their regions, an interesting example of the political exploitation of or resistance to church reforms. To maintain its independence from the crown, the clergy of Southern France continued to be closer to Rome than to the king. The clergy's most important opponent was not the king, however, but the *parlement* in Toulouse that was empowered by the estates. As early as the second decade of this century, the *parlement* limited clerical privileges, such as judgments against clerics who had committed crimes.

The demands for a council, as well as the intervention of secular authorities in ecclesiastical matters, were often based on a criticism of the church's current condition, with the papacy and the curia usually named as the chief culprits. If one examines the charges made against Benedict XIII and Gregory XII in Pisa, and even more so the ones raised against John XXIII in Constance, these wild criticisms present a horrific image of the "vicar of Christ," listing all the various sorts of things the popes at that time were believed to have done, which by far exceed the charges made against Benedict IX in 1046 and the condemnations in Dante's *Inferno*: Benedict XIII—and to almost the same degree Gregory XII—was accused not only of extending the schism by refusing to resign, but was also accused of perpetrating violent acts, of punishing curials who would not flatter him, of having such curials executed or sent to prison, of even favoring heresy and magic. John XXIII was supposedly even worse: from childhood on, he had fallen into a life of depravity —which says something about those who elected him—and as cardinal and pope he led a life of immorality. He was accused of having poisoned his predecessor, Alexander V, of being extremely greedy and a grand simonist, and of having sold off property of the church and the Papal States for his own profit.

What was damaging for the papacy as an institution was that many of these charges—as exaggerated and as personally prejudiced as they were—proved true, conditioned by the ecclesiastical system at that time and the exigencies of the schismatic period. Simony, as it was understood by contemporaries, was practiced by the Roman and Pisan popes in particular when, from the time of Boniface IX, they forced a trade in indulgences and tolerated or even encouraged simony in the curia, especially in the colleges (the college of *scriptores*, though perhaps also the *camera* notaries and cursors colleges). The gruesome punishment, from the time of Urban VI and Clement VII, of cardinals and curials who had fallen from favor can likewise be proved. More oppressive for the clergy of the various obediences, however, was the tax burden because of the existence of two curias, and even three after 1409. In their life-style and in their number of assistants, they were potentially just as improvident as the curia before the schism. For this reason, the councils of Constance and Basle, in particular, demanded and decided upon a reform of the curia and a limitation of papal prerogatives: to prevent the coronation of a heretical pope, every pontiff after 1417 was to affirm his faith with the so-called "Creed of Boniface VIII," bishops were not allowed to be transferred against their will, and the collection of money by the pope from spoils and procurations was forbidden. These demands were concluded on October 9, 1417, and accepted by Martin V after his election, but future popes were to undertake further reforms themselves. Through these reforms it was hoped that the papal right of reservation and with it the payment of *servitia* and annates could be curbed, as could the appellate system and other areas under the curia's jurisdiction. The payment of intercalary profits was to be reduced, or done away with altogether, as was the alienation of church property, the distribution of dispensations and indulgences, and the transferring of commendams (transferring of prelatures for administration). To bring this about, it was thought at the same time to change the system of provisions, to reduce quantitatively and improve qualitatively the College of Cardinals as well as to organize better the chancery and the Sacred Penitentary. Many of these suggestions were taken up again in Basle—especially as regards the conferring of benefices and curial revenue—and agreed upon. The two previously mentioned decrees concluded at Constance, *Haec sancta* and *Frequens,* in which the supremacy of the council over the pope and the regular convening of councils was announced, were almost unanimously recognized until the middle of the century as binding on all Christians, which aided the institutional anchoring of the church reforms in the structure of the church as a whole. Only the two popes, Martin V and Eugene IV, along with some of their supporters, clung to the idea of papal supremacy.

But despite their few numbers initially, the future was to belong to them. The councils had the disadvantage of not being able to be in session continuously, and the participants were not interested in having long-lasting councils in view of their obligations in their own dioceses. Moreover, prelates were in the minority at the Council of Basle, especially after 1438, and many participants wanted to reform others, but not themselves. And the longer the schism between the councils of Basle/Lausanne and Ferrara/Florence lasted, the wearier the higher clergy and most of the secular powers grew of councils. Because of these circumstances, the papacy gained the upper hand. In addition, none of the popes who were in power from 1409 seemed to have seriously considered a reform of their own institution. This was made quite clear by Alexander V, who as cardinal asked for a reform of both head and members in his opening sermon at the Council of Pisa, but immediately after his election went along with tradition in defending the papal position. Martin V acted in similar fashion. He abided by the decrees concluded in Constance only as much as he was bound to by the concordats; he did not venture any reforms that went beyond the decrees. Reforms were even less to be expected from Eugene IV, a nephew of Gregory XII, as can be seen in his conflict with the Council of Basle. The demands for reform of the electoral capitulation, which every pope since 1431 had implored, also remained empty rhetoric. The papacy's lack of interest in reform was also evident in its attitude toward the rest of the church reforms and the reforms of the monastic orders: as long as family interests were not at stake, as they were in the patronage given by Eugene IV to the reform monastery of S. Giustina in Padua, the popes merely reacted to the petitions presented by reform groups—like their predecessors in the twelfth century—without developing any initiatives of their own.

This determination to continue their position can be partly explained as a legacy of the schism and of the Council of Constance. Alexander V, and even more so Martin V, had to accept most of the curials from two or three obediences. But since the Council of Constance had limited the number of curials, there were numerous *supernumerarii* during Martin's pontificate, who received no income for their position, often having to wait quite long until a person holding a paid position retired. The majority of the curials came from the curia of Benedict XIII, thus guaranteeing a continuity marked by the Avignon experience in the administrative authorities, in the papal retinue and in the ceremonial. The most prominent example of this was François de Conzié, a sort of Talleyrand of the schism period, who received from Clement VII in 1386 the office of the chamberlain, so important for political correspondence, administration and finance, retaining this post after moving over to Alexander V and Martin V until his death in 1431. Though from the time of John XXIII he did stay in Avignon as papal representative, his influence on the curia remained intact for some time since his nephew, Louis Aleman, who became a cardinal in 1426, acted as vice chamberlain under Martin V and played an important role as an opponent of Eugene IV at the Council of Basle. But despite the dominance of the Avignon curials, not one of them became pope after 1409; in fact, all popes since Alexander V had been created cardinals by earlier

Roman popes: John XXIII by his compatriot Boniface IX, Alexander V and Martin V by Innocent VIII, Eugene IV by his uncle Gregory XII. Looked at in this way, it is understandable that, from 1417, the earlier Roman popes were more and more appreciated as the legitimate successors to Peter, while the Avignon popes were considered "antipopes." But it was not until the twentieth century that the Vatican designated the two Pisan pontiffs as antipopes. In this way, the Roman succession through Gregory XII was to become, even more clearly, the only legal line of popes.

In addition to curbing the number of curials, the Council of Constance also temporarily limited papal revenue, though in 1423, after the concordats had expired, Martin V was largely able to reobtain authority over benefices, except in England. His noble Roman origins notwithstanding, these curbs most likely might have stirred him to try and reconquer the Papal States. Like Boniface IX before him, whose good fortunes were ruined under his successors by the invasions from Naples, Martin V led numerous military campaigns, stabilizing his rule with the help of the Colonna, his family. During his pontificate, about two-thirds of the revenue came from the Papal States, though this money was also predominately spent for this region. Understandably, Eugene IV tried to break the power of the Colonna; at first, the Colonna were stronger, so that in 1434 he fled Rome, only able to return in 1443. His secular government, however, continued to be unstable. Finally, it was his successor, Nicholas V, who managed to strengthen papal rule in Rome and in the Papal States and put an end to the Basle schism.

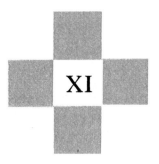

Restoration and Renaissance
(1447–1534)

Eugene IV's return to Rome came about primarily because of the military successes of Cardinal Vitelleschi (d. 1440), an army commander who was not exactly fussy about his methods. The secular rule of the pope remained quite unstable, however, dependent upon the balance of power among the Roman noble families. This was also the case after Eugene's death since the election of the cardinal Prospero Colonna, a nephew of Martin V, failed due to the opposition of the Orsini. The Tuscan Tommaso Parentucelli was then elected as a compromise candidate, giving himself the name of Nicholas V after his earlier patron, the cardinal Niccolò de'Albergati. An ardent promoter of science and art, Nicholas ushered in the epoch of the Renaissance papacy.

The new beginning manifested iteslf most clearly in the Vatican palace. From then on until today, the popes have preferred the Vatican over the Lateran as their residence, Martin V being the last one to promote the Lateran, which he chose as his grave site. Thus, over the course of the centuries, the palace name has been used as a synonom for papal government. Nicholas made plans for a completely new complex, including the tearing down of the more than one-thousand-year-old St. Peter's basilica and its replacement with a modern construction—one of the many examples that the "rebirth" of antiquity consisted first of all in the destruction of ancient buildings. But the pope was able to realize only a small part of his plans: for the time being, the basilica was to remain. Only the palace was expanded by adding a new residential wing, and was partly decorated; for security, a tower was added that is still standing today. The ensuing popes followed Nicholas's example. Particularly well known is the construction (or perhaps only a fundamental renovation) of the great palace chapel by Sixtus IV, the expansion and embellishment of the residential area and the representation rooms, mostly under Alexander VI and Julius II, additions to St. Peter's, such as a benediction loggia, and beginning with Julius II in 1506, the gradual tearing down of the old and the construction of the new St. Peter's basilica. The belvedere, begun by Innocent VIII, and the great courtyard for celebrations between the belvedere and the residential wing, reflected the new life-style. The new wall built around the palace during Julius' pontificate was for security, as was the reinforcement of the Castel Sant'Angelo, which was begun earlier, and its connecting wall to the Vatican.

Renewed papal control was likewise evinced by the numerous churches that were built, financed by popes, cardinals and the wealthier curials, and in the huge cardinal palaces, several of which—such as the Palazzo Capranica, the later so-called *cancelleria,* and the Palazzo Venezia—forced the demolition of older houses and the repositioning of streets. Even more so than from the time of Urban V, shops were set up near bridges over the Tiber by professionals—bankers, artists, artisans—who were important for the pope residing nearby in the Vatican. This business activity left its mark on the cityscape in that area. Particularly well known is the Florentine quarter just off the Castel Sant'Angelo bridge. Their competitors, the Genovese, settled as shippers mostly in the southern part of Trastevere near the great port. Around Piazza Navona and west of there, curials, artisans and pilgrims from other nations—Catalonians, Castilians, Germans, French—had their quarters, all of which were centered on their respective "national churches."

The various new buildings gave rise to new streets, with popes from the time of Sixtus IV intervening directly in city planning. Sixtus had a new bridge built on the foundation of one from antiquity (Ponte Sisto), but more importantly, he had a new street laid out connecting the Castel Sant'Angelo bridge to Piazza Navona (*Via del Governo Vecchio*). These projects, as well as changes in street layout under Alexander VI in Borgo San Pietro and in the Parione region, served the needs of the numerous pilgrims in the Holy Years 1475 and 1500. Julius II even had a completely new city plan in mind, but he ran into the opposition of the municipal administration and ended up being able to build a mere boulevard (*Via Giulia*).

These changes in the cityscape were so far-reaching, however, that they could have only taken place under increased papal influence over the Roman municipal government. Like Martin V and Eugene IV before them, Nicholas V and his successors until Paul II had no choice but to tolerate the municipal government, which was led by the mercantile upper class of Rome, and to rule in agreement with it. Eugene's lone achievement was that a *gubernator* took the place of the traditional city prefects, a position held for centuries by the noble family of de Vico, and which had to be ratified by the pope. And just how precarious the situation still was can be seen in the opposition of the Romans during his pontificate and his successors' to the coming of textile workers and merchants from Northern Italy, or in in the plot against Nicholas V in 1453 by the Roman Stefano Porcaro. In the end, it was Sixtus IV who, in 1473, was able, partly by violent means, to amend the municipal constitution and to place directly under himself the city magistrate of the *camera apostolica,* which also meant that, from that time onwards, the vice chamberlain was at the same time *governatore* of the city. Thus it was under Sixtus IV that the above-mentioned changes in the cityscape really began. And even if during the pontificate of his successor, Innocent VIII, the Romans tried to regain their autonomy, it was under Alexander VI, Julius II and Adrian VI that the papal municipal government grew stronger, increasingly to the detriment of municipal autonomy. One physical sign of this was Michelangelo's reconstruction of the Capitoline, the center of city, orderd by the pope, and the setting up of papal monuments in the Capitoline palace from the time of Leo X. In addition, there was the construction of a papal villa on the Capitoline during Paul III's pontificate. And even though the inscriptions on the Capitoline were patterned after the rhetoric of ancient Rome, and ancient Roman festivals such as the Festival of Pales (anniversary of the founding of Rome) were once again celebrated,

Rome was henceforth, more than ever before, securely in papal hands.

The cementing of papal control was also evident in the ceremonial. From the time of Sixtus IV in particular, the Vatican increasingly became the center of papal rituals, a fact that was influenced by developments that had taken place earlier in Avignon. From the time of Callistus III, papal elections took place in the Vatican; and from the palace the newly elected pope proceeded to his coronation in the nearby St. Peter's basilica. The only remnant of the earlier High Middle Ages was the procession to the Lateran (*posssesso*, meaning the "taking possession"), though it lost its significance in that, from the time of Julius II, it was made separate from the coronation, taking place several days later. The huge papal chapel took the place of the *statio* churches. Even St. Peter's basilica was now used for just a few big celebrations, under Leo X for only three. And just as in Avignon, the traditional processions only moved through the palace. Moreover, it was in the palace where the consecration of bishops and clerics usually took place. Exceptions to this included the procession of Corpus Christi, which went through the borgo, as well as the Carnival festivities.

At the same time, there were growing signs of a secularization of the papacy: when a pope moved through the city, secular attendants outnumbered ecclesiatical dignitaries. Instead of celebrating mass themselves, pontiffs increasingly left it up to cardinals and curial bishops. Popes were frequently absent even for important holidays, preferring to hunt or other such amusements instead. Even the liturgy itself contained profane elements: during a procession of Corpus Christi jesters beating on tambours danced in front of Alexander VI while he carried the pyx; and the chapel choir, employed to sing the liturgy, performed comedies for Leo X. It is not surprising, therefore, that Innocent VIII had his daughters married in the palace courtyard with great pageantry, that courtesans and upper class ladies, particularly from the time of Alexander VI, had access to the palace, and that during Alexander's pontificate, at one worship service in S. Agostino, prostitutes filled the chancel, impeding both the cardinals and the chapel choir.

Most of the popes of this epoch fit the picture of an Italian Renaissance prince that was common at this time—as for being the imitation of Christ, there remained only the title of *vicarius Christi*. This was related to the increased promotion of science and art.

Martin V integrated humanists into the curia who had been living in Constance or who were moving to Rome. As papal secretaries, humanists such as Flavio Biondo helped bring papal letters up to the stylistic standards of the day. Eugene IV likewise encouraged humanists, especially during his stay in Florence, as long as they were not too critical of him, as Lorenzo Valla was. But the biggest breakthrough came under Nicholas V, who not only increased the number of Italian humanists in the curia, but also enriched the library with the works of these humanists and classical texts. Pius II chose his papal name from the sobriquet of Virgil's Aeneas, "Pius Aeneas," and in so doing intensified the reference to antiquity in the given name he already had as a layman—Enea (Silvio Piccolomini). He himself was a humanist, and he founded, for his political friends in particular, a new college of abbreviators. Despite polemics to the contrary, his successor, Paul II, was not an enemy of the humanists, even though he had difficulties with the Pompomius Laetus academy of humanists. The founding of the papal library by Sixtus IV became famous, its first director being the humanist and chronicler of popes, Platina, whom Paul II had arrested. Just how strongly humanism had prevailed at the curia by the fifteenth century's end was evident in the use of the humanists' minuscle script as the standard not only for books but also for documents from the chancery. And since the sons of humanists followed their fathers as curials, and most of the later popes emulated the model of their predecessors, humanism was the predominant educational method in Rome throughout the entire epoch, with frequently even the priests in the pulpits orientating their sermons towards humanism. But while humanists of the first decades—such as Lorenzo Valla or Platina—were inclined to be critical towards the papacy, a devotional attitude towards the man who paid their salaries prevailed among their successors after the turn of the century.

For those who visit Rome today the extensive promotion of the fine arts by the popes is even more evident. Pontiffs turned to Florentine artists in particular, which can be explained by Florence's longtime dominance of the fine arts and the close ties of many popes to Florentine bankers. The tomb of Martin V was imported to Rome from Florence during the pontificate of Eugene IV; Nicholas V employed Fra Angelico, who also is buried in Rome; for the coronation of Pius II, Benozzo Gozzoli painted processional standards. Active during later pontificates were Ghirlandaio and Botticelli (under Sixtus IV), as well as Sangallo and, above all, Michelangelo (from the time of Julius II). But there were also other Italians who worked in Rome, including Signorelli (Sixtus IV) or Pinturicchio (Alexander VI). Artists from the Papal States were also called to Rome: Melozzo da Forlì and Perugino (Sixtus IV), and later Bramante and his protégé Raphael. As Raphael's frescoes such as the *Miracle of Leo IV*, the *Donation of Constantine* and others show, most of the artists followed the instructions of their employer even more than the humanists did. The well known exception was Michelangelo, the only one to keep his independence, and who became increasingly critical of the established church from the time of Clement VII. It was just this artistic activity that made Rome the center of the Italian Renaissance by the turn of the century, plainly showing just how much the city at that time had become the papal residence.

Just as the activity of the *Cosmati* in the Patrimonium Petri did two centuries earlier, the attraction of Rome for artists like Perugino, Melozzo and Bramante showed the extent to which papal rule had once again been secured in the Papal States after the middle of the fifteenth century. The actions of pontiffs in the Papal States reflected the traditional way of doing things there. Like their predecessors in earlier centuries, the Renaissance popes also by and large appointed relatives and compatriots as military leaders, and as heads of unstable areas in particular. The popes were then usually content with receiving recognition as overlord from the *signori* and the communes and with taking in taxes. Even more war-like pontiffs such as Alexander VI and Julius II followed this system. The only change was the technique of waging war, as the increased deployment of soldiers, the formation of standing troops by Nicholas V, and the use of cannons show. Even more so than earlier popes such as Boniface VIII had wanted, Pius II, Sixtus IV, Innocent VIII and Alexander VI were all bent on turning the traditional or newly conquered territories of the Papal States into independent domains for nephews and sons, which was not very conducive for consolidating ruling power. These aims ran not only into opposition in the College of Cardinals and in the affected areas (Urbino, Romagna, etc.), but they also made relations difficult with other Italian states. Equally ominous was the use of the papacy and the Papal States by popes Leo X and Clements VII, both members of the Medici family, to secure their family's domination in Florence or to reestablish it after the brief attempts at republican government.

With the exception of Nicholas V and the short-lived popes Pius III and Adrian VI, this usually extensive promoting of relatives and compatriots led to power struggles after the death of a particular pope, just as it did in earlier times. Besides the reoccurring feuds between the Colonna and the Orsini, there was the persecution of the "Catalans" after Callistus III's death, persecution of the Sienese after Pius II's, and persecution of the Genovese after Sixtus IV's; furthermore, there was the banishment of Sixtus IV's *nipote* Giuliano della Rovere under Alexander VI, as well as the the triumphant return of both Alexander's son, Ceasre Borgia, and Giuliano, after Alexander's death. Giuliano was elected to the papacy as Julius II. The origins of many of the popes showed— even more than in the thirteenth century—just how firmly nepotism had been established: Innocent VIII was a compatriot of his predecessor Sixtus IV, while Julius II was his *nipote*; Alexander VI, Pius III and Clement VII were relatives of the earlier popes Callistus III, Pius II and Leo X. Not counting Nicholas V, Paul II (*nipote* of Eugene IV) and Adrian VI, four families occupied the papal throne nine different times, the clique established by Sixtus IV being the most successful with three pontificates. If one considers that the Medici also rose to the papal office thanks indirectly to Sixtus IV in the sense that the future Leo X became cardinal in 1489 as a thirteen-year-old after his illegitimate sister had married the son of Innocent VIII, then the consequences of Sixtus IV's personnel policies and those of his successors can be put into sharper focus.

If the changes on the throne and nepotism led again and again to unrest in the Papal States, then so too did government measures taken by the papacy which ran counter to the interests of barons, especially those near Rome. Papal agrarian policies, in particular, deserve to be mentioned in this regard. Because families like the Colonna, Orsini, Savelli and Caetani cut back the production of grain on their estates in favor of pasture land, not only were many farmers driven off the land or reduced to seasonal work, but getting food to the ever increasing population of Rome was made more difficult. And while the amount of grain was cut back, the price the barons dictated went up. Sixtus IV countered by decreeing in 1476 that one third of all uncultivated land was to be

expropriated and to be assigned to landless farmers for the plant-
ing of grain. Beginning in 1480, the barons, and especially the
Colonna, resisted the measure, Innocent VIII eventually giving up
the plan because of his dependence on the support of the Colonna.
Julius II tried again when he introduced price controls over the
opposition of the barons. (Julius II showed just how little he
trusted the Roman nobility when he removed persons of this class
from the palace guard, replacing them with Swiss mercenaries—
the famous Swiss guards. What is more, he did not appoint a single
Roman as cardinal). Clement VII also made efforts to direct and
control the grain policies of the baronial estates, but the opposition
of the nobility also largely destroyed this effort.

The constantly increasing limitations on Roman autonomy from
the time of Sixtus IV to Adrian VI transformed the city more and
more into the official papal residence, while the Papal States continued to be an unstable creature which was continually being
fought for and which could only be secured by force. Five months
after the election of Nicholas V, Duke Filippo Maria Visconti of
Milan died without a male heir. Various pretenders battled for the
city, which for three years was ruled as a republic (the "Ambrosian
Republic" from 1447 to 1450). Finally, Filippo's son-in-law, Francesco Sforza emerged victorious and ruled the city as duke from
1450. His government continued to be challenged, however, by
Venice, Naples, the papacy and other states. Only under the pressure of Constantinople's conquest by the Turks in 1453 did Milan,
Florence and Venice conclude a peace in April 1454 in Lodi. Soon
after, Alfonso of Naples and Nichloas V also entered into the
accord. For the next forty years, this treaty assured the balance of
power among the five Italian "superpowers," an equilibrium that
was only disrupted by the lust for power of papal *nipoti*, by the
often hostile relations between the papacy and the new king of
Naples, Ferrante (1458–1494), and by Sixtus IV's involvement
from 1478 to 1480 in an assassination attempt against the Florentine Medici. It was in precisely these decades that science, art, and
commerce flowered in Italy.

The "forty happy years," as they were later referred to so glo-
riously, ended in 1494. The new duke of Milan, Lodovico il Moro,
eliminated the legitimate successor, a son-in-law of Ferrante of
Naples. To stabilize his control, he aided the new French king,
Charles VIII, in his plans to conquer Naples. A short while later
Ferrante died. Charles VIII claimed his throne, because the last

Angevin descendant, the "good King" René who had fled to Provence, had relinquished his right to rule to the Valois, who were governing France. At peace with the rulers of England, Germany and Spain, and backed by Milan, Charles blackmailed Florence into granting concessions and conquered Naples, driving out the Neapolitan king, Ferdinand II, in whose favor Alfonso II had earlier abdicated. The situation grew confusing with the banishment of the Medici from Florence—where from 1494 a republican government ruled with the backing of Savonarola—and with the designs on political power of the new pope, Alexander VI. Though Charles VIII left Italy in 1495 under pressure from a league that had been formed against him, his ambitions lived on. His successor, Louis XII, could count the Visconti among his ancestors and thus claimed not only Naples but also Milan. His campaign in Lower Italy in 1501, however, was a failure; it merely secured from 1505 the direct rule of Naples and Sicily by an Aragonese viceroy. Upper Italy, however, continued to be contested, especially over French claims to Milan. Ruling the duchy under frequent changes were the Sforza—Lodovico, Massimiliano and Francesco II—as well as the French kings Louis XII and Francis I. Finally, the new Spanish and German king, Charles V, intervened, beating Francis I near Pavia in 1525 and incorporating the duchy into Hapsburg territories for centuries. Moreover, by the end of the century, Venetian expansion on the mainland (the so-called *terra ferma*) was over. Venice could not be incorporated into the Hapsburg empire, however, as Emperor Maximilian I had planned.

The popes sought to exploit for their own purposes the invasions by non-Italian powers. During Alexander VI's pontificate, Alexander's son Cesare conquered parts of the Romagna and Emilia with French consent; he was, after all, in his capacity as the duke of Valence, a vassal of the French king. Julius II, on the other hand, having earlier been in exile in France himself, devoted his energy to freeing Italy from the "barbarians" and in so doing made himself an enemy of France. In conjunction with this stands the Council of Pisa, which opposing cardinals had convened under instructions from Louis XII. In Pisa, the decrees *Haec sancta* and *Frequens* of the Council of Constance were renewed, which induced Julius to inaugurate a council of his own in the Lateran in 1512. His successor, Leo X, was forced initially to rely again on the French, with whose help he was able to reestablish his family's control of Florence and to end the Council of Pisa. Later, he leaned more upon Spain. However, his efforts were directed towards keeping both France and Spain out of Italy. Therefore, in 1519, after the death of Maximilian, he came out against the election of a French or Spanish king as emperor of Germany; instead, he favored the elector of Saxony, Frederick the Wise. Paradoxically, Leo even made the offer of elevating to cardinal anyone whom Frederick might think acceptable—presumably Martin Luther!

The policies of Leo's uncle and second successor, Clement VII, proved in the end to be disastrous. Although Clement had been elected with Spanish support, he joined the League of Cognac, as did the resurrected Francesco II of Milan, along with France, Florence and Venice, against Charles V after his victory at Pavia in 1525. Only the duke of Ferrara, Alfonso d'Este, and the Colonna, continued on Charles' side. The Colonna laid waste to the Campagna south of Rome with the goal of expanding their sphere of influence. The situation became even more heated when German mercenaries marched on Rome and, after the death of their commander, conquered the city in May 1527 along with Spanish and Southern Italian mercenaries. Unbridled plundering during this so-called *sacco di Roma* led to the destruction of numerous works of art and archives, while the population was left to die by starvation or by the plague. Clement was forced to flee. He had to give up any claims to the Upper Italian cities of Piacenza, Parma and Modena, and then had to look on as the rule of his family in Florence fell apart. Even a renewed campaign by the French was unable to drive out Charles' troops. Finally, in 1529, France and Spain, and then Charles and the pope, concluded a peace. To finalize the agreement, Charles and Clement met in Bologna. In 1530 Clement crowned Charles first as king of Italy, after having already invested him with Naples the year before, and then, on February 22, Charles' birthday, Clement crowned him, again in Bologna, as the Holy Roman Emperor. This was to be the last imperial coronation by a pope. With the investiture and the coronations, Charles' dominance in Italy was now legally guaranteed, while the Papal States were now constricted even more than they had been under the Hohenstaufen. The descent of the papacy and its state to that of a minor power in Italy had begun.

It soon became clear that the papacy's relations with other European states were to be determined largely by papal ambitions in Italy. Moreover, there was the legacy of the councils of Constance and Basle. To end the schism at Basle, Nichloas V had concluded a concordat with the German king Frederick III in 1448, which cut back papal influence on appointments to bishoprics, as well as on the traditional revenue from benefices, in favor of the king. Through other papal concordats with the German electors, the electors' influence on the German church also grew. Because the balance of power had been altered, the trip made by the legation of Nicholas of Cusa in 1451, undertaken with papal approval to promote church reforms, was largely unsuccessful. The institutional ties between the papacy and Germany gradually decreased, though contacts did continue. Frederick III, for example, was crowned emperor in Rome in 1452, the last emperor to be crowned there, and visited Rome again in 1468; Maximilian I occasionally entertained the peculiar plan of becoming simultaneously both emperor and pope; from the turn of the century the Fugger of Augsburg acted as papal bankers; there was almost always at least one German member of the college of cardinals; and with Adrian VI, a Dutchman became pope. Increases were registered only in the flow of German pilgrims—especially in the Holy Years of 1450, 1475 and 1500, less so in 1525—and in the criticism leveled at the selling of Roman indulgences.

The relations of the papacy to France were subject to fluctuations. As long as he was alive, Cardinal Guillaume d'Estouteville (1439–1483), a relative of the royal family, used his influence on the curia to the benefit of the kings. Even he, however, was unable to prevent the continued strain in the relations between Charles VII and the pontiffs over the Pragmatic Sanction of Bourges of 1438. It was finally Charles's son, Louis XI, who for the most part decided not to implement the Pragmatic Sanction. The sanction did remain a welcome means of exerting pressure, however, as evinced in both Charles VIII's and Louis XII's willingness to keep it in force. Louis XI was principally concerned with securing his domestic control and with reducing the ever present threats from Burgundy and England. For these reasons, he tried to maintain peace with the other powers, as well as with the pope, whenever it was useful for him. In this, he was by and large successful, though towards the end of his reign he set the stage for the coming conflicts by assuming the claims of René of Anjou to Naples, as mentioned earlier. From the time of his successor, Charles VIII, the papal position towards France was usually determined by its Italian policies. The compromises during the Fifth Lateran Council (concordat of Bologna in 1516) became important, then, for the future inasmuch as they brought about the theoretical recognition of *Unam sanctam* even in France and the lifting of the Pragmatic Sanction, but left de facto ecclesiastical authority in France to the king. The pope, for the most part, waived his claim to appoint bishops or abbots as well as his claim on the lesser benefices and, in addition, did away with all reservations and expectatives for France. In this way, the influence of the French king on the "Gallic church," which had been visibly increasing, was from now on accepted by the pope. The only exception to this for the time being was the clergy in Southern France. Wanting to curtail royal influence as much as possible, and without great prospects of making a career with the crown's help, many of these clergymen used the opportunity to serve the pope as curials, and in so doing, to obtain posts as prelates back in their homeland.

Just as in the two preceding epochs, relations with the Spanish kingdom during the Renaissance remained relatively close. This was due not only to the two Aragonese popes, Callistus III and Alexander VI, but also to the presence of numerous Spaniards in the curia and to the relative weakness of most of the kings in the second half of the fifteenth century. One of the greatest defenders of papal restoration was the Castilian Juan de Torquemada; his nephew carried on his tradition as royal confidant and grand inquisitor. The papacy gained an important success when, at the beginning of the sixteenth century, the archbishop of Toledo, Francisco Ximénez de Cisneros, ordered the Roman rite to be obligatory in Castile and restricted the traditional Mozarabic rite to a few exceptions. And shortly before, in the treaty of Tordesillas of 1494, Alexander VI, after the discovery of America and in reference to the authority granted to him in the Donation of Constantine as lord of the "western islands"—that vaguely defined thus expandable territory Constantine had supposedly given to Pope Sylvester—drew the line of demarcation between the territories conquered by the Portuguese and the Spanish. One can still get an idea today of the tribute given to him for his service in the gilded coffers of Santa Maria Maggiore. The discovery a half century earlier by Nichloas of Cusa and Lorenzo Valla that the Donation of Constantine was fake did not disturb any of the parties involved. Soon after, the relations of the curia to Spain were also dominated by Italian policies. All this contact with Rome could not prevent Spain's national church from being directed more and more by the crown; a legacy of the great schism, this trend began in the fifteenth century, picking up steam from the time of the "Catholic monarchs," Isabella and Ferdinand.

The best example at this time, however, of a national church under royal direction was England. Though the position of the king was weakened during the War of the Roses, even towards the end of the war Edward IV was again filling bishoprics according to his own interests, which the new kings of the house of Tudor, Henry VII and Henry VIII, did even more so after 1485. Under these kings, a few of the archbishops of Canterbury became cardinals, which was hardly of any benefit to the papacy as these cardinals served, above all, the royal ecclesiatical authority. Henry VIII showed that the influence of the kings on the church was stronger than that of the church on the monarchy when he named Thomas More as lord chancellor, the first time a laymen had been appointed to this post. Even More could not prevent the king in 1534 from using the divorce from his first wife, Catherine of Aragon, as a pretext for breaking the English church away from the papacy once and for all, and for placing it definitively under his control.

The mostly hollow authority of the popes in other countries was also the reason behind the failure of their initially most important political project, the struggle against the Turks, who, with the help of cannons manufactured by Christians, conquered Constantinople in 1453, laying waste to the Byzantine empire. Under the shock of these events, Nichloas V tried even before the Peace of Lodi to unify the Italian rulers in an alliance against the Turks; furthermore, he gave financial backing to the Hungarians under John Hunyadi and to the Albanians under Skanderberg in their battles to defend against the Turks. Callistus III continued and even augmented these policies. To win over the European princes, he appointed the cardinal Caravajal as legate for a crusade and had the Franciscan John of Capestrano preach in support of the crusade. Something did come of all this in the end, and that was the expulsion of the Turks from the area around Belgrade in 1456 by an army led by Hunyadi and Capestrano. In the same year, a fleet led by Cardinal Ludovico Trevisan demonstrated the strength of the Christian front in the Aegean. To finance this undertaking, the pope pawned or sold jewels and books from the library that Nicholas V had assembled. Despite this, he had no lasting success, since the European princes were divided and even the pope himself offended those few Byzantine rulers who remained by advocating a union of the Greek and Roman churches under papal supremacy.

Failure also was in store for Pius II, who even before his election to the papacy had made a call to arms against the Turks. A congress for princes that he convened in Mantova in 1459 was attended by only a few rulers. And since Venice, whose fleet was needed, had concluded a peace shortly before with the Turkish sultan Mehmet II to safeguard its possessions, the basis for a successful undertaking was lacking. In 1464, Pius called again for a crusade, this time convincing Venice to participate. One year later, in view of the Venetian fleet sailing past Ancona, Pius died, and the Venetians turned around and headed back to their home port. Another plan, which the Bohemian king George of Podebrady had developed, failed partly on account of the pope himself: the unification of Europe into a federal state. Since this plan would have made the traditional powers—emperor and pope—secondary players, and since George had earlier in 1458 sworn to the Compacts of Prague (the offering of the chalice to the laity, free preaching, etc.), which had been approved by the Council of Basle but never recognized by the papacy, both Frederick III and Pius refused to support him. Paul II even called for a heresy crusade against him in 1466, though without success. Paul's plan for a new crusade against the Turks failed in 1470 after they had conquered the Venetian's last major posession in the Aegean, Negroponte (Evvia). During Sixtus IV's pontificate, the Turks even landed in Apulia; but even in the face of this the Italian rulers remained divided, not to mention those of other countries. The papal plan to unite the Russian church with Rome and to mobilize it against the Turks through the marriage of the grand prince of Moscow, Ivan III, with a niece of the last emperor, likewise yielded no results. The only consequence at all was that Ivan played himself up as the successor to the Byzantine Empire and built Moscow into the "third Rome."

The death of Mehmet II in 1481 reduced the Turkish threat. Because there was no legitimate successor, as is common in Islam, the new ruler, Bayazid II, had to go to great lengths to wipe out all potential rivals. For this reason, his brother Djem fled to Rhodes and was turned over to Innocent VIII as a hostage by the grand master of the Hospitallers, who was rewarded by being made a cardinal. To prevent Djem's return, Bayazid henceforth paid an annual sum to the pope and agreed not to invade Italy. Thus, in the end, the failure of Innocent VIII's and Leo X's crusade plans was not so grave for the papacy. When later Soliman II attacked Hungary, even threatening Vienna itself, Adrian VI planned a reform of both church and curia in order to lay a better foundation for a crusade against the Turks. But Adrian soon died, and his successor, Clement VII, was too wrapped up with his Italian policies and the political families of Italy to be able to carry on with Adrian's plans.

These papal plans for crusades, then, are some of the most impressive evidence we have to show that European rulers were far more interested in building their own states than in forging a common policy, with the consequence that it was no longer possible for the papacy to carry out its spiritual leadership of Christendom.

The renewed ideological anchoring of the papal position after the end of the Council of Basle did nothing to change this. If, on the one hand, it was the popes of the schism and council epoch who insisted upon their prerogatives, which, of course, was an expression of pure self-interest, then it was also former partisans of the Council of Basle like Nicholas of Cusa or Enea Silvio Piccolomini who from the end of the council period propagated papal supremacy. And even if they and other stricter "papilists"—such as Juan de Torquemada—continued to defend demands made by the councils for church reform, they also made it clear that the Universal Church was to be presided over by the pope alone, who was therefore the only competent authority for reforms as a whole. Two legates of Nichloas V, Guillaume d'Estouteville and Nicholas of Cusa, undertook to put this principle into practice in Germany and France. However, since in these two countries, as well as in Spain, the actual reforms were sustained by and dependent upon local authorities, and since the reforms of the papacy and the curia continued to be a long time in coming, it was precisely this widespread need for a reform, one that also included the papacy, that deepened the split between the papacy and the national churches. And even when the former council supporter Enea Silvio, as Pope Pius II, issued his bull *Execrabilis* forbidding any appeals to a council to thwart a future playing off of council ideas against the papacy, the possibility of convoking a council nevertheless remained a way of exerting political pressure for some rulers, especially in Germany and France, for which they could count on public approval. As a result, up until and including the period of the Council of Trent (1545–1563), there was a prevailing contrast within the church, namely, that the popes, by referring to antiquated texts, such as the Donation of Constantine, cultivated an "absolutist" position—an important factor for the so-called Counter-Reformation—while among rulers, prelates, orders and the faithful, the decrees of the councils of Constance and Basle lived on in various forms of intensity, depending on the intentions of each of these groups. And even when the attempt failed to form a council whose authority would stand above the pope's, to wit, the revival of the Council of Basle in 1482 and the Council of Pisa planned by Louis XII in 1511, then the meager response to the Fifth Lateran Council, which was largely to serve the ends of the papacy and was attended almost exclusively by Italians, showed that that contrast continued to exist.

Astonishingly enough, even the College of Cardinals was in favor of maintaining the council tradition. In contrast to the fourteenth century, and despite papal nepotism, the members of the various nations were united. There were the usual Italians of the five "great powers," Frenchmen, Spaniards, Germans, and an occasional Portuguese or Englishman, even a scattered Pole or Hungarian. Thus, superficially, one could speak of a representation of the entire Western church in the College of Cardinals. In practice, however, the influence of the cardinals who were related to the pope or were close to him for other reasons prevailed, the reason for this to be found in the policies towards the Papal States. Attempts, therefore, at church reform were usually limited to the opportune moment occasioned by a papal election: the electoral capitulations repeated well into the sixteenth century the demands that had first been forged at the councils of Constance and Basle. A few of the cardinals who lived to old age, such as Francesco Todeschini-Piccolomini, who, as nephew of Pius II, was created cardinal by him and in the end ruled for a short time himself as Pope Pius III, eagerly produced suggestions for reforms that usually ended up as waste paper. The same fate befell the reform tracts that were worked out for the Fifth Lateran Council. And even if some of the popes themselves wanted to reform the curia they had no great success: Pius II never published the detailed reform plans contained in the bull *Pastor aeternus;* Alexander VI quickly lost interest in a reform commission which he had appointed after the murder of his son Juan and the strange collapse of a roof in the Vatican, which was taken as an ominous sign of danger; Adrian VI failed due to his ignorance of the College of Cardinals and curia as well as due to their resistance. And many of the cardinals who participated in the electoral capitulations compromised themselves when they allowed themselves to be bought—as in the elections of Alexander VI and Julius II. In other words, they engaged in simony. According to canon law developed from the eleventh century, this made the elections invalid, though up to now it did not give rise to any concerns among supporters of the papal line of succession, unlike assessments of the Avignon popes after 1378 and of the Pisan popes.

Despite their lack of success, the various plans for reform are not without historical value inasmuch as they kept the reform tradition alive into the period of the Council of Trent, even at the papal court; moreover, they provide important information about the organization and the deplorable state of affairs of the Roman curia. This is especially important because the organization of administrative authorities in the Renaissance has not been investigated in as much detail as that of Avignon. The only exception is the chancery and some of the newly created institutions. The chancery continued to be under the direction of the vice chancellor—from Callistus III to Innocent VIII it was Rodrigo Borgia, who later became Alexander VI—while at the same time it was mostly made up of colleges which by and large appointed their own members, thus removing them from any supervision. The chancery's highest-ranking college, the protonotary (earlier called the notary), now held a rank equal to bishop, though it lost some of its actual importance. To maintain control over at least the important documents, the papacy strengthened the function of the referendary while creating, at the end of the century, the confidential position of *summator,* whose function was to personally present important texts to the pope. Simony increasingly permeated the colleges in the chancery from the time of Boniface IX. The regulation of simony was initially another possibility to place once again the positions in the chancery under the papal right of appointment, as was the transformation of existing positions into purchaseable ones with a fixed price of membership, as Pius II attempted with the College of Abbreviators. Simony will be dealt with in detail later.

Like the chancery, the *camera apostolica* largely kept its traditional organization, though it was now, as a result of developments since the pontificate of Martin V, still only nominally directed by the chamberlain, with the vice chamberlain being the actual person in charge. Under him were the *thesaurarius, camera* clerics, *camera* notaries, and secretaries, who were important for papal correspondence. In fact, the activity of the *camera* increased when Sixtus IV placed the Roman municipal government under the vice chamberlain as *governatore*, and with the increased financial exploitation of the Papal States, also on the rise from the time of Sixtus in particular. The actual management of the money, however, now lay exclusively in the hands of the general depositary, who, as an agent of mostly Tuscan financial houses (Medici, Chigi, Strozzi), also granted credit to the popes—the Fugger played less of a role—and in so doing had increasing influence on appointments to office as well as on the system of income and indulgences. Like the chancery and the *camera*, the organization of the Sacred Penitentiary and the various law courts continued to be modeled on the system developed in Avignon, even though their effectiveness was now curbed due to the decrees of the councils of Constance and Basle, or because new organs had been established. The papal chapel also followed the Avignon model, but was expanded beyond this. From the time of John Burckard (1483–1506), the masters of ceremonies for the chapel have left us valuable journals. During the pontificate of Eugene IV, and even more so from the time of Sixtus IV, the chapel's college of singers took in famous composers who made a considerable contribution to the beauty of the papal ceremonials.

The most important of the newly created offices was the datary. When Callistus III was pope, his compatriot, Cosmas of Montserrat, held this position. Cosmas was also papal *confessor*, and thus the adminstrator of the papal chambers, including the library, the archives, and the pope's private jewel case. When Pius II filled the two positions separately, the datary took over the confidential function of *confessor*. And even though the development of the position is difficult to follow precisely because it was a confidential position, it is clear nevertheless that, from the time of Pius II, the datary—often criticized and hated by many—gradually became involved in all the dealings of the church which, in terms of canon law, lay in the "gray zone." For example, the datary fixed the taxes for compositions involving dispensations, indulgences and the bestowing of curial positions. Consequently, the datary also set the prices for the purchaseable offices, and from the end of the fifteenth century directed the register for the payment of composition taxes and the register of selling prices. The datary was controlled, however, for a long time by the *camera*, which recorded the ordinances and mandates relating to the datary, accepted the monetarily renumerated resignations from offices, and, from the end of the fifteenth century, made up and publicized a list of the offices which could be bought.

The expansion of simony at the curia is a complicated issue. It ought not to be understood, as is often the case, as exclusively a method of raising capital for the popes; rather, the transformation of traditional colleges and individual positions into ones that could be bought was usually at the initiative of the incumbent, who wanted to gain a profit from the selling of his position. Only in the newly created colleges can papal initiative be confirmed; only with these positions was the profit from the first sale exclusively to the benefit of the papacy. Privations (the withdrawl of benefices), promotions or the sudden death of an office holder were further opportunities for pontiffs to receive the entire selling price. Usually, however, they had to be content with composition taxes, which, on average, amounted to ten percent of the purchase price.

Up to the time of Paul II, the positions that were especially available for purchase were those whose occupants lived from taxes (*scriptores*, abbreviators, various colleges of notaries) or fees ("voluntary" donations) and tips (cursors, *servientes armorum*, doorkeepers). Thus the free trade in these positions did not affect the papal budget. This was to change under Sixtus IV. As a result of the fiasco of his Florentine policies of 1478, he founded new colleges that could be purchased—244 positions altogether—and in so doing emphasized the financial exploitation, which is why from then on the positions were often called *portiones*. His successors proceeded in the same manner. In this same period, paid positions (*camera* clerics, and others) also became available for purchase, as did judicial or confidential positions (fiscal lawyer, *camera* judge, *summator*, and others). Their sale was actually a burden to the papal budget and lessened the influence of the popes on appointments to important positions. From the time of Julius II, colleges were founded that were purely for loans and whose members seldom exercised any real functions in the curia. And since the rate of return—an annual average of eight to ten percent of the purchase price—was not always enough for the buyers, not only was the revenue of the offices continually going up along with the purchase price until 1525, but new incentives were created by providing the purchaseable offices with privileges. If an office remained unavailable for purchase, thus guaranteeing the pope the right to fill that position, then the bestowing of office could still be exploited financially in that the new office holder had to make a down payment, which usually he never got back. If one considers that, from 1492 at the latest, payments were to be made to voters even in papal elections, then it is not surprising that from the time of Leo X positions were sold—even if secretly—in the College of Cardinals. The spiritual office of the grand penitentiary was also sold. Clearly these were simonistic practices. But in 1526, in the tradition of Italian savings institutions (*montes pietatis*), the Monte della Fede ("savings institutions of the faith") was founded in Rome. Its interest rates enticed many investors away from investing in simony, leading to a fall in prices. One year later, the *sacco di Roma* caused a collapse of even papal finances. Financial health was finally restored by Paul III and the following popes, who in doing so, however, continued to deal in simony, despite the "reforms" of the curia.

It is understandable that even at that time the practice of simony ran into much criticism. A further point of contention were the commendams. By this is meant, in particular, high benefices (bishoprics and abbeys), which were entrusted to an ecclesiastic for administration (*in commendam*). Already in use in the fourteenth century, and originally for a specific length of time, the conferring of commendations was practiced excessively by the popes despite all the criticism raised in Constance and Basle in the fifteenth and sixteenth centuries. Cardinals, nephews and other favorites in particular, but also relatives and protégés of rulers—they all received commendams, for personal and political reasons, to exploit them financially, usually without bothering about the duties that went with them. And the more the appointments to prelatures were filled by kings and emperors, as was the case in particular from the early sixteenth century, the more these rulers used this opportunity of commendation, especially in France and Spain.

Both simony and commendation contributed, at least in part, to the improvement in papal finances. Additional revenue flowed in from the Papal States. This income extended from the direct and indirect taxes or duties on the use of the salt-works at the mouth of the Tiber, to the monopoly on the alum mines near Tolfa discovered during Pius II's pontificate, as well as to the proceeds from the sale or lease of administrative positions in Rome and in the Papal States, and possibly even to fees paid by prostitutes and Jews in Rome for their protection. There was, in addition, the traditional revenue from benefices, though this source of income was limited in the period after the councils and the stronger position of many secular rulers that emerged from them. Income from the conferring of Holy Year privileges to other churches (the so-called "Rome privileges") increased in this period, as did income from the sale of indulgences, which was especially criticized, though priests, banks and often local rulers were also involved with money collected from indulgences. There is an extant register of revenue from the Papal States from the period of Sixtus IV; there are lists of offices available for purchase starting in 1497; under Clement VII a "budget" of the *camera* was drawn up in 1525. All of these documents have lacunae, however, with hardly any work having been done so far on total papal income and the various expenditures. For this reason we are, in contrast to the fourteenth century, less informed about papal finances of this epoch. What can be stated with certainty are the shifts in proportions. Under Leo X, for example, Germany (circa sixteen percent) and Italy (circa thirty-two percent) contributed more to papal revenue through *servitia* and annates than in the fourteenth century, while France's portion (circa thirty percent) went down. However, these sums of approximately 17,000 to 20,000 ducats annually were in any case much less than 150 years before. These amounts were probably surpassed by revenues from the Papal States and from the sale of offices and indulgences, though the exact relations are still not known.

Knowledge of the actual size of papal finances among most contemporary curials during the Renaissance was even less than what modern research can verify. This caused speculation to flourish all the more. The annual income from *servitia* and annates was estimated to be about 50,000 ducats or more, with the sums from the sale of indulgences and offices even higher. And just as in the fourteenth century, the inhabitants of some countries, including Germany, felt more cheated than they actually were. Thus these vague suspicions reinforced the criticism of the curia and the papal ecclesiastical authority. In addition, the life-style of the popes did not help strengthen their authority. And since the popes themselves were usually busy with securing the position of their family and the Papal States, they disregarded the warning signs. This becomes especially clear in Rome's reaction to Martin Luther. Leo

X, during whose pontificate Luther began his activity, slighted the Augustinian hermit, calling him a "little brother" and looking down on his controversy with Tetzel and other adversaries as a "monastic squabble." The trial and eventual condemnation of Luther was handed over to Cardinal Cajetan, who was in Germany, but at the curia it was not viewed with any special importance. In Germany, Luther's theological and moral reproaches found wide approval, but they did not lead to any self-reflection in Rome, except during the pontificate of Adrian VI, who had already served as an inquisitor in Spain. In the Roman view, Luther was merely one heretic among many. The German Christians' dissension over dogma and organization, which at the latest became clear in 1530 at the Diet of Augsburg, was not fully comprehended at the curia until the death of Clement VII. Zwingli's and other reformers' activity found even less of an echo among the Swiss at the papal court, not to mention the activity of Calvin which began towards the end of Clement VII's pontificate, nor the the English church's split from Rome that was underway and which became a reality shortly after Clement's death. Nor did Rome have any reaction to the demands of the German princes for a council in 1523, nor to John Eck's suggestions for reform to enable Rome to fight Martin Luther better.

Rome reacted in a similarly uninterested manner to the reforms in local churches and orders that were underway from the second half of the fifteenth century, especially in Italy and Spain, and to the new orders themselves. Rome finally took notice of the orders when the Cistercians, during Innocent VIII's pontificate, and later the Observants and the Capuchins from the Franciscan orders or the numerous other new brotherhoods and orders, requested privileges from the pope for their own safeguard. They had to pay dearly for these privileges, however. Under Innocent VIII, a bull in favor of Cistercian reform in France cost 6,000 ducats. And so it went for the Theatines from 1524, the Capuchins from 1528–1529, the Angelicals from 1530, the Barnabites from 1533, and for the Franciscan and Dominican chapters of the order in their efforts to reform their orders from the time of Julius II. Their reform activities were made even more difficult at the papal court by the fact that, for a long time, the Sacred Penitentiary followed the letter of the law in granting dispensations to members of reform-minded orders. Furthermore, understanding waned for the church's problems in other countries inasmuch as from the time of Julius II not only the popes—except for Adrian VI—but also most of the curials were Italian and whose interest in non-Italian events was usually confined within narrow limits. Thus it is hardly surprising that, for example, the Spanish national councils of Seville in 1478 and Burgos in 1511, which concerned church reform, did not look for papal cooperation; in fact, they only took the papacy into consideration when they had to decide upon defensive measures against papal intervention. Their partner was no longer the pope. It was now the king.

As a result, the *sacco di Roma* seemed to be due punishment for the papacy not only to the reformers, who condemned the pope as the antichrist, but also to many Catholics. In their eyes, the papacy had stirred up the wrath of God with its many abuses. And even though Luther, Calvin and other reformers succeeded through their own theological considerations in separating from the established church, and even though the English church's break from Rome originated in the personal and ecclesiatico-political calculations of Henry VIII, the papacy of the Renaissance nevertheless made its own significant contribution to the rise and entrenchment of the division in the church by disregarding the demands for reform of the "head and members" and by allowing abuses in Rome to take root.

Summary and Outlook

After Jerusalem's fall at the time of Emperor Vespasian, the Christian congregation in Rome, the center of the empire, gradually gained in prestige among fellow believers. Part of this prestige involved, starting in the second century, the cult of the two apostles Peter and Paul, the supposed founders of the Roman congregation. Starting in approximately the same period, the Roman congregation was presided over by a bishop, who—like in other congregations—obtained a "monarchial" position and who, during the persecutions of the Christians that started with Emperor Decius, was also respected in such other places as Carthage and Spain. To be sure, he still did not have any preeminence over other bishops, except perhaps in the congregations around Rome.

The end of the persecutions led, from the time of Constantine the Great, to a consolidation within Christendom of the local and supraregional organization, which also worked to the benefit of the bishop of Rome. The main task of the fourth-century Roman bishops was to Christianize their city once and for all as well as to unify it in liturgy and in faith. To this end, there was established not only the veneration of the martyrs, but also the apostolic succession and with it the emphasis on the cult of Peter. As a consequence of disputes regarding matters of faith (Donatists, Arians) in other congregations, in about A.D. 350 the bishops began using the claims they had made regarding Rome to emphasize Rome's preeminence over emperors and congregations in both the West and the East. After the upper political echelon had been Christianized around the year 400 and began exerting influence on the organization of the church, pontiffs such as Innocent I, Leo I, and Gelasius I furthered this tendency by formulating claims— also vis-à-vis the Eastern congregations—which, though usually not accepted, served as the theoretical basis for papal leadership of the Western church in the centuries to come in Rome and, to some extent, in the newly established German empire too. Among the papal claims was the assertion that the pope was successor, heir, and representative of Peter, and through this, the supreme head of the entire church. In addition, there was Gelasius' doctrine of two powers and the forgeries perpetrated under Symmachus, which stated that the pope was to be judged only by God. At the same time, the organization of the Roman clergy was consolidated, with the College of Presbyters and the College of Deacons at the head, and the board of administration. Their activities, as reflected in the *Liber pontificalis* and in papal correspondence, showed that by the end of this epoch, however, the papacy's only real influence was in Rome, in suburbicarian Italy, and in the patrimony of the Roman church.

After the power of the Goths had waned in the sixth century, Rome was incorporated into the Byzantine imperial church as a political outpost, its bishop by and large subordinate to the emperor. Consequently, the worship practices and organization of the congregation were remodeled along Byzantine lines; in Rome and its surroundings there formed a new class of leaders strongly shaped by Byzantine or at least Greek influences, and from which numerous popes of the seventh and eighth centuries came. In contrast, Roman contacts with the churches in North Africa and in the kingdoms of the Visigoths and the Franks slackened. Of significance for the future was the fact that territories of the Anglo-Saxons and the Jutes, partially under papal control, were missionized and organized on the Roman model.

The break with Byzantium became more prominent with the pontificate of Gregory II due to iconoclasm and to the measures of Emperor Leo III. Islam considerably reduced the importance of the North African and Visigothic churches, while Rome's contacts with the Frankish rulers grew closer thanks to Anglo-Saxon missionaries. Rome itself, however, was threatened by the Lombards more than ever before. For this reason, and because the ambitious Carolingians wanted papal consent for their new kingship, Pepin and Stephen II formed an alliance in 754 after earlier contacts in 750/751. This alliance was to grow closer in the future. The papacy looked to gain independence from its overlord, as is seen in statements from the Donation of Constantine, which was written at this time. In reality, however, the papacy had the Franks to thank for averting the Lombard threat and for its dominion in Central Italy (the future Papal States) as heir to the Byzantine exarchate. In turn, the Franks took up parts of the Roman model for worship, law, and organization for their growing realm of influence. And then in 800, Charlemagne had himself crowned emperor by Pope Leo III, deepening the cleft between East and West, though intensifying the ties between the papacy and the Frankish kingdom. Rome itself, however, continued to be modeled along Byzantine lines. The papacy endeavored to reduce its new dependence on the Frankish ruler.

In this, the papacy was successful due to the decline of Frankish rule in the second half of the ninth century. At the same time, however, the danger to Rome increased due to the power struggles of neighboring princes, the invasions by the Saracens, and later, to the renewed expansion of Byzantium in Lower Italy, to which there was a further loosening of ties during the Photian schism. Since the pope was also ruler of Rome, the papacy was increasingly sucked into the whirlpool of power struggles within the city. The situation was stabilized when "senator" Theophylact and his pope, Sergius III, seized power.

The following period, the so-called dark century, is characterized by the fact that the popes were largely dependent on whoever the current aristocratic ruler of Rome was, though in association with him the popes carried out both an ecclesiastical and secular reorganization of Rome and the surrounding territories, in this way shaping for the centuries to come the direction of papal politics largely according to Roman interests. On the other hand, more ecclesiastical institutions than ever before—especially abbeys in relatively recently Christianized areas like Germany or in politically unstable areas like France and Castile—made efforts to develop closer ties to the papacy through protective privileges and exemptions, an important precondition for the later expansion of papal authority. After Otto I was crowned emperor in 962, the papacy became more dependent on Germany. This also manifested itself in the liturgy. Except for the short period of Otto III, German influence in Rome itself, however, remained relatively slight as the city and its surroundings were ruled by the Crescentians, and later by the Tusculans, and their popes.

When the rule of these families came to an end in 1046, the dominance of the German ruler was evident once again. But even under Henry III, and even more so after his death, the pontiffs who came after Leo IX took a leading role in church reform, which they used to expand their own position and which they propagated with the support of a wide circle—monasteries, aristocracy, and some bishops, clerics, and lower laymen. From that point on, the papacy claimed imperial rights, preeminence over secular powers, and leadership of the church as a whole.

With the support of new assistants, the College of Cardinals and the curia, as well as with the backing of foreign reformers, canonists, and theologians, the popes succeeded, from the time of the so-called Investiture Controversy, in implementing, theoretically at least, their *plenitudo potestatis* in the church, in arranging the hierarchy under them, and in becoming the overlord of secular dominions through papal protection or through vassalage. On the other hand, their control over their own bishopric diminished appreciably, until finally, in 1144, Rome was ruled by a municipal government and the popes usually had to reside outside Rome. Their situation grew even more complicated due to the two schisms of 1130 and 1159. To be sure, the eventual success of the pretenders, Innocent II and Alexander III, demonstrated the extent to which papal claims to leadership had prevailed; disputed episcopal elections and squabbles within local churches were now being decided more and more at the curia. For this reason, canon law, which had been recently developed, bore a strong mark of the papacy, though compilers and commentators were only too eager to help. As a consequence of the Treaty of Benevento, the papacy came into a close association with the Norman empire in Southern Italy after 1156, and in so doing, made itself, Rome, and the Papal States dependent on the existing power structure there. This would determine papal policies time and again, not only toward the Hohenstaufen, but also vis-à-vis their successors and rivals from the middle of the thirteenth century until well into the sixteenth century.

From 1188 the popes were again the nominal overlords of Rome, and through nepotism and some adept policies, and even with violence when necessary, they tried to secure and entrench their control over Rome and the Papal States. Not only did the pontiffs run into conflict with the Hohenstaufen, but their policies toward Germany, as well as toward other countries, were now determined by their interests in Central Italy. In the church as a whole, papal authority was felt stronger than ever as the popes now directed the fight against the various heresies, with aid from the new mendicant orders, and they expanded the curia. Moreover, in the now revamped ceremonial, they showed off their elevated rank over rulers and ecclesiastics in an impressive fashion. They also increased their revenue and guaranteed their claims through the new collections of canon law. Although popes such as Innocent III and Innocent IV clearly demonstrated their leading role in the church, the papacy was already under Angevin influence by the time of Urban IV. Because of the overly close amalgamation of spiritual and secular interests, and in light of the abuses in the curia, the papacy increasingly ran into criticism, its claims to leadership questioned. And finally, Boniface VIII's conflict with Philip the Fair of France in particular proved that, although the papacy still enjoyed great prestige in wide circles of Christendom, as the first Holy Year of 1300 made evident, the universal papal claim was no longer fully accepted by the newly forming "nation-states."

In 1316, John XXII carried out the removal of the pope and the curia to Avignon, with the result that both government and ceremonial were concentrated more and more on the papal palace, increasing the distance between the pope and the average Christian. On the other hand, this guaranteed for the first time since the eleventh century a continuity in the curial administration. Thus, what previously had often merely been claimed, was now in fact obtained, especially when it came to fiscal matters. The Avignon period saw the most effective government, but it was also a period of exploitation of the Latin church by the papacy, which lasted until the Reformation. For this very reason, criticism of the papacy increased, especially in Germany and England, two countries where even at this time there was the danger of a split in the church. And these criticisms multiplied because of the papacy's political policies and its ties with France, often considered to be much too close. This development was ominous for another reason, namely, that the popes were now believed more capable of destroying the church rather than reforming it, with some of the popes appearing to be heretics in the eyes of contemporaries. Except for Benedict XII, the popes proved by their actions their lack of interest in church reform.

After many requests to do so, the papacy returned to Rome, first Urban V in 1365 and then Gregory XI in 1376, but not before Cardinal Gil Albornoz militarily "pacified" the Papal States and with his constitutions formed the basis for its system of government, which was to be fundamental for the following centuries. But the schism that broke out in 1378 led to renewed insecurity in Rome and its surroundings and to a low point in papal prestige. The various obediences were now dependent on rulers who used the opportunity to bring their national churches under their influence, as did princes and cities in Germany. The advocates of the "conciliar idea" disputed the papacy's claim of leadership over the Universal Church, which eventually led to the decrees *Haec sancta* and *Frequens* at the Council of Constance. Since these were accepted nearly everywhere, papal protests against them, especially from the time of Eugene IV, amounted to nothing more than factious commentaries that prevailed only from the late sixteenth century in those parts of Europe that had remained Catholic.

After the disaster of the schism period, which in Constance, and even more so in Basle, led to a cut in papal prerogatives and revenue, pontiffs beginning with Martin V endeavored to make Rome and the Papal States the center of their dominion. Henceforth, their designs in Italy determined, even more than in the thirteenth century, their policies vis-à-vis other rulers and other church institutions. To secure their dominion and to expand their residence in Rome, they curtailed Rome's autonomy, especially from the time of Sixtus IV, and subjugated most of the *signori* and communes of the Papal States. They demonstrated their love of art, as well as their power, by expanding and beautifying their capital city. To secure their dominion and to finance their political and artistic plans, they increased the revenue from the Papal States and from nepotism, exploited and expanded simony, and promoted the sale of Roman privileges and letters of indulgence, while the previously customary income from the clergy (*servitia, annates*) fell. Increasingly, these measures ran into criticism, as did the papal life-style and the lack of will for reform. These criticisms, along with the altered political situation in Italy after 1494, which eventually led to Spanish dominance, brought about a decline in papal authority. Under the two Medici popes, Leo X and Clement VII, large parts of Germany broke away from the papacy with the Reformation, followed by parts of Switzerland, and later by England and Scandinavia. At the same time, large areas of the Balkans and of Hungary fell to the Turks. Besides Poland and portions of Germany, the papacy was left with France, Spain, and Italy, whose southern and northern parts were also dominated by Spain. But since in France and Spain the national churches were now actually under the respective king rather than under the pope, the actual power of the pope was by and large limited to the Papal States at the end of the period described in this book, though the papal pretension to universality carried on.

Without going into the history of the papacy in the modern era, it should be pointed out that the political operations of the popes—in particular since the Peace of Westphalia of 1648—were concentrated even more on the Papal States, one of the most corrupt and most badly governed states in Europe (in particular in the eighteenth century) until its end in 1870. The Council of Trent in the late sixteenth century led to a reform of the church by accentuating papal authority, as evinced in the fixing of law and liturgy. However, this mostly benefited the consolidation of the curia, as long as new orders like the Jesuits, who were directly under the pope, were uneffective, since the activities of the papal nuncios in other countries were seldom efficacious because church power was in the hands of the national rulers. Nevertheless, the papal claims of supremacy that were developed in late antiquity and the Middle Ages continued, as did the concentration of the Catholic Church on the pope and his curia. In particular after the Napoleonic era and the break up of the Papal States, this tradition served as the basis for rebuilding papal prestige in the twentieth century in connection with the policies of the concordat decrees. Even if nowadays the theoretical foundation has changed—the Donation of Constantine and the Pseudo-Isidore Decretals survive for the most part indirectly in the *Codices iuris canonici* of 1917 and 1983—the papacy still largely stands on the accomplishments of its predecessors and of those who battled alongside them from late antiquity and the Middle Ages. Dogmatism, such as the renewed emphasis on Thomism in Rome since the nineteenth century, and the social and estate doctrines of the papacy developed from it, show just how strongly the Middle Ages still determines the present for the papacy. The same could be said for the precept of celibacy that was first handed down in the eleventh century and that continues to this day. The concentration of the curia in Rome, a noticeable trend at least from the time of Pius XII, and the dominance even today of Italians and other Europeans in the upper echelons of the curia despite the rising importance of the third world, are both a legacy of the epochs described in this book.

Appendix

Index of Roman Bishops and Popes from Peter to Clement VII

Prefatory remarks: The numbers in front of the names indicate those popes who are commonly recognized by the Vatican today, even though nowadays the *Annuario pontifico* no longer uses a numbering system because of the disputed recognition of some popes. "Antipopes" are listed under their opponents. The dates for the pontificates of bishops of the first to the early third centuries are based on fourth-century constructs, and for this reason they are followed by question marks. When known, the full date for election (el.), consecration or coronation (c.) are given. These dates are known more exactly after the eighth century. The full dates for death (ob.) as well as for deposition (d.) or resignation (r.) are also given.

1.	Peter	30?/33?–64?/67?
2.	Linus	64?/67?–76?/79?
3.	Anencletus (Cletus) (Anacletus I)	79?/–90?/92?
4.	Clement I	90?/92?–99?/101?
5.	Evaristus	99?/101?–107?
6.	Alexander I	107?–116?
7.	Sixtus I (Xysius)	116?–125?

8.	Telesphorus	125?–136?
9.	Hyginus	136?/138?–140?/142?
10.	Pius I	140?/142?–154?/155?
11.	Anicetus	154?/155?–166?
12.	Soter	166?–174?
13.	Eleutherius	174?–189?
14.	Victor I	189?–198?/199?
15.	Zephyrinus	198?/199?–217?
16.	Callistus I	217?–222
	Hippolytus	217?–235 (r.); 235/236 (ob.)
17.	Urban I	222–230
18.	Pontian	230–Sept. 28, 235 (r.), 235 (ob.)
19.	Anterus	235–Jan. 3, 236 (ob.)
20.	Fabian	Jan. 236–Jan. 20, 250 (ob.)
21.	Cornelius	March 251–June 253 (?)
	Novatian	251–258?
22.	Lucius I	253–March 5, 254 (ob.)
23.	Stephen I	May 12, 254–Aug. 2, 257 (ob.)
24.	Sixtus II (Xystus)	Aug. 30, 257–Aug. 6, 258 (ob.)
25.	Dionysius	July 22, 259/260–Dec. 26, 267/268 (ob.)
26.	Felix I	Jan. 5, 268/269–Dec. 30, 273/274 (ob.)
27.	Eutychian	274/275–282/283
28.	Caius	282/283–April 22, 295/296 (ob.)
29.	Marcellinus	June 30, 295(?)–Oct. 25, 304 (ob.)
30.	Marcellus I	May 307(?)–Jan. 16, 308(?) (ob.)
31.	Eusebius	April 18, 308/309/310–Aug. 17, 308/309/310 (ob.)
32.	Miltiades	July 2, 310/311–Jan. 11, 314 (ob.)
33.	Sylvester I	Jan. 31, 314–Dec. 31, 335 (ob.)
34.	Mark	Jan. 18, 336–Oct. 7, 336 (ob.)
35.	Julius I	Feb. 6, 337–April 12, 352 (ob.)
36.	Liberius	May 17, 352–Sept. 24, 366 (ob.)
	Felix II	355–358 (r.); Nov. 22, 365 (ob.)
37.	Damasus I	Oct. 1, 366–Dec. 11, 384 (ob.)
	Ursinus	366–Nov. 16, 367 (ob.)
38.	Siricius	Dec. 384–Nov. 26, 399 (ob.)
39.	Anastasius I	Nov. 27, 399–Dec. 401 (ob.)
40.	Innocent I	Dec. 21, 401–March 12, 417 (ob.)
41.	Zosimus	March 18, 417–Dec. 25, 418 (ob.)
42.	Boniface I	Dec. 29, 418–Sept. 4, 422 (ob.)
	Eulalius	418–419 (r.); 423 (ob.)

43.	Celestine I	Sept. 10, 422–July 27, 432 (ob.)
44.	Sixtus III (Xystus)	July 31, 432–Aug. 19, 440 (ob.)
45.	Leo I	Sept. 29, 440–Nov. 10, 461 (ob.)
46.	Hilarus	Nov. 13, 461–Feb. 29, 468 (ob.)
47.	Simplicius	March 3, 468–March 10, 483 (ob.)
48.	Felix III (II)	March 13, 483–March 1, 492 (ob.)
49.	Gelasius I	March 1, 492–Nov. 19, 496 (ob.)
50.	Anastasius II	Nov. 24, 496–Nov. 17, 498 (ob.)
51.	Symmachus	Nov. 22, 498–July 19, 514 (ob.)
	Lawrence	498–506 (r.); 506 (ob.)
52.	Hormisdas	July 20, 514–Aug. 6, 523 (ob.)
53.	John I	Aug. 13, 523–May 18, 526 (ob.)
54.	Felix IV (III)	July 12, 526–Sept. 22(?), 530 (ob.)
55.	Boniface II	Sept. 22, 530–Oct. 532 (ob.)
	Dioscorus	Sept. 22, 530–Oct. 14, 530 (ob.)
56.	John II	Jan. 2, 533–May 8, 535 (ob.)
	(orig.: Mercury)	
57.	Agapitus I	May 13, 535–April 22, 536 (ob.)
58.	Silverius	June 1(?), 536–Nov. 11, 537 (r.); Dec. 2, 537 (ob.)
59.	Vigilius	March 29, 537–June 7, 555 (ob.)
60.	Pelagius I	April 16, 556 (c.)–March 3/4, 561 (ob.)
61.	John III	July 17, 561 (c.)–July 13, 574 (ob.)
62.	Benedict I	June 2, 575 (c.)–July 30, 579 (ob.)
63.	Pelagius II	Nov. 26, 579 (c.)–Feb. 7, 590 (ob.)
64.	Gregory I	Sept. 3, 590 (c.)–March 12, 604 (ob.)
65.	Sabinian	Sept. 13, 604 (c.)–Feb. 22, 606 (ob.)
66.	Boniface III	Feb. 19, 607 (c.)–Nov. 12, 607 (ob.)
67.	Boniface IV	Aug. 25, 608 (c.)–May 8, 615 (ob.)
68.	Adeodatus (Deusedit) I	Oct. 19, 615 (c.)–Nov. 8, 618 (ob.)
69.	Boniface V	Dec. 23, 619 (c.)–Oct. 25, 625 (ob.)
70.	Honorius I	Oct. 27, 625 (el.)–Oct. 12, 638 (ob.)
71.	Severinus	May 28, 640 (c.)–Aug. 2, 640 (ob.)
72.	John IV	Dec. 24, 640 (c.)–Oct. 12, 642 (ob.)
73.	Theodore I	Nov. 24, 642 (c.)–May 14, 649 (ob.)
74.	Martin I	July 649 (c.)–June 17, 653 (d.); Sept. 16, 655 (ob.)
75.	Eugene I	Aug. 10, 654 (c.)–June 2, 657 (ob.)
76.	Vitalian	July 30, 657 (c.)–Jan. 27, 672 (ob.)
77.	Adeodatus II	April 11, 672 (c.)–June 17, 676 (ob.)
78.	Donus	Nov. 2, 676 (c.)–April 11, 678 (ob.)

79.	Agatho	June 27, 678 (c.)–Jan. 10, 681 (ob.)
80.	Leo II	Aug. 17, 682 (c.)–July 3, 683 (ob.)
81.	Benedict II	June 26, 684 (c.)–May 8, 685 (ob.)
82.	John V	July 23, 685 (c.)–Aug. 2, 686 (ob.)
83.	Conon	Oct. 21, 686 (c.)–Sept. 21, 687 (ob.)
	Theodore	687 (end)
	Paschal	687–692 (?) (ob.)
84.	Sergius I	Dec. 15, 687 (c.)–Sept. 8, 701 (ob.)
85.	John VI	Oct. 30, 701 (c.)–Jan. 11, 705 (ob.)
86.	John VII	March 1, 705 (c.)–Oct. 18, 707 (ob.)
87.	Sisinnius	Jan. 15, 708 (c.)–Feb. 4, 708 (ob.)
88.	Constantine I	March 25, 708 (c.)–April 9, 715 (ob.)
89.	Gregory II	May 19, 715 (c.)–Feb. 11, 731 (ob.)
90.	Gregory III	March 18, 731 (c.)–Nov. 741 (ob.)
91.	Zacharius	Dec. 10, 741 (c.)–March 22, 752 (ob.)
	Stephen (II)	March 23, 752 (el.)–March 25, 752 (ob.)
92.	Stephen II (III)	March 26, 752 (el.)–April 26, 757 (ob.)
93.	Paul I	April 757 (el.); Mai 29 (c.)–June 28, 767 (ob.)
	Constantine II	June 28, 767 (el.); July 5, (c.)–Aug. 6, 768 (d.), April 13, 769 (banished)
	Philip	July 31, 768 (el.)
94.	Stephen III (IV)	Aug. 1, 768 (el.); Aug. 7 (c.)–Jan. 24, 772 (ob.)
95.	Adrian I	Feb. 1, 772 (el.); Feb. 9 (c.)–Dec. 25, 795 (ob.)
96.	Leo III	Dec. 26, 795 (el.); Dec. 27 (c.)–June 12, 816 (ob.)
97.	Sephen IV (V)	June 22, 816 (el.)–Jan. 24, 817 (ob.)
98.	Paschal I	Jan. 25, 817 (el.)–Feb. 11, 824 (ob.)
99.	Eugene II	Feb./May, 824–Aug. 827 (ob.)
100.	Valentine	Aug. 827–Sept. 827 (ob.)
101.	Gregory IV	827 (end)–Jan. 844 (ob.)
	John	Jan. 844
102.	Sergius II	Jan. 844–Jan. 27, 847 (ob.)
103.	Leo IV	Jan. 847 (el.); April 10 (c.)–July 17, 855 (ob.)
104.	Benedict III	July 855 (el.); Sept. 29 (c.)–April 17, 858 (ob.)
	Anastasius Bibliothecarius	Aug. 855–Sept. 855 (banished), ca. 880 (ob.)

105.	Nicholas I	April 24, 858 (c.)–Nov. 13, 867 (ob.)
106.	Adrian II	Dec. 14, 867 (c.)–Dec. 14, 872 (ob.)
107.	John VIII	Dec. 14, 872 (el.)–Dec. 16, 882 (ob.)
108.	Marinus I	Dec. 16, 882 (el.)–May 15, 884 (ob.)
109.	Adrian III	May 17, 884 (el.)–Sept. 885 (ob.)
110.	Stephen V (VI)	Sept. 885–Sept. 14, 891 (ob.)
111.	Formosus	Oct. 6, 891–April 4, 896 (ob.)
112.	Boniface VI	April 896–April/May 896 (ob.)
113.	Stephen VI (VII)	May 896–Aug. 897 (ob.)
114.	Romanus	Aug. 897–Nov. 897 (ob.)
115.	Theodore II	Dec. 897–Dec. 897 (ob.)
116.	John IX	Jan. 898–Jan. 900 (ob.)
117.	Benedict IV	Jan./Feb. 900–July 903 (ob.)
118.	Leo V	July 903–Sept. 903
	Christopher	July/Sept. 903–Jan. 904 (banished)
119.	Sergius III	Jan. 29, 904–April 14, 911 (ob.)
120.	Anastasius III	April 911–June 913 (ob.)
121.	Lando	July 913–Feb. 914 (ob.)
122.	John X	March 914–May/June 928 (ob.)
123.	Leo VI	May 928–Dec. 928 (ob.)
124.	Stephen VII (VIII)	Dec. 928–Feb. 931 (ob.)
125.	John XI	Feb./March 931–Dec. 935 (ob.)
126.	Leo VII	Jan. 3, 936–July 13, 939 (ob.)
127.	Stephen VIII (IX)	July 14, 939–Oct. 942 (ob.)
128.	Marinus II	Oct. 30, 942–May 946 (ob.)
129.	Agapitus II	May 10, 946–Dec. 955 (ob.)
130.	John XII (originally: Octavian)	Dec. 16, 955–Dec. 4, 963 (d.); May 14, 964 (ob.)
131.	Leo VIII	Dec. 4, 963 (el.); Dec. 6 (c.)–March 1, 965 (ob.)
	Benedict V	May 22, 964–June 23, 964 (d.); July 4, 966 (ob.)
132.	John XIII	Oct. 1, 965–Sept. 6, 972 (ob.)
133.	Benedict VI	Jan. 19, 973–June 974 (ob.)
	Boniface VII	June 974–July 974 (banished), see below
134.	Benedict VII	Oct. 974–July 10, 983 (ob.)
135.	John XIV (originally: Peter)	Dec. 983–Aug. 20, 984 (ob.)
	Boniface VII (2d time)	Aug. 984–July 985 (ob.)

136. John XV   Aug. 985–March 996 (ob.)
137. Gregory V   May 3, 996–Feb. 18, 999 (ob.)
      (Bruno)
     John XVI   April 997–May 998 (d.); c. 1031 (ob.)
138. Sylvester II   April 2, 999–May 1003 (ob.)
      (Gerbert)
139. John XVII   May/June 1003–Nov. 6, 1003 (ob.)
140. John XVIII   Jan. 1004–June/July 1009 (ob.)
141. Sergius IV   July 31, 1009–May 12, 1012 (ob.)
      (Peter, called Os
      Porci)
142. Benedict VIII   May 18, 1012–April 9, 1024 (ob.)
      (Theophylact)
     Gregory (VI)   June 1012–Dec. 1012 (banished)
143. John XIX   April 19(?), 1024–1032 (ob.)
      (Romanus)
144. Benedict IX   Aug./Sept. 1032–1044 (banished), see
      (Theophylact)   below
     Sylvester III   Jan. 20, 1045–Feb. 10, 1045 (banished);
      (John)   Dec. 20, 1046 (ob.)
     Benedict IX (2d   April 10, 1045–May 1, 1045 (r.); Dec. 20,
      time)   1046 (d.)
     Gregory VI   May 5, 1045–Dec. 20, 1046 (d.), Nov. 1047
      (John Gratian)   (ob.)
     Clement II   Dec. 24, 1046 (el.); Dec. 25 (c.)–Oct. 9,
      (Suidger)   1047 (ob.)
     Benedict IX (3d   Nov. 8, 1047–July 17, 1048 (banished);
      time)   1055/56 (ob.)
145. Damasus II   Dec. 25, 1047 (nom.); July 17, 1048 (c.)–
      (Poppo)   Aug. 9, 1048 (ob.)
146. Leo IX   Dec. 1048 (nom.); Feb. 12, 1049 (c.)–April
      (Bruno)   19, 1054 (ob.)
147. Victor II   March 1055 (invest.); April 16 (c.)–July
      (Gebhard)   28, 1057 (ob.)
148. Stephen IX (X)   Aug. 2, 1057 (el.); Aug. 3 (c.)–March 29,
      (Frederick)   1058 (ob.)
     Benedict X   April 5, 1058 (el.)–Jan. 1059 (banished);
      (John)   April 1060 (d.)
149. Nicholas II   Dec. 6, 1058 (el.); Jan. 24, 1059 (c.)–July
      (Gerard)   27, 1061 (ob.)

150. Alexander II
(Anselm)
Oct. 1, 1061–April 21, 1073 (ob.)

Honorius II
(Cadalus)
Oct. 28, 1061–May 31, 1064 (d.); 1071/72
(ob.)

151. Gregory VII
(Hildebrand)
April 22, 1073 (el.); June 30 (c.)–May 25,
1085 (ob.)

Clement III
(Guibert)
June 25, 1080 (el.); March 24, 1084 (c.)–
Sept. 8, 1100 (ob.)

152. Victor III
(Desiderius)
May 24, 1086–Sept. 16, 1087 (ob.)

153. Urban II
(Odo)
March 12, 1088–July 29, 1099 (ob.)

154. Paschal II
(Rainerius)
Aug. 13, 1099 (el.); Aug. 14 (c.)–Jan. 21,
1118 (ob.)

Theodoric
Sept. 1110–Dec. 1100 (d.); 1102 (ob.)

Albert
Feb. 1102–March 1102 (d.)

Sylvester IV
(Maginulf)
Nov. 18, 1105–1111 (r.)

155. Gelasius II
(John)
Jan. 24, 1118 (el.); March 10 (c.)–Jan. 28,
1119 (ob.)

Gregory VIII
(Maurice
Burdinus)
March 8, 1118–1121 (d.)

156. Callistus II
(Guido)
Feb. 2, 1119 (el.); Feb. 9 (c.)–Dec. 13, 1124
(ob.)

Celestine II
(Teobaldo
Boccapecci)
Dec. 15, 1124 (el.); Dec. 16 (r.)

157. Honorius II
(Lamberto)
Dec. 15, 1124 (el.); Dec. 21 (c.)–Feb. 13,
1130 (ob.)

158. Innocent II
(Gregory
Papareschi)
Feb. 14, 1130 (el.); Feb. 23 (c.)–Sept. 24,
1143 (ob.)

Anacletus II
(Pietro Pierleoni)
Feb. 14, 1130 (el.); Feb. 23 (c.)–Jan. 25,
1138 (ob.)

Victor IV
(Gregory)
March 1138–May 29, 1138 (r.)

159. Celestine II
(Guido di
Castello)
Sept. 26, 1143 (el.); Oct. 3 (c.)–March 8,
1144 (ob.)

160. Lucius II
     (Gerardus)   March 12, 1144 (el.)–Feb. 15, 1145 (ob.)

161. Eugene III   Feb. 15, 1145 (el.); Feb. 18 (c.)–July 8,
     (Peter   1153 (ob.)
     Bernard)

162. Anastasius IV   July 12, 1153 (el.)–Dec. 3, 1154 (ob.)
     (Conradus de
     Subura)

163. Adrian IV   Dec. 4, 1154 (el.); Dec. 5 (c.)–Sept. 1, 1159
     (Nicholas   (ob.)
     Breakspear)

164. Alexander III   Sept. 7, 1159 (el.); Sept. 20 (c.)–Aug. 30,
     (Roland   1181 (ob.)
     Bandinelli)

     Victor IV   Sept. 7, 1159 (el.); Oct. 4 (c.)–April 20,
     (Octavian of   1164 (ob.)
     Monticelli)

     Paschal III   April 20, 1164 (el.); April 26 (c.)–Sept. 20,
     (Guido of   1168 (ob.)
     Crema)

     Callistus III   Sept. 1168–Aug. 29, 1178 (r.)
     (John of Struma)

     Innocent III   Sept. 29, 1179–Jan. 1180 (d.)
     (Lando of Sezze)

165. Lucius III   Sept. 1, 1181 (el.); Sept. 6 (c.)–Nov. 25,
     (Ubaldo   1185 (ob.)
     Allucingoli)

166. Urban III   Nov. 25, 1185 (el.); Dec. 1 (c.)–Oct. 20,
     (Umberto   1187 (ob.)
     Crivelli)

167. Gregory VIII   Oct. 21, 1187 (el.); Oct. 25 (c.)–Dec. 17,
     (Alberto of   1187 (ob.)
     Morra)

168. Clement III   Dec. 19, 1187 (el.); Dec. 20 (c.)–March
     (Paulo Scolari)   1191 (ob.)

169. Celestine III   March 30, 1191 (el.); April 14 (c.)–Jan. 8,
     (Hyacinth Bobo)   1198 (ob.)

170. Innocent III   Jan. 8, 1198 (e.); Feb. 22 (c.)–July 16, 1216
     (Lotario of Segni)   (ob.)

171. Honorius III   July 18, 1216 (el.); July 24 (c.)–March 18,
     (Cencius Savelli)   1227 (ob.)

172. Gregory IX (Ugolino of Segni) — March 19, 1227 (el.); March 21 (c.)–Aug. 22, 1241 (ob.)

173. Celestine IV (Goffredo da Castiglione) — Oct. 25, 1241 (el.); Oct. 28 (c.)–Nov. 10, 1214 (ob.)

174. Innocent IV (Sinibaldo Fieschi) — June 25, 1243 (el.); June 28 (c.)–Dec. 7, 1254 (ob.)

175. Alexander IV (Rinaldo of Segni) — Dec. 12, 1254 (el.); Dec. 20 (c.)–May 25, 1261 (ob.)

176. Urban IV (Jacques Pantaléon) — Aug. 29, 1261 (el.); Sept. 4 (c.)–Oct. 2, 1264 (ob.)

177. Clement IV (Guy le Gros) — Feb. 5, 1265 (el.); Feb. 15 (c.)–Nov. 29, 1268 (ob.)

178. Gregory X (Tedaldo Visconti) — Sept. 1, 1271 (el.); March 27, 1272 (c.)–Jan. 10, 1276 (ob.)

179. Innocent V (Pierre de Tarentaise) — Jan. 21, 1276 (el.); Feb. 22 (c.)–June 22, 1276 (ob.)

180. Adrian V (Ottobuono Fieschi) — July 11, 1276 (el.)–Aug. 18, 1276 (ob.)

181. John XXI (instead of XX) (Peter of Spain) — Sept. 8, 1276 (el.); Sept. 20 (c.)–May 20, 1277 (ob.)

182. Nicholas III (Giovanni Gaetano Orsini) — Nov. 25, 1277 (el.); Dec. 26 (c.)–Aug. 22, 1280 (ob.)

183. Martin IV (Simon de Brion) — Feb. 22, 1281 (el.); March 23 (c.)–March 28, 1285 (ob.)

184. Honorius IV (Giacomo Savelli) — April 2, 1285 (el.); May 20 (c.)–April 3, 1287 (ob.)

185. Nicholas IV (Girolamo Masci) — Feb. 22, 1288 (el.)–April 4, 1292 (ob.)

186. Celestine V (Pietro del Morrone) — July 5, 1294 (el.); Aug. 29 (c.)–Dec. 13, 1294 (r.); May 19, 1296 (ob.)

187. Boniface VIII   Dec. 24, 1294 (el.); Jan. 23, 1295 (c.)–Oct.
     (Benedetto   11, 1303 (ob.)
     Caetani)
188. Benedict XI   Oct. 22, 1303 (el.); Oct. 27 (c.)–July 7,
     (Niccolò   1304 (ob.)
     Boccasini)
189. Clement V   June 5, 1305 (el.); Nov. 14 (c.)–April 20,
     (Raymond   1314 (ob.)
     Bertrand de Got)
190. John XXII   Aug. 7, 1316 (el.); Sept. 5 (c.)–Dec. 4,
     (Jacques Arnaud   1334 (ob.)
     Duèze)
     Nicholas V   May 12, 1328 (el.); May 22 (c.)–Aug. 25,
     (Pietro di   1330 (r.); Oct. 16, 1333 (ob.)
     Corvaro)
191. Benedict XII   Dec. 20, 1334 (el.); Jan. 8, 1335 (c.)–April
     (Jacques   25, 1342 (ob.)
     Fournier)
192. Clement VI   May 7, 1342 (el.); May 19 (c.)–Dec. 6, 1352
     (Pierre Roger)   (ob.)
193. Innocent VI   Dec. 18, 1352 (el.); Dec. 30 (c.)–Sept. 12,
     (Étienne Aubert)   1362 (ob.)
194. Urban V   Sept. 28, 1362 (el.); Nov. 6 (c.)–Dec. 19,
     (Guillaume de   1370 (ob.)
     Grimoard)
195. Gregory XI   Dec. 30, 1370 (el.); Jan. 5, 1371 (c.)–
     (Pierre Roger)   March 26, 1378 (ob.)

Rome

196. Urban VI   April 8, 1378 (el.); April 18 (c.)–Oct. 15,
     (Bartolomeo   1389 (ob.)
     Prignani)
197. Boniface IX   Nov. 2, 1389 (el.); Nov. 9 (c.)–Oct. 1, 1404
     (Pietro   (ob.)
     Tomacelli)
198. Innocent VII   Oct. 17, 1404 (el.); Nov. 11 (c.)–Nov. 6,
     (Cosimo   1406 (ob.)
     Migliorati)

199. Gregory XII   Nov. 30, 1406 (el.); Dec. 19 (c.)–June 5,
     (Angelo Correr)   1409 (d.); July 4, 1415 (r.); Oct. 18,
                        1417 (ob.)

Avignon

Clement VII   Sept. 20, 1378 (el.); Oct. 31 (c.)–Sept. 16,
(Robert of   1394 (ob.)
Geneva)

Benedict XIII   Sept. 28, 1394 (el.); Oct. 11 (c.)–June 5,
(Pedro de Luna)   1409 (d.); July 26, 1417 (d.); May 23,
                     1423 (ob.)

Clement VIII   June 10, 1423 (el.); 1429 (r.)–Dec. 28,
(Gil Sanchez   1447 (ob.)
Muñoz)

Benedict XIV   Nov. 12, 1425–1430 (ob.)
(Bernard
Garnier)

Pisa

Alexander V   June 26, 1409 (el.); July 7 (c.)–May 3,
(Pietro Philarghi)   1410 (ob.)

John XXIII   May 17, 1410 (el.); May 25 (c.)–May 29,
(Baldassare   1415 (d.); Nov. 22, 1419 (ob.)
Cossa)

200. Martin V   Nov. 11, 1417 (el.); Nov. 21 (c.)–Feb. 20,
     (Oddone   1431 (ob.)
     Colonna)

201. Eugene IV   March 3, 1431 (el.); March 11 (c.)–June
     (Gabriele   25, 1439 (d.); Feb. 23, 1447 (ob.)
     Condulmaro)

Felix V   Nov. 5, 1439 (el.); July 24, 1440 (c.)–April
(Amadeus of   7, 1449 (r.); Jan. 7, 1451 (ob.)
Savoy)

202. Nicholas V   March 6, 1447 (el.); March 19 (c.)–March
     (Tommaso   24, 1455 (ob.)
     Parentucelli)

203. Callistus III
(Alonso Borja)
April 8, 1455 (el.); April 20 (c.)–Aug. 6, 1458 (ob.)

204. Pius II
(Enea Silvio Piccolomini)
Aug. 19, 1458 (el.); Sept. 3 (c.)–Aug. 15, 1464 (ob.)

205. Paul II
(Pietro Barbo)
Aug. 30, 1464 (el.); Sept. 16 (c.)–July 26, 1471 (ob.)

206. Sixtus IV
(Francesco della Rovere)
Aug. 9, 1471 (el.); Aug. 25 (c.)–Aug. 12, 1484 (ob.)

207. Innocent VIII
(Giovanni Battista Cibo)
Aug. 29, 1484 (el.); Sept. 12 (c.)–July 25, 1492 (ob.)

208. Alexander VI
(Roderigo Borja)
Aug. 11, 1492 (el.); Aug. 26 (c.)–Aug. 18, 1503 (ob.)

209. Pius III
(Francesco Todeschini Piccolomini)
Sept. 22, 1503 (el.); Oct. 1 (c.)–Oct. 18, 1503 (ob.)

210. Julius II
(Giuliano della Rovere)
Nov. 1, 1503 (el.); Nov. 26 (c.)–Feb. 21, 1513 (ob.)

211. Leo X
(Giovanni Medici)
March 9, 1513 (el.); March 19 (c.)–Dec. 1, 1521 (ob.)

212. Adrian V
(Adriaan Florensz)
Jan. 9, 1522 (el.); Aug. 31 (c.)–Sept. 14, 1523 (ob.)

213. Clement VII
(Giulio Medici)
Nov. 19, 1523 (el.); Nov. 26 (c.)–Sept. 25, 1534 (ob.)

Selected Bibliography

Since this book was originally primarily intended for German readers, the following bibliography contains mostly works in German. Works from other languages are included only when they are especially important for a particular chapter. Because of the limited range of the book, older works and sources had to be omitted. They are included only when reference is made to them in the text. If a text contains an especially extensive bibliography for a chapter, this is so noted. An excellent reference source for recently published works is the Archivum Historiae Pontificae, published in Rome since 1963, which contains an extensive bibliography. Works that cover several epochs appear under the heading "General." To save space, if a work is important for two chapters, it is cited only in the first one. For this same reason series titles are not given. If essay collections by a single author or conference publications contain several pertinent articles, then only the volume or issue number of the collection is cited.

Abbreviations for journals are as follows:

ADipl   Archiv für Diplomatik
AHC   Annuarium Historiae Conciliorum

AHPont	Archivum Historiae Pontificiae
AKG	Archiv für Kulturgeschichte
ALitKG	Archiv für Litteratur- und Kirchengeschichte
ASR	Archivio della (reale) società (or also: deputazione) romana di storia patria
AUF	Archiv für Urkundenforschung
AZ	Archivalische Zeitschrift
BasZG	Basler Zeitschrift für Geschichte
BiblChart	Bibliothèque de l'Ecole des Chartes
BIHBelgR	Bulletin de l'Institut Historique Belge de Rome
BISI	Bollettino dell'istituto storico italiano per il medioevo e archivio Muratoriano
BZ	Byzantinische Zeitschrift
CArch	Cahiers d'archéologie
CatHR	Catholic Historical Review
DA	Deutsches Archiv für Erforschung des Mittelalters
DumbOaP	Dumbarton Oaks Papers
EHR	English Historical Review
EL	Ephemerides liturgicae
EphIurCan	Ephemerides Iuris Canonici
EphThLov	Ephemerides Theologicae Lovanienses
FrühmSt	Frühmittelalterliche Studien
GWU	Geschichte in Wissenschaft und Unterricht
HJb	Historisches Jahrbuch
HZ	Historische Zeitschrift
JEH	Journal of Ecclesiastical History
JMedH	Journal of Medieval History
MélArchH	Mélanges d'archéologie et d'histoire (later: Mélanges de l'Ecole française de Rome. Moyen-Age)
MIÖG	Mitteilungen des Österreichischen Instituts für Geschichtsforschung
MNedHIR	Mededelingen van het Nederlands Historisch Instituut te Rome
OrChrPer	Oriens Christianus Periodica
OstkSt	Ostkirchliche Studien
QFIAB	Quellen und Forschungen aus italienischen Archiven und Bibliotheken
RDCan	Revue de droit canonique
RHEglF	Revue d'histoire de l'église de France
RHM	Römische Historische Mitteilungen
RömJbKG	Römisches Jahrbuch für Kunstgeschichte
RQ	Römische Quartalschrift für christliche Altertumskunde
RSChIt	Rivista di storia della chiesa in Italia
RSLetRel	Rivista di storia e letteratura religiosa
StudGreg	Studi Gregoriani

ThPQ	Theologisch-praktische Quartalsschrift
TransHSoc	Transactions of the Historical Society
VSWG	Vierteljahrsschrift für Sozial- und Wirtschaftsgeschichte
ZAachenG	Zeitschrift des Aachener Geschichtsvereins
ZBLG	Zeitschrift für bayerische Landesgeschichte
ZHF	Zeitschrift für historische Forschung
ZKG	Zeitschrift für Kirchengeschichte
ZNW	Zeitschrift für neutestamentliche Wissenschaft
ZRGKA	Zeitschrift für Rechtsgeschichte. Kanonistische Abteilung
ZThK	Zeitschrift für Theologie und Kirche

General Bibliography

General Information

Fliche, A. and V. Martin, eds. *Histoire de l'Eglise depuis les origines jusqu'à nos jours I-XVI.* Paris, 1934 ff.

Goez, W. *Grundzüge der Geschichte Italiens in Mittelalter und Renaissance.* Darmstadt, 1975.

Hartmann, L. M. *Geschichte Italiens im Mittelalter.* 4 of 6 vols. Gotha, 1897–1908. Italian history until the beginning of the eleventh century.

Jedin, H., ed. *Handbuch der Kirchengeschichte I-IV.* Freiburg 1962–1975. Includes extensive bibliography.

Mayer, H. E. *Geschichte der Kreuzzüge.* Stuttgart, 1965.

Schieder, Th., ed. *Handbuch der europäischen Geschichte I.* Stuttgart, 1976. European history up to the middle of the eleventh century.

Schmaus, M. et al., eds. *Handbuch der Dogmengeschichte III 3: Die Lehre von der Kirche.* 4 booklets. Freiburg, Basle, Vienna, 1970–1974.

Schramm, P. E. *Kaiser, Könige, und Päpste: Gesammelte Aufsätze zur Geschichte des Mittelalters.* 4 vols. Stuttgart, 1968–1970.

Wickham, Ch. *Early Medieval Italy: Central Power and Local Society, 400–1000.* London, Basingstoke, 1981.

Papal History

Barraclough, G. *The Medieval Papacy.* London, 1968.

Caspar, E. *Geschichte des Papsttums.* 2 vols. Tübingen, 1930–1933. Papal history up to the middle of the eighth century. One of the best sources available.

Fink, K. A. *Papsttum und Kirche im abendländischen Mittelalter.* Munich, 1981.

Franzen, A. and R. Bäumer. *Papstgeschichte: Das Petrusamt in seiner Idee und in seiner geschichtlichen Verwirklichung in der Kirche.* Freiburg, 1974.

Fuhrmann, H. *Von Petrus zu Johannes Paul II: Das Papsttum: Gestalt und Gestalten.* Munich, 1980.

Haidacher, A. *Geschichte der Päpste in Bildern. Mit einem geschichtlichen Überblick von J. Wodka: Eine Dokumentation zur Papstgeschichte von L. Frhr. von Pastor.* Heidelberg, 1965.

Haller, J. *Das Papsttum: Idee und Wirklichkeit.* 5 vols. 2d ed. Stuttgart, 1950–1953. Up to the beginning of the fourteenth century.

Hergemöller, B.-U. *Die Geschichte der Papstnamen.* Münster, 1980. Especially from the tenth century.

Mikat, P. "Papst, Papsttum." *Handwörterbuch zur deutschen Rechtsgeschichte.* 22d issue. Berlin, 1983, 1435–1476.

Pastor, L. von. *Geschichte der Päpste seit dem Ausgang des Mittelalters.* Vols. 1–5. Freiburg, Rome. Several editions since 1885 ff. Covers the period after 1378.

Seppelt, F. X. *Geschichte der Päpste.* Vols. 1–4. Munich, 1954–1957. Especially the 2d edition.

Seppelt, F. X. and G. Schwaiger. *Geschichte der Päpste von den Anfängen bis zur Gegenwart.* Munich, 1964.

Ullmann, W. *Kurze Geschichte des Papsttums im Mittelalter.* Berlin, 1978.

Zimmermann, H. *Das Papsttum im Mittelalter: Eine Papstgeschichte im Spiegel der Historiographie.* Stuttgart, 1981.

Institutions and Church Regiment

Alberigo, G. *Cardinalato e collegialità: Studi sull'ecclesiologia tra l'XI e il XIV secolo.* Florence, 1969.

Andrieu, M. "La carrière ecclésiastique des papes et les documents liturgiques du Moyen Age." *Rev. des Sciences reilg.* 21 (1974), 89–120.

Bauer, Cl. "Die Epochen der Papstfinanz." *HZ* 138 (1928), 457–503.

Benson, R. L. "Plenitudo potestatis: Evolution of a Formula from Gregory IV to Gratian." *Studia Gratiana* 14 (1967), 193–218.

Burn-Murdoch, H. "Titles of the Roman See." *The Church Quarterly Review* 159 (1958), 237–364.

Congar, Y. *Droit ancien et structures ecclésiales.* London, 1982.

Deér, J. *Byzanz und das abendländische Herrschertum: Ausgewählte Aufsätze.* Sigmaringen, 1977.

Delooz, P. *Sociologie et canonisations.* La Haye, 1969.

Duchesne, L. and C. Vogel, eds. *Le Liber Pontificalis.* 3 vols. 2d ed. Paris, 1955–1957.

Dumeige, G. and H. Bacht, eds. *Geschichte der ökumenischen Konzilien I-IX.* Mainz, 1963–1975.

Dvornik, F. *The Idea of Apostolicity in Byzantium and the Legend of the Apostle Andrew.* Cambridge, Mass., 1958.

Elze, R. *Päpste-Kaiser-Könige und die mittelalterliche Herrschaftssymbolik.* London, 1982.

Eubel, K., ed. *Hierarchia catholica I-III.* 2d ed. Münster, 1912 ff. Covers the period after 1198.

Fuhrmann, H. "Studien zur Geschichte mittelalterlicher Patriarchate." *ZRGKA* 39 (1953), 112–176; ibid. 40 (1954), 1–84; ibid. 41 (1955), 95–183.

Fuhrmann, H. "Die Wahl des Papstes-ein geschichtlicher Rückblick." *GWU* 9 (1958), 762–780.

Fürst, C. G. *Cardinalis: Prolegomena zu einer Rechtsgeschichte des römischen Kardinalskollegiums.* Munich, 1967.

Gatz, E., ed. *Römische Kurie. Kirchliche Finanzen: Vatikanisches Archiv. Studien zu Ehren von H. Hoberg.* 2 vols. Rome, 1979.

Giusti, M. *Studi sui registri di bolle papali.* Vatican City, 1979.

Goez, W. *Translatio Imperii, ein Beitrag zur Geschichte des Geschichtsdenkens und der politischen Theorie im Mittelalter und in der frühen Neuzeit.* Tübingen, 1958.

Göller, E. *Die päpstliche Pönitentiarie von ihrem Ursprung bis zu ihrer Umgestaltung unter Pius V.* 2 of 4 vols. Rome, 1907–1914.

Gutmann, F., *Die Wahlanzeigen der Päpste bis zum Ende der Avignonesischen Zeit.* Marburg, 1931.

Hefele, C. J. von and H. Leclercq. *Histoire des conciles.* Vols. 1–8. Paris, 1907–1917.

Jaffé, Ph. et al., eds. *Regesta pontificum Romanorum.* 2 vols. Leipzig, 1881–1888. Up to 1198.

Jordan, K. *Das Eindringen des Lehnswesens in das Rechtsleben der römischen Kurie.* Darmstadt, 1971.

Jordan, K. *Ausgewählte Aufsätze zur Geschichte des Mittelalters.* Stuttgart, 1980.

Kempf, F. "Die päpstliche Gewalt in der mittelalterlichen Welt." *Miscellanea Historiæ Pontificæ*, no. 21. Rome, 1959, 117–169.

Knabe, L. *Die gelasianische Zweigewaltentheorie bis zum Ende des Investiturstreites.* Berlin, 1936.

Kuttner, S. "Cardinalis: The History of a Canonical Concept." *The History of Ideas and Doctrines of Canon Law in the Middle Ages*, no. 9. London, 1980.

Ladner, G. B. *Die Papstbildnisse des Altertums und des Mittelalters.* 3 vols. Vatican City, 1941, 1970, and 1983.

Maccarrone, M. *Vicarius Christi: Storia del titolo papale.* Rome, 1952.

Mirbt, C. and K. Aland, eds. *Quellen zur Geschichte des Papsttums und des römischen Katholizismus.* 6th ed. Tübingen, 1967.

Paulus, N. *Geschichte des Ablasses im Mittelalter.* 3 vols. Paderborn, 1922–1923.

Rabikauskas, P. *Die römische Kuriale in der päpstilichen Kanzlei.* Rome, 1958.

Reinhard, W. "Nepotismus: Der Funktionswandel einer papstgeschichtlichen Konstanten." *ZKG* 86 (1975), 145–185.

Richard, J. *La Papauté et les missions d'Orient au Moyen Age.* Rome, 1977.

Santifaller, L. "Saggio di un elenco dei funzionari, impiegati e scrittori della Cancelleria Pontifica dall'inizio all'anno 1099." *BISI* 56 (1940), 1–473.

Schwaiger, G. *Päpstlicher Primat und Autorität der allgemeinen Konzilien im Spiegel der Geschichte.* Munich, Paderborn, Vienna, 1977.

Spinelli, L. *La vacanza della Sede Apostolica dalle origini al Concilio Tridentino.* Milan, 1955.

Tangl, G. *Die Teilnehmer an den allgemeinen Konzilien des Mittelalters.* Weimar, 1932; reprinted Darmstadt, 1969.

Tangl, M. *Die päpstlichen Kanzleiordnungen von 1200–1500.* Innsbruck, 1894; reprinted Aalen, 1959.

Tierney, B. *Foundations of the Conciliar Theory: The Contribution of the Medieval Canonists from Gratian to the Great Schism.* Cambridge, 1955.

Tierney B. *The Crisis of Church and State, 1050–1300.* Englewood Cliffs, N.J., 1964.

Tierney, B. *Origins of Papal Infallibility: Sovereignty and Tradition in the Middle Ages.* Leiden, 1972.

Ullmann, W. *Die Machtstellung des Papsttums im Mittelalter.* Graz, 1960.

Walther, H. G. *Imperiales Königtum, Konziliarismus, und Volkssouveränität.* Munich, 1976.

Wyduckel, D. *Princips legibus solutus: Eine Untersuchung zur frühmodernen Rechts-und Staatslehre.* Berlin, 1979.

Zimmermann, H. *Papstbesetzungen des Mittelalters.* Graz, Vienna, Cologne, 1968.

Canon Law

Brys, J. *De dispensatione in iure canonico praesertim apud decretistas et decrelistas usque ad medium seculum decimum quartum.* Brügge, Wetteren, 1925.

Feine, H.-E. *Kirchliche Rechtsgeschichte. I: Die katholiche Kirche.* 5th ed. Cologne, Graz, 1972.

Friedberg, Ae., ed. *Corpus Iuris Canonici.* 2 vols. Leipzig, 1879–1881.

Fuhrmann, H. *Einfluß und Verbreitung der pseudoisidorischen Fälschungen.* 3 vols. Stuttgart, 1972–1977.

Gagnér, S. *Studien zur Ideengeschichte der Gesetzgebung.* Stockholm, Upsala, Göteborg, 1960.

Gaudemet, J. *La formation du droit canonique médiéval.* London, 1980.

Le Bras, G., ed. *Histoire du Droit et des Institutions de l'Eglise en Occident.* Vols. 1 ff. Paris, 1955 ff.

Maffei, D. *La Donazione di Costantino nei giuristi medievali.* Milan, 1964.

Petersmann, J. "Die kanonistische Überlieferung des Constitutum Constantini bis zum Dekret Gratians." *DA* 30 (1974), 356–449.

Plöchl, W. M. *Geschichte des Kirchenrechts.* 3 vols. 2d ed. Vienna, Munich, 1960–1970.

Stickler, A. M. *Historia iuris canonici latini.* I: *Historia fontium.* Turin, 1950.

Ullmann, W. *The Church and the Law in the Early Middle Ages.* London, 1975.

Liturgy

Andrieu, M., ed. *Les Ordines Romani du haut moyen âge.* 5 vols. Löwen, 1931–1961.

Andrieu, M. *Le Pontifical romain au moyen-âge.* 4 vols. Vatican City, 1938–1941.

Cancellieri, F. *Storia de' solenni possessi de' Sommi Pontefici da Leone II a Pio VII.* Rome, 1802.

Dijk, S. J. P. van and J. H. Walker. *The Origins of the Modern Roman Liturgy.* London, 1960.

Duchesne, L. *Origines du Culte Chrétien: Etude sur la Liturgie Latine avant Charlemagne.* 5th ed. Paris, 1925.

Dykmans, M., ed. *Le cérémonial papal de la fin du moyen âge à la Renaissance.* 3 vols. so far. Brussels, Rome, 1977, 1981, and 1983.

Eichmann, E. *Die Kaiserkrönung im Abendland.* 2 vols. Würzburg, 1942.

Eichmann, E. *Weihe und Krönung des Papstes im Mittelalter.* Munich, 1951.

Grisar, H. *Das Missale im Lichte römischer Stadtgeschichte: Stationen, Perikopen, Gebräuche,* Freiburg, 1925.

Gussone, N. *Thron und Inthronisation des Papstes von den Anfängen bis zum 12. Jahrhundert: Zur Beziehung zwischen Herrschaftszeichen und bildhaften Begriffen, Recht und Liturgie im christlichen Verständnis von Wort und Wirklichkeit.* Bonn, 1978.

Jungmann, J. A. *Missarum sollemnia.* 2 vols. 5th ed. Vienna, 1962.

Kirsch, J. P. *Die römischen Titelkirchen im Altertum.* 2 vols. Paderborn, 1918.

Kirsch, J. P. *Die Stationskirchen des Missale Romanum.* Freiburg i. Br., 1926.

Ladner, G. B. "Der Ursprung und die mittelalterliche Entwicklung der päpstlichen Tiara." *Tainia (Festschrift für Roland Hampe).* Mainz, 1979, 449–481.

Maccarrone, M. "Die Cathedra Sancti Petri im Hochmittelalter: Vom Symbol des päpstlichen Amtes zum Kultobjekt." *RQ* 75 (1980), 171–207.

Richter, K. *Die Ordination des Bischofs von Rom: Eine Untersuchung zur Weiheliturgie.* Münster, 1976.

Schimmelpfennig, B. *Die Zeremonienbücher der römischen Kurie im Mittelalter.* Tübingen, 1973.

Schimmelpfennig, B. "Die Krönung des Papstes im Mittelalter, dargestellt am Beispiel der Krönung Pius' II (3.9.1458)." *QFIAB* 54 (1974), 192–270.

Träger, J. *Der reitende Papst: Ein Beitrag zur Ikonographie des Papsttums.* Münster, Zürich, 1970.

Vogel, C. *Introduction au sources de l'histoire du culte chrétien au moyen âge.* Spoleto, 1966.

Wasner, F. "De consecratione inthronizatione coronatione Summi Pontificis." *Apollinaris* 8 (1935), 86–125, 249–281, 428–439.

Zoepffel, R. *Die Papstwahlen und die mit ihnen im nächsten Zusammenhang stehenden Ceremonien in ihrer Entwicklung vom 11. bis zum 14. Jahrhundert.* Göttingen, 1872.

Rome and the Papal States

Benzinger, J. *Invectiva in Romam. Romkritik im Mittelalter vom 9. bis zum 12. Jahrhundert.* Lübeck, Hamburg, 1968.

Caravale, M. and A. Caracciolo. *Lo Stato pontificio da Martino V a Pio IX.* Turin, 1978.

Duchesne, L. *Scripta minora: Etudes de topographie romaine et de géographie ecclésiastique.* Rome, 1973.

Ferrari, G. *Early Roman Monasteries: Notes for the History of the Monasteries and Convents at Rome from the Vth through the Xth Century.* Vatican City, 1957.

Geertman, H. *More veterum: Il Liber Ponificalis e gli edifici ecclesiastici di Roma nella tarda antichità e nell'alto medioevo.* Groningen, 1975.

Graf, A. *Roma nella memoria e nelle immaginazioni del medioevo.* 2 vols. Turin, 1881–1882.

Gregorovius, F. *Geschichte der Stadt Rom im Mittelalter.* New ed., W. Kampf. 3 vols. Darmstadt, 1953–1957.

Halphen, L. *Etudes sur l'administration de Rome au moyen âge (751–1252).* Paris, 1907; reprinted Rome, 1972.

Hirschfeld, Th. "Das Gerichtswesen der Stadt Rom vom 8. bis 12. Jahrhundert wesentlich nach stadtrömischen Urkunden." *AUF* 4 (1912), 419–562.

Homo, L. *Rome médiévale 476–1420: Histoire, civilisation, vestiges.* Paris, 1934.

Krautheimer, R. *Rome: Profile of a City, 312–1308.* Princeton, N.J., 1980.

Lauer, Ph. *Le Palais de Latran.* Paris, 1911.

Partner, P. *The Lands of St. Peter: The Papal State in the Middle Ages and the Early Renaissance.* London, 1972.

Pressouyre, S. *Rome au fil de temps.* Boulogne, 1973. Includes city atlas.

Prodi, P. *Il sovrano pontefice. Un corpo e due anime: la monarchia papale nella prima età moderna.* Bologna, 1982.

Redig de Campos, D. *I palazzi Vaticani.* Bologna, 1967.

Reekmans, L. "Le développement topographique de la région du Vatican à la fin de l'Antiquité et au début du Moyen Age (300–850)." *Mélanges d'arch. et de l'art offerts auf prof. Jaques Lavalleye.* Löwen, 1970, 197–235.

Rodocanachi, E. *Les institutions communales de Rome sous la papauté.* Paris, 1901.

Schneider, F. *Rom und Romgedanke im Mittelalter: Die gestigen Grundlagen der Renaissance.* Munich, 1925; reprinted Darmstadt, 1959.

Solmi, A. *Il senato romano nell'alto medioevo.* Rome, 1944.

Tellenbach, G. "Kaiser, Rom, und Renovatio: Ein Beitrag zu einem großen Thema." In N. Kampf and J. Wallasch, eds., *Tradition als historische Kraft.* Berlin, New York, 1982, 231–253.

Toubert, P. *Les structures du Latium médiéval: Le Latium méridional et la Sabine du IXe siècle à la fin du XIIe siècle.* 2 vols. Rome, 1973.

Valentini, R. and G. Zucchetti, eds. *Codice topografico della Città di Roma.* 4 vols. Rome, 1940–1953.

Vielliard, R. *Recherches sur les origines de la Rome Chrétienne.* Mâcon, 1942; reprinted Rome, 1959.

Bibliography for Each Chapter

I. The Roman Congregation Before Constantine the Great

Andresen, C. *Die Kirchen der alten Christenheit.* Stuttgart, 1971.

Apollonj Ghetti, B. M. et al. *Esplorazioni sotto la confessione di S. Pietro in Vaticano.* Vatican City, 1951.

Bauer, W. *Rechtgläubigkeit und Ketzerei im ältesten Christentum.* 2d ed. Tübingen, 1964.

Blum, G. G. *Tradition und Sukzession: Studien zum Normbegriff des Apostolischen von Paulus bis Irenäus.* Berlin, Hamburg, 1963.

Blum, G. G. "Apostolische Tradition und Sukzession bei Hippolyt." *ZNW* 55 (1964), 95–116.

Campenhausen, H. Frhr. von. *Kirchliches Amt und geistliche Vollmacht in den ersten drei Jahrhunderten.* 2d ed. Tübingen, 1963.

Colson, J. *Klemens von Rom.* Stuttgart, 1962.

Gaudemet, J. "La décision de Callixte en matière de mariage." *Studi in onore di Ugo Enrico Paoli.* Florence, 1956, 333–344.

Grant, R. M. *Christen als Bürger im Römischen Reich.* Göttingen, 1981.

Grimm, B. "Untersuchungen zur sozialen Stellung der frühen Christen in der römischen Gesellschaft." Dissertation, Munich, 1975.

Henneke, G. "Kallist von Rom: Ein Beitrag zur Soziologie der römischen Gemeinde." *ZNW* 58 (1967), 102–121.

Künzle, P. "Sull'autenticità delle ossa ascritte recentemente a S. Pietro." *RSChIt* 21 (1967), 434–440.

Ludwig, J. *Die Primatworte Mt 16,18,19 in der altchristlichen Exegese.* Münster, 1952.

Maccarrone, M. *Apostolicità, episcopato e primato di Pietro: Ricerche e testimonianze dal II al V secolo.* Rome, 1976.

Maccarrone, M. "Il pellegrinaggio a San Pietro e il giubileo del 1300, p. 1." *RSChIt* 34 (1980), 363–429.

Marschall, W. *Karthago und Rom: Die Stellung der nordafrikanischen Kirche zum apostolischen Stuhl in Rom.* Stuttgart, 1971.

Molthagen, J. *Der römische Staat und die Christen im zweiten und dritten Jahrhundert.* Göttingen, 1970.

Pesch, R. *Simon-Petrus (á67): Geschichte und geschichtliche Bedeutung des ersten Jüngers Jesu Christi.* Stuttgart, 1980.

Schultze, B. "Epiphanius über Petrus." *AHPont* 17 (1979), 7–68.

Stockmeier, P. *Glaube und Religion in der frühen Kirche.* Freiburg, 1973.

Toynbee, J. C. and J. B. Ward-Perkins. *The Shrine of Saint Peter.* London, New York, Toronto, 1956.

Vogt, H. J. *Der Kirchenbegriff des Novatian und die Geschichte seiner Sonderkirche.* Bonn, 1968.

II. *The Papacy and Rome Until the Death of Theoderic (526)*

Alessandrini, A. "Teodorico e papa Simmaco durante lo scisma laurenziano." *ASR* 67 (1944), 153–207.

Anton, H. H. "Kaiserliches Selbstverständnis in der Religionsgesetzgebung der Spätantike und päpstliche Herrschaftsinterpretation im 5. Jahrhundert." *ZKG* 88 (1977), 38–84.

Ensslin, W. "Papst Johannes I als Gesandter Theoderichs d. Gr. bei Kaiser Justinos I." *BZ* 44 (1951), 127–134.

Ensslin, W. "Auctoritas und Potestas: Zur Zweigewaltenlehre des Papstes Gelasius I." *HJb* 74 (1955), 661–668.

Gaudemet, J. *L'église dans l'empire romain.* Paris, 1958.

Girardet, K. M. "Appellatio: Ein Kapitel kirchlicher Rechtsgeschichte in den Kanones des 4. Jahrhunderts." *Historia* 23 (1974), 98–127.

Grisar, H. *Geschichte Roms und der Päpste im Mittelalter. I: Rom beim Ausgang der antiken Welt.* Freiburg, 1901.

Heiler, F. *Altkirchliche Autonomie und päpstlicher Zentralismus.* Munich, 1941.

Huskinson, J. M. *Concordia Apostolorum. Christian Propaganda at Rome in the Fourth and Fifth Centuries: A Study in Early Christian Iconography and Iconology.* Oxford, 1982.

Joannou, P. P. *Die Ostkirche und die Cathedra Petri im 4. Jahrhundert.* Stuttgart, 1972.

Jones, A. H. M. "Church Finance in the Fifth and Sixth Centuries." *Journal of Theological Studies,* N.S. 11 (1960), 84–94.

Jones, A. H. M. *The Later Roman Empire, 284–602.* 2 vols. Oxford, 1964.

Klauser, Th. *Der Ursprung der bischöflichen Insignien und Ehrenrechte.* 2d ed. Krefeld, 1953.

Klinkenberg, H. M. "Papsttum und Reichskirche bei Leo d. Gr." *ZRGKA* 38 (1952), 37–112.

Koch, H. *Gelasius im kirchenpolitischen Dienst seiner Vorgänger, der Päpste Simplicius (468–483) und Felix III (483–492).* Munich, 1935.

Koeniger, A. M. "Prima sedes a nemine iudicatur." *Beiträge zur Geschichte des christlichen Altertums und der byzantinischen Literatur: Festgabe A. Ehrhard.* Bonn, 1922, 273–300.

Lippold, A. "Ursinus und Damasus." *Historia* 14 (1965), 105–128.

Llwellyn, P. "The Names of the Roman Clergy, 401–1046." *RSChIt* 35 (1981), 335–370.

Löwe, H. "Theoderich d. Gr. und Papst Johannes I." *HJb* 72 (1953), 83–100.

Matthews, J. *Western Aristocracies and Imperial Court, 364–425.* Oxford, 1975.

McShane, Ph. A. *La romanitas et le pape Léon le Grand: L'apport culturel des institutions impériales à la formation des structures ecclésiastiques.* Tournai, 1979.

Pietri, Ch. "Le sénat, le peuple chrétien et les partis du cirque à Rome sous le Pape Symmaque (498–514)." *MélArchH* 78 (1966), 123–139.

Pietri, Ch. *Roma Christiana: Recherches sur l'Eglise de Rome, sa organisation, sa politique, sa idéologie de Miltiade à Sixte III, 311–440.* Rome, 1976.

Stockmeier, P. *Leos I. d. Gr. Beurteilung der kaiserlichen Religionspolitik.* Munich, 1959.

Susman, F. "Il Culto di S. Pietro a Roma dalla morte di Leone Magno a Vitaliano (461–672)." *ASR* 84 (1961), 1–192.

Ullmann, W. "Der Grundsatz der Arbeitsteilung bei Gealsius I." *HJb* 97/98 (1979), 41–70.

Ullmann, W. *Gelasius I (492–496): Das Papsttum an der Wende der Spätantike zum Mittelalter.* Stuttgart, 1981.

Verrando, G. N. "Liberio-Felice: Osservazioni e rettifiche di carattere storico-agiografico." *RSChIt* 35 (1981), 91–125.

Vogel, C. "Le 'Liber Pontificalis' dans l'édition de Louis Duchesne." *Monsigneur Duchesne et son temps.* Rome, 1972, 99–127.

Vries, W. de. *Rom und die Patriarchate des Ostens.* Freiburg, Munich, 1963.

Vries, W. de. "Die Struktur der Kirche gemäß dem Konzil von Ephesos (431)." *AHC* 2 (1970), 22–55.

Wermelinger, O. *Rom und Pelagius: Die theologische Position der römischen Bischöfe im pelagianischen Streit in den Jahren 411–432.* Stuttgart, 1975.

Westenburger, G. *Der Symmachusprozeß von 501: Kirchenkrise und Papstdoktrin.* Tübingen, 1939.

Wojtowytsch, M. *Papsttum und Konzile von den Anfängen bis zu Leo I (440–*

461): Studien zur Entstehung der Überordnung des Papstes über Konzile.
Stuttgart, 1981.

III. The Papacy Under Byzantine Rule (Until 774)

Affeldt, W. "Untersuchungen zur Königserhebung Pippins: Das Papsttum und die Begründung des karolingischen Königtums im Jahre 751." *FrühmSt* 14 (1980), 95–187.

Angenendt, A. "Das geistliche Bündnis der Päpste mit den Karolingern (754–796)." *HJb* 100 (1980), 1–94.

Anton, H. H. *Studien zu den Klosterprivilegien der Päpste im frühen Mittelalter unter besonderer Berücksichtigung der Privilegierung von St. Maurice d'Agaune.* Berlin, New York, 1975.

Bavant, B. "Le duché byzantin de Rome: Origine, durée, et extension géographique," *MélArchH* 91 (1979), 41–88.

Bertolini, O. *Roma di fronte a Bisanzio e ai Longobardi (= Storia di Roma IX).* Bologna, 1941.

Bertolini, O. *Scritti scelti di storia medioevale.* Livorno, 1968.

Bertolini, O. *Roma e i Longobardi.* Rome, 1972.

Bock, F. "Bemerkungen zu den ältesten Papstregistern und zum 'Liber diurnus Romanorum Pontificum.' " *AZ* 57 (1961), 11–51.

Bognetti, G. P. *L'età longobarda.* 2 vols. Milan, 1966.

Caspar, E. *Pippin und die römische Kirche.* Berlin, 1914.

Le chiese nei regni dell'Europa occidentale e i loro rapporti con Roma sino all'800. Spoleto, 1960.

Conte, P. *Chiesa e primato nelle lettere dei papi del secolo VII.* Milan, 1971.

Conte, P. "Il significato del primato papale nei padri del VI concilio ecumenico." *AH Pont* 15 (1977), 7–111.

Delogu, P. et al. *Longobardi e Bizantini (= Storia d'Italia I).* Turin, 1980.

Dijk, S. J. P. van. "Gregory the Great, Founder of the Urban Schola Cantorum." *EL* 77 (1963), 335–356.

Drabek, A. M. *Die Verträge der fränkischen und deutschen Herrscher mit dem Papsttum von 754 bis 1020.* Vienna, 1976.

Fischer, E. H. "Gregor der Große und Byzanz." *ZRGKA* 36 (1950), 15–144.

Fritze, W. H. *Papst und Frankenkönig: Studien zu den päpstlich-fränkischen Rechtsbeziehungen von 754–824.* Sigmaringen, 1972.

Gibbs, M. "The Decrees of Agatho and the Gregorian Plan for York." *Speculum* 48 (1973), 213–246.

Giordano, O. *L'invasione longobarda e Gregorio Magno.* Bari, 1970.

Grotz, H. "Beobachtungen zu den zwei Briefen Papst Gregors II an Kaiser Leo III." *AHPont* 18 (1980), 9–40.

Guillou, A. *Régionalisme et indépendance dans l'empire byzantin au VIIe siècle: L'exemple de l'exarchat et de la pentapole d'Italie.* Rome, 1969.

Hallenbeck, J. T. "The Election of Pope Hadrian I." *Church History* 37 (1968), 261–270.

Hallenbeck, J. T. "Paul Afiarta and the Papacy." *AHPont* 12 (1974), 30–54.

Hallenbeck, J. T. "Pope Stephen III: Why Was He Elected?" *AHPont* 12 (1974), 287–299.

Hallenbeck, J. T. "Instances of Peace in Eighth-Century Lombard-Papal Relations." *AHPont* 18 (1980), 41–56.

Kreuzer, G. *Die Honoriusfrage im Mittelalter und in der Neuzeit.* Stuttgart, 1975.

Llewellyn, P. *Rome in the Dark Ages.* New York, 1971.

Losenno, N. L. "Il Pontefice come 'servus servorum Dei' nel 'Registrum' di San Gregorio Magno." Dissertation, University of S. Cuore, Milan, 1961.

Magi, L. *La Sede Romana nella corrispondenza degli imperatori e patriarchi bizantini (VI-VII sec.).* Löwen, Rome, 1972.

Meyendorff, J. "Justinian, the Empire, and the Church." *DumbOaP* 22 (1968), 43–60.

Miller, D. H. "Papal-Lombard Relations During the Pontificate of Pope Paul I: The Attainment of an Equilibrium of Power in Italy, 756–767." *CatHR* 55 (1969/1970), 358–376.

Miller, D. H. "The Roman Revolution of the Eighth Century: A Study of the Ideological Background of the Papal Separation from Byzantium and Alliance with the Franks." *Mediaeval Studies* 36 (1974), 79–133.

Miller, D. H. "Byzantine-Papal Relations During the Pontificate of Paul I: Confirmation and Completion of the Roman Revolution of the Eighth Century." *BZ* 68 (1975), 47–62.

I problemi dell'occidente nel secolo VIII. Spoleto, 1973.

Recchia, V. *Gregorio Magno e la società agricola.* Rome, 1978.

Richards, J. *The Popes and the Papacy in the Early Middle Ages, 476–752.* London, Boston, 1979.

Richards, J. *Consul of God: The Life and Times of Gregory the Great.* London, 1980.

Riedinger, R. "Aus den Akten der Lateransynode von 649." *BZ* 69 (1976), 17–38.

Riedinger, R. "Die Lateransynode von 649 und Maximos der Bekenner." *Maximus Confessor: Actes du Symposium sur Maxime le Confesseur Fribourg, 2–5 septembre 1980.* Fribourg, Switzerland, 1982, 111–121.

Santifaller, L. *Liber Diurnus: Studien und Forschungen.* Stuttgart, 1976.

Schieffer, Th. *Winfrid-Bonifatius und die christliche Grundlegung Europas.* Freiburg, 1954.

Schmid, K. "Zur Ablösung der Langobardenherrschaft durch die Franken." *QFIAB* 52 (1972), 1–36.

Sickel, Th., ed. *Liber Diurnus.* Vienna, 1889.

Zettinger, J. *Die Berichte über Rompilger aus dem Frankenreiche bis zum Jahre 800*. Rome, 1900.

Zettl, E. Die Bestätigung des V. Oekumenischen Konzils durch Papst Vigilius. *Untersuchungen über die Echtheit der Briefe "Scandala" und "Aetius."* Bonn, 1974.

IV. The Papacy Under Carolingian Rule (774–904)

Belting, H. "Die beiden Palastaulen Leos III im Lateran und die Entstehung einer Päpstlichen Programm-Kunst." *FrühmtSt* 12 (1978), 55–83.

Benz, K. J. " 'Cum ab oratione surgeret.' Überlegungen zur Kaiserkrönung Karls des Großen." *DA* 31 (1975), 337–369.

Beumann, H. et al. *Karolus Magnus et Leo papa: Ein Paderborder Epos vom Jahre 799*. Paderborn, 1966.

Borgolte, M. "Papst Leo III, Karl der Große, und der Filioque-Streit von Jerusalem." *Byzantina* 10 (1980), 401–427.

Boshof, E. and H. Wolter. *Rechtsgeschichtlich-diplomatische Studien zu frühmittelalterlichen Papsturkunden*. Cologne, Vienna, 1976.

Caspar, E. *Das Papsttum unter fränkischer Herrschaft*. Darmstadt, 1956.

Classen, P. *Karl der Große, das Papsttum und Byzanz*. Düsseldorf, 1968.

Duchesne, L. and G. Miccoli. *I primi tempi dello Stato pontifico*. 2d ed. Turin, 1967.

Dümmler, E. *Auxilius und Vulgarius: Quellen und Forschungen zur Geschichte des Papsttums im Anfange des zehnten Jahrhunderts*. Leipzig, 1866.

Dvornik, F. *The Photian Schism: History and Legend*. Cambridge, 1948.

Dvornik, F. *Byzanz und der römische Primat*. Stuttgart, 1966.

Falkenstein, L. *Der "Lateran" der karolingischen Pfalz zu Aachen*. Cologne, 1966.

Fried, J. "Boso von Vienne oder Ludwig der Stammler: Der Kaiserkandidat Johannes' VIII." *DA* 32 (1976), 193–208.

Fried, J. "Laienadel und Papst in der Frühzeit der französischen und deutschen Geschichte." In H. Beumann and W. Schröder, eds., *Nationes I*. Sigmaringen, 1978, 367–406.

Fuhrmann, H. "Das Papsttum und das kirchliche Leben in Frankreich." *Nascita dell'Europa ed Europa Carolingia: Un'equazione da verificare*. Spoleto, 1981, 419–456.

Grotz, H. *Erbe wider Willen: Hadrian II (867–872) und seine Zeit*. Vienna, 1970.

Heimbucher, M. *Die Papstwahlen unter den Karolingern*. Augsburg, 1889.

Heiser, L. "Die Responsa ad consulta Bulgarorum des Papstes Nikolaus (858–867)—ein Zeugnis päpstlicher Hirtensorge und ein Dokument unterschiedlicher Entwicklungen in den Kirchen von Rom und Konstantinopel." Dissertation, Münster, 1978.

Kempf, F. "Primatiale und episkopal-synodale Struktur der Kriche vor der gregorianischen Reform." *AHPont* 16 (1978), 27–66.

Kerner, M. "Der Reinigungseid Leo III vom Dezember 800. Die Frage seiner Echtheit und frühen kanonistischen Überlieferung. Eine Studie zum Problem der päpstlichen Immunität im früheren Mittelalter." *ZAachenG* 84/85 (1977/1978), 131–160.

Lapôtre, A. *Etudes sur la papauté au IXe siècle.* 2 vols. Turin, 1978.

Lohrmann, D. *Das Register Papst Johannes' VIII.* Tübingen, 1968.

Perels, E. *Papst Nikolaus I und Anastasius Bibliothecarius.* Berlin, 1920.

Peri, V. "Leo III e il 'Filioque.' Ancora un falso e l'autentico simbolo romano." *RSLerRel* 6 (1970), 268–297.

Roma e l'età carolingia. Rome, 1976.

Schneider, R. *Das Frankenreich.* Munich, Vienna, 1982.

Sefton, D. S. "The Pontificate of Hadrian I (772–795): Papal Theory and Political Reality in the Reign of Charlemagne." Dissertation, Michigan State University, 1975.

Sefton, D. S. "Pope Hadrian I and the Fall of the Kingdom of the Lombards." *CatHR* 65 (1979), 206–220.

Villoslada, R. G. "El himno al papa Juan (IX?) de las Laudes Cornomaniae." *Miscellanea Comillas* 32 (1974), 185–205.

Wallach, L. "The Greek and Latin Versions of II Nicaea (787) and the Synodica of Hadrian I." *JE* 2448. In Wallach, *Diplomatic Studies in Latin and Greek Documents from the Carolingian Age.* Ithaca, London, 1977, 3–46.

Zimmermann, H. "Imperatores Italiae." *Historische Forschungen für Walter Schlesinger.* Cologne, Vienna, 1974, 379–399.

V. The Papacy Under the Influence of the Roman Nobility (904–1046)

Beaufrère, A. *Gerbert, prêtre à Aurillac, pontife à Rome.* Aurillac, 1970.

Bulst, N. *Untersuchungen zu den Klosterreformen Wilhelms von Dijon (962–1031).* Bonn, 1973.

Duchesne, L. "Serge III e Jean XI." *MélArchH* 33 (1913), 25–64.

Eichengrün, F. *Gerbert (Silvester II) als Persönlichkeit.* Berlin, 1928; reprinted Hildesheim, 1972.

Engels, O., *Schutzgedanke und Landesherrschaft im östlichen Pyrenäenraum (9.-13. Jahrhundert).* Münster, 1970.

Erdmann, C. "Das ottonische Reich als Imperium Romanum." *DA* 6 (1943), 412–441.

Erdmann, C. *Forschungen zur politischen Ideenwelt des Frühmittelalters.* Berlin, 1951.

Fedele, P. "Ricerche per la storia di Roma e del papato." *ASR* 33 (1910), 174–247; ibid. 34 (1911), 75–115, 393–423.

Herrmann, K.-J. *Das Tuskulaner-Papsttum (1012–1046): Benedikt VIII, Johannes XIX, Benedikt IX.* Stuttgart, 1973.

Klinkenberg, H. M. "Der römische Primat im 10. Jahrhundert." *ZRGKA* 41 (1955), 1–57.

Kölmel, W. *Rom und der Kirchenstaat im 10. Jahrhundert bis in die Anfänge der Reform.* Berlin, 1935.

Moehs, T. E. *Pope Gregory V (996–999): A Biographical Study.* Stuttgart, 1972.

Santifaller, L. "Chronologisches Verzeichnis der Urkunden Papst Johanns XIX." *RHM* 1 (1956/1957), 35–76.

Santifaller, L. *Zur Geschichte des ottonisch-salischen Reichskirchensystems.* 2d ed. Vienna, 1962.

Schmale, F. J. "Die 'Absetzung' Gregors VI in Sutri und die synodale Tradition." *AHC* 11 (1979), 55–103.

Schramm, P. E. *Kaiser, Rom, und Renovatio.* 2 vols. Leipzig, 1929.

Venni, T. "Giovanni X." *ASR* 59 (1936), 1–136.

Vogel, C. and R. Elze, eds. *Le Pontifical Romano-Germanique du dixième siècle.* 3 vols. Vatican City, 1963, 1972.

Zimmermann, H. "Das Privilegium Ottonianum von 962 und seine Problemgeschichte." *MIÖG*, supplementary vol. 20 (1962), 147–190.

Zimmermann, H. *Papstregesten 911–1024 (= J. F. Böhmer, Regesta Imperii II 5).* Vienna, Cologne, Graz, 1969.

Zotz, Th. "Pallium et alia quaedam archiepiscopatus insignia: Zum Beziehungsgefüge und zu Rangfragen der Reichskirchen im Spiegel der päpstlichen Privilegierung des 10. und 11. Jahrhunderts." *Festschrift für Berent Schwineköper.* Sigmaringen, 1982, 155–175.

VI. The Papacy During the Investiture Contest

Becker, A. *Papst Urban II (1088–1099).* Vol. 1. Stuttgart 1964.

Blumenthal, U. R. *The Early Councils of Pope Paschal II, 1100–1110.* Toronto, 1978.

Blumenthal, U. R. "Opposition to Pope Paschal II: Some Comments on the Lateran Council of 1112." *AHC* 10 (1978), 82–98.

Blumenthal, U. R. "Paschal II and the Roman Primacy." *AHPont* 16 (1978), 67–92.

Blumenthal, U. R. *Der Investiturstreit.* Stuttgart, 1982. Extensive bibliography.

Boelens, M. *Die Klerikerehe in der Gesetzgebung der Kirche unter besonderer Berücksichtigung der Strafe: Eine rechtsgeschichtliche Untersuchung von den Anfängen der Kirche bis zum Jahre 1139.* Paderborn, 1968.

Brooke, Chr. N. L. "Gregorian Reform in Action: Clerical Marriage in England, 1050–1200." In Brooke, *Medieval Church and Society: Collected Essays.* London, 1971, 69–99.

Chiesa e riforma nella spiritualità del secolo XI. Todi, 1968.

Chodorow, S. A. "Ecclesiastical Politics and the Ending of the Investiture Contest: The Papal Election of 1119 and the Negotiations of Mouzon." *Speculum* 46 (1971), 613–640.

Cowdrey, H. E. C. *The Cluniacs and the Gregorian Reform.* Oxford, 1970.

Cowdrey, H. E. C. "The Papacy, the Patarenes, and the Church of Milan." *TransHSoc* 18 (1968), 25–48.

Dickerhoff, H. "Über die Staatsgründung des ersten Kreuzzugs." *HJb* 100 (1980), 95–130.

Drehmann, J. *Papst Leo IX und die Simonie: Ein Beitrag zur Untersuchung der Vorgeschichte des Investiturstreites.* Hildesheim, 1973.

Erdmann, C. *Die Entstehung des Kreuzzugsgedankens.* Stuttgart, 1935; reprinted Darmstadt, 1955.

L'eremitismo in occidente nei secoli XI e XII. Milan, 1965.

Fleckenstein, J., ed. *Investiturstreit und Reichsverfassung.* Sigmaringen, 1973.

Fliche, M. *La réforme grégorienne.* 3 vols. Paris, 1924–1937; reprinted Geneva, 1978.

Fonseca, C. D. *Medioevo canonicale.* Milan, 1970.

Fried, J. "Der Regalienbegriff im 11. und 12. Jahrhundert." *DA* 29 (1973), 450–528.

Fried, J. *Der päpstliche Schutz für Laienfürsten.* Heidelberg, 1980.

Fuhrmann, H. "Über die Heiligkeit des Papstes." *Jahrbuch der Akademie der Wissenschaften in Göttingen 1980* (1980), 28–43.

Gay, J., *Les papes du XIe siècle et la Chrétienté.* 2d ed. New York, 1974.

Gilchrist, J., "The Reception of Pope Gregory VII Into the Canon Law (1073–1141)." *ZRGKA* 59 (1973), 35–82; ibid. 66 (1980), 192–229.

Goez, W. "Zur Erhebung und ersten Absetzung Papst Gregors VII." *RQ* 63 (1968), 117–144.

Goez, W. "Papa qui et episcopus; Zum Selbstverständnis des Reformpapsttums im 11. Jharhundert." *AHPont* 8 (1970), 27–59.

Goez, W. "Zur Persönlichkeit Gregors VII." *RQ* 73 (1978), 193–216.

Graboïs, A. "Les séjours des papes en France au XIIe siècle et leurs rapports avec le développement de la fiscalité pontificale." In *Civilisation et société dans l'Occident médiéval.* London, 1983, no. II.

Hägermann, D. "Zur Vorgeschichte des Pontifikats Nicolaus' II." *ZKG* 81 (1970), 352–361.

Hägermann, D. "Untersuchungen zum Papstwahlendekret von 1059." *ZRGKA* 87 (1970), 157–193.

Herde, P. "Das Papsttum und die griechische Kirche in Süditalien vom 11. bis 13. Jahrhundert." *DA* 26 (1970), 1–46.

Hoffmann, H. "Langobarden, Normannen, Päpste: Zum Legitimitätsproblem in Unteritalien." *QFIAB* 58 (1978), 137–180.

Hübinger, P. E. *Die letzten Worte Papst Gregors VII.* Opladen, 1973.

Hüls, R., *Kardinäle, Klerus, und Kirchen Roms, 1049–1130.* Tübingen, 1977.

Le istituzioni ecclesiastiche della "Societas Christiana" dei secoli XI-XII: Papato, cardinalato ed episcopato. Milan, 1974.

Jordan, K. *Die Entstehung der römischen Kurie: Ein Versuch.* Darmstadt, 1973. With addendum.

Kempf, F. "Pier Damiani und das Papstwahldekret von 1059." *AHPont* 2 (1964), 73–89.

Kempf, F. "Die Eingliederung der überdiözesanen Hierarchie in das Papalsystem des kanonischen Rechts von der gregorianischen Reform bis zu Innozenz III." *AHPont* 18 (1980), 57–96.

Klewitz, H. W. *Reformpapsttum und Kardinalkolleg.* Darmstadt, 1957.

Krause, H.-G. *Das Papstwahldekret von 1059 und seine Rolle im Investiturstreit.* Rome, 1960.

Kupper, A. "Beiträge zum Problem der Simonie im 11. Jahrhundert." Dissertation, Mainz, 1953.

Loud, G. A. "Abbot Desiderius of Montecassino and the Gregorian Papacy." *JEH* 30 (1978), 305–326.

Meulenberg, L. F. J. *Der Primat der römischen Kirche im Denken und Handeln Gregors VII.* The Hague, 1965.

Miccoli, G. *Chiesa gregoriana: Ricerche sulla riforma del secolo XI.* Florence, 1966.

Minninger, M. *Von Clermont zum Wormser Konkordat: Die Auseinandersetzungen um den Lehnsnexus zwischen König und Episkopat.* Cologne, 1978.

Mirbt, C. *Die Publizistik im Zeitalter Gregors VII.* Leipzig, 1894; reprinted Leipzig, 1965.

Il monachesimo e la riforma ecclesiastica, 1049–1122. Milan, 1971.

Mordek, H. "Proprie auctoritates apostolice sedis. Ein zweiter Dictatus papae Gregors VII?" *DA* 28 (1972), 105–132.

Morghen, R. *Gregorio VII e la riforma della Chiesa nel secolo XI.* 2d ed. Rome, 1974.

Petrucci, E. *Rapporti di Leone IX con Constantinopoli. I: Per la storia dello scisma del 1054.* Rome, 1975.

Petrucci, E. *Ecclesiologia et politica di Leone IX.* Rome, 1977.

Robinson, I. S. " 'Periculosus homo': Pope Gregory VII and Episcopal Authority." *Viator* 9 (1978), 103–131.

Robinson, I. S. "Pope Gregory VII, the Princes, and the Pactum, 1077–1080." *EHR* 94 (1979), 721–756.

Runciman, S. *The Eastern Schism: A Study of the Papacy and the Eastern Churches During the 11th and 12th Centuries.* London, 1955; reprinted London, 1970.

Schieffer, R. "Spirituales latrones: Zu den Hintergründen der Simonieprozesse in Deutschland zwischen 1069 und 1075." *HJb* 92 (1972), 19–60.

Schieffer, R. "Gregor VII: Ein Versuch über die historische Größe." *HJb* 97/98 (1979), 87–107.

Schieffer, R. *Die Entstehung des päpstlichen Investiturverbots für den deutschen König.* Stuttgart, 1981.

Schimmelpfennig, B. "Zölibat und Lage der 'Priestersöhne' vom 11. bis 14. Jahrhundert." *HZ* 227 (1978), 1–44.

Schmale, F. J. "Papsttum und Kurie zwischen Gregor VII und Innocenz II." *HZ* 193 (1961), 265–285.

Schmale, F. J. "Synoden Papst Alexanders II (1061–1073): Anzahl, Termine, Entscheidungen." *AHC* 11 (1979), 307–338.

Schmid, P. *Der Begriff der kanonischen Wahl in den Anfängen des Investiturstreits.* Stuttgart, 1925.

Schmidt, T. "Die Kanonikerreform in Rom und Papst Alexander II, 1061–1073." *StudGreg* 9 (1972), 199–221.

Schmidt, T. *Alexander II (1061–1073) und die römische Reformgruppe seiner Zeit.* Stuttgart, 1977.

Schneider, Ch. *Prophetisches Sacerdotium und heilsgeschichtliches Regnum im Dialog, 1073–1077: Zur Geschichte Gregors VII und Heinrichs IV.* Münster, 1972.

Servatius, L. *Paschalis II (1099–1118): Studien zu seiner Person und seiner Politik.* Stuttgart, 1979.

Somerville, R. *The Councils of Urban II.* Vol. 1: *Decreta Claromontensia.* Amsterdam, 1972.

Stroll, M. "New Perspectives on the Struggle Between Guy of Vienne and Henry V." *AHPont* 18 (1980), 97–116.

Sydow, J. "Untersuchungen zur kurialen Verwaltungsgeschichte im Zeitalter des Reformpapsttums." *DA* 11 (1954/1955), 18–73.

Tellenbach, G. "Der Sturz des Abtes Pontius von Cluny und seine geschichtliche Bedeutung." *QFIAB* 42/43 (1963), 13–55.

Violante, C. *La Pataria Milanese e la riforma ecclesiastica I.* Rome, 1955.

Vollrath, H. "Kaisertum und Patriziat in den Anfängen des Investiturstreites." *ZKG* 85 (1974), 11–44.

Vones, L. *Die "Historia Compostellana" und die Kirchenpolitik des nordwestspanischen Raumes, 1070–1330: Ein Beitrag zur Geschichte der Beziehungen zwischen Spanien und dem Papsttum zu Beginn des 12. Jahrhunderts.* Cologne, Vienna, 1980.

Weitzel, J. *Begriff und Erscheinungsformen der Simonie bei Gratian und den Dekretisten.* Munich, 1967.

Ziese, J. *Wibert von Ravenna: Der Gegenpapst Clemens III, 1084–1100.* Stuttgart, 1982.

Zimmermann, H. *Der Canossagang von 1077: Wirkungen und Wirklichkeit.* Mainz, Wiesbaden, 1975.

VII. The Expansion of Papal Authority

Baaken, G. "Die Verhandlungen zwischen Papst Coelestin III und Kaiser Heinrich VI in den Jahren 1195–1197." *DA* 27 (1971), 457–513.

Baldwin, M. W. *Alexander III and the Twelfth Century*. New York, 1968.

Benson, R. L. *The Bishop Elect: A Study in Medieval Ecclesiastical Office*. Princeton, N.J., 1968.

Benson, R. L. and G. Constable, eds. *Renaissance and Renewal in the Twelfth Century*. Cambridge, Mass., 1982.

Cheney, C. R. "The Deaths of Popes and the Expiry of Legations in Twelfth-Century England." *RDCan* 28 (1978), 84–96.

Classen, P. "Zur Geschichte Papst Anastasius' IV." *QFIAB* 48 (1968), 36–63.

Deér, J. *The Dynastic Porphyry Tombs of the Norman Period in Sicily*. Cambridge, Mass., 1959.

Deér, J. *Papsttum und Normannen*. Cologne, Vienna, 1972.

Ehrle, F. "Die Frangipani und der Untergang des Archivs und der Bibliothek der Päpste am Anfang des 13. Jahrhunderts." *Mélanges M.E. Chatelain*. Paris, 1910, 448–483.

Engels, O. "Kardinal Boso als Geschichtsschreiber." *Konzil und Papst Festgabe für Hermann Tüchle*. Munich, Paderborn, Vienna, 1975, 147–168.

Enzensberger, H. "Der 'böse' und der 'gute' Wilhelm: Zur Kirchenpolitik der normannischen Könige von Sizilien nach dem Vertrag von Benevent (1156)." *DA* 36 (1980), 385–432.

Fabre, P. L. Duchesne, ed. *Le Liber Censuum de l'église romaine*. 3 vols. Paris, 1889, 1910, and 1952.

Ferri, G. "La Romana Fraternitas." *ASR* 26 (1903), 453–466.

Frugoni, A. *Arnaldo da Brescia nelle fonti del secolo XII*. Rome, 1954.

Geisthardt, I. *Der Kämmerer Boso*. Berlin, 1936.

Gleber, H. *Papst Eugen III unter besonderer Berücksichtigung seiner politischen Tätigkeit*. Jena, 1936.

Hageneder, O. "Die Häresie des Ungehorsams und das Entstehen des hierokratischen Papsttums." *RHM* 20 (1978), 29–47.

Häring, N. "Notes on the Council and the Consistory of Rheims, 1148." *Mediaeval Studies* 28 (1966), 39–59.

Häring, N. "Das Pariser Konsistorium Eugens III vom April 1147." *Studia Gratiana* 11 (1967), 91–117.

Heinemeyer, W. "Beneficium—non feudum sed bonum factum: Der Streit auf dem Reichstag zu Besançon." *ADipl* 15 (1969), 155–236.

Hoffmann, H. "Die beiden Schwerter im hohen Mittelalter." *DA* 20 (1965), 78–114.

Holtzmann, R. *Der Kaiser als Marschall des Papstes*. Berlin, Leipzig, 1928.

Inger, G. *Das kirchliche Visitationsinstitut im mittelalterlichen Schweden*. Lund, 1961.

Janssen, W. *Die päpslichen Legaten in Frankreich vom Schisma Anaklets II bis zum Tode Coelestins III, 1130–1198*. Cologne, Graz, 1962.

Jounel, P. *Le culte des saints dans les basiliques du Latran et du Vatican au douzième siècle*. Rome, 1977.

Kennan, E. "The De consideratione of St. Bernard of Clairvaux and the Papacy in the Mid-Twelfth Century." *Traditio* 23 (1967), 73–115,

Kuttner, S. *Repertorium der Kanonistik, 1140–1234.* Vatican City, 1937.

Maccarrone, M. *Papato e impero dalla elezione di Federico I alla morte di Adriano IV, 1152–1159.* Rome, 1959.

Madertoner, W. *Die zwiespältige Papstwahl des Jahres 1159.* Vienna, 1978.

Maleczek, W. "Das Kardinalkollegium unter Innocenz II und Anaklet II." *AHPont* 19 (1981), 27–78.

Maleczek, W. *Papst und Kardinalskolleg von 1191 bis 1261: Die Kardinäle unter Coelestin III und Innocenz III.* Rome, Vienna, c. 1984.

Moynihan, J. H. *Papal Immunity and Liability in the Writings of Medieval Canonists.* Rome, 1961.

Ohnsorge, W. *Die Legaten Alexanders III im ersten Jahrzehnt seines Pontifikats 1159–1169.* Berlin, 1928.

Olsen, G. W. "The Legal Definition of the Ecclesiastical Benefice During the Period of the Appearance of Papal Provisioning, 1140–1230." Ph.D. dissertation, University of Wisconsin, Madison, 1965.

Palumbo, P. F. *Lo scisma del MCXXX: I precedenti. La vicenda romana e le ripercussioni europee della lotta tra Anacleto e Innocenzo II.* Rome, 1942.

Petersohn, J. "Der Vertrag des römischen Senats mit Papst Clemens III (1188) und das Pactum Friedrich Barbarossas mit den Römern (1167)." *MIÖG* 82 (1974), 289–337.

Petersohn, J. "Papstschisma und Kirchenfrieden: Geistesgeschichtliche Stellung und stadtrömischer Hintergrund des Traktats 'De vera pace contra schisma sedis apostolicæ' aus dem Jahre 1171." *QFIAB* 59 (1979), 158–196.

Pfaff, V. "Papst Cölestin III." *ZRGKA* 47 (1961), 109–128.

Pfaff, V. "Die innere Verwaltung der Kirche unter Papst Coelestin III: Mit Nachträgen zu den Papstregesten, 1191–1198." *ADipl* 18 (1972), 342–398.

Pfaff, V. "Der Vorgänger: Das Wirken Coelestins III aus der Sicht von Innocenz III." *ZRGKA* 91 (1974), 121–167.

Pfaff, V. "Das Papsttum in der Weltpolitik des endenden 12. Jahrhunderts." *MIÖG* 82 (1974), 338–376.

Pfaff, V. "Das Papsttum un die Freiheit der Bischofsstädte im 12. Jahrhundert." *ADipl* 25 (1979), 59–104.

Pfaff, V. "Papst Clemens III (1187–1191): Mit einer Liste der Kardinalsunterschriften." *ZRGKA* 66 (1980), 261–316.

Pfaff, V. "Der Widerstand der Bischöfe gegen den päpstlichen Zentralismus um 1200." *ZRGKA* 66 (1980), 459–465.

Pfaff, V. "Sieben Jahre päpstliche Politik: Die Wirksamkeit der Päpste Lucius III, Urban III, Gregor VIII." *ZRGKA* 67 (1981), 148–221.

Pitz, E. *Papstreskript und Kaiserreskript im Mittelalter.* Tübingen, 1971.

Pitz, E. "Die römische Kurie als Thema der vergleichenden Sozialgeschichte." *QFIAB* 58 (1978), 216–359.

Rassow, P. *Honor Imperii.* Munich, 1940.

Saurwein, E. *Der Ursprung des Rechtsinstituts der päpstlichen Dispens von der nicht vollzogenen Ehe: Eine Interpretation der Dekretalen Alexanders III und Urbans III.* Rome, 1980.

Schimmelpfennig, B. "Zisterzienser, Papsttum, und Episkopat im Mittelalter." In *Die Zisterzienser: Ordensleben zwischen Ideal und Wirklichkeit.* Bonn, 1980, 69–85.

Schmale, F.-J. *Studien zum Schisma des Jahres 1130.* Cologne, Graz, 1961.

Schmale, F.-J. "Friedrich I und Ludwig VII im Sommer des Jahres 1162." *ZBLG* 31 (1968), 315–368.

Schwarzmaier, H. "Zur Familie Viktors IV in der Sabina." *QFIAB* 48 (1968), 64–79.

Sommerville, R. *Pope Alexander III and the Council of Tours 1163: A Study of Ecclesiastical Politics and Institutions in the Twelfth Century.* Berkeley, London, 1977.

Sydow, J. "Il Consistorium dopo lo scisma del 1130." *RSChIt* 9 (1955), 165–176.

Tillmann, H. *Die päpstlichen Legaten in England bis zur Beendigung der Legation Gualas.* Bonn, 1926.

Tillmann, H. "Ricerche sull'origine dei membri del collegio cardinalizio nel XII secolo." *RSChIt* 29 (1975), 363–402.

Ullmann, W. "The Pontificate of Adrian IV." *Cambridge Historical Journal* 11 (1955), 233–252.

Walter, C. "Papal Political Imagery in the Medieval Lateran Palace." *CArch* 20 (1970), 155–176.

Willoweit, D. "Die Entstehung exemter Bistümer im deutschen Reichsverband unter rechtsvergleichender Berücksichtigung ausländischer Parallelen." *ZRGKA* 52 (1966), 176–298.

Zenker, B. *Die Mitglieder des Kardinalkollegiums von 1130 bis 1159.* Würzburg, 1964.

Zerbi, P. *Papato, Impero, e "respublica christiana" dal 1187 al 1198.* 2d ed. Milan, 1980

VIII. The Papacy at the Peak of Its Power (1198–1303)

Baethgen, F. *Die Regentschaft Papst Innozenz' III im Königreich Sizilien.* Heidelberg, 1914.

Baethgen, F. "Quellen und Untersuchungen zur Geschichte der päpstlichen Hof- und Finanzverwaltung unter Bonifaz VIII." *QFIAB* 20 (1928/1929), 114–237.

Barbiche, B. "Les 'scriptores' de la Chancellerie Apostolique sous le pontificat de Boniface VIII, 1295–1303." *BiblChart* 128 (1970), 115–187.

Bautier, R. H. "Le Jubilé romain de 1300 et l'alliance Franco-pontificale au temps de Philippe le Bel et de Boniface VIII." *Le Moyen Age* 86 (1980), 189–216.

Bertram, M. "Die Abdankung Papst Cölestins V (1294) und die Kanonisten." *ZRGKA* 87 (1970), 1–101.

Brentano, R. *Rome Before Avignon: A Social History of Thirteenth-Century Rome.* London, 1974.

Buisson, L. *Potestas und Caritas: Die päpstliche Gewalt im Spätmittelalter.* Cologne, Graz, 1958.

Cheney, C. R. *Pope Innocent III and England.* Stuttgart, 1976.

Corvi, A. *Il processo di Bonifacio VIII.* Rome, 1948.

Digard, G. *Philippe le Bel et le Saint-Siège de 1258 à 1304.* Paris, 1936.

Dobson, C. J. "The Thirteenth-Century Papacy as Viewed by Those Outside the Roman Curia." Ph.D. dissertation, Michigan State University, 1975.

Dupré-Theseider, E. *Roma dal comune di popolo alla signoria pontificia, 1252–1327 (= Storia di Roma XI).* Bologna, 1952.

Dykmans, M. "D'Innocent III à Boniface VIII: Histoire des Conti et des Annibaldi." *BIHBelgR* 45 (1975), 19–211.

Dykmans, M. "Les transferts de la curie romaine du XIIIe au XVe siècle." *ASR* 103 (1980), 93–116.

Dykmans, M. Les pouvoirs des cardinaux pendant la vacance du Saint Siège d'après un nouveau manuscrit de Jacques Stefaneschi." *ASR* 104 (1981), 119–145.

Ermini, G. *I parlamenti dello Stato della Chiesa dalle origini al periodo Albornoziano.* Rome, 1930.

Finke, H. *Aus den Tagen Bonifaz' VIII.* Münster, 1902; reprinted Rome, 1964.

Foreville, R. "Innocent III et la Croisade des albigeois." *Gouvernement et Vie de l'Eglise au Moyen Age,* no. 13, London, 1979.

Ganzer, K. *Papsttum und Bistumsbesetzung in der Zeit von Gregor IX bis Bonifaz VIII Ein Beitrag zur Geschichte der päpstlichen Reservationen.* Cologne, Graz, 1969.

Gatto, L. *Il pontificato di Gregorio X, 1271–1276.* Rome, 1959.

Gottlob, A. *Die Servitientaxe im 13. Jahrhundert.* Stuttgart, 1903.

Hageneder, O. "Das päpstliche Recht der Fürstenabsetzung: Seine kanonistische Grundlegung." *AHPont* 1 (1963), 39–71.

Hageneder, O. "Studien zur Dekretalen 'Vergentis' (X.V 7.10): Ein Beitrag zur Häretikergesetzgebung Innocenz' III." *ZRGKA* 49 (1963), 138–173.

Hampe, K. *Urban IV und Manfred, 1261–1264.* Heidelberg, 1905; reprinted Nendeln, 1977.

Herde, P. *Beiträge zum päpstlichen Kanzlei- und Urkundenwesen im 13. Jahrhundert.* 2d ed. Kallmünz, 1967.

Herde, P. *Audientia litterarum contradictarum.* 2 vols. Tübingen, 1970.

Herde, P. *Cölestin V, 1294 (Peter von Morrone): Der Engelpapst.* Stuttgart, 1981. Includes an appendix and an edition of two *vitæ.*

Herde, P. "Die Entwicklung der Papstwahl im dreizehnten Jahrhundert." *Österr. Arch. f. Kirchenrecht* 32 (1981), 11–41.

Housley, N. *The Italian Crusades: The Papal-Angevin Alliance and the Crusades against Christian Lay Powers, 1254–1343.* Oxford, 1982.

Imkamp, W. *Das Kirchenbild Papst Innocenz' III, 1198–1216.* Stuttgart, 1983.

Kamp, N. *Kirche und Monarchie im staufischen Königreich Sizilien.* I: *Prosopographische Grundlegung: Bistümer und Bischöfe des Königreichs, 1194–1266.* 4 vols. Munich, 1973–1975, and 1982.

Kantorowicz, E. H. *The King's Two Bodies: A Study in Mediaeval Political Theology.* Princeton, N.J., 1957.

Kempf, F. *Papsttum und Kaisertum bei Innocenz III.* Rome, 1954.

Kempf, F. "Die Absetzung Friedrichs II im Lichte der Kanonistik." In J. Fleckenstein, ed., *Probleme um Friedrich II.* Sigmaringen, 1974, 345–360.

Kölmel, W. *Regimen christianum: Weg und Ergebnisse des Gewaltenverständnisses und des Gewaltenverhältnisses (8. bis 14. Jh.).* Berlin, 1970.

Kolmer, L. *Ad capiendas vulpes: Die Ketzerbekämpfung in Südfrankreich in der ersten Hälfte des 13. Jahrhunderts und die Ausbildung des Inquisitionsverfahrens.* Bonn, 1982.

Kuttner, S. "Universal Pope or Servant of God's Servants: The Canonists Papal Titles and Innocent III." *RDCan* 32 (1981), 109–149.

Laufs, M. *Politik und Recht bei Innozenz III, Kaiserprivilegien: Thronstreitregister und Egerer Goldbulle in der Reichs- und Rekuperationspolitik Papst Innozenz' III.* Cologne, 1980.

Linehan, P. *The Spanish Church and the Papacy in the Thirteenth Century.* Cambridge, 1971.

Lupprian, K. E. *Die Beziehungen der Päpste zu islamischen und mongolischen Herrschern im 13. Jahrhundert anhand ihres Briefwechsels.* Vatican City, 1981.

Maccarrone, M. *Studi su Innocenzo III.* Padua, 1972

Maisonneuve, H. *Etudes sur les origines de l'Inquisition.* 2d ed. Paris, 1960.

Miethke, J. "Die Traktate 'De potestate papæ.' Ein Typus politiktheoretischer Literatur im späten Mittelalter." *Les genres littéraires dans les sources théologiques et philosophiques médiévales.* Louvain-La-Neuve, 1982, 193–211.

Morghen, R. *Bonifacio VIII e il Giubileo del 1300 nella storiografia moderna.* Rome, 1975.

Nüske, G. F. "Untersuchungen über das Personal der päpstlichen Kanzlei, 1254–1304." *ADipl* 20 (1974), 39–240; ibid. 21 (1975), 249–431.

Pacaut, M. "L'autorité pontificale selon Innocent IV." *Le Moyen Age* 66 (1960), 85–119.

Packard, S. R. *Europe and the Church under Innocent III.* 2d ed. New York, 1968.

Paravicini Bagliani, A. *Cardinali di Curia e "familiæ" cardinalizie dal 1227 al 1254.* 2 vols. Padua, 1972.

Pásztor, E. "Censi e possessi della Chiesa Romana nel Duecento: Due registri pontifici inediti." *AHPont* 15 (1977), 139–193.

Pásztor, E. "La Guerra di Vespro e i suoi problemi: L'intervento di Martino IV." *Quaderni Catanesi* 1 (1979), 135–158.

Pennington, K. "Pope Innocent III's Views on Church and State: A Gloss to 'Per Venerabilem.'" In *Law, Church, and Society: Essays in Honor of S. Kuttner.* Philadelphia, University of Pennsylvania, 1977, 49–67.

Potthast, A., ed. *Regesta pontificum Romanorum inde ab a. post Christum natum MCXCVIII ad a. MCCCIV.* 2 vols. Berlin, 1874–1875.

Purcell, M. *Papal Crusading Policy, 1244–1291.* Leiden, 1975.

Rabikauskas, P. "'Auditor litterarum contradictarum' et Commissions de juges délégués sous le pontificat d'Honorius III." *BiblChart* 132 (1974), 213–244.

Rachewiltz, I. de. *Papal Envoys to the Great Khans.* London, 1971.

Ritzler, R. "I cardinali e i papi dei frati minori conventuali." *Miscellanea Franciscana* 71 (1971), 3–77.

Roché, D. *L'église romaine et les cathares albigeois.* Narbonne, 1969.

Roma anno 1300. Rome, 1983.

Roscher, H. *Papst Innocenz III und die Kreuzzüge.* Göttingen, 1969.

Rusch, B. *Die Behörden und Hofbeamten der päpstlichen Kurie des 13. Jahrhunderts.* Königsberg, Berlin, 1936.

Sayers, J. E. *Papal Judges Delegate in the Province of Canterbury, 1198–1254: A Study in Ecclesiastical Jurisdiction and Administration.* London, 1971.

Schatz, K. "Papsttum und partikularkirchliche Gewalt bei Innocenz III, 1198–1216." *AHPont* 8 (1970), 61–111.

Schiff, O. *Studien zur Geschichte Papst Nikolaus' IV.* Berlin, 1897; reprinted Vaduz, 1965.

Schimmelpfennig, B. "Das Prinzip der 'sanior pars' bei Bischofswahlen im Mittelalter." *Concilium* 16 (1980), 473–477.

Schöpp, N. *Papst Hadrian V. (Kardinal Ottobuono Fieschi).* Heidelberg, 1916; reprinted Nendeln, 1976.

Schwarz, B. *Die Organisation kurialer Schreiberkollegien.* Tübingen, 1972.

Selge, K. V. "Franz von Assisi und die römische Kirche." *ZThK* 67 (1970), 129–161.

Setton, K. M. *The Papacy and the Levant, 1204–1571.* I: *The Thirteenth and Fourteenth Centuries.* Philadelphia, 1976.

Schannon, A. C. *The Popes and Heresy in the Thirteenth Century.* Villanova, Pa., 1949.

Sternfeld, R. *Der Kardinal Johann Gaëtan Orsini (Papst Nikolaus III), 1244–1277: Ein Beitrag zur Geschichte der Römischen Kurie im 13. Jahrhundert.* Berlin, 1905; reprinted Vaduz, 1965.

Stickler, A. M. *Il Giubileo di Bonifacio VIII: Aspetti giuridico-pastorali.* Rome, 1977.

Tillmann, H. *Papst Innozenz III.* Bonn, 1954.

Ullmann, W. "Die Bulle Unam sanctam." *RHM* 16 (1974), 45–77.

Vries, W. de. "Innozenz III, 1198–1216, und der christliche Osten." *AHPont* 3 (1965), 87–126.

Vries, W. de. "Innozenz IV, 1243–1254, und der christliche Osten." *OstkSt* 12 (1963), 113–131.

Waley, D. *The Papal State in the Thirteenth Century.* London, 1961.

Watt, J. A. *The Theory of Papal Monarchy in the XIII Century: The Contribution of the Canonists.* New York, 1966.

Widmer, B. "Das Haus Aragon und Bonifaz VIII: Nachrichten aus dem Briefwechsel Jakobs II." *BasZG* 71 (1971), 37–78.

IX. The Papacy in Avignon (1303–1378)

Baethgen, F. "Der Anspruch des Papsttums auf das Reichsvikariat." *Mediaevalia.* Stuttgart, 1960, 110–185.

Baluze, E. and G. Mollat, eds. *Vitæ paparum Avenionensium.* 4 vols. 2d ed. Paris, 1914–1922.

Barraclough, G. *Papal Provisions.* Oxford, 1935.

Bock, F. "Studien zum politischen Inquisitionsprozeβ Johannes' XXII." *QFIAB* 26 (1935/1936), 21–142.

Bock, F. "Einführung in das Registerwesen des avignonesischen Papsttums." *QFIAB* 31 (1941), complete vol.

Boehm, L. "Papst Benedikt XII als Förderer der Ordensstudien: Restaurator Reformator oder Deformator regularer Lebensform?" *Secundum regulam vivere Festschrift für N. Backmund.* Windberg, 1978, 281–310.

Bowsky, W. M. "Clement V and the Emperor Elect." *Mediaevalia et Humanistica* 12 (1958), 52–69.

Caggese, E. *Roberto d'Angiò e i suoi tempi.* 2 vols. Florence, 1922–1935.

Caillet, L. *La Papauté d'Avignon et l'Eglise de France: La politique bénéficiale du pape Jean XXII en France, 1316–1334.* Paris, 1975.

Colliva, P. *Il cardinale Albornoz, lo Stato della Chiesa, le "Constitutiones Aegidianæ," 1353–1357.* Bologna, 1977.

Dehio, L. "Der Übergang von Natural- zu Geldbesoldung an der Kurie." *VSWG* 8 (1910), 56–78.

Deprez, E. *Les préliminaires de la guerre de Cent ans: La Papauté, la France, et l'Angleterre, 1328–1342.* Paris, 1902; reprinted Geneva, 1975.

Dupré-Theseider, E. *I papi di Avignone e la questione romana.* Florence, 1939.

Dupré-Theseider, E. *Problemi del papato avignonese.* Bologna, 1961.

Dykmans, M., ed. *Jean XXII: Les sermons sur la vision béatifique.* Rome, 1973.

Ehrle. F. "Der Nachlass Clemens' V und der in Betreff desselben von Johann XXII, 1318–1321 geführte Prozeβ." *ALitKG* 5 (1889), 1–158.

Erler. A. *Aegidius Albornoz als Gesetzgeber des Kirchenstaates.* Berlin, 1970.

Esch, A. *Die Ehedispense Johanns XXII und ihre Beziehung zur Politik.* Berlin, 1929; reprinted Vaduz, 1965.

Gagnière. S. "Le palais des papes d'Avignon." *Caisse nat. de mon. hist.,* 1965.

Genèse et débuts du Grand Schisme d'Occident, 1362–1394. Paris, 1980.

Guillemain. B. *La Cour pontificale d'Avignon, 1309–1376: Étude d'une société.* Paris 1962. Includes extensive bibliography.

Lulvès. J. "Päpstliche Wahlkapitulationen: Ein Beitrag zur Entwicklungsgeschichte des Kardinalats." *QFIAB,* 12 (1909), 12–35.

Lulvès, J. "Die Machtbestrebungen des Kardinalats bis zur Aufstellung der ersten päpstlichen Wahlkapitulation." *QFIAB* 13 (1910), 73–102.

Lunt, W. E. *Papal Revenues in the Middle Ages.* 2 vols. New York, 1934; reprinted New York, 1965.

Lunt, W. E. *Financial Relations of the Papacy with England, 1327–1534.* Cambridge, Mass., 1962.

Miethke, J. *Ockhams Weg zur Sozialphilosophie.* Berlin, 1969.

Miethke, J. "Kaiser und Papst im Spätmittelalter: Zu den Ausgleichsbemühungen zwischen Ludwig dem Bayern und der Kurie in Avignon." *ZHF* 10 (1983), 421–446.

Mollat, G. *La collation des bénéfices ecclésiastiques par les papes d'Avignon, 1305–1378.* Paris, 1921.

Mollat, G. *Les papes d'Avignon, 1305–1378.* 10th ed. Paris, 1965. Includes extensive bibliography.

Müller, E. *Das Konzil von Vienne, 1311–1312: Seine Quellen und seine Geschichte.* Münster, 1934.

Muldoon, J. "The Avignon Papacy and the Frontiers of Christendom: The Evidence of Vatican Register 62." *AHPont* 17 (1979), 125—195.

Piola Caselli, F. *La costruzione del palazzo dei papi di Avignone, 1316–1367.* Milan, 1981.

Renouard, Y. *Les relations des papes d'Avignon et des compagnies commerciales et bancaires de 1316 à 1378.* Paris, 1941.

Renouard, Y. *La papauté à Avignon.* 2d ed. Paris, 1962.

Samaran C. and G. Mollat. *La fiscalité pontificale en France au XIVe siècle: Période d'Avignon et du Grand Schisme d'Occident.* Paris, 1905.

Schimmelpfennig, B. "Die Organisation der päpstlichen Kapelle in Avignon." *QFIAB* 50 (1971), 80–111.

Schimmelpfennig, B. "Zisterzienserideal und Kirchenreform: Benedikt XII, 1334–1342 als Reformpapst." *Zisterzienser-Studien* 3, Berlin, 1976, 11–43.

Schmitt, C. *Un pape réformateur et défenseur de l'unité de l'Eglise: Benoit XII et l'Ordre des Frères-Mineurs, 1334–1342.* Quaracchi, Florence, 1959.

Schormann, G. A. "Beiträge zur Ehepolitik der Päpste von Benedikt XII bis Gregor XI." Ph.D. dissertation, Bonn, 1969.

Schütz, A. *Die Prokuratorien und Instruktionen Ludwigs des Bayern für die*

Kurie, 1331–1354: Ein Beitrag zu seinem Absolutionsprozeß. Kallmünz, 1973.

Schwöbel, H. O. *Der diplomatische Kampf zwischen Ludwig dem Bayern und der römischen Kurie im Rahmen des kanonistischen Absolutionsprozesses.* Weimar, 1968.

Tabacco, G. *La casa di Francia nell'azione politica di papa Giovanni XXII.* Rome, 1953.

Thier, L. *Kreuzzugsbemühungen unter Papst Clemens V.* Werl, 1973.

Tomasello, A. "Musical Culture in Papal Avignon, 1309–1403." Ph.D. dissertation, Yale University, 1982.

Trexler, R. C. "Rome on the Eve of the Great Schism." *Speculum* 42 (1967), 489–509.

Turley, Th. "Infallibilists in the Curia of Pope John XXII." *JMedH* 1 (1975), 71–101.

Ullmann, W. "The Legal Validity of the Papal Electoral Pacts." *EphIurCan* 12 (1956), 3–35.

Vries, W. de. "Die Päpste von Avignon und der christliche Osten." *OrChrPer* 30 (1964), 85–128.

Walsh, K. "Papal Policy and Local Reform." *RHM* 21 (1979), 35–57.

Weakland, J. E. "John XXII Before His Pontificate." *AHPont* 10 (1972), 161–185.

Wright, J. R. *The Church and the English Crown, 1305–1334: A Study Based on the Register of Archbishop Walter Reynolds.* Toronto, 1980.

Zacour, N. P. *Talleyrand, the Cardinal of Perigord, 1301–1364.* Philadelphia, 1960.

X. Schism and Reform (1378–1447)

Alberigo. G. *Chiesa Conciliare: Identità e significato del conciliarismo.* Brescia, 1981.

Alvarez Palenzuela, V. A. *Extinción del cisma de occidente: La legación del cardenal Pedro de Foix en Aragón, 1425–1430.* Madrid, 1977.

Bäumer R., ed. *Die Entwicklung des Konziliarismus: Werden und Nachwirken der konziliaren Idee.* Darmstadt, 1976.

Bérence, F. *Les papes de la renaissance: Du Concile de Constance au Concile de Trente.* Paris, 1966.

Brandmüller, W. "Der Übergang vom Pontifikat Martins V zu Eugen IV." *QFIAB* 47 (1967), 596–629.

Brandmüller, W. "Zur Frage nach der Gültigkeit der Wahl Urban VI: Quellen und Quellenkritik." *AHC* 6 (1974), 78–120.

Brandmüller, W. "Die Gesandtschaft Benedikts XIII an das Konzil von Pisa." *Konzil und Papst: Festgabe für Hermann Tüchle.* Munich, Paderborn, Vienna, 1975, 169–205.

Caggese, R. *Re Ladislao d'Angiò-Durazzo.* 2 vols. Milan, 1936.

Delaruelle, E. et al. *L'Eglise au temps du Grand Schisme et de la crise conciliaire, 1378–1499* (=*Histoire de l'Eglise* 14). Paris, 1962–1964.

Diener, H. "Zur Persönlichkeit des Johannes de Segovia: Ein Beitrag zur Methode der Auswertung päpstlicher Register des späten Mittelalters." *QFIAB* 44 (1964), 289–365.

Dykmans, M. "D'Avignon à Rome: Martin V et le cortège apostolique." *BIHBelgR* 39 (1968), 203–309.

Dykmans, M. "La bulle de Grégoire XI à la veille du Grand Schisme." *MélArchH* 89 (1977), 485–495.

Esch, A. "Bankiers der Kirche im Großen Schisma." *QFIAB* 46 (1966), 277–394.

Esch, A. *Bonifaz IX und der Kirchenstaat.* Tübingen, 1969.

Esch, A. "Das Papsttum unter der Herrschaft der Neapolitaner: Die führende Gruppe Neapolitaner Familien an der Kurie während des Schismas, 1378–1415." *Festschrift für H. Heimpel II.* Göttingen, 1972, 713–800.

Esch, A. "Simonie-Geschäft in Rom, 1400: 'Kein Papst wird das tun was dieser tut.'" *VSWG* 61 (1974), 433–457.

Favier, J. *Les finances pontificales à l'époque du Grand Schisme d'Occident, 1378–1409.* Paris, 1966. Includes extensive bibliography.

Fink, K. A. *Martin V und Aragon.* Berlin, 1938.

Franzen, A. and W. Müller, eds. *Das Konzil von Konstanz.* Freiburg, Basel, Vienna, 1964.

Ganzer, K. "Päpstliche Gesetzgebungsgewalt und kirchlicher Konsens: Zur Verwendung eines Dictum in der Concordantia Catholica des Nikolaus von Kues." *Von Konstanz nach Trient: Festgabe für A. Franzen.* Munich, Paderborn, Vienna, 1972, 171–188.

Gill, J. *Eugenius IV: Pope of Christian Unity.* Westminster, Md., 1961.

Girgensohn, D. "Wie wird man Kardinal? Kuriale und außerkuriale Karrieren an der Wende des 14. zum 15. Jahrhundert." *QFIAB* 57 (1977), 138–162.

Haller, J. *Papsttum und Kirchenreform 1.* 2d ed. Berlin, 1966.

Hofmann, W. von. *Forschungen zur Geschichte der kurialen Behörden vom Schisma bis zur Reformation.* 2 vols. Rome, 1914.

Immenkötter, H. "Ein avignonesischer Bericht zur Unionspolitik Benedikts XIII." *AHC* 8 (1976), 200–249.

Lenzenweger, J. "Das Kardinalskollegium und die Papstwahlen, 1378." *ThPQ* 126 (1978), 316–325.

Logoz, R. Ch. *Clément VII (Robert de Genève): Sa chancellerie et le clergé romand au début du Grand Schisme, 1378–1394.* Lausanne, 1974.

Lombardo, M. L. *La Camera Urbis: Premesse per uno studio sulla organizzazione amministrativa della città di Roma durante il pontificato di Martino V.* Rome, 1970.

Partner, P. *The Papal State Under Martin V: The Administration and Government of the Temporal Power in the Early Fifteenth Century.* London, 1958.

Petersohn, J. "Papst Gregors XII: Flucht aus Cividale (1409) und die Sicherstellung des päpstlichen Paramentenschatzes." *RQ* 58 (1963), 51–70.

Prerovsky, O. *L'elezione di Urbano VI e l'insorgere dello Scisma d'Occiente.* Rome, 1960.

Puig y Puig, S. *Pedro de Luna: Ultimo papa de Aviñón, 1387–1430.* Barcelona, 1920.

Reinhard, W. "Papa Pius: Prolegomena zu einer Sozialgeschichte des Papsttums." *Von Konstanz nach Trient. Festgabe für A. Franzen.* Munich, Paderborn, Vienna, 1972, 262–289.

Reinhard, W. "Herkunft und Karriere der Päpste, 1417–1963: Beiträge zu einer historischen Soziologie der römischen Kurie." *MNedHIR* 38 (1976), 87–108.

Schwarz, B. "Die Abbreviatoren unter Eugen IV: Päpstliches Reservationsrecht Konkordatspolitik und kuriale Ämterorganisation." *QFIAB* 60 (1980), 200–274. Includes two appendixes: Konkordate Eugens IV; Aufstellung der Bewerber.

Seidlmayer M. *Die Anfänge des großen abendländischen Schismas: Studien zur Kirchenpolitik insbesondere der spanischen Staaten und zu den geistigen Kämpfen der Zeit.* Münster, 1940.

Setz, W. *Lorenzo Vallas Schrift gegen die Konstantinische Schenkung De falso credita et ementita Constantini donatione: Zur Interpretation und Wirkungsgeschichte.* Tübingen, 1975.

Souchon, M. *Die Papstwahlen in der Zeit des großen Schismas: Entwicklung der Verfassungskämpfe des Kardinalates von 1378 bis 1417.* 2 vols. Braunschweig, 1898/1899; reprinted Aalen, 1970.

Thomson, J. A. F. *Popes and Princes, 1417–1517.* London, 1980.

Ullmann, W. *Origins of the Great Schism.* 2d ed. Hamden, 1967.

Vincke, J. *Der König von Aragon und die Camera apostolica in den Anfängen des Großen Schismas.* Münster, 1938.

Waldmüller, L. "Materialien zur Geschichte Johannes' XXIII, 1410–1414." *AHC* 7 (1976), 229–237.

De Weese Jr., M. L. "A Study of Decision-Making in France During the Reign of Charles VI (The Rejection of the Avignon Papacy, 1395)." Ph.D. dissertation, University of Washington, 1973.

XI. Restoration and Renaissance (1447–1534)

Babinger, F. *Mehmed der Eroberer und seine Zeit.* Munich, 1953.

Bauer, C. "Studi per la storia delle finanze papali durante il pontificato di Sisto IV." *ASR* 50 (1927), 319–400.

Berglar, P. "Die kirchliche und politische Bedeutung des Pontifikats Hadrians VI." *AKG* 54 (1972), 97–112.

Bignami-Odier, J. *La bibliothèque Vaticane de Sixte IV à Pie XI.* Vatican City, 1973.

Brandi, K. *Kaiser Karl V.* 2 vols. Munich, 1937–1941.

Cardini, F. "La Repubblica di Firenze e la crociata di Pio II." *RSChIt* 33 (1979), 455–482.

D'Amico, J. F. "Papal History and Curial Reform in the Renaissance: Raffaele Maffei's 'Brevis Historia' of Julius II and Leo X." *AHPont* 18 (1980), 157–210.

Dupré-Theseider, E. "I Papi Medicei e la loro politica domestica." *Studi Fiorentini*. Florence, 1963, 271–324.

Esch A. and D. Esch. "Die Grabplatte Martins V und andere Importstücke in den römischen Zollregistern der Frührenaissance." *RömJbKG* 17 (1978), 209–217.

Ettlinger. L. D. *The Sistine Chapel Before Michelangelo: Religious Imagery and Papal Primacy*. Oxford, 1965.

Fink. K. A. "Das Scheitern der Kirchenreform im 15. Jahrhundert." *Mediaevalia Bohemica* 3 (1970), 237–244.

Frenz. Th. "Humanistische Schriftformen in der päpstlichen Kurie im 15. Jahrhundert." *ADipl* 19 (1973), 287–418; ibid. 20 (1974), 384–506.

Frenz, Th. "Die Gründung des Abbreviatorenkollegs durch Pius II und Sixtus IV." *Miscellanea in onore di M. Giusti I*. Vatican City, 1978, 279–329.

Frommel, C. L. "Die Petruskirche unter Papst Julius II im Lichte neuer Dokumente." *RömJbKG* 16 (1976), 57–136.

Gazzaniga, J.-L. *L'église du Midi à la fin du règne de Charles VII, 1444–1461, d'après la jurisprudence du Parlement de Toulouse*. Paris, 1976.

Gilbert, F. *The Pope, His Banker, and Venice*. Cambridge, Mass., 1980.

Gottlob, A. *Aus der Camera Apostolica des 15. Jahrhunderts*. Innsbruck, 1889.

Halkin, L. E. "Adrien VI et la Réforme de l'Eglise." *EphThLov* 35 (1959), 534–542.

Hoberg, H. "Die Einnahmen der Apostolischen Kammer am Vorabend der Glaubensspaltung." *RQ* Suppl. 35 (1977), 69–85.

Hofmann, G. "Papst Kalixt III und die Frage der Kircheneinheit im Osten." *Miscellanea G. Mercati III*. Rome, 1946, 209–237.

Izbicki, Th. M. *Protector of the Faith: Cardinal Johannes de Turrecremata and the Defense of the Institutional Church*. Washington, D.C., 1981.

Le Bross, O. de. *Le Pape et le Concile: La comparaison de leurs pouvoirs à la veille de la Réforme*. Paris, 1965.

Lee, E. *Sixtus IV and Men of Letters*. Rome, 1978.

Leturia, P. de. *Relaciones entre la S. Sede e Hispanoamérica I*. Rome, 1959.

Marc-Bonnet, H. *Les Papes de la Renaissance, 1447–1527*. 2d ed. Paris, 1969.

McCready, W. D. "Papal Plenitudio potestatis and the Source of Temporal Authority in the Late Medieval Papal Hierocratic Theory." *Traditio* 30 (1974), 325–349.

McCready, W. B. "Papalists and Antipapalists: Aspects of Church/State Controversy in the Later Middle Ages." *Viator* 6 (1975), 241–273.

McNally, R. E. "Pope Hadrian VI (1522–1523) and Church Reform." *AHPont* 7 (1969), 253–285.

Monaco, M. "Le finanze pontificie al tempo di Clemente VII, 1523–1534." *Studi Romani* 6 (1958), 278–296.

Monaco, M. "Il primo debito pubblico pontificio: Il Monte della Fede (1526)." *Studi Romani* 8 (1960), 553–569.

Monaco, M. *La situazione della reverenda camera apostolica nell'anno 1525.* Rome, 1960.

Müller, G. *Die römische Kurie und die Reformation, 1523–1534: Kirche und Politik während des Pontifikats Clemens' VII.* Gütersloh, 1969.

O'Malley, J. W. *Praise and Blame in Renaissance Rome.* Durham, N.C., 1979.

Palermino, R. J. "The Roman Academy, the Catacombs, and the Conspiracy of 1468." *AHPont* 18 (1980), 117–210.

Partner, P. "The 'Budget' of the Roman Church in the Renaissance Period." In E. F. Jacob, ed., *Italian Renaissance Studies: A Tribute to the Late Cecilia M. Ady.* London, 1960, 256–278.

Partner, P. *Renaissance Rome, 1500–1559: A Portrait of a Society.* Berkeley, Calif., 1976.

Partner, P. "Papal Financial Policy in the Renaissance and Counter-Reformation." *Past and Present* 88 (1980), 17–62.

Pfeffermann, H. *Die Zusammenarbeit der Renaissancepäpste mit den Türken.* Winterthur, 1946.

Pitz, E. *Supplikensignatur und Briefexpedition an der Römischen Kurie im Pontifikat Papst Calixts III.* Tübingen, 1972.

Ranke, L. von. *Die römischen Päpste in den letzten vier Jahrhunderten I.* 8th ed. Leipzig, 1885.

Re, N. del. *Monsignor Governatore di Roma.* Rome, 1972.

Rodocanachi, E. *Histoire de Rome. Une cour princière au Vatican pendant la Renaissance: Sixte IV, Innocent VIII, Alexandre VI Borgia.* Paris, 1925.

Roover, R. de. *The Rise and Decline of the Medici Bank, 1397–1494.* Cambridge, Mass., 1968.

Ruysschaert, J. "Sixte IV Fondateur de la Bibliothèque Vaticane (15 juin 1475)." *AHPont* 7 (1969), 513–524.

Sägmüller, J. B. *Die Papstwahlen und die Staaten von 1447–1555 (Nikolaus V bis Paul IV): Eine kirchenrechtlich-historische Untersuchung über den Anfang des staatlichen Rechtes der Exklusive in der Papstwahl.* Tübingen, 1890; reprinted Aalen, 1967.

Schimmelpfennig, B. "Der Ämterhandel an der römischen Kurie von Pius II bis zum Sacco di Roma, 1458–1527." In I. Mieck, ed., *Ämterhandel im Spätmittelalter und 16. Jahrhundert.* Berlin, 1984.

Schüller-Piroli, S. *Die Borgia-Päpste: Kalixt III und Alexander VI.* Munich, 1980.

Schürmeyer, W. *Das Kardinalskollegium unter Pius II.* Berlin, 1914; reprinted Vaduz, 1965.

Schulte, A. *Die Fugger in Rom, 1495–1523.* 2 vols. Leipzig, 1904.

Setton, K. M. *The Papacy and the Levant, 1204–1571.* II: *The Fifteenth Century.* Philadelphia, 1978.

Stieber, J. W. *Pope Eugenius IV, the Council of Basel, and the Secular and Ecclesiastical Authorities in the Empire: The Conflict Over Supreme Authority and Power in the Church.* Leiden, 1978.

Storti, N. *La Storia e il diritto della dataria apostolica dalle origini ai nostri giorni.* Naples, 1969.

Strnad, A. "Francesco Todeschini-Piccolomini: Politik und Mäzenatentum im Quattrocento." *RHM* 8/9 (1964/1966), 101–425.

Strnad, A. "Johannes Hinderbachs Obödienz-Ansprache vor Papst Pius II: Päpstliche und kaiserliche Politik in der Mitte des Quattrocento." *RHM* 10 (1966/1967), 43–183.

Valentini, G. "La Crociata da Eugenio IV a Callisto III (dai documenti d'archivio di Venezia)." *AHPont* 12 (1974), 91–123.

Vaughan, H. M. *The Medici Popes (Leo X and Clement VII).* Port Washington, N.Y., 1971.

Voigt, G. *Enea Silvio de' Piccolomini als Papst Pius II und sein Zeitalter.* 3 vols. Berlin, 1856–1863; reprinted Berlin, 1967.

Westfall, C. W. *In This Most Perfect Paradise: Alberti, Nicholas V, and the Invention of Conscious Urban Planning in Rome, 1447–1455.* University Park, Pennsylvania State University, 1974.

Wiesflecker, H. "Neue Beiträge zur Frage des Kaiser-Papstplanes Maximilians I im Jahre 1511." *MIÖG* 71 (1963), 311–332.

Index

Persons and place names are given as completely as possible. Concepts, however, are often included under the appropriate general concept. For example, under "chancery" one will find all the officials that are a part of the chancery. Ideas associated with the key-words "curia," "papacy," and "Rome" will by and large be found under these headings.